Sales Force Management

Joe L. Welch

**Vice President
Savitz Research Center and
Visiting Associate Professor
North Texas State University**

Charles L. Lapp

**Professor Emeritus
Washington University**

Published by

S53 SOUTH-WESTERN PUBLISHING CO.

CINCINNATI   WEST CHICAGO, ILL.   DALLAS   PELHAM MANOR, N.Y.   PALO ALTO, CALIF.

ISBN: 0-538-19530-4

Library of Congress Catalog Number: 82-50577

1 2 3 4 5 6 7 D 9 8 7 6 5 4 3

Printed in the United States of America

Preface

Sales Force Management is designed to provide practitioners and students with both the most contemporary concepts in sales management and the more traditional supervisory practices. It integrates theory and practice into an informative and useful text. Although the practice of sales management has generally surpassed empirical investigation of the efficacy of sales management activities, recent research has helped to narrow the gap. *Sales Force Management* helps to bring both perspectives into focus. The book is logically organized into sections that reflect the sales management process. It deals with all of the major functions: planning, organizing, staffing, developing, controlling, motivating, and compensating. Company profiles are presented in each chapter. Each profile describes the procedure utilized by a major company in handling the managerial functions described in the chapter. Cases of varying length and complexity appear at the end of each part and provide students the opportunity to test their understanding of ideas and concepts presented in the preceding chapters.

Because of personal selling's close relationship to sales force management, an introductory chapter, Basics of Personal Selling, is included to permit students an opportunity to review the fundamentals of this important topic. Instructors may wish to skip this review chapter if students have successfully completed a course in personal selling. Part 1 then examines the environment within which sales managers must operate. Not only are economic, political, social, and competitive contingencies examined, but a marketing concept framework for adapting to the complexities of the environment is established. Part 2 deals with the planning functions of sales management. It presents a logical planning procedure and discusses the following specific planning problems: demand analysis, forecasting, financial planning, quota setting, and territory decisions. Part 3 covers the organizing and staffing functions of sales force management. Part 4 examines the development and maintenance of salespeople. Discussion focuses on initial training, continuous training, in-field coaching, and performance review. (Two appendices in this part deal specifically with coaching and evaluating the sales force.) Part 5 looks closely at the motivational aspects of sales management including communications, motivational theory, and compensation. The final section, Part 6, deals with information systems and future challenges.

The authors are grateful for the editorial input provided by Professor George Trebbi of Xavier University, and for case material donated by Professor William Stanton of the University of Colorado. We also genuinely appreciate the invaluable editorial and administrative assistance provided by Lydia Welch, and the typing assistance given by Estelle Doyle and Susan Martin.

Contents

Developing and Maintaining Salespeople

4

Motivational Aspects of Sales Management

5

Future-Oriented Considerations

6

Cases

List of Tables

List of Figures

Introduction _____

Basics of Personal Selling

After completing this chapter, you will be able to:

- Outline and discuss the basics of personal selling that a salesperson should practice in order to have a successful career in sales.

- Indicate some newer trends and countertrends in personal selling.

- Suggest some of the steps involved in personal selling.

Salespeople are *not* born; rather, if they have the appropriate characteristics, salespeople can acquire the knowledge, skills, work habits, and attitudes necessary to be successful.[1] At the same time, however, it should be acknowledged that selling is both a *science* and an *art*, consisting of both a specific body of knowledge and principles of empathy and insight that must be understood and practiced. The specific knowledge necessary to become a salesperson can be learned through training. The empathy, sensitivity, and understanding that is necessary to sell one's self involves extensive personal evaluation and practice. Although the art of empathizing may seem ambiguous and unclear, it is the most critical element in sales. Salespeople cannot be successful until they learn to sell themselves. Once they learn to do that, the scientific application of sales and marketing principles becomes much easier to implement.

The aim of this chapter, then, is to identify both the scientific principles of personal selling and the attitudes and sensitivities necessary to sell one's self.

Personal selling can be defined as a process of informing customers and persuading them to purchase products and services they need, can pay for, and/or want through personal interaction in an exchange situation.

Personal selling is not a matter of some rare, unusual gift that a person has, which can be turned on and off at will. It is, rather, a combination of careful planning, good training, attention to procedures and details, an ability to analyze a buyer's problems, and the ability to

---

[1] Charles L. Lapp and William W. Frank, *How to Outsell the Born Salesman* (New York: Collier Books, a Division of MacMillan Publishing Company, 1962).

explain to the buyer how problems can be solved by purchasing a particular product or service.

REQUIREMENTS FOR PROFESSIONAL SELLING

There are a number of characteristics that are especially well suited to the field of professional selling. This section discusses some of the more important ones.

Professional Attitude

It is evident that salespeople, in order to win increasing respect from the general public, competitive salespeople, and other businesspeople, must be professional in every way. The professional salesperson is one who is constantly striving to improve. A professional attitude is evident when a salesperson wants to become a champion salesperson in order to serve customers better. This requires constant study of new products and new sales techniques as well as an awareness of changing attitudes and requirements of buyers.

In other words, professional salespeople must genuinely believe that satisfaction of customer needs is the single most important function that can be performed. In fact, they should understand that customer satisfaction is the reason their companies are in business. This attitude must exist and be internalized before success can be achieved.

Product Knowledge

In addition to having a genuine sensitivity for customer needs, professional salespeople must have a thorough knowledge of product characteristics and applications. They should also be aware of competitive products and the advantages realized by each product line on the market. Also, it is an absolute necessity that salespeople feel that their product is making a significant contribution to society. Although it is often difficult to devote the time necessary to acquire such in-depth knowledge and develop such an attitude, the benefits far outweigh the investment of time and energy.

One of the most significant disservices a sales manager can render for salespeople is to get them involved in customer activities before they have developed an overall sense of professionalism and product knowledge. If new salespeople are not properly oriented and trained, they may receive a large amount of negative feedback from customers, become frustrated, and eventually question their own abilities. This leads to demotivation and increased turnover.

As was indicated previously, a professional salesperson satisfies needs and does not simply sell products. Nothing will destroy a salesperson's credibility faster than presenting a product that is totally inconsistent with a customer's requirements. Conversely, one of the best ways to build credibility and confidence is to say, "an evaluation of your company's requirements suggests that my product is possibly not the best alternative." For example, some airline companies fully cook steaks before they are placed on airplanes and then hold the steaks in a heating unit for two or three hours before they are served to passengers. Such an operational system of maintaining the temperature of meat may cause it to become tough. These airline companies, therefore, must utilize the most tender cuts of meat available (i.e., tenderloin). It would be unwise for a meat salesperson to approach these companies with other cuts of meat. Not only would the salesperson fail to make a sale, but the buyer would know that the salesperson does not have a complete understanding of the buyer's requirements and unique operational problems.

Work Orientation

Another quality of the professional salesperson is a desire and willingness to work hard. Knowledge and ability will not be of much value unless a salesperson has a willingness and the energy to work hard. In fact, the following old cliché has a great deal of application: "It's not what you know that is important, but it's what you do with what you know that is most critical." Although it is certainly important to have a knowledge of customers and products, such knowledge is of little value unless the salesperson shares it with prospective customers.

Ability to Sell One's Self

The fourth quality of professional salespeople is their ability and desire to sell themselves. If a particular buyer does not like or respect a salesperson, it is unlikely that the buyer will consider the salesperson's company as a potential vendor, regardless of the value associated with the product. On the other hand, a buyer that likes, trusts, or respects a salesperson may utilize the salesperson's service even if it is not economically justified.

In terms of the mechanics of selling, therefore, selling one's self is a prerequisite to selling a product. In fact, a good salesperson will not even begin a product presentation until this task is accomplished.

Enthusiasm

Enthusiasm is a fundamental personality trait which is often confused with the showy or flashy characteristics of pep or energy. Enthusiasm should be thought of as a strong feeling for a cause or product. A salesperson that is enthusiastic will have a keen, intense commitment to the total offer being made to prospects. Genuine enthusiasm results from a knowledge of and respect for selling, what is being sold, and the people to whom the sale is being made. Such enthusiasm invariably will be transferred to prospective buyers.

Positive Mental Attitude

In order for salespeople to be successful, they must have a knowledge of their product line, understand customer requirements, skillfully utilize selling tools and principles, and genuinely believe that they can sell to everyone. There is no room for negative beliefs or lack of confidence in selling. A negative mental attitude will lead to frustration and sales resistance. Negative thinkers will find an endless number of excuses for not calling on new prospects. For example, salespeople with a negative mental attitude might call a potential prospect and silently hope that the prospect will not answer. Salespeople with a positive attitude, on the other hand, will continuously look for new and creative ways to meet new prospects.

A positive mental attitude and the motivation that results from such an attitude is developed through training and positive reinforcement. Training prepares salespeople to employ the most effective techniques in the sales process. Training improves the probability of success and serves as a useful and positive source of reinforcement. Salespeople that are thrown into their jobs in a sink or swim fashion will probably experience a significant amount of frustration and eventually become overwhelmed. The constant rejection and negative reinforcement can seriously impair even the most positive mental attitude.

Empathy

Salespeople must empathize, i.e., put themselves in the shoes of customers, in order to understand and react positively to the buyers' feelings and needs. Although it may be easier to look at situations from one's own perspective, it is more rewarding, both personally and professionally, to consider the other person's needs and experiences as the basis of discussion. Not only do people appreciate the fact that you are interested in their ideas and experiences, but such a perspective also minimizes the probability of argument and conflict.

The key to empathy is being understanding and sensitive to the unique needs, desires, and beliefs of each prospect or customer. Salespeople must physically and mentally place themselves in the prospect's environment. This, combined with technical expertise and other sales skills, equips salespeople to effectively satisfy customer needs, which, of course, is the goal of personal selling.

Personal Appearance

The necessity of good personal appearance seems obvious. A salesperson should take the attitude that to do or say anything that creates unnecessary resistance is unprofessional. The general rule is that salespeople should dress and appear in accordance with expectations of customers in a particular industry. For example, a successful stereo equipment representative may be appropriately more casual in appearance than a computer salesperson. Again, as in so many aspects of sales, customer expectation is the critical variable in deciding what to do. Salespeople must attempt to satisfy those expectations.

Loyalty

Every sale should benefit the customer, the salesperson, the salesperson's company, and society. Disloyalty, or anything that can be interpreted as such, toward the salesperson's company, other salespeople, or the customer may cause the prospect to be distrustful and suspicious. Disloyal and derogatory comments both on and off the job will invite disrespect from everyone. A feeling of dedication and loyalty must always be shown naturally and enthusiastically. In fact, one of the primary variables that is used by sales managers when recruiting and selecting salespeople is their attitude toward their current employer. If recruits are derogatory toward their present company, their chances of being hired may be reduced.

Honesty

Never lie or exaggerate to a prospect or customer. Not only can it cause a person to lose immediate sales but it can have a long-term, widespread negative impact on a salesperson's credibility.

Dishonesty or deception is sometimes used by salespeople to build up expectations and, therefore, close the sale. If the company cannot perform to the expected level of performance, however, a long-term association may not be possible. All companies experience problems periodically. The customer should understand that there may be problems, and not be led to believe that the salesperson's company can do all things perfectly.

Persistence[2]

There's no power in selling that equals persistence. It wears down prospect resistance and makes it easier for a salesperson to close a sale. Every highly successful salesperson is everlastingly persistent. No one has respect for a quitter. A salesperson who too readily takes no for an answer or is quickly defeated by resistance earns little or no respect or admiration.

Many a sale has been lost, and many a business friendship nipped in the bud by salespeople who left too soon because they were afraid to impose too much on the prospect's time. They passed out of the picture just when the last barrier to a sale was about to crumble.

Most good buyers are normally loyal to suppliers that perform well and see no reason why they should change to a new supplier or try

---

[2] Charles L. Lapp, "Persistence," *Salesman's Opportunity* (March, 1981).

something that is new to them. Salespeople lacking persistence seldom secure any of these choice accounts. The objective of any salesperson is to create desire. If the salesperson does not do a thorough selling job, future calls are of no value. A lot of talking can be done without creating desire for a product or an idea. Also, a lot of good selling can be wasted through failure to follow-up on initial calls.

SEQUENTIAL STEPS IN A SALE

The sequential steps in a sale may vary depending on the prospect or customer contacted, the industry, the product or service sold, and the situational environment in which personal selling takes place. No two salespeople sell exactly alike and no two sales situations are alike. Consciously or unconsciously, however, a successful salesperson develops a format to follow in making sales. Typical of most personal selling are the following sequential steps:

Step One: Overall Preparation

In the chain of activities leading to a sale, the first step is for a salesperson to be thoroughly familiar with the state of the economy, industry developments, specific area market factors and trends, strategies, policies, procedures, and product selling points of competitors, as well as of the company or companies the salesperson represents. Thus, the salesperson must not only become knowledgeable, but also develop the right mental attitude, the skills of handling sales techniques, the proper work habits, and the motivation to succeed.

Salespeople must be well acquainted with their own strengths and weaknesses, the product lines and specific products being sold, the various markets to be served and their respective likenesses and differences, the various types of buyers that will be confronted, what competitors have to offer, and the specifics for making their offerings. Mastery of the selling techniques necessary to handle the varied situations and people a salesperson encounters is very important.

Step Two: Prospecting—Locating Potential Buyers

Prospecting for potential buyers should enable salespeople to bring the right products in contact with the right buyers at the right time and in the right light. **Prospects** are qualified, profitable opportunities for a sale. Prospecting can be broken down into three activities:

1. Formulating criteria for identifying a prospect. One set of criteria may be as follows: (a) high volume usage of products that can be mass produced, (b) headquarters decision-making, (c) satisfactory credit rating, (d) capacity for sound growth, and (e) high integrity and loyalty.

2. Searching for potential buyers based on the above criteria.
3. Qualifying leads to insure that they are *bona fide* prospects based on the above requirements.

Prospecting is a major activity for some types of salespeople such as those selling insurance and real estate in contrast to retail selling where prospect generation is largely done through advertising. In some companies, prospecting is made a functional specialty, wherein one part of the salesforce generates new business and another part of the salesforce concentrates on account relationships and maintenance. It is not uncommon in direct selling for a salesperson to have a number of **bird dogs**, i.e., individuals who generate leads and set up appointments for the salesperson to make sales presentations.

Prospecting is very often the downfall of many salespeople. An example of the prospecting techniques which may be utilized for some products include acquisition of nearby high school, college, or junior college graduation lists. A personal letter to each of the graduates extending your congratulations and inviting them to see your product may bring in new customers. Similar letters might be sent to families with new births or to new residents. Let's look at some additional sources helpful to prospecting.

Prospecting Sources.   Typical prospecting sources include the following:

- Directories of companies or other organizations doing business or functioning in a territory. There are directories published by trade and professional associations, by chambers of commerce and boards of trade, and by professional directory publishers. A good librarian can be an excellent guide to the kinds of directories needed.

- The yellow pages of the local telephone directory.

- Various industry, commerce, and professional periodicals containing articles and advertisements capable of providing valuable leads.

- Daily newspapers.

- Observation of industrial, commercial, or professional buildings, and directories of tenants of office buildings.

- Information provided by a prospect or customer whom a salesperson is about to leave.

- Conversations with business associates.

- Attendance at various business or professional meetings.

- Noncompetitive salespeople. In most cities, salespeople have organized tip clubs. These clubs normally consist of one salesperson from each industry in the area. For example, a club's membership may be comprised of an insurance salesperson, a real estate agent, a business machines salesperson, a new car dealer, a stock broker, and so on. If the real estate agent meets a new resident in the area, he or she may then pass the name along to the other members of the club. Also, most of the clubs have a quota of referrals that must be made by each member.

Qualifying the Prospect.   Once prospects are identified, based on a predetermined set of criteria, it is necessary to further qualify prospects to determine if they have the capacity and authority to buy. First, the salesperson must determine if there is an immediate need to buy. If the need is not immediate, the salesperson should complete a prospect card and follow up at the appropriate time. Second, the salesperson should identify the decision-maker. When selling to large companies it is often difficult to identify the decision-maker. Although a purchasing agent may appear to be the decision-maker, the real decision-maker may be a marketing manager, engineer, research and development director, or a committee. Finally, the salesperson must determine if the company or individual can afford to buy. This can sometimes be accomplished through credit checks; however, it is necessary to make personal contact before an assessment of financial status can be determined. Once the salesperson is in front of the prospect, it is possible to ask the person about similar expenditures, budgets, and financial growth. If it appears that a decision cannot be made because of financial constraints, it may be advisable to focus attention on other prospects.

Prospect Follow Up Card.   Salespeople should complete a prospect follow up card on each company or individual that meets the preestablished criteria. As indicated in Figure I-1, information included on a prospect card would depend on the classification of the prospect, business or consumer. For business prospects, the salesperson should primarily be interested in identifying products they could utilize, key decision-makers, their role in the firm, and their career objectives. For consumers, the salesperson needs to maintain any information that can help in developing a strong rapport. For example, anniversary and birthday cards can be mailed, or the salesperson may see an opportunity to help a potential customer accomplish a career or personal objective.

Step Three: Pre-Call Preparation

After developing a list of qualified prospects but before contacting them, a salesperson should engage in some pre-call activities. This step involves answering the following questions: What are the buyer's specific needs and/or wants? How does the buyer want to buy? and, how will the buyer react to a likely sales presentation? The planned sales interview should then be tailored to fit specific situations and prospects. Pre-

Business Prospect Card	**Consumer Prospect Card**
Company Name: _____ Address: _____ _____ Phone Number: _____ Size of Business: _____ Products Potentially Used: _____ _____ Primary Decision Maker: _____ _____ Other Decision Makers and their Role: _____ _____ _____ Career Objectives of the Decision- Maker: _____ _____ Credit Status: _____ _____ Special Notes: _____ _____ _____	Name: _____ Address: _____ _____ Home Phone: _____ Business Phone: _____ Age: _____ Income:$ _____ Credit Status: _____ Name of Spouse: _____ Name of Children: _____ _____ Birthdate: _____ Anniversary Date: _____ Special Hobbies & Interests: _____ _____ _____ Best Time to Meet: _____ Career Goals: _____ _____ Other Notes: _____ _____

Figure I-1
Prospect Follow Up
Cards

call activities might well be organized around the acronym, ACME. "A" stands for *aim*. A determination should be made as to what should be accomplished on each call. The aim may be to introduce one's self, to get a commitment for future business, to obtain the specifications or needs of a prospect, to present a proposal, to handle a complaint, or to finalize a sale on selected items.

"C" represents the *content* necessary to accomplish the selected aim or aims. Once it is determined that the prospect's interest is genuine, the salesperson should match buying motives to the content of the presentation. Which features, advantages, and benefits should be stressed in the presentation? The "M" involves a decision as to the *methods* of presentation to be used. The following should be answered.

- Is a demonstration feasible?

- Should testimonials be used?

- What supporting sales literature should one have available?

- Which products or product lines should be represented?

"E" stands for *evaluate*. An evaluation of the type of individual a salesperson will be dealing with should be made.

The following questions should be considered in profiling a prospect as:

- Will the prospect be dominant or submissive?

- Will the prospect be warm or hostile?

- Will the prospect be slow and analytical or aggressive and impulsive?

- What selling situations are apt to occur and what alternatives are there in handling them?

- Will there be more than one person involved in the buying decision and, if so, who are they?

As part of the precall preparation, salespeople should precondition themselves to react properly under the probable situations that they might confront. This includes being certain that sales literature, samples, and order blanks are organized. Then, too, a decision should be made as to whether an advance appointment for the sales call can be made.

Step Four: Approach and Getting Attention

Whether a buyer comes to an establishment to buy, or the salesperson calls on customers, attention must be obtained and the process of qualifying a prospect started (or continued if covered in pre-call preparation). If a salesperson must go through a receptionist, that person should be treated with respect. Although the receptionist should be respected, little information should be given, especially if it is a cold call. The receptionist does not make final purchasing decisions, but can put up obstacles to protect the potential buyer. A receptionist who has no idea why the salesperson wants to see the prospect, however, cannot as easily block the salesperson's visit.

The manner in which salespeople conduct themselves in the prospect's home or office is important. If customers or prospects are busy taking care of some detail, wait until they are free before attempting to get attention. Some salespeople have even found it quite effective to wait for the prospect to start the conversation.

Step Five: Opening Remarks and Establishing Rapport

The objectives of this step should be:

- To gain the prospect's attention.

- To get the prospect to listen or react.

- To find the prospect's level of acceptance of one's self, company, and general line of products or services offered.

After approaching prospects or customers with confidence, salespeople should introduce themselves in as pleasant a manner as possible. Also, a salesperson must remember that prospective customers are very cautious, skeptical, and sometimes irritable because they fear they are going to part with some of their hard earned money. An introduction such as "What can I do for you?" may be too often interpreted as "What can I *do you* for?"

When a potential buyer offers his or her name, the salesperson should be sure to get it right. The salesperson should use the prospect's name, as it makes the prospect feel more important and will also get other attention. Mispronouncing or forgetting a buyer's name will cause irritation. The main purpose of the introduction is to meet the prospect, establish rapport, and give the prospect or customer a reason to listen.

It is also a good idea to begin by discussing subjects in which the prospect is interested. Look around the office for clues such as pictures, awards, special fixtures and accessories such as an ashtray with a golf ball on it. Also look for pins, rings, or other indicators of special interest. Remember, salespeople sell themselves first and the product second. If salespeople do not effectively sell themselves they will not effectively sell products. The personal relationship may, therefore, be the most critical aspect of the sales process.

Step Six: Telling a Sales Story and Conducting a Sales Interview

At this stage everything should be done to assure that two-way conversation takes place. A professional salesperson listens to the buyer's ideas, probes for buying motives, and, in general, attempts to identify the buyer's needs. The salesperson can then focus attention on important product benefits and ignore the unimportant aspects of the planned presentation. This means that the sales presentation will change for different prospects. Some additional aids to professional salespeople include the following suggestions:

- Vary the speed of speech to the voice speed of each customer. People listen and comprehend at different rates. The appropriate rate is often indicated by voice speed.

- Vary voice inflection to highlight important ideas or benefits.

- Help prospects make the right decision in terms of need satisfaction, rather than pressure them into an inappropriate decision.

- Attempt to read body language signals.

- Ask questions instead of presuming things about the prospect's needs.

Step Seven: Demonstrating and Dramatizing The Offer

A touch of showmanship aids in getting and holding a prospect's interest and assuring conviction. Showing a product or picture of a product often tells a sales story much better than talking at length. A simple pad and pencil can be used to prove points, to draw diagrams or graphs, and to rough out sketches of the application of a product.

Step Eight: Handling Objections

The perceptive salesperson recognizes an objection as a vital part of selling. Without objections and resistance, a salesperson could be replaced by an order-taking machine. The objection stated may not be the real one, such as when a buyer states that the price is too high. The buyer may really be saying, "I don't have the resources now to make a purchase." A real **objection** can be defined as an argument offered in good faith by a prospect who is still interested but doubtful about some particular aspects of an offer. Excuses are really disguised refusals and indicate that the prospect is no longer interested. An excuse calls for an arousal of interest. Objections, however, must be met and dealt with if the presentation is to continue. Objections can tell the salesperson just how much further to go before trying for a close.

Objections normally result because (1) the customer does not have a complete understanding of the value associated with conducting business with the salesperson's company, (2) the customer is not willing to abandon traditional ways of doing business, (3) the customer does not want to take the risk associated with making a decision, (4) the customer is unable to effectively relate to the salesperson, (5) the customer is negotiating for a better deal, (6) the customer is not really the final decision-maker, or (7) the salesperson has not effectively communicated benefits that are consistent with the customer's needs.

How can objections be handled most effectively? Consider the following steps:

Listen to the Objection.   When confronted by the prospect, listen to and understand the objection. The customer is communicating his or her needs, and these needs should be evaluated carefully. In order to insure that everything is understood and that the client has related all aspects of the objection, there are several things that the salesperson can do.

- Keep the customer talking. One effective way to do this is to repeat the last several words of a statement in a questioning or puzzling manner. This will cause the prospect to continue talking and rephrase the objection in other terms. If there are other issues involved, they should become evident.

- Directly ask for additional information surrounding the objection.

- Make a note of the objection. This not only shows that you are genuinely interested in customer input, but it also gives you more time to formulate an effective answer.

Restate the Objection.   In order to insure that you accurately and completely understand the real objection, you should restate it in your own words.

If the salesperson has developed a solid relationship with the customer, a pricing objection, for example, is a request for justification of a price differential. The customer wants the salesperson to provide input that justifies a decision to purchase a higher priced item. After the prospect agrees to the question for more information, you are then in a position to provide that information.

Agree With the Prospect. A salesperson cannot win any argument with the prospect. If the salesperson proves that the customer is wrong, then the salesperson loses because the prospect won't buy. If the salesperson loses the argument then the potential for a sale disappears with the disagreement. It is, therefore, critical that the salesperson at least partially agree with any objection that the customer mentions.

Answer the Objection. A customer's objection should be handled by emphasizing and reemphasizing the benefits of doing business with your company. Common objections and methods of handling objections are mentioned in a subsequent section.

Obtain Agreement. Once the objection is handled, it is important that the customer agree with the salesperson's assessment. Therefore, the salesperson should complete his or her defense with a question: "Doesn't that make sense?" or "Don't you agree that the additional services we can offer you are worth $25.00?"

Postpone the Answer. In some cases it is not necessary to answer a question. It may be more important to provide additional background or support information before the objection is handled. When this situation arises, the salesperson might simply say, "that's an important question, and in just a few minutes I will provide you with some information that will help answer it."

The Pricing Objection. The pricing objection is basically a question about the value/cost relationship. The salesperson has not effectively built value to the point that it is perceived to be greater than cost. It is, therefore, necessary to simultaneously build value and reduce perceived cost. The following three suggestions can help the salesperson deal with a pricing objection:

- Keep the customer talking to insure that the objection is a legitimate one. Ask if the price is too high. Normally, the prospect will provide more than just yes for an answer.

- Restate the objection and agree that the price may be higher than some competitive prices. As was indicated earlier, the salesperson must show concern, restate the objection, and obtain agreement with the restatement.

- Answer the objection by building value and reducing the perceived cost. Try to find out how much too high the price is. Assume the customer says $600. The salesperson should then ask how long the customer plans to use the machine. If the prospect indicates three years, the salesperson is then in a position to reduce the $600 cost differential to a daily differential (see Figure I-2). "In essense then we are talking about an 83 cents price differential per day. Don't you agree that it is worth 83 cents per day to have (1) immediate service attention through the largest national service network in the industry, (2) a machine that is 10 percent faster than competitive machines, (3) additional options such as automatic dialing.... ?" (keep building value through benefits).

Figure I-2
Worksheet For
Reducing Price to
Daily Differential

Price Differential:	$600.00
Product Life:	3 years
Price Differential (per year):	$200.00
Price Differential (per month):	$ 16.67
Price Differential (per week):	$ 4.17
Price Differential (per day):	$ .83

The Loyalty-to-a-Competitor Objection.   First, agree that it is important to have a solid, long-term relationship with a supplier, and that you would not ask anyone to switch suppliers unless there were some overriding reasons to do so. Second, point out the advantages of doing business with your company. Third, ask the prospect to test the product for a limited time to compare the overall effectiveness of alternative suppliers.

It may also be feasible to suggest that the customer utilize your company for one or two items. This will stimulate competitive pricing and reduce the risks associated with having one supplier (i.e., the current supplier may not be able to provide all products for a period of time).

The I-Have-Had-Service-Problems-With-Your-Company-in-the-Past Objection. First, find out what specific problems have occurred in the past. Second, ask the prospect what he or she would do if confronted with a similar problem. After the prospect suggests what should have been done, indicate that your firm was aware of the problems, and did what the prospect has suggested to improve the situation.

The I-Just-Want-to-Think-it-Over Objection.   The think-it-over objection is a cover-up, and the real objection must be identified. If the prospect refuses to make a decision, try to set up a specific follow-up appointment.

Step Nine: Closing the Sale or Getting a Commitment

Closing the sale is usually the ultimate objective of a salesperson. To make most sales, a salesperson must ask (through various closing techniques) a buyer to buy. A salesperson should ask for the order and then wait until the prospect responds.

There are many closing techniques. Trial and error will reveal which technique a salesperson will be able to employ most effectively. The close that is utilized should be consistent with the salesperson's personality. It is difficult, therefore, to categorically establish that a particular close should be utilized in a particular situation by all salespeople.

Not only can salespeople ask for an order several different ways, but they can ask several times during the selling process. In fact, some managers suggest that salespeople ask for the order five or six times before giving up. Some of the techniques that may be utilized include the following:

- Assume the prospect is going to buy. Start completing the order blank and continue until the customer objects.

- Give the prospect several different choices. If the prospect begins making selections as to color or quantity, for example, you have probably made the sale.

- Close on a summary of all major points discussed in the interview.

- Close by listing all the pros and cons of the decision. Help the prospect develop the list, and point out that the positives outweigh the negatives.

- Close by relating a parable (particularly effective if the buyer is mainly an emotional buyer). Tell a story about someone else who made a positive decision and benefited from it.

If a salesperson has done a good job of qualifying, approaching, and working with the prospect, the close is nearly automatic. No sophisticated techniques need to be applied. The salesperson only has to ask for the order.

When a prospect has a legitimate objection and the salesperson cannot close, it is important to be courteous and keep the door open for future negotiations. Thank the buyer for showing an interest and maintain contact.

Step Ten: Post-Sale Follow Up and Servicing

Involvement in the selling process by a salesperson doesn't end when a sale is written. Most buyers need reassurance that they have made the right decision. Buyers need to be mentally conditioned for future sales. Also, there are many follow-up details that a salesperson must handle. The salesperson should give more emphasis to post-sale follow up and servicing which may include a call or letter to a new purchaser asking for comments, complaints, or suggestions. Favorable letters received from the customer can thus be used in making sales presentations to other customers. Unfavorable letters should be investigated.

The professional salesperson doesn't forget to give a little attention to employees other than the buyer in an establishment, and will try to win the goodwill not only of buyers but of anyone else who may influence the buying decision. The salesperson will do everything possible to help these people succeed. For example, the buyer may select a product that saves the company a significant amount of money. The salesperson may write the buyer congratulating him or her on the successful decision and send a copy of the letter to the buyer's superior. The salesperson will also identify the buyer's needs and interests and do things to satisfy these needs.

THE NEW ERA OF PERSONAL SELLING

A new era and a new challenge has come to professional selling to remove the cloud of doubt, uncertainty, and questionable practices that have been characteristic of this reputable profession. As complicated as the causes of recession and/or inflation may be, most people agree that the real cure is greater productivity. Constant dedication to greater productivity is the primary objective of professional sales. Since most salespeople are compensated on a commission basis, they are not rewarded if they are not productive. Also, additional rewards are contingent upon their ability to become more productive. The need for greater productivity will cause salespeople of the future to give greater attention to:

1. The work patterns or routes followed to cover their territories that yield the maximum return for effort and money expended.
2. Analyzing their prospects and customers to identify the most viable and profitable people with which to do business.
3. Recognizing problems of those to whom they sell and being capable of acting as business counselors.
4. Developing more concise and objective presentations in order to say just what prospects want to hear.
5. Recognizing that every buyer is different and must be assisted to buy accordingly.
6. Improving the use of psychology in their sales effort.
7. Building long-run sales rather than just securing the immediate order.
8. Providing feedback to their superiors on what they learn and observe in the field.

9. Assisting the buyer by suggesting any new or unusual uses for application or resale of their products.
10. Making certain they sell more than their product line or lines. They must sell themselves, their competitive advantages, their suppliers, and their companies' policies and leadership.
11. Knowing competitive products and policies as well as they know their own.
12. Improving their ability to hold group meetings and to do effective group selling.

In profit, non-profit, private, and government organizations, leaders must get a group of people to work willingly and effectively together in order to obtain greater productivity. This requires a consultative type of selling in which the manager consults and negotiates with subordinates to get them to sacrifice their own whims and peculiarities to work with the manager as a team toward a common goal of greater productivity.

The salesperson attempts to do the same thing with customers. In consultative selling, it is true that the salesperson still controls the interview. However, the control is more subtle and less blatantly manipulative. The new era salesperson controls the selling effort by asking more questions, listening, and then attempting to react appropriately on an individualized basis.

The consultative new era salesperson establishes such a relationship that clients become less sensitive to competitive proposals, less price sensitive, but more profit sensitive, i.e., they will take a broader view of situations. The consultative new era salesperson is more future-oriented and assists customers in becoming more future-oriented.

This new era of selling is not confined to managers selling concepts and programs, nor to salespeople selling goods and services. This new era of consultative-negotiative selling is becoming more prevalent among all types of professional people in their relationships with clients. For example, dentists must sell patients on the idea of using a private practitioner instead of a franchised dental clinic. Unless they practice consultative selling, they will be out of business.

Salespeople in the future will be faced with complex changes in their customer relationships. Customers are acquiring more knowledge and becoming more sophisticated, and salespeople must meet this challenge with greater attention to training and personal development.

Tomorrow's salespeople will also have a consultant's role in many aspects of a customer's business. Salespeople will be called upon to give advice on customers' marketing programs, operating systems, and distribution procedures. Salespeople truly become consultants. They acquire more knowledge of sales promotion, advertising, merchandising, public relations, and other aspects of their customers' business.

New era salespeople will also be accompanied by new era sales managers, a group of people who recognize the necessity of selling salespeople on their ideas rather than intimidating them into accepting their programs. They are managers that motivate through training and greater sensitivity rather than through meetings, contests, and criticism.

If, in this world of change, the selling force is to remain the vanguard of corporate progress, it must resist continuance of the status quo. It must recognize that there is a better way, a better approach, and seek change with energy and determination as apostles of constructive discontent.

SUMMARY

Selling is both an art and a science. The art of selling can be acquired only through constant attention to empathy and continuous practice to perfect selling techniques. Professional salespeople will be knowledgeable, possess a willingness to work hard, and have a desire to sell themselves, their product, and their company. Professional salespeople will make an attempt to acquire such qualities as enthusiasm, confidence, tact, acceptable appearance, sense of humor, loyalty, and honesty.

A salesperson's activities can be viewed as before-the-sale, during-the-sale, and after-the-sale. New era salespeople will recognize that their role will be that of a consultant, who helps customers meet their own objectives.

QUESTIONS

1. Is selling an art or a science? Explain.

2. What is the single most important characteristic that a salesperson should possess? Justify your answer.

3. What are the major steps of a sale? In what cases would a salesperson deviate from that model?

4. For the following industries, where would a salesperson go to generate prospects?
   a. Electronic component manufacturer.
   b. Full line industrial distributor.
   c. Life insurance.
   d. Consulting.
   e. Banking.

5. Develop a telephone procedure for setting appointments utilizing sound principles of selling.

6. How would you handle the following objections?
   a. "Your price is higher than competitive prices."
   b. "One of your salespeople called on me several months ago and was extremely rude."
   c. "I am not interested."

7. If a secretary asked you why you wanted to see her boss, what would you say?

8. In what ways is the profession of selling changing?

9. What is the most important rule associated with closing a sale?

10. Evaluate the following statement: Salespeople are born and not made.

Part 1

Environment of Sales Management

1. SALES FORCE MANAGEMENT IN A BALANCED MARKETING
   FIRM
2. SCIENTIFIC APPROACH TO SALES FORCE MANAGEMENT
   CASES

Chapter 1 _____

Sales Force Management in a Balanced Marketing Firm

After completing this chapter, you will be able to:

- Trace marketing thought through various stages of development.

- Explain the marketing concept and the variables that comprise its essence.

- Identify the importance of communication in development of the marketing concept.

- Define sales management, the scope of sales management, and the interrelationship between sales management and the marketing concept.

Science has brought many blessings to the twentieth century, including, in recent years, the implementation of the scientific method by companies to improve the marketing of goods and services. Forces both inside and outside companies have been responsible for advancing the science of marketing and the concept of marketing management as it is known today. Some of the internal forces which have impacted upon marketing procedures include consumer orientation, greater need for accurate planning, and need for better coordination of the elements of marketing with other functional areas of business. Some of the external forces known to have influenced the marketing science are the scientific management movement, competitive changes in the economy, and the newer and more active role of governmental agencies.

No areas of business have been more profoundly influenced by the scientific method or in need of a more systematic approach to problem solving than the sales and sales management functions. Not only does personal contact remain as the primary means of bringing buyers and sellers together, but it is still one of the most difficult activities to manage. The sales manager must not only attempt to allocate financial resources efficiently to various markets, but the manager must also attempt to allocate, maintain, direct, and control a large group of human resources that are oftentimes either independent businesspeople or employees who are not in direct contact with management.

HISTORICAL PERSPECTIVE

In the early development of modern business, firms were primarily production-oriented because of the large and independent demand for products relative to the available supplies. Since there was little need to stimulate demand, companies utilized their time and resources to develop more efficient methods of generating more output with the same input. As competition and supply expanded, however, the need to identify and penetrate available markets became mandatory for long-run survival. Concurrent with this new awareness and challenge came numerous innovations in sales and marketing such as:

- The move from sales agent utilization to the development of company-owned sales forces.

- The adoption of company policies which made the consumer's desires and needs the primary consideration for development of sales and marketing programs.

- The development of more effective consumer monitoring.

- Improvement in the organizational status of sales and marketing.

- The incorporation of social, cultural, and governmental goals into the sales and marketing plan.

Evolution of Marketing Thought

Although the need for more efficient marketing procedures paralleled the changes in supply/demand relationships, actual implementation of such systems was relatively slow because of the need for a better ideological understanding of marketing's role in business. For example, the first focus of marketing was a commodity focus within which people were primarily concerned with the movement of various types of products from the point of production to the point of consumption. Proponents of the commodity approach, therefore, envisioned marketing as the process of concentration, equalization, and dispersion of products. The next philosophy of marketing focused on the institutions involved in moving broad categories of products (i.e., consumer and industrial) from producer to consumer. The institutional approach emphasized that marketing institutions added value to goods and services by creating time, place, and possession utilities. Since the commodity and institutional approaches were not generally accepted, a functional approach evolved with primary emphasis on the various activities which are vital for efficient movement of goods and services. While the previous marketing philosophies were largely descriptive in nature, the functional approach can be thought of as the *process of marketing*.

Finally, marketing became a normative science involving the efficient creation and offering of wanted buyer values to stimulate desired transactions. Thus, marketing management became not just a descriptive account, or merely functions to be performed, or even a set of prescribed answers, generalizations, or guidelines; but it became an orderly set of questions with which the marketer determines the best course of action in each situation. This new contingency approach emphasizes that there are numerous, interrelated influences, variables, or contingencies that operate on and within the marketing system. It is not only necessary to identify the contingencies but also understand the impact which contingencies have on the system. The contingency approach, therefore, abandons the simplistic descriptive and functional approaches and advances the theory that all situations are different, and that the appropriate marketing procedure is dependent on external demands and internal goals.

A New Era of Awareness

In recent years, marketers have determined that the primary contingency impacting on market strategies and procedures is the ultimate consumer. In fact, according to Stanton, "The consumer's want-satisfaction is the economic and social justification of the company's existence."[1] Known as the marketing concept, this philosophy suggests that firms:

1. Find out what the consumers want; then attempt to satisfy those wants.
2. Consider the impact of all internal and external contingencies on marketing decisions.
3. Operate to realize a profit.

As one of the early practitioners of the marketing concept, General Electric's marketing executive indicated in 1957 that fundamental to this philosophy is the recognition and acceptance of a consumer-oriented way of doing business. Under marketing, the consumer becomes the fulcrum, the pivot point about which the business moves in operating for the balanced best interests of all concerned. Subsequent sections of the chapter elaborate on this basic marketing philosophy and indicate some basic procedures which are fundamental to its implementation.

PHASES OF THE MARKETING CONCEPT

In order to understand the role of sales management, it is necessary to completely understand the meaning and scope of the marketing concept. Since the marketing concept is a consciousness which permeates the entire organization, it influences and directs the behavior of all employees, including sales managers. Figure 1-1 shows the interrelationship of variables that comprise the essence of this significant concept.

---

[1] William J. Stanton, *Fundamentals of Marketing* (6th ed.; New York: McGraw-Hill Book Company, 1981), p. 10.

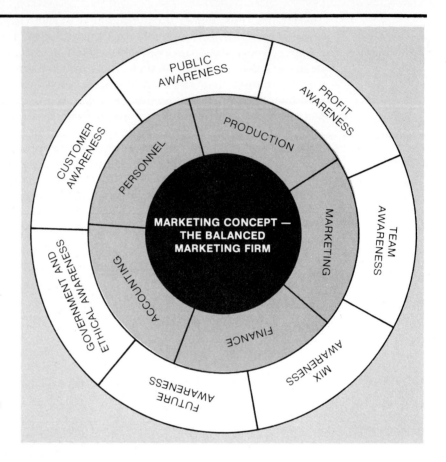

Figure 1-1
Interrelationships of
the Marketing
Concept.

The outer circle reflects the consciousness which must be understood
and assumed by all company divisions (inner circle) to implement the
marketing concept.

Customer Awareness

Customer awareness is the pivotal phase of the marketing concept
and has two primary aspects. First, everyone in the company must direct
their efforts toward identifying and satisfying the customer's needs,
wants and/or desires. Second, within their functional area, everyone in
the company must concentrate on persuading prospective customers to
purchase the company's products or services as well as insure that the
customer is subsequently satisfied with the purchase. This customer orientation is certainly not new to all firms. For example, in the early 1920s,
John H. Patterson told all National Cash Register employees the following: "Don't talk machines, don't talk cash registers, talk the customer's
business." In implementing this customer awareness phase of the marketing concept, one does not think, "How can I sell this widget to this

individual?", but rather, "How can I best assist this person in solving a problem?" Practically stated, it is easier to assist buyers in purchasing something they want, the way they want to buy it, than to sell them something you want to sell them the way you want to sell it.

In order to satisfy the customer awareness criteria, therefore, the marketer must be proficient in at least two analytical skills. First, the marketer must identify the appropriate target market segments and obtain all demographic and psychographic information that is necessary for development of an understanding of the target customer (i.e., market analysis). Second, the marketer must identify customer attitudes toward the company's product lines and understand what additional needs can be satisfied through development of related products (i.e., product analysis). The successful companies of the future are going to be sensitive to these needs by developing both internal and external information systems which facilitate the accomplishment of market and product analysis.

Profit Awareness

Although it is necessary to be customer oriented, it is also vital that the company do so at a profit. Companies exist to satisfy the needs of customers as well as to provide a reasonable financial return to investors. Satisfaction of one goal while compromising the other contradicts the basic ideology of the marketing concept. Not only can companies not afford to sacrifice customer satisfaction for profit, they cannot sacrifice profit to achieve greater customer satisfaction.

The total profit approach to evaluating alternative, strategic plans requires that the marketing executive forecast potential revenues and develop cost projections for each market strategy. By identifying the profitability of alternative strategies, it may become evident that some plans provide higher returns on invested capital. Also, the total profit approach will indicate the amount of risk associated with various plans, the extent to which resources will be tied up, the cost of tying up various human, financial, and physical resources, and the effect of tying up resources on flexibility.

Team Awareness

Successful implementation of sales and marketing plans requires the cooperation of groups of people working together toward a common objective. In addition to intergroup and intragroup cooperation, it is also critical that individuals sense that their personal goals are being fulfilled while cooperating to fulfill the common, company goals.

Team building consists of periodic attempts by a group of people whose jobs are interrelated to examine how effectively they function as a team, to identify barriers to effective collaboration, and to cooperatively reduce or eliminate the barriers. Effective interaction and cooperation among employees can trigger a synergistic effect which results in a situation where total output is greater than individual inputs. The team concept does, however, have some hazards which should be guarded against. First, when the team concept is used for problem solving; it can, at least initially, be very time consuming. Second, new members that subsequently join the team sometimes have a difficult time catching up with and being accepted by the existing team members. To have effective team building, therefore, attention must be given to organization structure, organization staffing, and organization motivation. Closely related to team building is mix awareness.

Mix Awareness

Not only must there be proper coordination between company goals and personal and organizational goals of employees, there must also be effective coordination of various elements of the marketing mix. Popularized by McCarthy, the four primary elements of the marketing mix include: (1) development of the right *product* for the target market; (2) utilization of the right *place* (distribution channel); (3) identification of the proper *price*; and (4) development of effective *promotion* strategy.[2] All four elements of the marketing mix are essential and interdependent. Thus, when a marketing mix is selected, all decisions about the elements should be made at the same time to assure compatibility. For example, if a company recognizes a need for a new, patented product that has primary appeal among a small, relatively affluent segment of the population, it may be a good idea to price the product high, utilize a selective or an exclusive distribution channel, and implement a promotional program that educates and supports the dealer as well as selectively appeals to the appropriate target market (i.e., magazines, direct mail). Of course, numerous additional variables would impact upon the financial marketing mix decision, but the point is that the decisions should be consistent and interrelated.

Future Awareness

As firms get larger, markets become more complicated and interrelationships increase at a geometric rate. Coupled with this growth is the need for future awareness. It is on this very basis that some authorities have differentiated selling and marketing. As Carlyle F. Barnes stated, "Sales is getting orders today." Marketing involves what is needed "to produce sales tomorrow."[3] Since change is one of the certainties of business, it is necessary for all personnel to anticipate changes, to attempt to understand the possible effects of changes on their organization, and to

---

[2] For a more comprehensive discussion of this mix concept, see Jerome McCarthy, *Basic Marketing* (6th ed.; Homewood, Ill.: Richard D. Irwin, Inc., 1978), pp. 39-43.

[3] Carlyle F. Barnes, "Modern Marketing Concepts: How They Contribute to Business Profits," *Marketing Insights* (February 9, 1968).

prepare for changes by implementing appropriate policies, procedures, and strategies.

The pervasiveness of change has provided impetus for some practitioners to develop more reliable and valid forecasting techniques. Although some success has been realized in development of demographic and sales forecasting models, there is still a critical deficiency of effective economic, political, and cultural forecasting procedures. With change in all these areas profoundly influencing many marketing decisions, it is critical that companies and researchers improve the state of the art in forecasting change. Without a future awareness there will be a tendency to promote short-term profits and survival at the expense of long-term growth and survival which are (or should be) two primary goals of business.

Public Awareness

Each person in a company must have an awareness of the importance and impact of internal and external publics. Philip Kotler defines a public as a distinct group of people and/or organizations that has an actual or potential impact on an organization.[4] The following publics can be roughly classified as external publics:

- Supporter publics who lend resources, i.e., money, time, and encouragement.

- Supplier publics who sell material goods and services to the company.

- General publics who have no direct relationship but can bring pressure on other publics and government regulatory agencies.

There are also internal publics that should be considered. These include:

- Employees.

- Spouses of employees.

- Shareholders.

- Informal cliques.

Government and Ethical Awareness

Because of the proliferation of governmental agencies which have been commissioned to regulate business, marketers have not only had to consider the impact of decisions on employees, customers, suppliers,

---

[4] Philip Kotler, *Marketing for Nonprofit Organizations* (Englewood Cliffs, N.J.: Prentice-Hall, Inc., 1975), p. 17.

and owners, but have also had to assess the legal implications of all decisions. It has become mandatory for all companies, large and small, to develop policies and implement procedures for handling government regulations. For example, all salespeople should be trained in basic anti-trust provisions. They should be aware of the fact that they cannot coerce customers to sell a certain product for a particular price or grant a discriminatory price for a product to certain, favored customers. Cursory training in appropriate areas of the law and specific legal counsel should be a prerequisite to development of a new business.

Communication—The Vital Catalyst

The catalyst for customer, profit, team, mix, future, public, and governmental awareness is efficient communication. If the marketing management concept is to be a reality rather than a mouthed philosophy, it is necessary that management encourage free and efficient communication between functional areas. This way a philosophical balance is achieved throughout the entire firm. In order to inform and instruct more effectively, the following steps should be followed:

Step 1: Carefully identify and think through the key points of the proposed communication.
Step 2: List all related points to be covered.
Step 3: Anticipate questions and objections, and think of answers to clarify them.
Step 4: Make sure that the message to be conveyed has reached the intended audience.

The total communication process will be discussed in Chapter 11.

Marketing Concept and The Sales Function

Before development of the marketing concept, a salesperson was regarded simply as an individual who pushed a particular product or product line. Very little consideration was given to the customer's needs or the product's ability to satisfy those needs. Today, however, with development of the balanced marketing concept, the salesperson is concerned with customer desires as well as the total distribution process. Such involvement begins with products designed to fit customer needs and continues through sales promotions activities, advertising, the final sales, and after-sale service to insure customer satisfaction.

As technology advances, the salesperson's role assumes greater importance. Marketing no longer means only the sale of a product; it becomes the sale of a bundle of buyer benefits. A customer does not seek, for example, to purchase just a machine, but rather is interested in acquiring greater production. The seller, therefore, must be prepared not only to sell the machine but also to install it, to advise on ways to optimize its use, and to service the machine after it has been installed.

A Company Profile

Mary Kay Cosmetics is a $235 million manufacturer and international marketer of cosmetics and skin care products. From its headquarters and manufacturing plant in Dallas, Texas, Mary Kay's management team directs almost 150,000 beauty consultants, 3,400 sales directors, 31 national sales directors, 5 domestic distribution centers, and 3 international operations located in Australia, Canada, and Argentina.

In order to maintain control over quality, Mary Kay is extremely selective in the development of new products. New product ideas proceed through an intensive product and market testing procedure before reaching the market place. The result is that after nineteen years, Mary Kay Cosmetics currently markets a selective line of only 45 different products. With the exception of eyebrow pencils, all of these products are manufactured in the 300,000 square foot plant located near the Mary Kay's Dallas headquarters.

The marketing and distribution structures have played an important role in the success of Mary Kay. Only one form of wholesale distributor, the beauty consultant or director, stands between the company and the consumer. Beauty consultants are not employees of Mary Kay, but are independent contractors, buying their products wholesale from Mary Kay, and then selling those products at retail to the consumer. The sales strategy primarily involves the utilization of beauty shows. These shows are given in the home of a hostess who has invited no more than five women to participate in a two-hour beauty session. The beauty consultant takes her guests through a step-by-step Mary Kay Skin-Care Program.

She offers personalized counseling, fashion tips, and demonstrates proper application of the Mary Kay products. Because most Mary Kay consultants maintain an inventory of products, orders can usually be taken and filled immediately at the show.

Beauty consultants are continuously supported by Mary Kay with training, advertising, sales aids, and frequent meetings designed to keep them informed of new developments. With a proven record of sales and sales recruiting, a beauty consultant may advance to sales director. Approximately 3,400 independent sales directors provide motivation, leadership, and training to beauty consultants throughout the world.

The highest achievement in Mary Kay's sales organization is becoming a National Sales Director. Each of the 31 National Sales Directors manages and provides motivation, leadership, and guidance to a group of sales directors.

In 1963 Mary Kay Cosmetics developed a long range sales and marketing plan that still serves as the basis for the firm's marketing programs and orientation. First, Mary Kay is dedicated to the development of products that are consistent with consumer needs and desires. The relatively narrow product line helps Mary Kay maintain excellent quality control and continue to improve the present product line. Second, Mary Kay serves the consumer with one-on-one, direct contact and service. They also provide immediate delivery of orders. Third, Mary Kay's marketing research department studies customer needs, monitors attitudes, and identifies opportunities. Marketing research also studies, analyzes and disseminates to management input from beauty consultants and directors.

In addition, Mary Kay Cosmetics is a teaching-oriented company. The beauty show, where company products are demonstrated, is designed to teach scientific methods of skin care. Although beauty consultants conduct beauty shows in a personalized way, the company provides a steady flow of information and suggestions. Beauty consultants also receive instruction on skin care so that they can then provide each consumer with reliable and helpful information on the care of her skin.

Finally, Mary Kay's customer orientation is reflected in several of its distribution and manufacturing policies. The company maintains complete control over the quality and timing of delivery by utilizing its own trucks. Also, products are supplied to consultants from one of five regional distribution centers that are owned and managed by Mary Kay Cosmetics, Inc. Also, products are normally manufactured during the day shift. Although it is expensive to avoid utilization of a night shift, Mary Kay believes that such a policy enhances quality control.

SALES MANAGEMENT TERMINOLOGY DEFINED

The focus of this book is the management of the critical function of personal selling. We use the terms management of the personal selling function, sales force management, and sales management interchangeably. We do, however, distinguish between the terms marketing management and management of the personal selling function. **Marketing management** is much broader in scope than sales management, encompassing interrelated business management of all activities involved in (1) planning and developing a product and/or service to be offered, (2) pricing of such a value, (3) promoting the value offered, and (4) selecting, evaluating, and managing appropriate channels of distribution.

Marketing management from a functional standpoint is usually considered to involve the following management activities: buying, selling (in the broader promotional sense), transporting, storing (sometimes including inventory control), financing, risking, standardizing and grading (the inspection function), and gathering and disseminating market information. Although the various marketing management functions are interrelated and have some impact on each other, our primary focus will be management of the sales function. The broad aspects of marketing management will, therefore, only be referred to when some significant interrelationship with management of the personal selling function exists.

It is appropriate then to define management and personal selling. According to Lawrence A. Appley, **management** is "getting things done through other people."[5] A broader and possibly more useful concept of management is that it is a process required to optimize the return from a specific commitment of the company's assets (including technical, finan-

---

[5] *Formula For Success* (New York: American Management Association, 1974), p. 1.

cial, human and/or mechanical) when other possible alternative commitments exist. **Personal selling** is the ability to interpret products and service features in terms of benefits and advantages to the buyer and to persuade and motivate the buyer to purchase the right quantity and quality of product or service.[6]

We shall identify and discuss activities and challenges associated with management of outside salespeople. **Outside salespeople** are those who call at the establishment or home of the customers as contrasted to inside retail salespeople, counter salespeople, and/or sales correspondents for wholesaling of manufacturing firms. Even though we focus on the activities and problems of outside salespeople, much of the material has a much wider application, with some adaptation on the part of the reader.

THE SCOPE OF SALES MANAGEMENT

As was previously indicated, sales and sales management are critical to successful allocation of scarce resources in a free, competitive enterprise economy. Since sales is a primary consideration in resource allocation, the way in which companies envision the role and position of the sales function will impact significantly on company profit, growth, and survival. This section identifies the various perspectives of sales and sales management.

The Narrow View

In many firms, the sales manager's primary function is to increase sales with little or no concern given to maximizing profit. Companies that maintain a narrow perspective also show little concern for maintaining consistent employment levels throughout the company or monitoring the interrelated effect that sales has on other functional areas. Pricing, distribution, product development, information collection and dissemination, and advertising normally receive only cursory consideration; and the sales manager is envisioned as nothing more than a glofified sales representative.

The Broader View

In today's more progressive firms, a broader view of the sales management function is taken. Firms recognize that the management of the personal selling function is related not only to advertising and other marketing activities but also to all other business activities. The contemporary sales manager also recognizes the necessity of making sales at a

---

[6] Kenneth B. Haas and John W. Ernest, *Creative Salesmanship* (2d ed.; Beverly Hills: Glencoe Press, 1974), p. 10.

profit, monitoring customer and supplier reactions to company products, services, and policies, and understanding buyer attitudes toward
the sales methods employed by each sales representative.

If one attempted to describe the sales manager's job in different
industries, companies, geographical areas, or at different levels within
an organization, one would find quite a diversity in the job activities
performed. Because of these significant differences, the emphasis in our
text will be on what constitutes the area of sales management regardless
of who may be performing the activities or at what level activities are
performed, rather than on the sales management job as performed under
differing circumstances or the activities which are assigned to a particular sales manager.

Functions of Sales Management

When defining the sales manager's role from a broad perspective,
numerous marketing management functions become at least partially the
responsibility of the sales manager. Figure 1-2 lists activites representative of the additional functions of the sales executive under the broad
view.

Figure 1–2
Sales Manager
Responsibilities—
The Broad View

1. Selecting and/or recruiting salespeople.
2. Initial and continuous training of salespeople.
3. Directing company-owned stores.
4. Managing office personnel (the supervisor may have as many as two to five times more office personnel than salespeople to manage).
5. Selling in an assigned territory or to certain selected accounts.
6. Coordinating such functions as service, engineering, buying, credit, financing, and warehousing.
7. Handling advertising and/or promotional work.
8. Acting as a substitute salesperson in uncovered territories.
9. Testing field presentations of promotions with customers.

Sales executives must assume the responsibility of training salespeople; familiarizing them with company plans, policies, products, and
methods; making certain that they call on the right customers at the
appropriate time; and making sure that they utilize appropriate sales
presentations. In performing these functions, the manager must continually train, motivate, control, and communicate with the sales force. Specific duties, however, are contingent upon such factors as the size of the
company, number of sales representatives, attitude of executives toward
marketing, types of distribution channels, and characteristics of the
market.

After specific supervisory duties have been delegated to the sales manager, the company must determine how many additional duties can be assigned without impairing the sales manager's efficiency in supervising a sales force. For example, should sales managers be required to sell in an assigned territory? Although it generally depends on the size of the company, the trend is away from loading down managers with too much direct selling responsibility. Generally, they call on accounts when a salesperson is sick or cover territories prior to hiring new salespeople.

Because of the myriad of activities that can be performed by sales managers, it is important that management identify and assign priorities to the specific functions that are critical to the success of the organization. If priorities are not specifically identified, it is easy for executives to conclude that the sales staff is properly supervised simply because someone has the title of sales manager. Identifying someone as sales manager, however, does not assure that salespeople will be given continuous training, proper direction, and the personal control necessary to bring about efficient sales performance. Sales management, therefore, must be approached functionally. Utilization of a functional approach makes it possible for executives to determine if management of the sales force is being performed efficiently and effectively and to specifically identify weaknesses in the sales force.

THE TOTAL-BALANCED-MARKETING PROGRAM

The primary objective of Chapter 1 has been to provide a brief understanding of sales management, the role of sales managers, the position of sales management in the marketing organization, and the philosophical basis for marketing strategy development (i.e., marketing concept). Although it is vital to understand the significance of a marketing concept ideology and to conceptualize the position that the sales and marketing functions should assume in a business organization, it is also critical that managers realize the necessity of developing a total-balanced-marketing program. The **total-balanced-marketing program** is a master marketing plan which reflects a sensitivity to the needs, priorities, and problems of other functional areas of the firm, all channel members, the consuming public, and governmental agencies. It is also a flexible plan; one that, like people, changes and is uniquely individual. Most important, however, the total-balanced-marketing program balances the needs of all significant groups and variables to arrive at a program that represents the optimum allocation of resources to accomplish organizational goals.

Balancing the many variables that impact on the achievement of organizational objectives requires the cooperation of all employees, channel members, and facilitating agencies. If someone compromises achievement of organizational goals in order to satisfy an individual or division goal, then the marketing program may become imbalanced; and if the practice becomes too widespread, inefficiency may result. For example, many firms allow sales representatives to negotiate price with customers. The same firms may also reward salespeople with a commission which is based on total sales volume. Since employees oftentimes sacrifice company goals in order to satisfy personal goals, the sales representative will possibly attempt to make sales, even if it means selling the item at a loss. Decentralizing decision-making relative to price also makes the firm vulnerable to antitrust violations such as price fixing and price discrimination.

Less than total-balanced-marketing will result if employees and channel members fail to accept a manufacturer's objectives as their own. Although it is impossible to achieve, a goal of the organization should be to strive toward such a balanced program. The firm should implement training programs, employee and channel communication systems, and control devices which effectively motivate people to understand and cooperate with the firm's short- and long-range plans. For example, intermediaries are too often thought of as computer codes, numbers, or pins on a map rather than as companies with unique needs and objectives. Rather than just impersonally dealing with channel members, the manufacturer should attempt to recognize their needs and objectives and utilize personal communications, employee education programs, and effective motivation to help them achieve their goals and, consequently, cooperate with the manufacturer's programs.

SUMMARY

Marketing and sales management ideology has progressed through numerous profound states which have made it more logical, objective, and consistent with society's needs. The result of this development is the marketing concept which emphasizes that the consumer is the focus of business decision-making and activity. In order to implement the marketing concept, a firm must have customer awareness, profit awareness, team awareness, future awareness, and government awareness.

Sales management is the process of optimally collecting, allocating, directing, and controlling resources related to the personal selling function. Some of the more important functions of sales managers are: (1) selecting salespeople, (2) training salespeople, (3) directing company-owned stores, (4) managing office personnel, (5) motivating salespeople, and (6) compensating salespeople. Also, it is critical that these functions be interrelated with other marketing activities in order to achieve a total-balanced-marketing program. In other words, sales should be interrelated with marketing which reflects a sensitivity to the needs, priorities, and problems of other functional areas of the firm, all channel members, the consuming public, and governmental agencies.

QUESTIONS

1. What are the two analytical skills in which marketers must be proficient in order to satisfy the customer awareness criteria?

2. Discuss two hazards of the team concept and what attention must be given in order to have effective team building?

3. What are the four primary elements of the marketing mix?

4. Why is it necessary to build a total-balanced-marketing-program?

5. List six phases of the marketing concept.

6. Define management and personal selling.

7. What are the functions of sales management?

8. Are marketing management and management of the personal selling force the same thing? Explain.

9. What might be the difference in activities performed by the chief marketing executive and an operational sales executive directly responsible for execution of the sales plan?

10. Some salespeople are designated as account managers or territorial managers. What management activities would be performed by these salespeople?

11. In this chapter under the heading "Historical Perspectives," five trends or innovations were suggested. What additional trends or innovations can you think of?

Chapter 2 _____

Scientific Approach to Sales Force Management

After completing this chapter, you will be able to:

- Identify the importance of scientific planning in business decision-making.

- Examine the sales planning procedure and variables that impact on its implementation.

- Identify and analyze marketing laws that impact on sales planning activity.

The competitive nature of the economic environment plus political uncertainties make survival difficult, even for companies which have service or technological superiority. In such an environment, firms often have difficulty translating the needs of complex and sometimes indifferent consumers into product or service opportunities. Firms enter markets too late, do not anticipate the effect of competitive behavior on market position, do not monitor changes in consumer characteristics, are insensitive to government policymaking and, in general, do not study the impact of various contingencies on future strategy decisions. Firms that are insensitive to these contingencies and do not systematically examine environmental factors in decision-making will generally be less able to translate their assets into want-satisfying goods and services—a prerequisite for long-term survival and growth.

Therefore, simply increasing selling effort in an unsystematic, random manner is unjustifiable and inconsistent with long-term company goals. In fact, such behavior may generate needless sales effort at greater costs thereby resulting in lower profits. It is the sales executive's responsibility to examine present and future opportunities, identify variables which may impact on those opportunities, coordinate sales effort with other marketing activities to insure that opportunities are efficiently taken advantage of, and direct sales effort into areas of maximum productivity.

The key factor in achieving long-term, manageable growth and survival, therefore, is systematic, scientific planning and decision-making. Without a systematic planning procedure, decisions are made in an environment of uncertainty; information which significantly impacts on accuracy of the decision is lost; and the influence of key individuals becomes more important than logic and objectivity. This chapter presents a scientific planning and decision-making procedure for sales managers. It is also designed to familiarize the reader with the legal environment of sales and sales management which must be carefully examined before any long-range plans are developed.

PLANNING SALES ACTIVITY

While the marketing plan deals with all marketing activities, a **sales plan** is a delineation of opportunities, strategies, and factors which impact on the sales function. It furnishes an outlook on *what, where, how, by whom,* and *why* actions should be taken to achieve the most effective results. The primary difference between a sales plan and a marketing plan is that the marketing plan is broader in scope. The sales plan is a subset of the marketing plan and must be interrelated with the marketing plan in order to achieve overall company objectives.

Specifically, the steps in the sales planning process are as follows:

Step 1: Analysis of the environment.
Step 2: Identification of opportunities and problems.
Step 3: Determination of organizational and individual goals.
Step 4: Determination of strategies to achieve objectives.
Step 5: Development of plans of action.
Step 6: Determination of the budget and resource allocation.
Step 7: Establishment of control and review procedures.
Step 8: Submission of the plan for review and approval.

Although the planning procedure appears somewhat overwhelming, its value relates to the extent to which it promotes simplicity. The sales planning process is a logical step-by-step process which facilitates an orderly flow of decision-making. There is an important continuity established by the sequence, with each step building from the former and then providing the basis for the succeeding activity. Most of the steps consist of familiar procedures, many of which are often currently being performed. But when performed out of sequence, or without prior or succeeding steps, the process can become costly and confusing. Thus, orderliness and sequence in the steps are as important as the steps themselves.

Step 1: Analysis of the Environment

The sales or market planner must set objectives, define strategies, and determine action plans to reach identified objectives. This must be done in a complex environment characterized by numerous internal and external contingencies. **Internal environmental contingencies** are factors which are within the firm and include (1) financial strength of the firm, (2) market position relative to competition, (3) managerial and technical expertise, (4) managerial philosophy and orientation (i.e., marketing or production orientation), and (5) company image. **External environmental contingencies** are factors which are beyond the scope of the firm's control and include (1) legal environment, (2) distribution channel structure, (3) competitive behavior, (4) technological state of the art, (5) market demand behavior and characteristics, and (6) cultural characteristics of the economy.

Environmental analysis is an organized method of collecting pertinent environmental data, analyzing the data, and determining its possible effect on business activity. Although sales executives cannot change these environmental factors, they can take advantage of opportunities and alleviate problems which are associated with these factors.

The key to effective environmental analysis is development of a system for collecting and evaluating information which impacts on company objectives. Internal information which indicates potential problems should be objectively analyzed to insure that organizational structure, strength, and philosophy are compatible with corporate growth objectives. Also, external information should be collected and disseminated to various decision points so that problems and opportunities are recognized.

In many large firms, it is feasible to establish a marketing intelligence or research group to collect and distribute information which is requested by the sales executive. The research group may distribute a questionnaire to the sales executive to help determine what information is needed by the executive in order to make effective decisions (see Figure 2-1 for a sample questionnaire). Information is then systematically collected and disseminated to the executive in an efficient and timely manner.

Figure 2–1
Sample
Questionnaire for
Determining
Marketing
Information Needs

1. What types of decisions are you regularly called upon to make?
2. What types of information do you need to make these decisions?
3. What types of information do you regularly get?
4. What types of special studies do you periodically request?
5. What types of information would you like to get which you are not now getting?
6. What information would you want daily? weekly? monthly? yearly?
7. What magazines and trade reports would you like to see routed to you on a regular basis?
8. What specific topics would you like to be kept informed of?
9. What types of data analysis programs would you like to see made available?
10. What do you think would be the four most helpful improvements that could be made in the present marketing information system.?

Source: Philip Kotler, "A Design for the Firm's Marketing Nerve Center," *Business Horizons*, Vol. 9 (Fall, 1966), p. 70.

For other firms, environmental analysis is left up to individual executives. The sales executive must identify information sources and set up a system for collecting, monitoring, and acting upon important data. For example, salespeople may be used to identify competitive activity, technological advances, and customer changes. This type of grass roots research is often neglected but can be a source of invaluable information. Although salespeople may not initially cooperate, compensation incentives can be tied to this research activity to help encourage cooperation.

Investigation of the environmental situation serves as the basis for the next decision area - identification of opportunties and problems.

Step 2: Identification of Opportunities and Problems

An organized environmental analysis will disclose the strengths and weaknesses of an organization relative to its opportunties, capabilities, and resources. The market planner must study that information and determine what it means to the company in terms of long-term growth. One of the major weaknesses of many plans is the failure to select opportunities which are most promising in terms of user need and satisfaction. Similarly, significant obstacles to growth go undetected and are not acted upon until the firm realizes irreparable harm. The market planner must answer such questions as: What are the major problems that are restricting or impeding growth? What problems have existed in the past? What problems are likely to exist in the future? What opportunities are there for overcoming these problems? What can be done to increase user satisfaction? What may be the reaction of competition to any plan set forth? What government regulations must be considered?

The answers to such questions can aid in identifying the variety of opportunities which are available and the major obstacles with which the firm must deal. A clear understanding of opportunities and problems serves as the basis for establishing clear and concise objectives. Objectives will reflect the identification of major opportunity areas and be modified by the potential influence of obstacles.

One way a firm can realize growth is to identify market segments (i.e., segmentation analysis) which are not being completely satisfied by existing sales effort. Resulting from the environmental analysis, the planner must decide which market segments should receive primary focus in the market or sales plan. Thus, the planner's frame of reference must be as follows: What is the nature, scope, and variety of segments to which the organization's marketing effort must be directed? Stated another way, the planner must consider every market segment which justifies a specialized marketing effort and, hence, requires a special plan. For example, a marketing plan for selling a piece of equipment to a farmer must be different than a marketing plan for selling the same equipment to a construction company.

The planner must begin by considering the profile of the market or markets served. There are usually numerous market segments for a product or service, each having its own unique set of characteristics. Too often planners lump too many market segments into broad market groups. They do not identify the unique demographic, psychographic, or life-style characteristics which characterize a specific segment. The resultant plans are, therefore, too general; they do not lend themselves to effective implementation because they are not adapted to the unique needs, wants, and desires of each customer group. The primary ways consumers and industrial users may be grouped are presented in Figure 2-2.

Consumer Segmentation

- Demographic - Population characteristics such as age, income, size of household, race, stage in family life cycle, occupation, education level, nationality, and sex.

- Geographic - Location of consumers.

- Life Style - Opinions and behavior relative to various activities and special interests.

- Personality - Individual self-concept and behavior pattern.

- Benefits - Benefits consumers desire to receive from a product.

- Usage Rate - Extent to which consumers use a product (i.e., light, medium, heavy).

- Loyalty - Degree of loyalty consumers have for a product or store.

- User Status - Past and present usage behavior of consumers (i.e., non-user, exuser).

- Social Class - Class level; upper-upper, lower-upper, upper-middle, lower-middle, upper-lower, lower-lower.

Industrial Segmentation

- Size - Number of employees, sales volume.

- Standard Industrial Classification - Customer classification based on primary type of product sold by the business and the business' position in the distribution channel (i.e., manufacturer, wholesaler, retailer).

- Account Status - National account or local account.

- Geographic benefits, usage rate, loyalty, user status.

Figure 2-2
Basis for
Segmenting
Customers

Step 3: Determination of Organizational Objectives _____

While previous phases in the planning process have been concerned with the compilation, analysis, and synthesis of data, this is the *first phase of key decision making*. At this point in the process, objectives which will serve as the basis for resource allocation and strategy selection are identified.

Objectives are specific, measurable results of organizational effort for a specific time period. They express a set of desired conditions—accomplishments to be realized at a given point in time. They do not specify the actions or means of arriving at the desired situation, but express a concrete achievement. For example, the following objective might be established for a sales force: Each member of the sales team will increase by 10 percent the number of accounts handled before July 1. This objective does not state how an expansion in the customer base will be accomplished; it simply delineates the desired final situation on July 1.

Types of Decisions Required.   There are three major dimensions to any objective:

1. The type or kind of result to be achieved—*What?*
2. The amount or quantity of achievement—*How much?*
3. The time by which it will be achieved—*When?*

The type and amount of result which a firm can reasonably expect to achieve depends on several factors: (1) the nature of market opportunities available to the firm; (2) the possible elimination, reduction, or modification of problems; (3) the limits placed on the firm by the external environment; (4) the extent to which managerial and technical expertise exists and can be utilized to pursue stated objectives; (5) the availability of financial and labor resources to pursue opportunities.

The time dimension of objectives is usually designated in one of three ways: long-term, intermediate, and short-term. Long-term objectives normally cover a period of time which is greater than five years. Intermediate objectives are usually accomplished within one to five years and short-term objectives are accomplished within one year. While long-term objectives are designed to establish basic growth patterns, short-term objectives are designed to help the firm hit immediate targets. Short-term objectives should obviously be related to long-term objectives, i.e., a current year's accomplishments should be part of the planned long-term results.

Purpose of Specific Objectives.   The purpose of the objective-setting phase is to establish a direction for the allocation of organizational efforts and resources. Stating the precise objectives to be accomplished implies both the strategy and course of action to be taken. This, in turn, determines the way in which activities are to be concentrated and how resources are to be deployed. It is critical, therefore, that objectives be established only after careful examination of environmental factors, potential opportunties, and problems.

Step 4: Determination of Strategies to Achieve Objectives

A **strategy** is the basic system of ideas to be employed to attain an objective. Strategies determine the nature and direction of support activities which are required in the plan of action. Determining strategies to be followed in achieving objectives is a critical aspect of the planning process. It is at this point that the nature and direction of the general approach to achieving objectives is identified. While it is important to collect environmental information and identify opportunties and goals, it is also important and necessary to translate these opportunties into strategies.

Tactics, on the other hand, are the individual actions required to implement strategies. Therefore, tactics are narrower in scope than strategies. For example, a firm may find that dealer effort to push its products is marginal. In order to solve the problem, the firm may employ a **push strategy** (i.e., direct contact with the dealer to encourage the dealer to push the product) as well as a **pull strategy** (i.e., contacting consumers to encourage them to use the product). The push strategy could incorporate several possible tactics: (1) increase salesperson contact to get dealers to carry more inventory; (2) provide dealers with displays and/or demonstrators; (3) sell for the dealers; (4) offer the dealers free merchandise; or (5) set up a contest to encourage additional sales effort. The pull strategy, on the other hand, might call for different tactics: (1) advertising directed at consumers to encourage them to try the product; (2) free samples; or (3) coupons.

Strategies, while they must be flexible, remain somewhat fixed and usually operate over long periods of time. Tactics or action plans, however, change more frequently. Many different tactics can be used to support a basic strategy. Also, until a specific strategy is defined, a meaningful action plan cannot be developed.

Although tactics are an important aspect of the total planning process, they are only as good as the information with which they are developed. Tactics are, however, the focal point of any sales or marketing plan and are critical to successful accomplishment of objectives.

Step 5: Development of Plans of Action

The **plan of action** is the logical step-by-step description of actions to be taken to properly implement the strategy and to attain performance of organizational objectives. This phase specifies the *how to, by whom, by when, with the help of, the timing of,* and other pertinent details of the execution of the marketing policy. In general, it specifies the work to be done, sets forth the sequence of work activities, and allocates tasks among employees. In other words, when strategies and tactics are accepted as accurate representations of company goals, they become the blueprint for operating the firm.

Since the plan of action is the detailed method for implementing strategy, it can be derived only after a strategy has been established. The strategy determines not only the direction of various actions to be taken, but also describes the amount of dollars to be spent and the purpose for which they are to be spent. Developed in this context, the phases required to make the plan effective become readily apparent. When developed out of the context of a predetermined strategy, the plan will usually be ineffective in accomplishing the desired goals. Succeeding steps are corollaries to this step since they describe the requirements for putting the plans to work and keeping performance on target.

Step 6: Determination of the Budget and Resource Allocation

In a sense, the resource allocation phase is simply a continuation of developing strategies and tactics. It entails the identification of financial factors which impact on plan development, the specification of costs which are related to each action, and the identification of resources required to perform identified activities. Although these actions are a continuation of Step 5, the nature and importance of these further considerations warrant special attention as a separate step.

It is important that the marketing director first determine all plans of action which are necessary to achieve objectives without being preoccupied with cost considerations. If the executive is overly concerned with costs, it is possible that the optimum plan to achieve objectives will never be developed. When developing a plan, it is best to identify the ideal course of action as an initial point of departure. Then costs can be considered to serve as a basis for modifying the ideal. Also, if the ideal is significantly better than alternatives, in terms of goal achievement, the marketing executive may be successful at selling management on additional funding.

Step 7: Establishment of Control and Review Procedures

Although development of a thorough and well conceived plan is important, it is equally critical that details of the plan be implemented in such a way that basic objectives of the plan be preserved. Specifically, this means that (1) the plan be implemented according to details of the action plan, (2) results be analyzed and monitored to insure that they are consistent with objectives, and (3) corrective action be taken if results deviate from stated goals.

The basic reason for building a control procedure into the marketing plan is to insure that execution of the plan is consistent with the predetermined time schedule and is measured in terms of its contribution to objectives. An organized control procedure provides for constant, *orderly feedback* of information which improves the quality of day-to-day implementation of the plan by the responsible manager. The importance of the feedback aspect will be discussed in Chapter 11.

Identification of performance factors to be controlled is determined by the established objectives. The marketing director must identify key performance factors which influence achievement of these objectives and establish a systematic measurement procedure. Objectives must be stated in a manner which facilitates effective control, and they must be quantified on a time scale so that in-progress measurements can be made. Tactics and strategies must also be stated in terms of goals. If objectives are well defined and goal-oriented strategies, and tactics are stated specifically, the design of an effective control procedure is greatly simplified.

Step 8: Submission of Proposed Plan for Review and Approval

If a plan is developed according to the recommended procedure, it should generate a complete document which represents the conditions and realities of the market. The completed document actually becomes a proposal of the best course of action based upon existing circumstances. It is not necessarily the final plan. When submitted to the chief executive officer or executive committee, the plan may be modified in order to make it more consistent with higher objectives.

In order to minimize the number of changes and, at the same time, insure that the basic direction of the plan is not lost, it is critical that marketing personnel interact directly with the review authority during plan development phases. Political problems should be identified, personal preferences should be considered, and executive cooperation should be obtained so that valuable ideas and time are not lost.

CONSIDERING THE LEGAL ENVIRONMENT IN SALES FORCE PLANNING AND DECISION-MAKING

As indicated previously, the first step in development of a plan is analysis of the environment. The firm must identify and examine all contingencies which impact on opportunities and strategies. Although all environmental factors are important to decision making, the legal contingency is rapidly becoming one of the most critical, constraining, and uncertain factors.

Sales and marketing executives are constantly working with distribution channel members in order to facilitate product movement to ultimate consumers or industrial users. When planning marketing strategy, sales executives have numerous potential strategies which may be employed to make these channel relationships more rewarding, productive, and consistent with corporate strategy. This section identifies distribution patterns that are regulated by government and the laws which influence sales force management.[1]

A Company Profile

Jimmy Dean Meat Company began operations in Plainview, Texas in May, 1969. After five years of continuous growth, the company expanded its $60 million dollar per year operation to Osceola, Iowa. During its early years, the Jimmy Dean Meat Company became the only company distributing fresh pork sausage nationally. Part of this impressive growth and development was attributed to Jimmy Dean's uncompromising philosophy: "Appeal to the people with quality and honesty—you'll win their confidence. Maintain quality and honesty, and you'll keep it."

From 1974 to 1977 the Jimmy Dean Meat Company experienced a significant decline in sales. One of the primary reasons for this decline was a problem with developing and maintaining distributor relationships. As a result, Jimmy Dean became more personally involved in day to day operations. He acquired control of the company, restructured the organization, appointed a new management team, and rededicated the company to its original mission: "to produce and market a high quality line of meat products in order to create and maintain satisfied customers, with an acceptable level of profit to the company and its distribution network allowing continued progress and growth."

The new management group also made important decisions to reverse the downward spiral in sales and profits. Texas and Mississippi plants were closed, and production was consolidated at the Osceola, Iowa facility. The food service program was temporarily suspended to free resources for development of new products and package sizes. Management also developed an organization structure that was more responsive to a competitive and complex market. The Executive Committee, including the vice president of sales and marketing and the vice president of operations, reports directly to Jimmy Dean, the President and chief executive officer. Reporting to the vice president of marketing are the product manager, the manager of sales and marketing administration (including promotions), and the vice president of sales.

Jimmy Dean's distributes its products on a fleet of 30 trucks. The company's promotional program includes television and newspaper advertising, newspaper couponing, and joint cooperative advertising with firms selling compatible products. Many of these activities are coordinated with an advertising agency. An independent public relations firm coordinates both marketing activities and Jimmy Dean's personal efforts.

Marketing planning has also become an ingredient in Jimmy Dean Meat Company's success. Planning is initiated by the marketing department. Regional sales managers submit sales activies and quarterly forecasts to the product manager. Marketing then accumulates vital marketing data in order to establish strategic priorities and forecasts. Data evaluated by marketing includes: location, strategies, and market position of competitors; trends in the industry and economy; hog prices; pricing strategies and levels; distribution programs and strategies; advertising and public relations activities; and attitudes and behaviors of present and potential customers.

After the marketing department identifies the company's present position, the executive committee determines its future courses of action. At the same time, each regional manager sets his or her own objectives. The product manager then considers *headquarter objectives and regional objectives, and establishes marketing priorities.*

Marketing strategies, therefore, result from interplay between top management, marketing, and sales. Sales provides input on strategies and programs that are consistent with the needs of each region. Marketing evaluates activities in each region and provides additional impact on regional strategies. Marketing also analyzes market data as well as data on new product tests, customer studies, pricing, competition, and distribution penetration. Top management established overall company goals and objectives. Marketing subsequently utilizes this input to finalize marketing strategies. In light of regional and national strategies, forecasts and budgets for each operating division are established.

Regulated Distribution Practices

Although companies are free to engage in most channel activities, certain sets of circumstances may cause some activities to be in violation of the law. Specifically, channel activities which are scrutinized by enforcement agencies include exclusive dealing contracts, tying contracts, requirements contracts, reciprocity, and vertical and horizontal division of the markets.

Exclusive Dealing Contracts. Exclusive dealing contracts involve situations where the seller agrees to sell only through one agency and the agency reciprocates by agreeing to sell the product of only one manufacturer. Although exclusive dealing contracts are not illegal per se, they are normally considered illegal if (1) the manufacturer's sales volume represents a substantial percent of the total sales volume for a particular product class in the affected market or (2) competition is substantially lessened because the dealer involved in the exclusive deal has a dominant position in the market. In other words, if a dealer has a significant share of the market and only one manufacturer can sell to that dealer, then penetration of that market is virtually closed to competing manufacturers.

Tying Contracts. A tying contract is a situation in which the seller agrees to sell one product, the tying product, only if the buyer agrees to buy the seller's other product(s), the tied product(s). If the tying product is a patented product, the arrangement is always illegal (i.e., illegal per

[1]This section is adapted from Joe. L. Welch, *Marketing Law* (Tulsa, OK: Petroleum Publishing Company, 1980).

[2] *See Moore v. Matthews and Co.* in: "Legal Developments in Marketing," *Journal of Marketing* Vol. 41, No. 4 (October, 1977), p. 108.

[3] *Times-Picayune Publishing Company v. United States,* 345 U.S. 594 (1953); See also: Malcolm E. Wheeler, "Some Observations on Tie-Ins, the Single Product Defense, Exclusive Dealing and Regulated Industries," *California Law Review,* Vol. 60, No. 6 (November, 1972), pp. 1558-1562.

[4] Lee N. Abrams, "Tying Arrangements and Exclusive Dealing Contracts," *Chicago Bar Record,* Vol. 53, No. 2 (November, 1971), p. 78.

se). If a patented product is not involved, tying contracts are illegal unless the tying product is neither unique nor attractive enough to restrain competition in the tied market.[2] Specific situations which may serve as justification for using tying contracts are as follows:

- No economic power exists because the tying product is not sufficiently unique.

- The tying contract is necessary to control the quality image of the tying product (e.g., in some franchising operations).

- Two distinct products do not exist; for example, the Times-Picayune Publishing Company will publish both a morning and evening newspaper. In order to purchase advertising space in one of the editions, the advertiser had to buy space in the other edition. The court ruled that the products (morning and evening editions) and markets were the same; therefore, there was no dominant tying product which gave the publisher economic leverage in the tied market.[3]

- The "use of the tying product is essential to the efficient operation of the tied product."[4]

Requirements Contracts. A requirements contract maintains that the buyer must buy or lease all or part of its requirements from one seller for a specified time period. Although they are not illegal per se, requirements contracts may be considered illegal if they restrain trade or substantially lessen competition. In other words, a requirements contract is illegal only "if it forecloses competition in a substantial share of the market."[5]

Reciprocity. Reciprocity involves a situation where Buyer A agrees to buy from Buyer B only if Buyer B agrees to reciprocate by purchasing from Buyer A. In other words, "if you will buy from me, I will buy from you". According to Moyer, there are at least two advantates of using reciprocity.[6] First, it reduces selling costs because of the minimum selling effort required. Second, costs of searching for sources of supply and outlets for merchandise disposal are reduced.

Although reciprocity is a widely accepted method of conducting business, it is not immune from examination by the courts. As with other forms of exclusive agreements, reciprocity can be attached under the Sherman Act, Section 3 of the Clayton Act, or Section 5 of the Federal Trade Commission Act.

In the early 1960s, General Motors was accused in both criminal and civil court of utilizing its size and related bargaining power to exert

---

[5] *Ibid.*, pp. 80-81.
[6] Reed Moyer, "Reciprocity: Retrospect and Prospect," *Journal of Marketing*, Vol. 34, No. 4 (October, 1970), p. 52.

pressure on railroads to engage in a reciprocal agreement.[7] GM formed a subsidiary company which manufactured locomotives. Because of the volume of business GM transacted with the railroads, it could force the railroads to purchase its locomotives by threatening to ship through other railroads if competing locomotives were purchased. As a result of this conspiracy, General Motors captured 84 percent of locomotive business. The courts found this activity in violation of the Clayton and Sherman Acts and sought divestiture of the locomotive division by GM. Anticompetitive reciprocity, therefore, involves a situation where one firm can use its market strength to coerce companies into compliance with the reciprocal agreement.

Division of Markets.   There are two types of market divisions: horizontal and vertical. Horizontal divisions involve situations where two or more companies on the same level of distribution conspire to allocate geographic territories or product markets among themselves. A vertical division is one in which the manufacturer gives dealers or distributors the right to sell in a specified territory. Although horizontal divisions are illegal per se, vertical divisions are only illegal if the agreement substantially lessens competition.

Major Legislation Affecting Distribution Practices

Three major pieces of legislation profoundly influence distribution planning and decision-making of marketing executives. They include the Sherman Act, the Clayton Act, and the Federal Trade Commission Act. A summary of these and other statutes is presented in Figure 2-3.

Sherman Act.   The Sherman Act, passed in 1890, may also be applied to control certain distribution activities. The act requires that businesses act independently rather than in concert with competing businesses. Proponents of the act wanted to maintain free competition by eliminating unfair accumulations of power. This was generally accomplished by prohibiting (1) "Every contract, combination, or conspiracy, in restraint of trade or commerce among the several states, or with foreign nations" (Section 1) and (2) "Monopolies or attempts to monopolize" (Section 2).

The primary problem with the Sherman Act in regulating distribution is that the activity must involve monopolization, an attempt to monopolize, or conspiracies to restrain trade unreasonably. Specific activities which may be in violation of the Sherman Act are mergers, tying contracts, division of markets, and price fixing. The Antitrust Division of the Department of Justice has sole responsibility for investigating and prosecuting companies which violate the Sherman Act and

---

[7] *U.S. v. General Motors Corporation*, Criminal Action 61-CR-365 (April 12, 1961): *U.S. v. General Motors Corporation*, Civil Action 63C80 (January 14, 1963).

1890 — **Sherman Antitrust Act.** Outlaws monopolies as well as contracts, combinations, and conspiracies that restrain trade.

1914 — **Clayton Act.** Regulates price discrimination, tying contracts, exclusive dealing arrangements, requirements contracts, reciprocal deals, and acquisition of stock of another company.
AMENDMENTS TO CLAYTON ACT
    1936 — *Robinson-Patman Act.* Regulates seller-induced price discrimination, buyer-induced price discrimination, and price discounts (i.e., advertising allowances, broker's discounts).
    1950 — *Celler-Kefauver Amendment.* Regulates acquisition of assets as well as stock of another company.
    1976 — *Hart-Scott-Rodino Antitrust Improvement Act.* Requires large firms to prenotify FTC of their intentions to merge.

1914 — **Federal Trade Commission Act.** Declares unfair methods of competition to be illegal; established the Federal Trade Commission.
AMENDMENTS TO FTC ACT
    1938 — *Wheeler-Lea Act.* Prohibits deceptive acts and practices as well as unfair methods of competition.
    1973 — *Alaska Pipeline Act.* Increases penalty for violating a cease and desist order; allows injunctive relief.
    1975 — *FTC Improvement Act.* Expands idea of trade regulation rules; expands remedial powers of FTC.

1966 — **Fair Packaging and Labeling Act.** Prevents deceptive packaging and labeling practices; facilitates price comparisons.

1968 — **Consumer Credit Protection Act.** Requires full disclosure of credit terms. Includes Truth-in-Lending Act, Equal Credit Opportunity Act, Fair Credit Billing Act, Fair Credit Reporting Act, Fair Debt Collection Practices Act, and Consumer Leasing Act.

1972 — **Consumer Product Safety Act.** Regulates activities related to product safety such as adopting safety standards for products; banning hazardous products; recalling defective products; established Consumer Product Safety Commission.
AMENDMENTS TO CPSA
    1976 — *Consumer Product Safety Commission Improvements Act.* Permits consumers to sue Customer Product Safety Commission; expands authority of CPSC.

1975 — **Magnuson-Moss Warranty Act.** Requires disclosure of warranty terms in easily understood language.

Figure 2–3
Significant
Legislative
Enactments

joint responsibility with the Federal Trade Commission for monitoring activities delineated in the Clayton Act.

Clayton Act.   The law which was specifically designed to regulate distribution channel relationships is the Clayton Act. Passed in 1914 to give the courts more specific guidelines with regard to anticompetitive restraints of trade, the Clayton Act prohibited the following practices "where the effect of the practice may be to substantially lessen competition or tend to create a monopoly in any line of commerce."

- Price Discrimination (Section 2)

- Exclusive Agreements, including tying contracts, requirements contracts, and reciprocity (Section 3).

- Acquisition of stock of another company (merging)—Section 7.

In 1950, Section 7 of the Clayton Act was amended by the Celler-Kefauver Act to prohibit acquisition of assets as well as the stock of another company when the effect of the acquisition is to lessen competition substantially or to create a monopoly. Prior to passage of this amendment, only acquisition of stock was illegal. The Celler-Kefauver Amendment plugged this loophole in the law.

Federal Trade Commission Act.   The Federal Trade Commission Act (FTC Act) of 1914 may also be used to attack some distribution activities as "unfair methods of competition." Specifically, the FTC Act (1) declared unfair methods of competition to be illegal, and (2) established the FTC as an investigative and regulatory agency. In 1938, the FTC Act was amended by the Wheeler-Lea Act to make deceptive acts and practices illegal too. Because of the broad scope and general nature of the law, the FTC has flexibility to investigate numerous business activities such as advertising, preticketing, lotteries, pricing practices, and distributing activities.

Regulation of Pricing

Since salespeople oftentimes use price to stimulate purchasing behavior, it behooves sales managers to inform salespeople of the laws which regulate pricing activity. In fact, when training new members of the sales force a special session should be devoted to price-oriented laws.

Price fixing.   Price fixing involves a scheme between competitors to raise, lower, or stabilize prices directly through personal interaction or indirectly by (1) taking distress merchandise out of deviant market channels, (2) rotating bids, (3) distributing price lists to competitors, or (4) agreeing on standard markups or discounts. The court's attitude toward these direct and indirect schemes to fix prices is very clear. They are, under all circumstances, illegal even if the fixed prices are reasonable and even if the conspirators are small and control an insignificant proportion of the market.

In order for the FTC and Justice Department to utilize their resources effectively to uncover price-fixing schemes, it is important for them first to identify industries where the probability of a conspiracy is greatest. In an attempt to identify such industries, the following conditions have been suggested as being most favorable to price-fixing schemes: (1) existence of an oligopolistic market structure; (2) insignificance of a competitive fringe (i.e., small firms that when taken together, command a relatively large market share—20 percent; (3) a small number of close product substitutes; (4) a high ratio of fixed costs to total costs; (5) decentralization of decision-making; (6) a history of price-fixing schemes in industry; (7) availability of a trade association.

Price Discrimination.   Discrimination in price may assume several forms and have negative competitive effects at various levels of the distribution channel. A manufacturer might give a lower price to customers in one geographic area in order to run a competitor in that area out of business. On the other hand, the manufacturer might give a lower price to a potential customer simply to get that customer's business. The effect may be to reduce competition between the favored customer and other customers that pay higher prices for the same items. Price discrimination may also result from providing one customer with proportionally more advertising dollars or promotional support than competing customers. Finally, discriminatory pricing may be accomplished by giving a broker discount to a buyer that performs the broker's function but is not a *bona fide* independent broker.

Price discrimination is regulated by the Robinson-Patman Act of 1936 which amended Section 2 of the Clayton Act. Specifically, the Robinson-Patman Act makes it unlawful to discriminate in price where the effect of such discrimination may substantially lessen competition or tend to create a monopoly on any level of the distribution channel. The law also requires that advertising allowances and promotional support be given on proportionally equal terms to all competing customers. In addition, the Robinson-Patman Act requires that broker discounts only be given to brokers who are independent of both the buyer and seller.

Although price discrimination is illegal where competition is reduced, it is not illegal per se. There are, therefore, several conditions which, when present, serve as justification for discriminatory pricing. These defenses are as follows:

- The seller can show that a cost savings was realized from selling to a particular customer.

- The seller is meeting the equally low price of a competitor.

- The price differential was caused by normal market/price fluctuations.

- The product being sold at a discount is not of like grade and quality as other products that are being sold by the manufacturer.

- The transaction does not involve interstate commerce.

- Buyers are not in competition.

- The item being sold is not a commodity.

Regulation of Sales Promotion

Although most governmental regulatory activity has been directed at advertising, several statutes also affect personal salespeople. According to the FTC Act, as amended by the Wheeler-Lea Act, "unfair methods of competition" and "deceptive acts and practices" are illegal. Some activities which are considered to be unfair or deceptive are as follows:

- Making fraudulent statements or introductions. For example, stating the salesperson is conducting research to get in the door; then, once in the door, attempting to sell a product or service.

- Using in-store switch tactics by using an advertisement to lure people to the store, then (1) refusing to sell the product as advertised, (2) disparaging the product, (3) failing to maintain a reasonable level of inventory, (4) refusing to deliver the product within a reasonable time period, (5) showing a defective product, or (6) using compensation methods which discourage salespeople from selling the product.

- Using after-sale switch tactics. Although the retail store may apparently offer and sell an advertised product in good faith, it may use after-sale tactics to cause the consumer to cancel the purchase; e.g. switching to a higher priced item, failing to make delivery within a reasonable period of time, delivering defective merchandise, or using after-sale disparagement of the product.

- Misrepresenting the nature or quality of a product. For example, land companies misrepresenting the quality and potential of land developments.

In addition to the FTC Act, several other statutes have been advanced to help alleviate unfair sales tactics. First, some municipalities enforce "Green River Ordinances," which require the salespeople be invited by the occupant of a residence before any sales call is made. Second, the FTC adopted a trade regulation rule, *Cooling-Off Period for*

Door-to-Door Sales, which requires that sellers print the following statement on contracts for the sale of consumer goods and services:

You, the buyer, may cancel this transaction at any time prior to midnight of the third business day after the date of this transaction.

Third, some states require that salespeople identify themselves as salespeople when contacting personal residences. Finally, the FTC has required that some companies disclose positive as well as negative product information. Such affirmative disclosure orders have been given to land companies, computer schools, hair replacement centers, and tobacco companies (e.g., health warning on cigarette packages).

SUMMARY

In order to achieve long-term growth and survival, firms should develop a systematic and scientific sales planning procedure. Steps that should be included in the planning procedure include: (1) analysis of the environment; (2) identification of opportunities and problems; (3) determination of organizational and individual goals; (4) determination of strategies to achieve objectives; (5) development of plans of action; (6) determination of the budget and resource allocation; (7) establishment of control and review procedures; (8) submission of the plan for review and approval.

Although all environmental factors are important to decision-making, the legal contingency is rapidly becoming one of the most critical, constraining, and uncertain factors. Laws with which sales managers should be particularly familiar include the Sherman Antitrust Act, the Clayton Act, the Federal Trade Commission Act and the various consumer-oriented laws. The purpose of these laws is to require that firms operate independently and honestly.

QUESTIONS

1. Discuss long-term, intermediate, and short-term organizational objectives.

2. Discuss the difference between *strategy* and *tactic*.

3. List the steps in the sales planning process.

4. Discuss the legality of exclusive dealing contracts and tying contracts.

5. Discuss the two types of market divisions.

6. What are the conditions that have been suggested as being most favorabe to price-fixing schemes?

7. Discuss two advantages of using reciprocity. What are the legal implications of such a strategy?

8. Discuss the function of the sales executive.

9. When is a merger illegal?

10. What factors should be considered in environmental analysis?

11. Discuss the validity of the statement: "The consideration of budgeted costs should be of primary importance when determining plans of action."

Case 1–1

Sure-
Remove
Company

Roberta Brownfield, an M.B.A. graduate of Northwestern University, took over two months ago as president of a small firm, Sure-Remove, in Springfield, Missouri. The firm sells a combination of hand cleaner and spot remover through both company salespeople and independent sales agents. Prior to attending Northwestern, Ms. Brownfield, an undergraduate with a Liberal Arts degree from Southwest Missouri State University, had been a regional sales manager of a large, well-known pharmaceutical firm.

Ms. Brownfield selected as her sales manager Mr. Pershing Bell, a friend who was a student with her at Southwest State and later, a salesman with her when she was regional manager.

Mr. Bell feels it is his main responsibility to sell the product and get as great a sales volume as possible regardless of the price, cost of sales, or customer reached. The company's sales force consists of twenty of its own salespeople, plus fifteen sales agents. All are paid on commission.

James Addison, the Controller, Finance Officer, Chief Accountant, and Legal Advisor agrees with the sales manager that sales volume is the all-important goal. He believes that if the sales manager could get the volume, he would be able to manipulate finances to assure a profit. Addison has the final say about prices and all terms of sales. He is also solely responsible for forecasting and budgeting.

The production manager assured everyone that the product should sell itself since the lanolin base made the combination hand cleaner and spot remover the best product on the market. The competitors, of course, feel differently about the product, and suggest that it is a high priced cosmetic; not really a hand cleaner/spot remover.

Pedro Sanchez, another Southwest Missouri State graduate, was given the responsibility of handling both purchasing and credit and collections. Mr. Sanchez believes tighter controls, particularly on purchasing, personal selling, advertising, and credit granting, could significantly help the company avoid financial losses.

Roberta Brownfield had been introduced to the marketing concept at Northwestern University and felt that the concept had not been used in the past, but that it should be implemented within and throughout the Sure-Remove Company. She believes that an updated view of the marketing concept requires that she and the sales manager be customer-oriented and profit-oriented, and that all company activities be coordinated.

Mr. Bell is afraid that if too much emphasis is placed on the marketing concept, day-to-day implementation of sales programs would be neglected. Though interested in planning and coordinating activities, Mr. Bell is convinced that only increased sales can pave the way to higher profits.

1. What is your opinion of Sure-Remove Company's attitude toward marketing, in general, and sales, in particular?

2. What organizational and philosophical developments would have to accompany implementation of the marketing concept?

3. Does the firm have a clear and accurate understanding of the total-balanced-marketing concept? Explain.

Case 1–2

Stevenson's Candy Company

Jack C. Stevenson, founder and chief operating officer for Stevenson's Candy Company, recently attended an American Marketing Association seminar on the realities of the marketing concept in U.S. business. His company's growth had recently gone from an annualized rate of 27 percent to a negative 5 percent during the past two years. Part of the reason for this decline was that two products accounted for most of the growth during the past 20 years. Decline in the growth of these two products could have been directly correlated to decline in overall corporate growth.

In order to reverse this negative growth pattern, Mr. Stevenson decided to hire a Vice President of Sales that would be responsible for increasing sales of existing products and developing new products for existing markets. This person would report directly to Mr. Stevenson.

Mr. Stevenson also hired a research director that would be responsible for monitoring the penetration of existing markets, monitoring market share, identifying customer attitudes and needs, and testing the acceptability and feasibility of new product ideas.

1. Do you think Mr. Stevenson came away from the seminar with a good understanding of the marketing concept? Explain.

2. What additional questions should be answered by a company that is attempting to develop a marketing orientation?

Case 2–1

Hollywood-at-Home, Inc.: Promoting In-Home Movies

Hollywood-at-Home, Inc. (HAH) was incorporated in January, 1976, to engage in the subscription T.V. business. The public had been exposed to current, unedited, commercial-free movies in hotels and motels, and early tests disclosed that apartment and condominium dwellers were willing to pay a fee to receive these films in their homes.

Television programming has moved increasingly to movies since 1961 when they were first shown regularly in prime-time. Industry spokepersons were of the opinion that uninterrupted, more up-to-date, uncensored movies would cut into free T.V. audiences or else force a change in programming. Television did not kill radio, as some people predicted it would, but it forced a change in programming. Apparently, the same is proving true of pay versus free T.V.

In mid-1975, 10 million homes were hooked up to one or another of the nation's 3,240 cable systems. But cable penetration in each market—the proportion of people who can sign up for cable who actually do—was not what cable operators had hoped for. In New York, it was about 30 percent. As with *load factors* in the airline industry, *penetration* is crucial in the cable business. "Once you rip up the streets, lay the cable, and endure additional costs of central overhead, the cost of

Hollywood-at-Home case published in *Marketing Management: Strategies & Cases* by Delozier and Woodside. Reprinted by permission of Charles E. Merrill Publishing Company, Columbus, Ohio.

hooking up new subscribers—particularly in an already-wired building—is minimal."[1]

A major objective of the cable system is to provide acceptable T.V. reception in areas where the reception of conventional T.V. signals is less than satisfactory, or where consumers perceive the number of available channels as inadequate. These problems are not as prevalent in major metropolitan areas as they are in rural or remote locations. Yet when *Home Box Office* introduced its current, unedited movie offerings in 1972, cable subscription increased dramatically in affluent New York areas.

At the time of inception of HAH, the home T.V. movie industry was in its infancy, dating back approximately four years. Accordingly, there was no substantial track record upon which to rely and no reliable record of profitablity in the industry. The HAH operation was typical of similar organizations throughout the country who placed major emphasis on the hotel/motel market and subsequently found that the greatest potential for expansion lay in the residential apartment/condominium market.

Selling Problems

HAH's most optimistic forecast was that it could ultimately acquire 60,000 subscribers, 12 percent of the 500,000 apartment units in the greater metropolitan area. By mid-1977, the firm had approximately 3,500 subscribers and revenues of nearly $550,000 per year. Profits were at the breakeven point. In July, 1977, Henry Newhouse, HAH's founder and President, was in the process of coordinating the elements of the firm's promotional program, especially the personal selling effort. In particular, Newhouse was concerned with formulation of the optimal remarketing program, for example, the method of obtaining additional subscribers in buildings where the HAH system had been operative for some time.

For reasons that will be explained in the following section, sales force turnover was excessively high and recruiting and training new sales force members was a continuous process. Sales Manager Lucy Mora reported to work each day at noon, performed administrative and planning functions during the day, recruited and trained new salespeople during the late afternoon and early evening, and was out in the field with her salespeople each evening. She was also quite active most Saturdays and Sundays since prospective subscribers were available for contact on weekends. Lucy had the authority to control her own working hours but because of her conscientious nature, she seldom took time off. Yet she was both physically and mentally exhausted and was giving serious thought to submitting her resignation.

The Promotional System

Company marketing efforts were aimed at two distinct groups: (1) individuals who reside in "fresh" buildings; that is, buildings in which the HAH television network is being introduced for the first time, and (2) individuals who reside in "exposed" buildings; that is, buildings in which HAH already has a substantial number of subscribers.

Fresh Buildings

After receiving formal permission from building management, HAH erects a parabolic receiving dish on the building roof. The system is then connected into the "head end" of the building's master antenna. This connection technically permits each resident to receive HAH programs assuming the resident's T.V. set is con-

---

[1] Andrew Tobias, "Are You Ready for Super T.V.?" *New York Magazine* (August 4, 1973), pp. 25-32.

nected to the building's master antenna. The resident is offered a choice of subscribing or not. A subscriber pays a small installation charge and a $10.00 deposit for a small box on his T.V. set that "unscrambles" or "decodes" the HAH signal. The programs appear on an unused T.V. channel during specified hours each day, usually 6:00 pm to 2:00 am. An added benefit to the subscriber is that installation usually improves T.V. reception on all channels.

The monthly subscription rate is $12.00 and the subscriber may view current, uncut movies without commercials. *Uncut* movies are those with the same explicit materials that appear in the theaters. The decoder box is equiped with a parental guidance key that permits parents to prevent children from viewing the private channel.

Prior to any personal selling activities, HAH places attractive signs in strategic building locations to advise residents that the service will be available. A notice is then mailed to each resident, on the letterhead of the building, advising the prospective subscriber that a HAH representative will call to explain the service and respond to questions. Representatives are well-trained, well-dressed young men and women who make evening sales calls to prospective subscribers who have been sent the prenotification letter.

The in-home sales presentation is brief (about ten minutes in duration) but quite exciting due to the unique appeal of the product. Every evening on the HAH television network, two and sometimes three features are presented. Each month, eight premier feature films and four previously-shown films are available. In addition, a number of monthly specials, including music, cultural, sports, and night club events, are offered. Salespeople emphasize that subscribers can enjoy the same movies currently showing at local theaters while avoiding the hassle of driving, parking, standing in line, paying babysitters, and spending $3.00 or more per person. Moreover, the subscriber is not involved in a lease or long-term commitment. The service may be cancelled with a 30-day written notice, and the decoder box will be removed and the $10.00 deposit refunded.

HAH salespeople are either students or young men and women who are employed elsewhere during the day. They represent HAH several evenings a week and often on weekends. Salespeople earn between $100 and $200 a month based on an average sales commission of $7.00 per order.

Typical door-to-door selling problems prevail. It is the policy of some buildings to forbid such direct solicitation or to require that the salesperson be announced from the lobby. At least 30 percent of the prospective subscribers are not at home when first contacted. Recruiting is difficult due to the perceived negative features of a job that requires door-to-door contacts on a straight commission basis. Sales force turnover is high since those who do not experience immediate success terminate quickly. Therefore, recruiting and training are never-ending processes frustrating to management.

Exposed Buildings

Company records show that the initial concentrated selling effort in a fresh building results in sales of 8 to 20 percent of the tenants depending upon building demographics. The remaining residents do not subscribe either because the sales proposal is rejected or because the salesperson, for one or more reasons, fails to make contact with the prospect in order to deliver a sales presentation. Moreover, approximately 6 percent of all subscribers terminate their service each month because of move-outs, dissatisfaction with the movies, financial, or other personal reasons.

Clearly, then, there are a large number of nonsubscribers in all exposed buildings at all times. Due to the limited number of available fresh buildings, and HAH's substantial capital and labor costs in "opening" a fresh building, the remarketing program in exposed buildings is of paramount importance.

Currently, HAH is operating more than 80 apartment buildings, approximately 25,000 apartment units. Using a three percent monthly move rate, 750 fresh prospects are available each month in exposed buildings.

Mr. Newhouse notes that new move-ins (NMIs) are usually good prospects for company offerings:

NMIs possess all three characteristics of a great prospect for our product. They have *buying power* since in most cases they are working couples with double-incomes. Second, since the wife works all day, she has *less sales resistance* than the typical housewife who is confronted by numerous door-knockers every day of the week. Moreover, many NMIs are new-marrieds or singles who have had *limited exposure to salespeople* and therefore are not canvass-wise as yet. Finally, young people under the age of 36 *welcome modern films that strike at realism in all forms.* The enjoy westerns, crime dramas, and story lines that involve intellectually mature content.

Despite the perceived high quality of NMIs as HAH prospects, there are certain sales logistics problems when 750 prospects are spread throughout 80 or more buildings. The salesperson must drive from building to building, park, ride up and down elevators, and suffer disappointment when many of these prospects are not at home or will not answer the door. Thus, despite a relatively high rate of conversion of presentations into sales, fewer presentations and sales are possible in a given evening.

Incumbent tenants in an exposed building represent an even more formidable selling hurdle. These people either rejected the HAH proposition at an earlier date or could not be reached previously. Unlike NMIs or those who live in a fresh building, these people may already know the HAH story. They may have been exposed to the negative comments of former subscribers who have since discontinued service. They may know the price of the service and may have developed firm reasons opposing subscription. A high level of sales resistance by this group may require persuasive or creative selling.

Previous Remarketing Efforts

When Lucy Mora came to work for HAH, she was convinced by Mr. Newhouse that the door-to-door selling method would be appropriate for HAH operation. For more than a year she devoted herself completely to the task of building a sales force. She visualized the ultimate development of two or three unit field managers each of whom would work with small groups of salespeople.

To date, Lucy has not been successful in developing a single dependable assistant. She finds it more difficult to "sell recruits the job" than to sell subscriptions for the HAH program. She has read many articles and reports about successful direct-selling companies, but she now is quite doubtful that direct-to-consumer personal selling is the correct approach for HAH:

'No Canvassing' signs are now posted in most buildings. Residents are reluctant to open doors because of high crime rates or unwillingness to talk to salespeople. The unit sale and earned commission are so small that the sales agent's gasoline costs often exceed earnings. It is getting so that applicants will not even answer our ads and it is like pulling teeth to get someone to try out the job for a few days. Our product is great, but there must be a better way to sell it.

Mr. Newhouse did not overtly agree with Lucy, but since he had no direct selling experience himself, he was not in a position to make any suggestions to ease her burden. He did, however, agree to experiment with other selling methods that would be supplementary to the direct-to-consumer approach. He felt, inwardly, that direct selling was suitable for selling in "fresh" buildings but difficult, to say the least, in "exposed" buildings.

HAH attempted to employ building resident managers, rental clerks, and other apartment building employees as part-time salespeople. In general, these people exhibited a major reluctance to sell. They felt that efforts to sell to tenants would interfere with their primary occupations and that there should be a sharp separation between building services and HAH programs.

The company spent several thousand dollars to create a multi-color direct mailing piece which included a postage-free return card to be sent to residents. The return rate was a miniscule four percent. The company then attempted to improve the response rate by directing a telephone call to individuals who had failed to return the reply card. The phone message included mention of a 50 percent reduction of the installation fee. The telephone follow-up did little to improve the return rate.

The Free Trial

Following some amount of dissatisfaction with the ventures described above, HAH executives were convinced that the remarketing program should be spearheaded by an offer to expose nonsubscribers to seven days of HAH movies without charge. The underlying assumption is that once exposed to theater-like movies on a living room level, residents would be reluctant to give up this luxury.

Two types of free trial hookups are possible. The first is a *private connection* including a decoder, the same currently used by present subscribers. This type of hookup includes a special wall plate and involves a company cost of $13.00 per unit including labor, supplies, and equipment. The resident is required to put up a refundable deposit of $27.00. At the conclusion of the free trial, the prospect can elect to:

1. Subscribe at the standard rate of $12.00 per month, plus a $15.00 installation charge. These charges have been covered by the $27.00 deposit. An additional deposit of $10.00 for the decoder box is billed the following month.
2. Reject the subscription and receive a refund of $27.00 when the decoder box is returned and the connection to the wall plate is removed.
3. Reject the subscription but retain the wall plate and private connection in order to improve T.V. reception on all channels. The previously collected $27.00 pays for installation.

The second type of free trial hookup is a *mass connection* whereby all T.V. sets in the building are connected to the master antenna that would automatically receive HAH programs on a predetermined channel. For example, for a seven-day period, all regular programs on Channel 45 would be aborted between the hours of 6:00 pm and 2:00 am, so that HAH programs could be shown. In these cases, HAH programs could be viewed without the need of a special wall plate or decoder box. The company unit cost of installation is negligible and tenants would not be subject to installation charges or deposits. Following the free trial period, the HAH signal is removed and those who wish to subscribe must have the private connection.

Clearly, the private connection requires prior permission from the building management but not from the resident. However, its effectiveness as a promotional tactic requires that the prospective subscriber is aware of and responsive to the promotion. This responsiveness may be solicited by a personal visit or a telephone call[2] and, to a lesser degree, by mailing the resident an announcement of the impending free trial.

Additionally, each month attractive program guides are left at the desk of each exposed building to be taken by residents. Large (10 × 16) promotional displays are put in laundry rooms, bulletin boards, and the reception desk in the lobby.

Remarketing Suggestions

Following a series of meetings of HAH executives and their advisors, the following promotional ideas were under consideration:

1. New move-ins (NMIs) would be telephoned and notified that the HAH program is active in their building, and that they are eligible for a seven-day free trial on a private connection basis. The telephone correspondent would inform NMIs that information describing the HAH program and the free trial will be mailed along with a guide of current movies being shown. The NMI is told that he or she will be contacted by telephone in a few days to see if he or she is willing to authorize a free trial.

2. If the NMI completely rejects the HAH program and the free trial, no literature is mailed. It is estimated that about 80 percent of those contacted by telephone will be willing to look over the literature.

3. The second phone call would inform the NMI about the enthusiastic response to the free trial offer, and the phone correspondent would offer to answer any questions the NMI might have. Assuming the prospect wishes to authorize the free trial, he or she may return the free trial agreement along with a credit card number or check for $27.00. A private connection will be made within a few days. It is estimated that about half of those who receive the literature and the second telephone call will authorize the free trial.

The agreeement indicates that if the NMI decides not to subscribe to HAH service after the free trial, the NMI may so notify the company and receive a refund of $27.00 when the decoder and installation material are recovered or may purchase the installation only. HAH will recover the decoder, and the deposit (27.00) will pay for the installation. The company estimates that of those authorizing the free trial, 50 percent will subscribe, 20 percent will retain the private connection, and 30 percent will buy nothing. Thus, the forecast calls for subscriptions from 20 percent of those who received the original phone call.

4. Incumbent tennants (ITs) in exposed buildings would be approached in a parallel but somewhat different way than that used to promote subscriptions from NMIs. Since ITs in a given building far outnumbered NMIs, the former could be best converted into subscribers by use of a mass connection approach. ITs would be telephoned and informed that on a given date the entire building will have the benefit of a seven-day free showing of HAH programs. The purpose of the phone call is to announce the event and to inform the tenant that information describing the HAH

---

[2] HAH's experience with telephone promotional programs has not been satisfactory because phone numbers are difficult and costly to obtain. Lists supplied by buildings do not include phone numbers. Many phone numbers are not listed in the directory, especially those of NMIs and people who desire unlisted numbers. Telephone company information operators will give out only one or two phone numbers at a time.

program, including a movie guide, is being mailed. The ITs are told that they will be recontacted at or near the conclusion of the trial period so that questions pertaining to HAH service can be answered.

    5. The literature is mailed and a second phone call is made as the trial period nears completion. Those who wish to subscribe would be asked to fill in a brief agreement and return it along with a credit card number or check for an installation fee, decoder box deposit, and the first month's subscription.

    6. When the payment has been received, a private connection will be made. HAH officials predict that 12 percent of the contacted ITs will subscribe.

Sales Force Recruitment

    The telephone selling system would be manned by part-time people to be recruited from the following sources:

1. Salespeople who are presently contacting residents of fresh buildings on a door-to-door basis.
2. Newspaper ads.
3. On-site representatives to be enlisted by advertisements on the HAH T.V. screen. These are satisfied customers who are familiar with the HAH service. Each person will be assigned a logistically acceptable area within 5 to 10 minutes driving time of their own apartment house.

1. Is HAH's product offering well conceived?

2. Evaluate the proposed remarketing suggestions.

3. HAH management has identified three separate and distinct marketing segments: residents of fresh buildings, NMIs, and ITs. Do you agree that three separate and distinct selling approaches should be used to reach these segments?

4. What is your appraisal of the future potential of the HAH operation?

Case 2–2

Johnson Manufacturing Company

Johnson Manufacturing is a 65 year old firm that sells ball bearings. The firm sells primarily through distributors, both domestically and internationally. Recently, the president of Steiner Machine Company, a large user of Johnson ball bearings, indicated to one of the company's salespeople, John Jackson, that Johnson's pricing was out of line with competitors' prices and wanted Jackson to remedy the situation. Otherwise, the president hinted, Steiner would have to consider switching brands.

    This development presented a serious problem for Jackson. He had worked with the distributor that handles the Steiner account for a number of years, but had never gotten too much cooperation. In fact, the distributor had just recently increased its mark up by eight percent. Although the distributor was not particularly well managed, it had a number of excellent contracts. It also was the only distributor in the market area that was not carrying competitive products. Also, the distributor had an exclusive agreement with Johnson Manufacturing Company which required that Johnson give six months' notice before changing distributors.

    Mr. Jackson desperately needed to quote a lower price to Steiner Machine, but, at the same time, knew that the distributor would probably not cooperate in lowering its price to Steiner. He also knew that Johnson Manufacturing would lose money if he lowered the price to the distributor. Although Jackson could sell directly to the customer and bypass the distributor, he would alienate the distributor and possibly lose its support for the numerous small customers that could not feasibly be handled on a direct basis. After considering his alternatives, Jackson finally decided to threaten the distributor with termination if its prices were not lowered by two percent.

1. What additional alternatives are available to Mr. Jackson?

2. What is the legal status of Jackson's decision?

3. Evaluate Johnson Manufacturing Company's weaknesses as evidenced by this situation.

Part 2

Planning

3. SALES FORECASTING

4. FINANCIAL PLANNING AND QUOTA SETTING

5. TERRITORY MANAGEMENT

   CASES

Chapter 3 _____

Sales Forecasting

After completing this chapter, you will be able to:

- Emphasize the importance of sales forecasting.
- Discuss the methods and procedures for forecasting sales.
- Consider the uses of forecasting in various departments.

Sales forecasting represents one of the most important activities in the areas of marketing and sales management. Not only is forecasting a necessity for effective development of marketing plans, it is the cornerstone for all company planning. Specifically, executives use sales forecasts to (1) prepare budgetary programs, (2) determine production loads, (3) develop financial controls, (4) anticipate purchasing requirements, (5) set quotas, (6) plan promotional programs, (7) determine new product needs, and (8) allocate financial and human resources. Because of the apparent impact sales forecasts have on organizational effectiveness, sales and marketing executives must be aware of procedures to follow for successful accomplishment of this vital activity.

DEFINITIONS OF SALES FORECASTING AND OTHER RELEVANT TERMS

One author defines the **sales forecast** as the amount of a product or service which, it is estimated, will actually be sold over some defined future period in the light of existing marketing methods of one company.[1] Furthermore, sales forecasting can be defined as a group of business activities which produce periodic estimates of future sales. The estimate of future sales must be consistent with market forces and should result from an examination of planned company activities, competitive reactions, and economic conditions. In addition, the sales forecast should be stated in specific quantitative terms. It should not be an ambiguous statement of intentions such as sales will be up a little. There are some related terms which should be distinguished from sales forecasting but are important for accurate estimation of sales. A **market fac-**

---

[1] D. M. Phelps and J. H. Westing, *Marketing Management* (Homewood, Ill.: Richard D. Irwin, Inc., 1960), p. 238.

tor is some reality existent in the market that causes demand for a product and/or service. A **market index** is a mathematical expression of one or more market factors that underlie the demand for a given product. **Market potential** is a calculation of the maximum sales opportunities for *all* sellers of a good or service during a stated period of time. **Sales potential** is the share of market potential which an individual company under ideal conditions, could achieve. For further distinctions see Figure 3-1.

A manufacturer of facsimile equipment[2] (e.g., Quip, Telecopier), for example, may identify that there are 33 million telephone lines in United States businesses. The *market potential*, therefore, would be 33 million units. An analysis of all segments would reveal, however, that some businesses would not have a need for facsimile devices (i.e., small, single location companies). Subtraction of these segments from the total base of business firms may leave 10 million telephones which would represent the *market forecast*. Under ideal conditions, Amco Electronics may decide that it can achieve a 10 percent share of the market or 1 million units. One million units would be Amco's *sales potential*. In 1983, however, Amco figures that it can realistically sell or lease 100,000 units (i.e., *sales forecast*). In order to achieve the sales forecast, Amco must establish a *sales quota* or goal of 30,000 units for its Northeastern region, 10,000 units for its Southeastern region, 5,000 units for the Southern region, 25,000 units for the Midwestern region, 10,000 units for its Southwestern region, and 20,000 units for its Western region.

APPROACHES TO SALES FORECASTING

There are five widely accepted methods of forecasting sales. They are:

- Jury of executive opinion.
- Sales force composite method.
- Survey method.
- Trend analysis.
- Regression analysis.

When reviewing these approaches to forecasting sales, it should be remembered that they are simply tools and not complete procedures. Each one of the approaches or tools must be integrated into a comprehensive procedure. In a football game, for example, the long pass may be utilized as part of the overall game plan. To be effective, it must be

---

[2] A device that electronically sends copies along telephone lines from one terminal to another.

	Expectations	**Opportunities**
Firm (Micro Measure)	Sales Forecast Sales Quota	Sales Potential
Industry (Macro Measure)	Market Forecast	Market Potential

Sales Forecast — an estimate of dollar or unit sales for a specified future period under a proposed marketing program.

Sales Potential — the share of a market potential which a company, under ideal conditions, could achieve.

Market Forecast — an estimate of the amount that will be sold by an entire industry.

Market Potential — the amount of sales that would result for an entire industry if all possible customers for all possible uses were accommodated.

Figure 3–1
Relationship
Between Forecast
and Potential

Sales Quota — a sales goal assigned to a marketing unit for use in the management of sales efforts.

utilized at the appropriate time in the overall plan. A procedure for forecasting sales and an explanation as to how each tool fits into the procedure is presented in the next major section of this chapter.

Jury of Executive Opinion

One of the simplest, but most widely utilized methods of forecasting sales is executive opinion. As indicated by a Conference Board study, executive opinion was applied by approximately 80 percent of all companies surveyed.[3] Although relatively subjective, the executive opinion procedure can serve as a valuable input into the final dollar or unit forecast. The procedure involves three basic steps.

Step 1: *Solicit several independent forecasts from a number of executives.* The request for anticipated sales can be initiated by the marketing director, another appointed top executive, or a forecasting committee. Since

---

[3] *Sales Forecasting Practices* (New York: The Conference Board Experiences in Marketing Management, Nov. 25, 1970), p. 10.

most executives will consider a number of factors such as past sales, economic conditions, competitive strengths, and anticipated marketing strategies in arriving at a reasonable estimate of sales, the executive opinion approach is often more sophisticated than a simple hunch or guess. Rather, it takes on the appearance of an informal mathematical modeling approach.

Step 2: *Examine, by means of a forecasting jury or committee, independent executive forecasts and supporting data.* Since there will obviously be some differences of opinion, it is mandatory for the company to develop a procedure for reconciling the differences. An effective way to accomplish this reconciliation is to bring the group of executives together to discuss their estimates. Discussion may bring out new ideas and lead some executives to modify their estimates. Another way by which reconciliation can be accomplished is through application of the **Delphi Method**. Under this method, forecasts of key executives are first reviewed by a person who is designated as forecasting analyst.[4] This person then aggregates the forecasts by weighting each forecast. The amount of weight given a particular executive's forecast may be based on the executive's perceived competence in forecasting or success in past forecasting activities. On the other hand, individual forecasts may simply be averaged with each estimate receiving the same weight. After the weighting and averaging procedure is accomplished, the averaged forecast is returned to each executive, who is then asked to make another sales prediction.[5] Several iterations of the forecasting and averaging procedure will result in a concensus of opinion.

The Delphi Method of executive opinion has been proven to be effective by reducing the forecasting error for numerous companies. For example, American Hoist and Derrick reduced forecasting error from over 20 percent to less than one-third of one percent by using the Delphi Method.[6]

Step 3: *Arrive at a final forecast.* After examining independent forecasts and making modifications from jury input, the forecasting committee or designated analyst must select a reasonable sales forecast.

There are several advantages of the executive opinion approach that account for its widespread popularity. First, it is fast and can be relatively simple. Companies that lack resources or sophistication can, therefore, utilize the approach. Second, it forces key management people to study and maintain an awareness of factors that may impact on their business's future. Third, no one procedure can consider all factors that may impact on sales. The executive opinion approach gives management the opportunity to identify and assess the effect of unusual or extraordi-

---

[4] A group or panel of experts, instead of only one analyst, can also assume the role of forecast analyst.

[5] Donald S. Tull and Del I. Hawkins, *Marketing Research: Meaning, Measurement, and Method* (New York: MacMillan Publishing Company, 1976), pp. 615–616.

[6] Shankar Basu and Roger Schroeder, "Incorporating Judgments in Sales Forecasts: Application of the Delphi Method at American Hoist and Derrick," *Interfaces*, VII, No. 3, (May, 1977), p. 23.

nary factors on market behavior. Fourth, decision-making is improved by the interaction and combined thinking of key executives. Also, new opportunities and threats may be uncovered during the decision-making process.

Sales Force Composite Method

The sales force composite method is similar to the previous method. However, instead of having the company's top executives estimate sales, the sales force makes the estimates. Salespeople estimate next year's sales for their particular territory by product and, in some cases, by customer. These individual estimates are subsequently aggregated by the marketing director into a future sales forecast.

This method has the advantage of letting the salespeople have a part in developing their own sales goals instead of simply receiving a quota into which they have had no input. This method also tends to help salespeople feel a part of the team and gives them a greater sense of responsibility for accomplishment of the forecasted volume. They may also be more willing to accept bonus and incentive plans which are often based on the relationship between forecasted and actual sales.[7]

A second advantage of the sales force composite method is that estimates are made by the individuals most intimately in touch with local situations. They can take into account problems and opportunities which might not be recognized by home office personnel. This procedure of assessing each account individually is especially applicable to industrial organizations where the number of customers is often limited, and the salespeople can stay abreast of the individual needs and problems of each firm.

Estimates made by the sales force also have several limitations. As a group, salespeople will tend to be overly optimistic or pessimistic as conditions change. If their forecasts are used as a basis for determining quotas, salespeople tend to understate their potential volume in order to minimize the chances of not making quota. This shortcoming can, in part, be overcome by tying expense to forecasted sales. Salespeople are also unlikely to have sufficient knowledge of basic economic trends, information sources, and company changes that may influence sales results. There is the additional disadvantage that forecasting is not the saleperson's specialty. Time spent in forecasting might be better spent in selling. On the other hand, it has been found that many of these disadvantages disappear when the sales force composite method is formalized. This formalization procedure involves giving salespeople information on anticipated marketing programs, economic conditions, and other data relevant to each salesperson's territory.[8]

---

[7] For an application of the sales forces composite, see: Harold W. Rakes, "Grass Roots Forecasting" *Management Accounting*, LVI, No. 3 (September, 1974) pp. 38–40.

[8] Thomas R. Wotruba and Michael L. Thurlow, "Sales Force Participation in Quota Setting and Sales Forecasting," *Journal of Marketing*, XXXX (April, 1976), pp. 15–16.

Survey Method

Another way to forecast future sales is to simply ask present and potential customers how much they anticipate purchasing during some future period. Responses to such a survey of buyer intentions are subsequently aggregated to arrive at a forecast. The Conference Board study on sales forecasting practices suggested that surveys are utilized by 59 percent of industrial goods manufacturers and 37 percent of consumer goods manufacturers.[9] A more recent study indicated that 32 percent of business people in the Midwest apply survey techniques to forecasting problems.[10]

Although surveys of buyer intentions have primarily been applied to forecasting sales of industrial goods, some studies have been conducted for consumer goods. For example, the Bureau of the Census conducted a Quarterly Survey of Buyer Intentions and the University of Michigan computes an Index of Consumer Attitudes which is based on consumer surveys. The number of such intention surveys for consumer goods, however, is limited. There are several reasons why intention surveys are not as popular as other methods:

- Survey costs are excessive, especially when the market size is large (i.e., consumer goods firms).

- Persons or companies surveyed often do not purchase what they intend to purchase.

- Forecasting error is often high. One study suggested that error is highest among companies utilizing surveys as a regular forecasting method.[11]

Time Series Method

Time series forecasting involves making future predictions from an analysis of past data—usually past sales data. Projecting future sales from historical sales information is a popular and widely utilized procedure because of its relative high degree of accuracy and simplicity.

It is accurate for both long and short-run forecasting. Along with the *Box-Jenkins Model,* which uses the computer to select from all alternative time series models the one model which best fits the historic data,[12] time series methods (e.g., trend analyses) are considered to be the most accurate forecasting procedures for long-range forecasts. Time series methods are also very good for short-range forecasting.[13]

[9] Conference Board, *loc. cit.*

[10] Douglas J. Dalrymple, "Sales Forecasting Methods and Accuracy," *Business Horizons*, Vol. XVII, No. 6 (December, 1975), p. 71.

[11] *Ibid.*, p. 73.

[12] G.E.D. Box and G.M. Jenkins, *Time Series Analysis, Forecasting and Control,* (San Francisco: Holden-Day, Inc., 1970).

[13] Alan Leyshon, "The Sales Forecast is a Top Management Problem," *The Director*, Vol. XXV, No. 10 (April, 1973), p. 95.

Time series methods are easier to apply and understand than more sophisticated procedures. Although some executives may be concerned that a certain amount of accuracy is lost with simple models, there is some evidence suggesting that no relationship exists between perceived sophistication of forecasting techniques and forecasting accuracy.[14]

Any time series, such as sales, consists of four factors: (1) long-run trends, (2) cyclical variations, (3) seasonal variations, and (4) irregular variations. *Long-run trends*, if identifiable, can serve as the basis for accurate, long-run forecasting. *Cyclical variations*, on the other hand, are normally random, more frequent fluctuations which, when identified, can serve as significant input to intermediate forecasting. *Seasonal variations* are frequent, repetitive variations that correspond to holidays, weather changes, or other uncontrollable, but predictable, environmental events. Finally, *irregular variations* are unexplained fluctuations resulting from such events as natural disasters, unexpected bad weather, or strikes.[15]

The objective in time series forecasting is to separate trend, cyclical, and seasonal variations from the irregular variations. Although a discussion of the actual separation of time series data is beyond the scope of this text, it can be accomplished by statistical calculations such as least squares and moving average explained in many statistics texts or by utilizing computer models designed to analyze and describe the various trends.

One relatively simple method for calculating trends is the moving average. When projecting trends of sales data, a **moving average** is the average sales value for the preceding X periods (weeks, months, or quarters). It is primarily used by companies that are predicting sales for only one period, and is normally applied by companies which have relatively stable sales. Long-run predictions or predictions by companies with significant seasonal and irregular variations are normally not precise when utilizing moving averages.

One of the primary disadvantages of the moving average method is that all periods used in the trend calculations are weighted equally. Sales of the most recent period which might reflect a new innovative marketing strategy are not considered to be more important than sales of previous months which were not influenced by such marketing programs. This disadvantage of the moving average is particularly significant when forecasting retail sales where next month's sales are particularly dependent upon the previous two or three month's sales.

One way to overcome the weighting problem of moving average is to utilize **exponential smoothing,** a time series technique which assigns

---

[14] Judy Pan, Donald Nichols, and O. Maurice Joy, "Sales Forecasting Practices of Large U.S. Industrial Firms," *Financial Management*, VI, No. 3 (Fall, 1973), p. 75.

[15] For a discussion of irregular variations and how to handle them, see: Michael D. Geurts, "Documented Sales Data Improves Forecasting," *Journal of Systems Management*, XXIV, No. 8 (August, 1973), pp. 32–34.

a higher value to the most recent data.[16] A smoothed forecast of next period's sales can be calculated by using the following formula:

$$\bar{S}_t = aS_t + (1 - a)(S_t - 1)$$

Where:

$\bar{S}_t$ = sales forecast for the next period
a = smoothing constant
S_t = present sales
$S_t - 1$ = smoothed sales for present period

The first step in exponential smoothing is to arbitrarily select a smoothing constant which is between 0 and 1.0. To determine the most appropriate value for "a", one should apply "a" values to historical data to see what would have happened to forecasting accuracy of the particular value utilized. If sales change slowly and consistently, the value of "a" will be small (i.e., 0.1, 0.2, 0.3, . . . 0.5). If sales are erratic and fluctuate widely, the value of "a" will be relatively large.

The second step in exponential smoothing is to use the smoothing equation to forecast next period sales (i.e., next period sales = "a" (this period sales) + (1 − a) (this period smoothed forecast)). For example:

this period sales:	$250,000
this period smoothed forecast:	$320,000
smoothing constant:	0.8

$\bar{S}_t$ = .8(250,000) + .2(320,000)
$\bar{S}_t$ = 200,000 + 64,000
$\bar{S}_t$ = $264,000

The primary decision that must be made by the committee or individual making the forecast is identification of an appropriate smoothing constant. This is normally done by testing all possible constants between 0 and 1 to determine which one provides the best sales forecasting model. The analyst can use sales data of previous years to test the predictive accuracy of the model since actual as well as historical sales are known.

Regression Models

Regression analysis is a statistical technique designed to identify the relationship between one variable, the criterion variable (e.g., sales), and one or numerous other variables, the predictor variables. In simplest terms, the regression equation is $Y = a + bx$ where Y is the criterion variable (sales), a is the intercept (volume of sales when x = 0), b represents the effect of the predictor variable on sales, and x is the value of the predictor variable. The formula $Y = a + bx$ not only represents the model for simple regression, but is also the formula for conducting sta-

---

[16] See R.G. Brown, *Smoothing, Forecasting, and Prediction of Discrete Time Series* (Englewood Cliffs, N.J.: Prentice-Hall, Inc., 1963).

tistical trend analysis. The only difference in the two procedures is the character of the predictor variable. With trend analysis, x represents time (i.e., number of weeks, months, quarters, or years) and does not show a cause and effect relationship. The regression approach, however, may imply a casual relationship — x represents a predictor variable such as GNP, disposable income, or some other variable, which does affect sales volume. In some cases, a regression model may appear to reflect a casual relationship between the predictor and the criterion variable when, in fact, there is only an association between the two variables. For example, sales of a domestic steel company (the criterion variable) may be correlated to changes in weather conditions in Brazil (the predictor variable). Although there is an associative relationship between the two variables, weather conditions in Brazil are not the cause of changes in sales of a U.S. steel company. In other words, the model is merely associative, not casual.

There is another important point that forecasters should remember when identifying and evaluating the predictive value of x. Specifically, the predictor value, x, is only useful in forecasting sales if (1) it is easier to predict than sales or (2) recent values of x reflect future sales levels (i.e., a lend-lag relationship with the dependent variable). For example, although changes in GNP may be correlated to changes in sales, forecasting GNP for the next quarter or year may be more difficult than predicting sales levels. However, if changes in GNP precede changes in sales by one quarter, then GNP would be a useful predictor variable. The firm could monitor GNP in Quarter 1, for example, and use the information to predict sales in Quarter 2.

The objective of the simple regression method is to find the values of a and b that provide the best fit of the trend line to the data. This can be accomplished by either plotting the data on a graph and drawing the line of best fit, or computing the values of a and b using least squares procedures. Calculation of regression coefficients is discussed in most basic statistics texts.

Although simple regression can be used for forecasting sales, it is unusual to find one variable which explains enough of the variation in sales to be a reliable predictor. Normally, accurate prediction can be accomplished only by identifying several variables which impact upon sales. The procedure for identifying the relationship between multiple predictor variables and one criterion variable (sales) is referred to as multiple regression analysis and is presented in the following form:

$$Y = a + b_1 x_1 + b_2 x_2 + \ldots b_n x_n$$

Although the computer calculates the regression equation simply and easily, a trained statistician should be employed to analyze the data since manipulation and interpretation of the data is necessary at various stages of the computational process. For example, before the coefficients (a and b) are calculated, one must test to see if the relationship between the variables is linear or curvilinear. If a relationship is curvilinear, then the affected variable must be presented in logarithmic form. Other problems with the data may also be experienced and must be identified.

In addition to identification of a regression equation, the regression procedure for forecasting sales also involves the utilization of correlation procedures. After the regression model is developed, correlation analysis is used to determine the strength of the relationship between the predictor variables and sales. One such correlation statistic is r^2 (the coefficient of determination) which shows the percent of the variation in sales that is explained by the predictor variables. The value of r^2 will be between 0 and 1. For example, an r^2 value of .75 means that 75 percent of the variation in sales is explained by the predictor variables. The closer the value is to one, the better the regression fits the sample data.

The calculation of r^2 is not particularly difficult. Assume, for example, that Y (the criterion or dependent variable) relates to sales and X (the predictor or independent variable) relates to disposable income in the market area. The objective is to determine the amount of variability in Y that is explained by X. The equation for calculating r^2 is as follows:

$$r^2 = \frac{b^2 \left[\Sigma X_1^2 - (\Sigma X_1)^2/n \right]}{\Sigma Y_1^2 - (\Sigma Y_1)^2/n}$$

where n = number of periods of data

$$\text{and } b = \frac{n\Sigma X_1 Y_1 - \Sigma X_1 Y_1}{n\Sigma X_1^2 - (\Sigma X_1)^2}$$

Y = sales (thousands)
X = disposable income (millions)

Computations for a sample regression analysis problem are shown in the following shaded area.

Year	X	X²	Y	Y²	XY
1975	80	6,400	122	14,884	9,760
1976	86	7,396	134	17,956	11,524
1977	92	8,464	148	21,904	13,616
1978	90	8,100	144	20,736	12,960
1979	104	10,816	162	26,244	16,848
1980	108	11,664	174	30,276	18,792
1981	112	12,544	206	42,436	23,072
1982	132	17,424	225	50,625	29,700
TOTAL	804	82,808	1,315	225,061	136,272

$$b = \frac{8(136,272) - 804(1,315)}{8(82,808) - (804)^2} = \frac{32,916}{16,048} = 2.051$$

$$r^2 = \frac{(2.051)^2 \left[82,808 - (804)^2/8 \right]}{225,061 - (1,315)^2/8} = .95$$

Therefore, changes in disposable income explain 95 percent of the changes in sales volume.

Many companies have found regression analysis to be an extremely useful tool for forecasting sales. For example, American Can Company identified that beer can demand is correlated to income levels, number of drinking establishments per thousand persons, and age distribution of the population. Eli Lilly found a correlation between sales of pharmaceuticals and disposable income. Also, by using regression, Armour and Company was able to predict the number of cattle to slaughter by monitoring range-grass conditions and steer-corn price ratios.[17] Although the preceding examples indicate the application of regression by large firms, regression techniques can be used by firms of all sizes. For example, Interroyal Corporation uses regression to forecast sales of commercial and institutional furniture.[18]

Combination of Methods

Although the various forecasting methods were explained separately, we are not suggesting that companies use either one method or another. It is best to use numerous techniques at various decision points in the forecasting procedure. In fact, all techniques can be used to forecast sales: regression can be used to study the effect of external factors on sales; surveys can be utilized to study the effect of new marketing programs on sales; trend analysis is a feasible starting point for calculating a preliminary forecast; sales force composite methods help provide insight into competitive programs and customer activities; executive opinion can be utilized to summarize and evaluate information collected by the other techniques.

PROCEDURE FOR DEVELOPING A FORECAST

We must now integrate the techniques of forecasting into a model for determining an actual forecast. The techniques identified in the previous section are important, but they are only important if applied at the appropriate time during the forecasting procedure. The procedure and techniques for forecasting sales are presented in Figure 3-2.

Preliminary Forecast

The preliminary forecast is simply a starting point upon which forecasters can build. The firm should apply simple time series analysis and identify future sales based upon an assessment of past sales. By tracking past sales, the firm is identifying what would happen in the future if everything stayed the same. Since the status quo cannot be maintained, however, several modifications must be made in this preliminary forecast.

---

[17] George G.C. Parker and Edillerto L. Segura, "How to Get a Better Forecast," *Harvard Business Review*, Vol. XLIX, No. 2 (March-April, 1971),

[18] Richard M. Kahn, "You Don't Have to be a Colossus to Forecast Accurately," *Sales and Marketing Management*, Vol. 115, No. 9 (November 17, 1975), pp. 7–11.

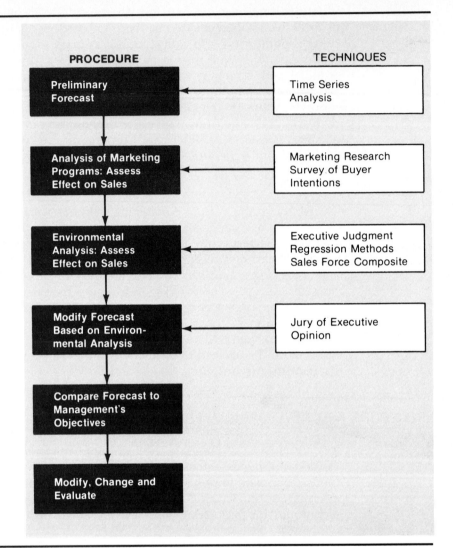

Figure 3–2
Procedure for
Forecasting Sales

Analysis of Marketing Programs: Assess Effect on Sales

After a preliminary forecast is made, the firm must begin analyzing the impact of internal contingencies on future sales. What impact will new marketing strategies have on sales? The firm may be introducing a new product line, extending an old product line to include new models, modifying an advertising campaign, dropping obsolete products, changing price, changing package design, increasing in-store promotion, expanding geographically, or adding new distributors. Any of these changes will affect sales and the firm should use marketing research and buyer intention surveys to identify their actual impact.

A Company Profile

O*riginated over 60 years ago by Milton P. Levy, Sr., NCH Corporation is a major manufacturer of commercial maintenance products such as floor care products, cleaners and degreasers, lubricants, insecticides and coolants. NCH markets over $370 million of these products each year to industries, institutions, and government entities throughout the world.*

A significant part of NCH Corporation's success can be attributed to its philosophy of looking ahead, and building on past strengths. It can also largely be attributed to the development and maintenance of a well-trained and professional sales organization. Not only is the sales force responsible for developing new accounts and servicing existing customers, but it is also responsible for implementing a variety of other activities. NCH was, in fact, established on the principle that the company exists because of its salespeople.

Salespeople at NCH are involved in training, planning, and teambuilding at all levels. They must learn how to set goals and establish strategies on an individual basis to collectively reach overall corporate goals. They are also involved in providing management with grassroots research information on customer maintenance problems that is oftentimes translated into new product ideas and market opportunities.

Each year salespeople are involved in the establishment of corporate goals including sales forecasting. Until recently, NCH employed a top-down approach to forecasting. The National Sales Manager based his forecast on three factors: (1) the increase or decrease in size of the sales force (i.e., new recruits minus terminations), (2) gross sales volume, and (3) the average number of orders filled during the preceding year. Top management, after evaluating these factors, would dictate to lower level managers and salespeople that they were expected to increase sales volume, number of orders, and, in some cases, number of salespeople by a specified amount. Subordinates would then engage in strategies and programs that were designed to meet the sales forecast that was mandated by top management.

Although the top-down approach was relatively effective while NCH was small and top management was able to accurately assess customer trends and needs, its effectiveness diminished as NCH developed into a $350 million company. Management became too far removed from the market to accurately determine customer needs, monitor sales trends, and assess the impact of internal and external variables on sales.

The forecasting procedure has, therefore, evolved into a bottom-up approach. In general, sales managers monitor the sales performance of each salesperson, discuss with each person the reasons for performance levels, and evaluate the probability that a particular sales level can be achieved during the next year. The first variable examined is the number of salespeople that have been employed by NCH for various lengths of time: less than three months, three to twelve months, and over twelve months. Since there is a higher probability that turnover will primarily take place among the newest employees, their productivity must be adjusted in order to reflect this potential attrition. Since the sales forecast is directly impacted by the size of the sales force, an estimate of changes in each category is a logical starting point in estimating future sales potential.

Sales managers also evaluate such variables as number of calls per day, number of closes as a percent of calls, and dollar volume per order. Since these are calculated for each category of salesperson (i.e., 0-3 months, 3-12 months, and over 12 months), a precise estimate of the impact of hiring policies as well as attrition can be assessed. Such an assessment is facilitated by a computer simulation model.

With quantitative information on the performance of each salesperson, sales managers then work directly with each person to develop individual sales plans and volume expectations. Each plan is accumulated into a master plan that is presented to top management for review and evaluation. If management is not satisfied with the resultant growth potential, it will send the plans back to sales managers. Sales managers may then modify their plans so that their expected sales are more consistent with top management expectations. For example, they may plan to hire more salespeople or assign a larger quota of calls per day to each salesperson. Once new programs are developed and plans are revised, a new set of projections are submitted to management. The interaction between management and sales continues until realistic and optimum sales plans and forecasts are developed.

NCH perceives the bottom-up approach to be an important key to more accurate sales forecasting in the future. It not only provides more control over the company's growth, but provides more realistic goals than could be accomplished with the top-down approach.

For example, the Universe Candy Company might conduct focus group interviews to see if there are any potential customer groups that have a unique desire or need that is not being fulfilled by existing products. The group interviews suggest that there is a group that wants a creamy candy with fruit chunks blended into the product. Subsequent research of a nationwide group of consumers confirm the preliminary hypothesis developed in the group interview. The research is followed by development of numerous product alternatives which are tested and evaluated by consumers. After an acceptable product is identified, Universe Candy Company introduces the product into two regional test markets. The test markets reveal that the product is purchased and repurchased by 3 percent of the market, or 1.5 million people if extrapolated to the entire country. Further analysis indicates that total sales in the upcoming year will be $2.2 million—a finding that will have a profound effect on the sales forecast for that year. Universe Candy Company can conduct similar market tests on new package designs, revised advertising copy, and other aspects of the marketing mix to get an even better idea of future sales.

Analyzing the effect of marketing programs on sales is critical to any forecasting procedure. Strategy development is a controllable variable and should be treated as such. Some firms, however, treat it as an uncontrollable factor. They estimate sales based upon judgment or some crude analysis of economic conditions, then use this to determine how much money the marketing department can have to develop new programs. By approaching forecasting in this manner, marketing strategy becomes a result of the forecast rather than an input variable into the forecasting procedure.

Environmental Analysis: Assess Effect on Sales

In addition to assessing the impact of marketing programs on sales, it is important to calculate the effect of uncontrollable, environmental factors on sales. Factors such as GNP, disposable income, discretionary income, government regulations, competitive strategies, and technological innovation may influence future sales.

Regression techniques are extremely useful for assessing the effect of national and regional economic conditions on sales. With quantitative models, the firm can study economic conditions as well as identify the extent to which changes in conditions will affect sales. Without such models, an examination of economic conditions is much less useful.

Although the sales force composite method is not extremely useful for estimating future sales precisely, it is helpful for identifying competitive and market conditions in territories. Salespeople are close to customers and are oftentimes the first ones to know if customers are cutting back or expanding operations. They are also generally aware of competitive programs and strategies through interaction with competitors, customers, and other salespeople. Therefore, it is critical that firms collect information from salespeople on market trends and competitive strategy.

Modify Forecast

After data on internal and external conditions are collected, the firm must use this data to modify the preliminary forecast. All information must be disseminated to appropriate executives to serve as input to forecast identification or it may be utilized by a forecasting department or committee as input to a forecasting model.

Compare to Management Objectives

At this point, the forecast is evaluated by management and compared with objectives. If forecasted growth is not consistent with expected or necessary growth, management may decide to modify marketing programs to achieve marketing objectives.

Evaluate, Modify, and Change

Forecasting is a continuous process. Conditions change, opportunities emerge, and programs oftentimes do not meet expectations. Because of the dynamic aspect of business coupled with the need to adapt to change, it is mandatory that firms constantly monitor factors which may affect accomplishment of the forecast. If it is observed that a firm will sell more or less than expected, it must adapt as soon as possible.

TYPES AND SOURCES OF BASIC DATA FOR SALES FORECASTING

Although there are no set rules for establishing forecasting systems, there are, nevertheless, basic groupings of data required which can be applied to virtually every company. There are four basic groupings:[19]

- Economic data.
- Industry data.
- Data on competition.
- Data on the company making the forecast.

Economic Data

Economic data are necessary to forecast the economic climate in which the company will be operating during the forecast period. Data concerning gross national product,[20] personal income, and disposable personal income, for example, are often useful for this purpose. All businesses are affected, to some degree, by changes in the national economic outlook. The scope of change cannot be predicted with certainty, but an understanding of the various economic principles and relationships that affect business behavior will aid in evaluating the general business climate for some small time beyond the present. This will be utilized in the environmental analysis section of the procedure for forecasting sales. Some of the more popular governmental sources of economic data are presented in Figure 3-3.

Industry Data

Industry data provide essential information concerning the past history of a given industry and how it responds to changes in the pertinent economic indicators mentioned above. An attempt should be made to determine the stage in the growth cycle of the industry; that is, whether growth is increasing, decreasing, or leveling off. This can be determined through the techniques mentioned previously. Good sources of industry data are:

Industry trade associations. Statistical figures on growth of industry, number of manufacturers, personnel employed.

Industry trade journals. Information on management changes, diversifications and expansions, product announcements, industry statistics.

Tariff Commission report (by industry). Reports on tariffs and foreign trade matters.

Monthly retail trade reports. Bureau of the Census, U.S. Depart-

---

[19] American Management Association, *Sales Forecasting: Uses, Techniques, and Trends*, American Management Association, Inc., 1515 Broadway, Times Square, New York 36, N.Y., 1956, Special No. 16.

[20] See: Harlow Osborne, "Characteristics of Sales Forecasts Based on Gross National Product," *Financial Analysts Journal*, XXVI, No. 5 (September-October, 1970), pp. 39–60.

Economic Indicators, U.S. Government Printing Office, Washington, D.C. A monthly series of basic charts and tables presenting a concise and meaningful picture of current economic trends and developments. (gross national product, personal income, disposable income)

Monthly Labor Review, Bureau of Labor Statistics, Washington, D.C. Statistics by month and by industry for employment, payroll, hours, etc.; weekly and hourly earnings by months, cities, and commodities (for prices and cost of living); work stoppages, and building and maintenance costs.

Survey of Current Business, U.S. Department of Commerce, Office of Business Economics, Washington, D.C. A monthly survey comprising 2,500 different statistical series, including national income, personal and farm income, retail and wholesale sales indices, manufacturer's orders and inventory, production, prices, and shipments.

Federal Reserve Bulletin, United States Board of Governors of the Federal Reserve System, Washington, D.C. A monthly compilation of statistics on numerous phases of finance, industry, commerce, and economics.

Weekly Desk Sheet on Business Indicators, National Industrial Conference Board, Inc., 246 Park Avenue, New York City. Data on production, wholesale prices, federal cash surplus, deposits adjusted, and department store sales.

"Survey of Buying Power," *Sales Management Magazine,* New York City. Marketing data by regions, states, counties, and cities.

Figure 3–3
Government
Sources of
Economic Data

ment of Commerce, Washington, D.C. Monthly sales for retail stores by census region for most industries.

Data on Competition

Data on competition actually are a type of industry data which should include information on the company's sales and also those of its competitors. Any change in the relative position of one or more competitors could result in a company gaining or losing a portion of total industry sales. All available data on competitors' growing strengths or weaknesses should be studied in order to predict more accurately the company's estimated share of industry sales during the forecast period. Data on competition can be secured from the following sources.

Stockholders' reports. Progress made by company; new product information; future plans; total sales and profits.

Commercial audits and surveys. Nielson Index, Dun & Bradstreet. Invoice and inventory audits on food, drugs, television, etc.

Wall Street Journal. 44 Broad Street, New York City. Often carries relevant information such as company plans, expansion and diversification, new product announcements, and financial notes and comments.

Data on Company Making the Forecast

Data on the company making the forecast are also important, since a sensitivity index to changes in economic indicators should be established for the individual company, as well as for the industry. As a rule, there will be very little change between the weighting for the industry and that of individual companies making up the industry. The factor of the forecaster's judgment is probably more important at this level than at any other point in the forecast in evaluating the effect of such factors as major decisions, additional new products, and obsolescence of older products on the company's total sales during the forecasted period. Company information may be derived largely from internal records, such as sales statistics, accounting records, top management's plans for the future, market research data, and sales plans for the future, particularly including policy changes relevant to the marketing mix of product, promotion channels, and price.

It can be seen that almost any forecast will require data of the several types mentioned above. In addition to those data, one of the best single sources of general information covering data for forecasting purposes is the booklet, *Market Research Sources*, compiled by the U.S. Department of Commerce, Office of Industry and Commerce. This booklet covers a wide list of available publications in the following areas: (1) the federal government, (2) state and local governments, (3) colleges and universities, (4) chambers of commerce, (5) associations, foundations, and cooperatives, (6) commercial organizations, and (7) publishing companies. Another excellent general reference is the *Federal Statistical Directory*, published annually by the Bureau of Budget. This publication lists the personnel in the Federal agencies engaged in statistical activities, including reporting, planning, research, data collection, and analysis.

DEPARTMENTS USING SALES FORECASTS

The sales forecast is the factor around which most business planning is centered. Figure 3-4 represents a list of the principal departments that can use sales forecasts in their own planning operations and the nature of their uses.[21]

The categories in Figure 3-4 are quite broad, and in the process, some department may have been eclipsed. However, all basic functions of business management are to be considered in the sales forecast. The

---

[21] *Ibid.*, Special No. 16.

1. **Production Department**	4. **Financial Department**
a. Scheduling plant operations.	a. Cash inflow.
b. Expansion requirements.	b. Profit position.
c. Traffic management.	c. Capital requirements.
2. **Personnel Department**	5. **Marketing Department**
a. New hires necessary.	a. Changing trends.
b. Terminations.	b. Profit items.
c. Promotions required.	c. Advertising and promotion.
3. **Purchasing Department**	d. Human resource needs.
a. Raw material requirements.	
b. Other supplies.	

Figure 3–4
Departments Using
Sales Forecasts

need for comprehensive and integrative planning cannot be overemphasized.

Production Department

A successful manufacturing business depends largely upon the coordination of two main functions—production and marketing. For this reason, the production department can often find more useful information in the sales forecast than can any other department. In fact, the sales forecast could really serve as the production schedule, assuming that the forecast is accurate.

The way in which the production department can use this information depends a great deal upon the type of business. In a job-order shop, for example, nothing is produced without an order. The level of plant operations depends upon the backlog of orders. If the business is cyclical, it is most important for the plant to know whether business will increase or decrease, and what the timing of the turning point will be. Only experience and diligent research in sales forecasting can answer these questions.

Another example is the warehousing operation, where the sales forecast indicates the drain on warehouses and thus, the production required to bring warehouse stocks to a proper level. This can become quite complicated with seasonal products, which require different inventory levels in different seasons, and which also have different production runs in different seasons. The importance of the sales forecast in coordinating the production of such a business should be quite obvious.

These questions of coordinating production with sales are of a short-term nature. Long-term forecasts, extending beyond two years, cannot generally be prepared with sufficient accuracy and in necessary detail to use in scheduling production. They are vital, however, for measuring production capacity against sales demand in determining any required expansion of facilities and to help project the competitive situation. The

latter may indicate which production economies or product improvements must be made if the firm is to maintain its position in the
industry.

Another use of sales forecasts is in the area of traffic management.
Transportation costs are often a very large part of the cost of distributing
products. In companies that move a considerable volume of product,
traffic coordination is a big problem, and the best guide for alleviating
the problem is the sales forecast. The transportation function of any
company will be aided greatly in coordinating its service with production and sales by being kept fully informed of sales expectations. This
includes not only increases and decreases in volume, but also geographical shifting of markets involving changes in types of transportation, destination, and other such related problems. A good sales-forecasting function should be capable of being broken down into geographical detail to
supply such needed information for planning.

Personnel Department

Personnel requirements in many industries fluctuate a great deal.
Accurate sales forecasts in these industries can help management prepare for shifts in personnel requirements that accompany increasing or
decreasing production and sales levels. Not only is such information of
use to individual plant personnel managers, but it also aids centralized
departments in large companies. Long-term forecasts show the need for
additional personnel and indicate the size of the hiring and training programs that may be involved in successfully reaching planned objectives.
These are especially necessary in companies that are experiencing significant market expansions, as well as those companies that are primarily
labor intensive.

Purchasing Department

The primary interest of the purchasing department in the sales forecast is for determining material requirements for production and/or
stocking for resale. Obviously, in coordinating production with sales,
production must have the materials required to produce when needed.
The sales forecast is the best and easiest way for the purchasing department to keep abreast of changes in requirements. The forecast, of
course, must be translated into purchasing functions before it can
become part of any detailed planning for material requirements. The
forecast will also help in judging the needs for regular supplies of all
types.

Financial Department

The fourth principal department which can make use of the sales
forecast is the financial department, which supervises the expenditure of
money. The basic use of sales forecasting for the financial department is,

of course, in determining the cash inflow. Every business must know how much money is coming into the firm in order to judge its operation. The cash inflow is primarily dependent upon sales, shipments, and collections.

The financial department is also interested in the forecast, particularly the long-term forecast, for determining capital requirements. Careful planning of financial requirements is particularly important to businesses in periods of rapid expansion. Still another area of interest for the financial department is in establishing profit level and dividend policy. Here, of course, the cash inflow is balanced with expenditures to determine the relative area of profitability. Policy decisions to pay dividends and to increase or decrease them are made on this basis. All of this information should be tied very closely to the sales forecast.

Marketing Department

The marketing department relies on the forecast for developing new product expansion plans, allocating human resources and setting sales quotas, developing sales force compensation programs, and coordinating sales and advertising activities.

Plans to develop new products are largely dependent on the anticipated sales potential of existing products (e.g., their position in the product life cycle), competitive trends, and consumer trends (e.g., age distributions, income trends, attitude changes, life style developments, and so on).

The importance of developing forecasts by territory becomes evident when management endeavors to allocate human resources. Unless anticipated sales are known with certainty in various geographical areas, it is virtually impossible to *efficiently* determine human resource needs in those various territories. Not only is it difficult to determine human resource needs without territorial forecasts, it is also equally difficult to set sales quotas and allocate advertising and promotion dollars to various markets.

SUMMARY

Forecasting is a necessity for market and corporate planning. It is an estimate of future sales and results from an examination of planned company activities, competitive reactions, and economic conditions. In order to accurately assess future sales, firms should (1) develop a preliminary forecast, (2) analyze the impact of marketing programs on future sales, (3) assess the effect of environmental factors on sales, (4) modify the preliminary forecast, (5) compare the forecast to management objectives, and (6) modify, change, and evaluate the forecast.

Tools that can be utilized to implement the forecasting procedure include the survey, jury of executive opinion, sales force composite, trend analysis, and regression analysis. Once a final forecast is developed, it is utilized by the production, personnel, purchasing, financial, and marketing departments in making operating decisions.

QUESTIONS

1. What basic determinations or assumptions should be considered when making a sales forecast?

2. Why would the jury of executive opinion and salesforce composite methods of forecasting be used instead of quantitative, statistical methods?

3. If the sales forecast is the basic cornerstone for planning in all departments of a business, why shouldn't such a forecast be called a business forecast?

4. Is it easier to forecast sales for an industry or for an individual product in a product line for a company?

5. Under what conditions should the sales manager attempt to obtain a sales volume that is greater than those forecasted? Are there cases where obtaining sales that are considerably beyond the forecast level could be detrimental to the firm?

6. "The number of forecasting assumptions is inversely proportional to the degree of forecast exactness." Please comment.

7. Elaborate on the statement, "Management deals entirely with the future."

8. Discuss at least four of the basic indices that can be used in determining potential sales volume for consumer items.

9. Discuss the difference between "market potential" and "sales potential."

10. Discuss the general procedure for forecasting sales?

11. What are the advantages and disadvantages of using sales force composite method?

12. Of all methods of forecasting sales that have been discussed in this chapter, which method is the best method for a company to utilize? Justify your answer.

13. Why is sales forecasting an important ingredient in the overall marketing plan?

Chapter 4

Financial Planning and Quota Setting

After completing this chapter, you will be able to:

- Define sales budgeting and identify the importance and principles of budgeting.
- Present alternative budgeting methods and formats.
- Discuss the procedure for developing sales budgets.
- Identify the types of quotas utilized by sales organizations.
- Identify procedures for establishing quotas and discuss the importance of salespeople participating in quota setting.

Inherent in the sales management planning process is financial planning and quota setting. Financial planning involves the translation of forecasts into goals and performance indexes for each area of the sales organization (i.e., budgets). Quota-setting involves the allocation of the forecast (i.e., revenue) to each salesperson. Budgets, therefore, are primarily concerned with the planning of expenses and quotas are related to revenue planning. Both activities, however, are designed to facilitate the development of goals and performance indexes.

SALES BUDGETING[1]

After firms establish objectives, analyze external and internal factors that impact on future performance, and arrive at forecasted revenue, they must allocate projected revenue to each department. This allocation procedure involves the development of a reporting system that allows firms to analyze, direct, and control the flow of resources through each organizational jurisdiction. This reporting system is referred to as **the sales budget**.

The purpose of the sales budget is to help management direct resources toward accomplishment of company goals and objectives. It is a future oriented procedure that utilizes accounting terminology and for-

---

[1] The authors genuinely appreciate the invaluable assistance of Ms. Virginia Duke, University of Dallas, in development of this section on Sales Budgeting.

mat to reflect this course. The budget report is a tool that facilitates analysis of current performance, aids in projection of future performance, and directs and controls resources so that optimum efficiency can be maintained.

Fundamental Principles of Sales Budgeting

There are several principles of sales budgeting that management should be aware of prior to development of a budgeting policy and system.

Budgeting is an on-going process. It is not simply a report form that is completed once a year and filed away until next year. It is a reporting method which is utilized to compare actual performance to desired performance on a daily, monthly, or quarterly basis, depending on management needs.

Sales budgets must be flexible. Since external and internal conditions change it is necessary to make the budget flexible enough to adapt to these changes. The budget is primarily a guide—not an inflexible mechanism of control. An example of a budget form that allows for quarterly revisions is presented in Table 4–1.

Employees at every level of the sales and marketing organization should be involved in sales budgeting. When subordinates are consulted for their input into budget formulation, a spirit of cooperation can be established. Employee cooperation can be a

Table 4–1
Budget Performance Report: Allowing for Revisions Which are Consistent with Changing Conditions

Expense	1980	1981	Current 1982	First Quarter Revision	Second Quarter Revision	Third Quarter Revision	Fourth Quarter Revision
Sales Office (rent)							
Office Salaries							
Insurance							
Depreciation							
Sales Salaries							
Sales Commissions							
Office Supplies							
Telephone							
Automobile Expense							
Travel Expense*							
Sales Meetings & Conventions							
Training Expense							

*Travel expenses can be broken down further into food, lodging, entertainment, cleaning, and transportation.

critical variable in gaining acceptance of the budget at the implementation stage.

Sales budgets should serve as a control mechanism.   Performance
standards for expenses and revenue are reflected in the budget.
Deviations from these standards can be identified monthly and
corrective action can be taken to correct these deviations. Table
4–2 presents a budget form which can aid in performance of the
control function.

All variances in the budget performance report must be evaluated
immediately. There is the possibility that conditions have changed significantly since the budget was prepared. In this case, the budget must
be updated to accurately reflect current conditions. It also helps management identify problems that are outside the control of supervisors (e.g.,
changing economic conditions, raw material price increases, changes in
dealer inventories, etc.).

Sales Budgeting Procedure

The procedure for developing a sales budget is as follows:

1. Identify company objectives.
2. Prepare a sales forecast by reviewing environmental data, internal
   factors, and future company strategies.
3. Determine sales budget of revenue and relevant expenses.
4. Review budgets.
5. Authorize budgets.

Step 1: Identify Company Objectives.   Top management, along with the
Board of Directors, should review long-range company goals. Utilizing
these goals as a guide, each operating division should then establish
their goals and present them to management. Operating objectives are
then reviewed by top management in order to determine if divisional
goals are consistent with long term objectives in terms of company philosophy, anticipated growth, product diversification, etc. Goals are
resubmitted to operating divisions for analysis and revision and, after
this review, are again presented to top management. Recycling of this
procedure insures a convergence between top management goals and
operating management objectives.

Step 2: Prepare the Sales Forecast.   After company goals are established,
the firm must identify future sales volume expectations. As was indicated in Chapter 3, development of the sales forecast involves an analysis of
economic factors, competitive programs, technological developments,
changes in distribution channels, anticipated promotional programs,
new product developments, anticipated pricing strategies, international
money markets, and political factors.

Table 4–2
Budget Form: Controlling Revenue and Expenses (Bi-Monthly)

Sales and Costs	Jan. Budget	DEV*	Mar. Budget	DEV	May Budget	DEV	July Budget	DEV	Sept. Budget	DEV	Nov. Budget	DEV
Sales Revenue												
Sales Office												
Office Salaries												
Insurance												
Depreciation												
Sales Salaries												
Sales Commissions												
Office Supplies												
Telephone												
Automobile												
Travel Expense												
Sales Meetings and Conventions												
Training Expense												

*DEV = Deviation from budget.

Step 3: Determine Budget of Revenues and Expenses. There are several types of budgets that a firm may utilize: operating budgets, financial budgets, and capital budgets. An in-depth discussion of financial and capital budgets, however, is beyond the scope of this text. Sales budgets, on the other hand, are part of the operating budget—i.e., a reflection of projected revenues and expenses for a given period of time. Similar to other departmental budgets, budgetary expenses must be divided into fixed and variable expenses. Variable expenses fluctuate with fluctuations in sales while fixed expenses are not influenced by sales volume changes.

Estimating fixed expense budgets is highly procedural and based on managerial judgment and past experience. The manager begins by examining last year's performance record. An analysis of the recent past as well as the present performance indicates areas of efficiency and inefficiency. To improve efficiency, for example, the manager may identify a need for another secretary or clerk. After each expense is evaluated and needed changes are noted, expenses which accompany those changes are added to or subtracted from last period's budget.

Fixed expense budgets are prepared on a yearly basis with monthly, quarterly, or annual dollar extensions for each item. This information is completed on a worksheet which contains a section for last year's expenditures by account. The projected or budgeted amounts are placed in the second section. A third section usually shows the percent increase/decrease between current and projected expenses. A fourth section is a "remarks" column where the increase or decrease can be explained or justified (see Table 4–3 for example of a fixed expense budget).

Table 4–3
Fixed Expense
Budget Estimate—
1982

Classification*	Previous Year Actual		Current Year Budgeted							
	Year	1st Qtr.	1st Qtr.	2nd Qtr.	3rd Qtr.	4th Qtr.	Year Total	% Inc. (Dec.)	Remarks
Adm. Salaries									
Clerical Salaries									
Office Supplies									
Rent									
Depreciation									
Insurance									
Misc.									

*This would be accompanied by a detailed breakdown of each classification.

Flexible budgeting (i.e., sales budgeting) is more complex than simple fixed expense budgeting. In flexible budgeting, expenses must be classified as fixed costs and variable costs. Fixed costs are handled in the manner described in the preceding paragraph. Variable costs, on the other hand, will fluctuate with changes in sales volume. If sales drop, for example, routes may be terminated and the sales force may be reduced. Other, related expenses such as travel expense and automobile expense may also be reduced. Each manager, therefore, must conduct an in-depth analysis of his or her operation and estimate variable expenses over a range of expected sales levels (see Table 4–4).

Table 4–4
Flexible Expense
Budget—January,
19--

	Units Sold		
	40,000	50,000	60,000
Fixed Costs			
Office salaries	$ 2,000	$ 2,000	$ 2,000
Depreciation	400	400	400
Insurance	600	600	600
Rent	1,000	1,000	1,000
Total fixed costs	$ 4,000	$ 4,000	$ 4,000
Variable costs			
Sales salaries	$ 4,000	$ 5,000	$ 6,000
Office supplies	200	300	400
Repairs	100	150	200
Travel Expense	1,500	2,000	2,500
Misc.	50	75	100
Total variable costs	$ 5,850	$ 7,525	$ 9,200
Total operating expenses	$ 9,850	$11,525	$13,200

Step 4: Review Budgets.   After the sales departments have prepared their flexible budget estimates, they are reviewed at the divisional or regional level and then sent to top management or the budget committee. Top management first reviews its own economic assumptions to be sure they are valid and then reviews budget estimates of each sales department. Top management checks estimates for reliability and compliance with company goals and guidelines. If adjustments or modifications of the estimates are necessary, they are accomplished at the department level with input from management.

Step 5: Authorize budgets.   After budgets are approved, they are authorized and compiled into the Company Operating Budget for inclusion in the Master Budget (i.e., operating, financial, and capital budget).

Budget Preparation Worksheet

A detailed procedure for estimating sales expenses is presented in

Figure 4–1. This worksheet can help the sales manager calculate sales costs for each territory as well as indicate whether sales goals are consistent with corporate profit objectives. Instead of breaking it down by city, as is suggested in Column 1, expenses may be broken down by account, subregion, or market segment.

Major expense categories include lodging, food, auto rental, personal auto expense, other travel, entertainment, parking, tips, promotional material, and miscellaneous. These expenses are added to budgeted salaries and allocated overhead such as rent, utilities, maintenance, etc. The total expense package is then subtracted from forecasted sales to give a gross dollar return on sales. If anticipated return is not consistent with company goals, expense budgets may be revised until they are acceptable.

Supplementary Budget Forms

In addition to general budget forms, special budget forms can be employed to help sales managers calculate item expenses. For example, Figure 4–2 presents a procedure for calculating costs associated with sales meetings. It includes a form which itemizes all potential costs as well as a step-by-step guide for preparing sales meeting budgets. Utilization of such a format can help insure that all expenses are accounted for and that the manager is consistent in estimating costs for each meeting. Formats can also be developed for other activities such as training, travel, trade shows, special promotions, and contests.

QUOTA SETTING

After the forecasts have been developed, the firm must translate the estimate of future sales into sales quotas. A **sales quota** is defined as that portion of the sales forecast which is allocated to a particular salesperson, territory, or sales group during a specified time period. It represents a realistically attainable and fairly developed goal to be accomplished by a sales territory. If properly developed, the quota should (1) provide salespeople with a target sales goal which may serve as the basis for allocation of sales effort, (2) provide management with a performance index for control of sales activity, and (3) serve as the basis for determining incentive pay.

Types of Quotas

Although this section will primarily focus on sales and profit quotas, remember that quotas may also be established to reflect other objectives. In fact, any time performance goals are established, quotas may be developed. The most common quota types are sales or unit quotas, profit quotas, activity quotas, and expense quotas.

Sales or Unit Quotas.   As you might expect, there are both benefits and

Figure 4–1
Step-by-Step Sequence in Preparing a Sales Cost Budget

TERRITORY _____
PERIOD _____

1. Major Cities	2. Forecast Sales	3. Budgeted Salaries	FORECAST OF FIELD SELLING EXPENSES							
			4. Lodging	5. Food And Drink	6. Auto Rental	7. Misc. (Parking, Taxi, Tips)	8. Entertainment	9. Other Travel	10. Promotional	11. Total City Expenses
12. Total $										
13. % Total Territory	%		%	%	%	%	%	%	%	%
14. Total Territory $										
15. Budgeted Salaries $										
16. Forecast Expenses $										
17. Total $										

Forecast Sales $ _____ ÷
Gross Dollar Return $ _____ = On Sales _____ %

1. List the major cities in your territory that are included in Section II: Metro Sales Costs.

2. Enter the forecast sales for each city.

3. List in total only the budgeted salaries of the territory sales manager and salespeople as fixed costs.

4. Estimate the number of nights to be spent in each city and multiply by the lodging averages shown in Section II.

5. Estimate the number of meals and drinks per day in each city (S&MM assumes an allowance of two drinks per day per salesperson) and multiply by the appropriate food and drink medians that are shown in Section II.

6. If an auto will be rented, estimate the number of miles per week. *Multiply* the number of days by the rate per day, *add* the sum of the number of miles times the rate per mile, *add* insurance of $2 per day, and subtract your company discount (if any). Auto-rental data are in Sections II and VI.

7. Estimate the miscellaneous expenses.

8. Add entertainment costs by multiplying the dinner and drink rates (for each city) by the number of clients or customers entertained.

9. Estimate other travel expenses—air, train, or bus fares—that may be incurred in trips to the home office or the sales meeting.

10. Estimate promotion expenses by including advertising, sales promotion, trade shows, meetings, and so on that may be charged to the territory.

11. Total expenses across columns 4 to 10 to derive expenses by city.

12. Total all expenses shown in columns 4 to 11.

13. Calculate the percent of the territory's sales that will be accounted for by total sales of the cities listed; do the same for expenses. *A possible short-cut:* Assume that a city's percentage of total territory sales will be the same as its share of total territory expenses.

14. Enter the expected total sales of the territory.

15. Enter total budgeted salaries.

16. Enter total forecast expenses for the cities from column 11. Total salaries and expenses should be adjusted for any overhead—rent, utilities, secretarial expenses—charged to the sales office.

17. Add salaries (item 15) and expenses (item 16). Subtract total expenses (item 17) from forecasted sales (item 12), giving the gross dollar return on sales. This gross dollar return can then be converted to a percentage figure by dividing by the forecast sales total. Comparing the percent shown here with your company's targeted profit ratio tells you if you are on target. If you are not, analysis of the data may suggest the reasons why.

Source: *Sales and Marketing Management* (February 27, 1978), p. 43.

Figure 4–2
Step-by-Step Sequence in Preparing a Sales Meeting Budget

	1. City (Write In)	2. No. Of Meeting Participants	3. No. Of Times Cost is Incurred	4. Cost Per Person	11. Total Cost Per Meeting
Hotel costs					
5. Lodging					
6. Meals					
B					
L					
D					
7. Coffee breaks					
8. Cocktail party					
9. Meeting room					
10. Hospitality-suite rental					
12. Subtotal (Hotel costs)					
Supplementary costs					
13. Audiovisual rental					
14. Meals away from hotel					
15. Transportation from airport to meeting site					
16. Automobile rental					
17. Transportation to and from meeting					
18. Entertainment, printed materials, handouts, etc.					
19. Subtotal (Supplementary costs)					
20. Grand Total					
21. Number of participants					
22. Average cost per participant					

Hotel costs

1. Enter name of city in which meeting will be held.
2. Determine number of persons who will attend each function in items 5 through 8.
3. Estimate length of meeting time, that is, number of nights requiring sleeping rooms, number of meals, and coffee breaks and cocktail party, if any.
4. Enter estimated per-person cost incurred in functions 5–8 by referring to Table IV-5.
5. List group-lodging rates for meeting-site city after deciding type of rooms to be used (single or double, higher or lower priced).
6. List average breakfast, lunch, and dinner prices for meeting-site city for meals to be included in the meeting.
7. Add additional charge per person for each coffee break.
8. Enter hotel charges per person for receptions and cocktail parties.
9. If a one-day, or shorter, meeting is planned, requiring no sleeping rooms or planned meals, add cost of meeting-room rental in column 11.
10. If a one-day, or shorter, meeting is planned, requiring no sleeping rooms or meals, add cost of hospitality-suite rental in column 11.
11. Calculate total costs of items 5–8 by multiplying columns 2, 3, and 4.
12. Add totals for each cost item in column 11 for subtotal of hotel costs.

Supplementary costs

13. Add other costs to be incurred, such as audiovisual rental (Section V).
14. Add meals away from hotel (Section II).
15. If necessary, add taxi or limousine fares from airport to downtown of meeting-site city (Section II).
16. Add automobile rental (Section II or VI).
17. Add transportation to and from meeting, such as airline fares (Section VI).
18. Provide for other items: speakers' fees, entertainment, printed materials, etc.
19. Add all supplementary costs for subtotal.
20. Add hotel costs subtotal and supplementary costs subtotal for grand total.
21. Enter number of meeting attendees.
22. Divide item 20 by item 21 to derive average cost per participant.

Source: *Sales and Marketing Management* (February 27, 1978), p. 73.

disadvantages associated with the use of sales quotas. The primary benefits of sales quotas are that they are easy to understand and control, and they are consistent with corporate revenue goals (if they are properly developed). The primary problem with quotas which are simply based on sales volume is that they do not reflect profitability, generally the most significant corporate goal. In fact, most companies that utilize quota-setting procedures have some products that contribute significantly to profit and others that are low profit items. Since it may be easier to sell the low profit items, salespeople focus their attention on those items at the expense of high profit items. One way to overcome this is to establish separate quotas for each product line.

Another problem with sales volume quotas is that they are often inequitable. Quotas are often based on historical sales and, therefore, do not reflect differences in territory potential, experiences of salespeople in territories, advertising support in various territories, travel time required to contact customers, or tasks which must be performed to satisfy customer needs. Although this problem may partially result from inadequate administration of the quota setting procedure, anytime a forecast of sales is involved, errors and inequities may result.

Another problem, which also applies to other types of quotas, is that the sales quota may be too conservative to effectively motivate salespeople. Although the sales manager can monitor this and attempt to eliminate overly conservative estimates of sales volume, it is often difficult to identify this problem. A study by Winer suggested that salespeople are quota achievers and, therefore, primarily attempt to attain quota instead of maximize income or sales volume.[2] If quotas are set too low, salespeople will only work hard enough to achieve quota. On the other hand, if quotas are set too high, there is a risk that the quota will lose meaning and not serve as an effective motivational tool. In fact, inability to achieve quota may be a source of demotivation.

Although sales quotas have several limitations, they are useful. For example, when an industrial firm develops a new product and, therefore, has dominance early in the product's life cycle, it is critical that the firm attempt to maintain dominance until the product approaches market saturation. For such products, firms will gladly sacrifice short term profits in order to achieve long run dominance. Profits which accompany long run dominance will always significantly outweigh profits during introduction and growth stages of the life cycle. In this case, it is critical to develop and monitor sales objectives.

Profit Quotas.   In order to overcome weaknesses associated with sales quotas, some firms base quotas on profit objectives. For each product, a unit profit margin is calculated. Management then directs salesperson

---

[2] Leon Winer, "The Effect of Production Sales Quotas on Sales Force Productivity," *Journal of Marketing Research*, Vol. X (May, 1973), p. 183.

A Company Profile

Bennett Printing Company is a multimillion dollar regional printer employing both letterpress and offset capabilities. The company was established by Paul Bennett who began business in 1889, in Paris, Texas and relocated its operations to Dallas in 1927. In 1952, Bennett was sold to Sammons Corporation, a major conglomerate owning hotels, a travel wholesaler, a communications company, an industrial distributor, and numerous other companies.

Marketing its products in Texas, Arkansas, and Oklahoma, Bennett traditionally maintained a slow but consistent growth of 10 to 15 percent. In order to maintain a high quality product, Bennett focused efforts on two major markets, banking with a variety of products and county tax units with record books that are used for handposting.

In 1979, the company decided to expand its markets and production capabilities in order to realize a higher than average growth rate. It hired several salespeople to concentrate on penetrating the advertising industry, developed a supporting bindery operation, and added two two color presses, one four color press, and one five color press. At the same time, it maintained the corporate philosophy of giving high quality work at a reasonable price (i.e., a dollars worth of printing for a dollar).

Bennett Printing Company utilizes seven territory salespeople, eight city salespeople, and two independent brokers to market its products in the Southwest. The city salespeople only concentrate on accounts in the Dallas/Fort Worth metropolitan area while territory salespeople cover all other areas in their market. They also employ two sales managers, one for each of the two major markets, that report directly to the company's president. All salespeople are compensated with a salary for their first three to six months of orientation, training, and market development. At the end of this time period each person's income then becomes a function of productivity. Although they are paid a straight commission, each person draws an established income each month that is applied against commissions. If commissions exceed a salesperson's monthly draw the person receives a check for the difference.

In order to give salespeople an incentive and the sales managers a basis for measuring performance Bennett has established sales, activity, and expense quotas. Quotas are established through one-on-one interaction between salespeople and sales managers. The process begins with a list of all customers and prospects. Each salesperson complies a list of existing customers as well as accounts that they expect to contact during the following year. For existing customers, the sales managers and salespeople get together and analyze expected volumes associated with each account. In addition to evaluating the preceding year's sales volume for each account, the sales managers study the impact of the economy and anticipated marketing plans on volume. Evaluation of this information results in a target sales quota.

Salespeople also have a quota for the number of new prospects contacted during the year. After developing a list of prospects, salespeople divide each list into sublists that reflect monthly call plans. They are then required to make approximately three new prospect calls each month. Of course the quota varies by salesperson. While an established salesperson may spend more time on account maintenance than account development, a new person may *primarily concentrate on developing new customers.*

Finally, salespeople have an expense ceiling that is monitored by management. Similar to other quotas, as long as salespeople do not exceed the expense quota, sales managers take no action. However, each expenditure that is not established in the quota plan must be approved by management. By controlling expenses, monitoring sales, and encouraging new business development, Bennett believes that the principle elements of their formula for success are accounted for in the quota plan. Not only does this serve as the basis for evaluating performance but it also helps management identify who needs special attention and training. The quota system, therefore, gives the sales managers input on how their time should be allocated among the sales force.

activity toward those products that contribute most to profit. This may be accomplished in several ways. Management may establish a unit sales quota for each line which, when combined with all other lines, reflects overall profit objectives. Another alternative is to simply establish profit objectives for each salesperson. Then each salesperson personally allocates sales effort to various products in order to accomplish objectives.

Although profit quotas are useful and, to many managers, desirable there are several problems that one should be aware of. First, it is not unusual for companies to change the way they calculate contribution from year to year. This is particularly true for younger, rapidly growing firms. One company with which the authors are familiar calculated each salesperson's contribution in 1979 by subtracting from sales the following: cost of goods sold, storage, transportation, allocated labor, direct labor, and allocated overhead. In 1980, they began to subtract maintenance in addition to the other expenses to arrive at contribution. Since compensation was based on quota attainment and quotas were based on the previous year's contribution, an unfair and difficult situation developed. Salespeople had to both maintain a reasonable growth and make up for the change in profit determination in order to maintain their compensation level.

Another problem with profit quotas is the inherent assumption that low profit sales should be avoided. If a plant is operating at 60 percent capacity, it may be advisable to pursue sales that do not cover all overhead expenses. Referred to as variable cost pricing, a sale may be priced to simply cover variable costs (i.e., cost of goods sold, direct labor, packaging, transportation, and storage) and contribute a small amount to overhead or fixed costs. Since the fixed costs are present whether the sales are made or not made, it makes sense to contribute some money to keep paying for these fixed expenses.

Activity Quotas. Whenever goals are established it is important to divide the larger, more general goals into smaller, more operational goals. Businesses are extremely complex entities involving the interaction of dozens of activities. Although the general goal of business is to optimize profits, firms must identify activities which must be accomplished in order to achieve profits; then establish quotas or goals for each activity. Some activities for which quotas should be established are (1) development of new accounts, (2) sales penetration of existing accounts, (3) development of displays and other dealer sales aids, (4) call frequency, (5) number of demonstrations, or (6) any activities which characterize the selling environment of a particular industry.

Combination of Quotas.   Since most firms have unique products and policies, it is possible to have numerous, feasible combinations of quotas. For companies that give salespeople authority to establish price, for example, it is probably best to establish profit quotas. If sales quotas were utilized, there may be a tendency to concentrate on sales at the expense of profits. The same firm, however, will not want to completely ignore sales and growth. Therefore, it may want to have activity quotas for number of new accounts, number of calls, and number of demonstrations.

Establishing Quotas

Establishing optimum quotas is difficult because of the numerous variables and tradeoffs which impact on the decision.[3] As mentioned earlier, quotas must be set high enough to motivate performance but not be set too high to lose meaning. To complicate matters even further, a reward system is generally attached to quota setting. If quotas are attained, salespeople receive a material reward. The reward must be high enough to motivate and low enough to help the company maintain acceptable profits. The effect of these factors is generally not considered in establishing quotas. Rather, it is normally a subjective judgment of the sales executive.

Quota as a Percent of Market Potential.   One method for setting quota levels is to multiply company sales forecast times each territory's relative market potential. If XYZ Company forecasts sales to be $10 million, then that $10 million is allocated to each territory in an amount which corresponds to the territories' market potential as a percent of total market potential. For example:

$$\text{Quota for Territory A} = \$10 \text{ Million} \times \frac{\text{Market Potential (Territory A)}}{\text{Market Potential (All Markets)}}$$

Therefore, if total market potential is $50 million and $5 million of that potential exists in territory A, the sales quota for territory A would be:

---

[3] For an additional discussion of trade offs, see: Rene Y. Darmon, "Setting Sales Quotas with Conjoint Analysis," *Journal of Marketing Research*, Vol. XVI (February, 1979), pp. 133–140.

$$\$10 \text{ Million} \times \frac{\$5 \text{ Million}}{\$50 \text{ Million}} \text{ or } \$1 \text{ Million}$$

Although the method is simple and easily administered it does not take into consideration the maturity of various territories, the intensity of competition in each territory, or the amount of promotional support given each territory. However, it can serve as a starting point and be subjectively modified by these other factors.

Other quotas can also be set by making minor modifications in the formula. For example, if one wanted to set a quota for new accounts, the formula would be:

$$\text{Quota for Accounts in Territory A} = \frac{\substack{\text{Total Goal for Developing} \\ \text{New Accounts} \times \text{Potential} \\ \text{New Accounts (Territory A)}}}{\substack{\text{Potential New Accounts} \\ \text{(All Markets)}}}$$

If territories are not effectively balanced, however, some territories may have larger accounts that require more time to sell. This would partially invalidate this calculation. On the other hand, it is a starting point from which goals can be consistently established.

Mathematical Modeling.   Another major problem with calculating a quota as percentage of market potential is that it does not take into consideration the impact of a reward system for achieving quota. If a reward system is effective it should most likely effect selling behavior and, therefore, the corresponding quota level. One approach that integrates market potential, reward systems, and salesperson attitude toward risk in order to determine optimal quota and reward levels is an operational quota-setting procedure based on conjoint analysis.[4] In order to implement this procedure, the sales manager must present each salesperson with a series of compensation plans which include quota levels and bonus levels. The salesperson is then asked to rank the compensation schemes in order of preference. By doing this, the salesperson is identifying how he or she would react to a change in compensation schemes. Some salespeople might increase work time to achieve higher income levels, some might reduce work time if quota levels are perceived as unattainable, and some may maintain constant work levels irrespective of changes in income possibilities. In other words, by considering the salesperson's attitude toward risk and the utility the salesperson attaches to additional work, the sales manager can determine a quota and bonus plan that both "maximizes the firm's profits and gives each salesperson the desired satisfaction level.[5]

---

[4] This section is based on Darmon, *Ibid.*
[5] *Ibid.*, p. 137.

Salesperson Participation.   In addition to the advantages associated with objectively calculating an optimum quota and bonus level for each salesperson, Darmon's conjoint approach requires that the sales force participate in the quota setting activity. In a study by Wotruba and Thurlow it was found that sales managers have more confidence in the accuracy of quotas when salespeople are asked to participate in quota-setting. Specifically, 77 percent of firms which allow salesperson participation and 59 percent of the firms that do not allow participation believe that quota estimates for their firm do not deviate by more than 10 percent of reality.[6] They also found that quota setting took place in 74 percent of the firms studied.[7]

Evaluating Quotas

One of the primary uses of quotas is in controlling salesperson performance. Sales managers can compare expected performance in terms of quota achievement with actual performance at any time during the sales period in order to determine if problems exist. Salespeople can also use the calculation to monitor their performance and correct performance problems before they impact on earnings and standing within the firm.

The calculation required to evaluate quota achievement is quite simple. When one is comparing quota to a performance variable (e.g., sales volume, number of calls, number of new accounts, number of displays, etc.) actual performance is simply divided by quota.

$$\text{Performance Index} = \frac{\text{Actual Performance}}{\text{Quota}} \times 100$$

If salesperson A, therefore, had a sales volume quota of $150,000 and a year-end performance of $139,000, then Salesperson A's performance index for sales volume is .93 (93 percent). The same calculation can be utilized for all activities except expenses. If a firm has an expense quota, the performance index is calculated by dividing quota by actual expenses.

In addition to evaluating the performance index of each activity, it is also possible to aggregate the sales activities into an overall salesperson performance index. This is accomplished by (1) weighting each activity, (2) multiplying each weight by the performance index of each activity (provides a weighted index), (3) aggregating the weighted indexes, (4) dividing the sum of the weighted indexes by the total weighting factor (provides a rating index), and (5) comparing the rating index to 100. If the rating index is less than 100, the salesperson is under quota, and if it is over 100, the salesperson exceeded quota. Although this overall rating index gives top management a tool for quickly and easily evaluating performance, it should not be utilized by sales managers as a substitute for

[6] Thomas R. Wotruba and Michael L. Thurlow "Sales Force Participation in Quota Setting and Sales Forecasting," *Journal of Marketing*, Vol. 40 (April, 1976) p. 16.
[7] *Ibid.*, p. 13.

evaluating performance of each activity. For example, the overall rating index of a salesperson may be 100. As indicated in Table 4-5, however, this could be caused by higher than expected sales volume and expenses and lower than expected profits. The high expenses were partially caused by a larger than normal number of calls and a relatively low closing rate (i.e., relationship between call frequency and demonstrations). Salesperson A, therefore, possibly needs some training on closing techniques.

Activity	Quota	Actual Performance	Performance Index	Weight	Weighted Index
Sales Volume	$100,000	$120,000	120	2	240
Expenses	40,000	65,000	62	2	124
Profit	60,000	55,000	92	3	276
New Accounts	10	10	100	1	100
Call Frequency	250	400	160	1	160
Demonstrations	50	50	100	1	100
				10	1,000

$$\text{Rating Index} = \frac{1,000}{10} = 100$$

Table 4–5
Evaluation of Quota Performance for Salesperson A

SUMMARY

Inherent in the sales management planning process is budgeting and quota-setting. The sales budget is a reporting system that allows firms to analyze, direct, and control the flow of resources through each organizational jurisdiction. It is a flexible, on-going, control procedure involving employees at every level of the sales and marketing organizations. The sales budget procedure involves the following steps: (1) identify company objectives, (2) prepare a sales forecast, (3) determine sales budget of revenue and expenses, (4) review budgets, and (5) authorize budgets.

A sales quota is defined as that portion of the sales forecast which is allocated to a partic-

ular salesperson, territory, or sales group during a specified time period. It represents a realistically attainable and fairly developed goal to be accomplished by a sales territory. The most commonly used quotas are sales quotas, profit quotas, activity quotas, and expense quotas. Irregardless of the type of quota utilized, it must be high enough to motivate performance but not too high to lose meaning. Also, the reward system that is generally attached to quota performance must provide rewards high enough to motivate but low enough to help the company maintain acceptable profits.

QUESTIONS

1. What are the fundamental principles of sales budgeting?

2. Define "sales quota" and its primary advantages.

3. How would a sales executive establish optimum quotas?

4. What are the advantages of a properly established quota?

5. Discuss the sales budgeting procedure.

6. Why should top management review the goals of operating divisions as a part of the sales budgeting procedure?

7. Why is flexible budgeting more complex than fixed budgeting?

8. List some activites for which quotas should be established.

9. Should quotas be based on past performance or on measures of potential? Support your opinion.

10. How would a sales manager evaluate quota achievement?

Chapter 5 _____

Territory Management

After completing this chapter, you will be able to:

- Identify the procedure for designing new territories or reassessing old territorial boundaries.
- Discuss the procedures for calculating market potential for industrial and consumer goods.
- Present procedures for determining the amount of market potential that can feasibly be handled by a salesperson.
- Identify factors which impact on sales force routing and present a procedure for actually routing salespeople.

With increases in costs of automobile travel, air travel, lodging, and food it becomes more critical that salespeople utilize their selling time efficiently. Travel routes between customers should be established so that travel distance and time is minimized. Profitability analysis should be performed on each customer to determine the feasibility of personally calling on customers. The size of territories should be established so that they can be adequately covered within a minimum time frame and with minimum travel, especially overnight travel. Also, management must identify the optimum number of salespeople that are necessary to adequately cover territories.

All of these decision making areas are included in territory management. It is the activity of optimally designing territorial boundaries, identifying sales force size and mix, and determining appropriate sales routes. The objective of this chapter is to facilitate understanding of specific procedures associated with territorial management.

DESIGNING TERRITORIES

Whether a firm is designing new territories or reassessing old territorial boundaries it is critical to employ a systematic procedure of evaluation. The firm must (1) identify market potential of each area in the firm's overall geographic market, (2) determine the market size that can optimally be handled by a salesperson (i.e. territory size) and, therefore, the number of salespeople that are needed to adequately cover all potential markets, (3) examine extraneous factors that may affect territory design such as number of key accounts (customers that account for a significant percent of the firm's total sales), customer concentration or dispersion, market support allocated to areas and strength of competition, and (4) design territories.

Identify Market Potential

As was indicated in Chapter 3, market potential is a calculation of the maximum sales opportunities for all sellers of a good or service if all possible customers and all possible users were accommodated. Not only does market potential serve as an equitable basis for dividing territories but it is significantly related to actual sales. This correlation between sales and market potential was proven in a study of a major ready-to-wear apparel company.[1]

Industrial Goods. Calculation of an estimate of market potential for industrial goods is best accomplished by the SIC (standard industrial classification) Method. Utilization of the SIC Method involves the following steps.

Step 1: Assign a SIC code to all actual and potential customers. The SIC code is a four digit coding system established by the Federal Government to uniformly categorize all businesses into industry groupings. For example, all firms that manufacture fur goods will have as their SIC code 2371. A firm such as Dun & Bradstreet can economically assign SIC codes to a firm's customers as well as provide a computer listing of all potential customers.

Step 2: Check listing of actual and potential customers for accuracy and completeness. Salespeople should be asked to check the list of customers in their respective territories to make sure that all actual and potential customers are listed with the accurate SIC code.

Step 3: Identify the size of each actual and potential customer in terms of number of employees. Numerous firms that maintain information files on companies can provide this information. Also, accuracy and completeness should be checked by sales managers and salespeople.

Step 4: Determine consumption estimates per employee for each industry category (i.e., SIC category). This can be done by examining the consumption rate of existing customers that buy all of their requirements from the firm conducting the study. If the firm does not have a represen-

---

[1] Henry C. Lucas, Jr., Charles B. Weinberg, and Kenneth W. Clowes, "Sales Response as a Function of Territorial Potential and Sales Representative Workload," *Journal of Marketing Research*, Vol. XII (August, 1975), pp. 298-305.

tative number of such customers in each SIC category, then marketing research should be done in light and medium users to identify the percent of their total purchases made from the supplier conducting the study. For example, if a company buys 25 percent of its requirements from the supplier, then one can simply multiply consumption by four to arrive at total consumption. Total consumption is divided by the number of employees in the firm. The result of this calculation is average consumption per employee. The company, therefore, ends up with a separate average consumption figure for each SIC category. Consumption per employee estimates for each SIC category are reviewed and analyzed to arrive at a consumption estimate which can be applied to every firm in each SIC category.

Step 5: Multiply the number of employees by consumption per employee for each firm. Aggregation of these customer potential estimates will result in an estimate of market potential. Although the result may not be a precise estimate of market potential, it will be accurate enough for designing territories. Since all territories are evaluated consistently with the same procedure, the relative market potential of territories will be extremely accurate, which is, of course, the objective of market potential estimation for territory management.

Table 5–1 illustrates the output of the SIC procedure. The firm conducting the market potential analysis has three primary market areas, San Diego, Kansas City, and Dallas, with each area having three potential customers. For each customer, consumption per employee associated with the customer's SIC code is multiplied times the number of employees to arrive at market potential. For example, companies with a SIC code of 7213 (i.e., American Textile Supply) consume about $19.82 of product per employee. Since American Textile has 68 employees, it can potentially purchase $1347.96 of product. Consumption figures of each company in each trade area are aggregated to provide a potential for each market. The total market potential for the San Diego trade area, for example, is $7267.92.

Consumer Goods.   The most appropriate method for estimating market potential for consumer goods is the Buying Power Index Method (BPI). Published annually in the *Sales and Marketing Management* magazine, the BPI is an indicator of market demand for specific market areas in the United States. For each State, County, and Standard Metropolitan Statistical Area (SMSA)[2], *Sales and Marketing Management* evaluates estimates of population, income, and retail sales to arrive at an index which reflects consumer demand in that area. Specifically, the BPI is calculated using the following formula:

---

[2] An SMSA consists of a county or a group of contiguous counties with a total population of at least 100,000 and a central city with a minimum population of 50,000 (or two closely located cities with a combined population of 50,000).

Table 5–1
SIC Method for Determining Market Potential

SIC Code	Firm Name	Firm Address	Number of Employees	Consumption per Employee	Emp. X Consumption Market Potential
7213	American Textile Supply	San Diego	68	$19.823	$1,347.96
3811	Cubic Western Data	San Diego	550	8.965	4,930.75
3662	Interocean Systems, Inc.	San Diego	105	9.421	989.21
4924	Gas Service Co.	KC, Mo.	2530	3.984	10,079.52
4213	Riss Int. Corp.	KC, Mo.	1200	5.921	7,105.20
2648	Stuart Hall Co.	KC, Mo.	300	12.624	3,787.20
5931	Jackson Arms	Dallas	5	29.821	149.11
5065	Norvell Electronics	Dallas	40	1.495	59.80
4899	Sammons Communications	Dallas	500	2.645	1,322.50

Summary—Market potential by trade area:

Trade Area I (San Diego, Ca.) .... $ 7,267.92
Trade Area II (Dallas, Tx.) .... $ 1,531.41
Trade Area III (Kansas City, Mo.) $20,971.92

$$BPI = \frac{5(\text{Income}) + 3(\text{Retail Sales}) + 2(\text{Population})}{10}$$

Income is weighted by a factor of 5 and represents the effective buying income of the specific area as a percent of total United States income. Similarly, retail sales represents the percentage of United States retail sales and population is the population of the area as a percent of total United States population.

Table 5–2 presents the buying power index, effective buying income, retail sales, and population for the New England States. Connecticut, for example, has 1.6677 percent of the total effective buying income in the United States, 1.4116 percent of retail sales, 1.4415 percent of the population, and 1.5457 percent of total buying power. Buying power index for Connecticut was calculated as follows:

$$\frac{1.6677(5) + 1.4116(3) + 1.4415(2)}{10} = 1.5457$$

If a firm used BPI figures to allocate salespeople to territories it would, therefore, divide the sales force along the lines of relative size (i.e., in terms of BPI). Since a buying power index is also calculated for counties and SMSA's, a consumer goods firm could use the data to allocate salespeople to these smaller geographic units. Also, *Sales and Marketing Management* recently began publishing an Industrial Survey of Buying Power which could be used instead of the SIC Method to allocate industrial goods salespeople to territories.

The primary problem with the buying power index method is that the weighting procedure (i.e., 5 for income, 3 for retail sales, and 2 for population) is not appropriate for all firms. These weights are established through regression analysis and primarily apply to nationally distributed convenience goods. It is recommended that each firm use the

Table 5–2
Buying Power Index
Method by State

State	Effective Buying Income (% of U.S. Income)	Retail Sales (% of U.S.)	Population (% of U.S.)	Buying Power Index
Connecticut	1.6677	1.4116	1.4415	1.5457
Maine	.4293	.4652	.5014	.4546
Massachusetts	2.7281	2.6563	2.6725	2.6955
New Hampshire	.3676	.4113	.3892	.3850
Rhode Island	.4361	.4071	.4298	.4260
Vermont	.1905	.2238	.2232	.2070
Total—New England	5.8193	5.5753	5.6576	5.7138

Source: *Sales and Marketing Management* (July 24, 1978), pp. B-3, B-5, B-7.

available data to identify variables and calculate weights that are appropriate for each product line.

Determine Optimum Territory Size and Number of Salespeople _____

Once market potentials have been established for each trade area it is necessary to determine the amount of market potential that can feasibly be handled by a salesperson. This can be accomplished by simple trial and error procedures or can be done quantitatively. Although new companies with limited data bases may feasibly utilize subjective procedures, more mature firms should always solve territorial size problems quantitatively. The decision is far too critical for guesswork.

Semlow's Model. One of the most popular techniques for determining optimum territory size was developed by Walter Semlow.[3] Semlow's approach deals with the following question: How many salespeople can a firm add to a sales force before the cost of adding another salesperson is greater than expected revenue? For example, Salesperson A who sells in a territory which represents 5 percent of total market potential may have a sales volume of $250,000. Salesperson A would, therefore, have a sales volume per 1 percent potential of $50,000 ($\frac{250,000}{5 \text{ percent potential}}$). Salesperson B, on the other hand, produces $160,000 per year in a territory that has 2 percent of total market potential (i.e., $80,000 per 1 percent potential). Obviously, Salesperson B is more productive per 1 percent potential than Salesperson A. Among other things, this may be caused by the fact that a salesperson cannot adequately handle a 5 percent territory. If salespeople cannot handle larger territories, it may be advisable to reduce the size of territories to a more manageable level. If territory size is reduced, however, what effect will the change have on sales volume? Are sales volume increases negated by hiring, training, and maintenance costs? What territory size is most profitable?

In order to answer the preceding questions, Semlow suggested that firms utilize the following procedure:

Step 1: Determine sales potential for each salesperson's territory.
Step 2: Compute dollar sales performance in each territory for which a potential was determined.
Step 3: Divide dollar sales performances (Step 2) by sales potential (Step 1) for each territory to arrive at dollar sales performance per 1 percent potential. As indicated in Figure 5-1, as territory size increases, sales performance per 1 percent potential decreases.
Step 4: Take into consideration differences in sales ability of individual salespeople and territory maturity by fitting a trend line to the data on sales performance per 1 percent potential (see Figure 5-1). This smoothed data on sales performance should be used in subsequent steps of the analysis.

---

[3] Walter Semlow, "How Many Salesmen do You Need?" *Harvard Business Review*, Vol. 32 (May-June, 1959), pp. 126-132.

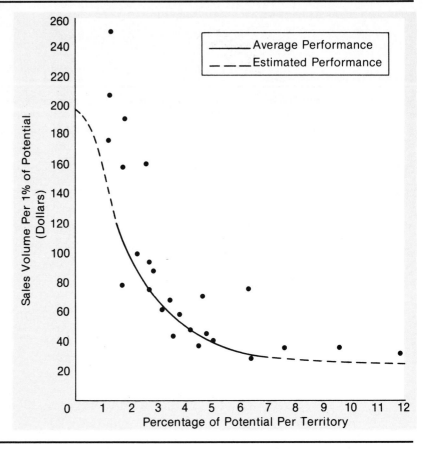

Figure 5–1
Relationship
Between Sales
Potential Per
Territory and Sales
Volume Per 1
Percent of Potential

Source: Reprinted by permission of the Harvard Business Review. Exhibit from "How Many Salesmen Do You Need" by Walter J. Semlow (May-June, 1959). Copyright © 1959 by the President and Fellows of Harvard College; all rights reserved.

Step 5: At first glance, it may seem to be appropriate to hire more sales-people and, therefore, reduce territory size in order to achieve a higher sales volume. However, keep in mind that increases in the size of a sales force will lead to both a higher sales volume and higher overhead and operating costs, such as additional management, hiring costs, new plant and equipment, etc. All direct and indirect costs associated with a change in territory size should be considered in this calculation of profit.

Step 6: Select the territory size and, therefore, sales force size that maximizes profit.

Although Semlow's approach to calculating territory size is widely accepted by sales managers, it does have several limitations. First, it can only be utilized if the firm has numerous sales territories from which a data base can be developed. Second, Semlow did not prove a relationship between market potential and actual sales.[4] Although this relationship may exist, Semlow did not resolve the issue. If there is no correlation between market potential and actual sales, than the procedure does not have any significant application.

Lucas-Weinberg-Clowes Model. In order to provide more insight into the relationship between sales performance and territory potential, a study of 248 salespeople of a major ready-to-wear apparel company was conducted. Results of the survey indicated that sales performance is positively correlated to market potential and negatively correlated to workload (i.e., number of calls necessary and amount of travel between accounts).[5]

In applying the Lucas-Weinberg-Clowes study results, the following model was developed that can be used to identify optimum sales force size.[6]

$$\text{Maximum } Z = mnf \frac{P}{n} \cdot \frac{W}{n} - cn$$

Where:
    m = profit margin per unit
    n = number of salespeople
    c = cost per salesperson (not including commissions which are deducted from m)
    p = total corporate potential
    w = total corporate workload

The objective is to find a value for n which maximizes Z. Once an optimum sales force size is identified the firm can divide size into market potential to identify the optimum size of each territory.

Talley's Workload Method. Talley's method utilizes workload as the primary variable for determining sales force size. Specifically, the objective of Talley's method is to equalize workload (i.e., "the amount of time required by a salesperson to service adequately his customer's needs").[7] The procedure for calculating sales force size is as follows:[8] (see Table 5–3 for output of the procedure).

    Step 1. Divide customers into size categories.
    Step 2. Determine a call frequency (i.e, the number of times per period a customer wants to be contacted) for each customer class. This can be accomplished with customer surveys.

    [4] Charles B. Weinberg and Henry C. Lucas, Jr., "Letters to the Editor," *Journal of Marketing,* Vol. 41 (April, 1977), pp. 146–147.
    [5] Henry C. Lucas, Jr., Charles B. Weinberg, and Kenneth W. Clowes, "Sales Response as a Function of Territorial Potential and Sales Representative Workload," *Journal of Marketing Research*, Vol. XII (August, 1975), pp. 298–305.
    [6] *Ibid.,* p. 303.
    [7] Walter J. Talley, Jr., "How to Design Sales Territories," *Journal of Marketing*, Vol. 25 (January, 1961), p. 8.
    [8] *Ibid.,* p. 8.

	(1) Customer Classification (by size)	(2) Yearly call frequency for each class	(3) Number of Customers (Actual & Potential)	(2) X (3) Workload
I.	(0–99 Employees)	8	1000	8,000
II.	(100–999)	10	800	8,000
III.	(1000–4999)	14	250	3,500
IV.	(5000 and over)	17	85	1,445
		Total Workload		20,945

Table 5–3
Determining Sales
Force Size by
Analyzing Workload

$$\text{Sales Force Size} = \frac{\text{Total Workload}}{\text{Calls per salesperson}} = \frac{20,945}{600}$$

$$\text{Sales force size} = 34.9 \text{ or } 35$$

can be accomplished with customer surveys.

Step 3. Multiply call frequency per account times the number of potential accounts for each customer classification. Adding the resulting workload for each customer class provides total workload.

Step 4. Determine the number of calls that could feasibly be made by the average salesperson. In order to do this, the sales manager must consider holidays, vacations, sick days, time for sales meetings, training, travel time, and waiting time. In Table 5–3 it is assumed that the average salesperson can make 600 calls per year.

Step 5. Divide total workload (Step 3) by yearly call frequency (Step 4).

Examine Extraneous Factors

Although quantitative models for calculating territory size and sales force size serve as a good starting point for designing territories, they are certainly not a panacea. Some areas have more **key accounts** (i.e., accounts that are established and represent a significant portion of the total sales); some areas receive more or less promotional assistance; areas require varying amounts of travel; also, trade areas have varying amounts of competition. The size of a salesperson's territory should reflect differences in these factors. Sales territories that contain larger, more concentrated trade areas should be smaller in terms of market potential than territories which have numerous, small, geographically dispersed markets.

Design Territories

To this point, the sales manager should have developed the following information: (1) market potential of each trade area (i.e., trade areas being counties, SMSAs, census tracts, or parts of these units); (2) number of salespeople needed to adequately cover territories; (3) recommended size of each territory; and (4) unique characteristics of each trade area (in terms of volume of business per customer, number of key accounts, dispersion of customers, extent of competition, and amount of marketing support). Once this information is collected and evaluated for completeness and accuracy, it is time to establish territorial boundaries; i.e., design territories.

The best procedure for designing territories is the build-up approach. The sales manager simply puts trade areas together according to the rules established in the previous analysis. First, the size of each territory should be approximately the same in terms of market potential and workload. Although it is impossible to perfectly distribute potential and workload among territories, it should be a constant objective. Also, if a territory requires more work in terms of travel and call frequency, it should be allocated more potential. Second, each territory should have approximately the same number of key accounts. Third, the characteristics of each territory should conform to guidelines established in the analysis of market potential, workload, and extraneous factors. Fourth, areas that cannot be profitably serviced by salespeople should be excluded when designing territories. Firms should possibly contract with independent agents to handle such territories.

Figure 5–2 illustrates how FMC Corporation's Machinery Group changed its territorial design to conform to the rules identified in this chapter.[9] As indicated in Figure 5–2 the Southeastern United States was uncovered prior to the territory redesign procedure. Since salespeople were not given adequate direction in their selling activity, they had simply considered this area to be unimportant. Market potential analysis indicated that the area accounted for approximately 20 percent of the firm's total market potential. Analysis also indicated that Montana, Wyoming, South Dakota, and North Dakota had a negligible number of potential customers. A salesperson was therefore assigned to the Southeastern region and the North Central was left uncovered.

Consideration of market potential and workload led to a more equitable distribution of territory potential (see Table 5–4). Before the customer analysis, territory potential ranged from 2 percent to 22 percent. After the analytical procedure was implemented, territory potential ranged from 8 percent to 16 percent with most of the territories containing 11 or 12 percent of their total potential.

SALES FORCE ROUTING

Most managers will agree that the identification of optimum travel schedules is not a high priority activity for most salespeople. They will oftentimes spend too much time socializing with certain friendly cus-

---

[9] Michael S. Heschel, "Effective Sales Territory Development," *Journal of Marketing*, Vol. 41 (April, 1977), pp. 39–43.

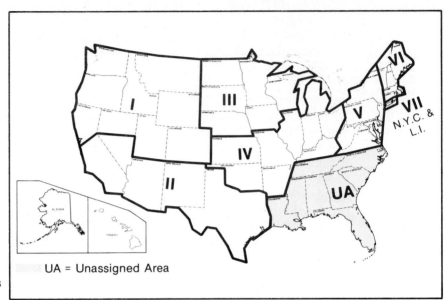

Figure 5–2a
Sales Territories
Before

UA = Unassigned Area

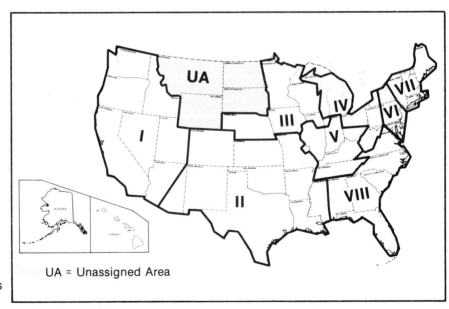

Figure 5–2b
Sales Territories
After

UA = Unassigned Area

BEFORE		AFTER	
Territory	Percent	Territory	Percent
I	8%	I	11%
II	11	II	15
III	11	III	11
IV	21	IV	12
V	22	V	12
VI	2	VI	15
VII	5	VII	8
		VIII	16
Unassigned	20%	Unassigned	Negligible
Weightings are percent of the total estimated U.S. market potential			

Figure 5–2c
Territory Weightings

Source: Michael S. Heschel, "Effective Sales Territory Development," *Journal of Marketing*, Vol. 41 (April, 1977), pp. 42–43.

tomers, utilize familiar routes too often, and not devote enough time exploring unfamiliar areas of their territory.

Since routing is largely neglected by salespeople, it is important that this necessary function be accomplished through a co-operative effort between the salesperson and sales manager. At the same time, however, the salesperson should feel like he or she is primarily responsible for development of optimum routes.

Call Routing Factors

A number of considerations and rules are important when planning and implementing a salesperson's routing so as to properly control travel and call activity. Some of these factors are as follows:

- All actual customers and potential prospects must be contacted at predetermined intervals.

- Calls must be lined up or clustered in order to minimize travel time and expense.

- If calls are to be made at regular intervals, time preferences and buying habits of the customers should be considered.

- If calls are to be at irregular or on a once-around basis, appointments must be used whenever possible. Although some salespeople prefer to make their own appointments, this time consuming activity may be delegated to clerical or para-sales personnel.

- Planned calls and proposed routes should be regularly devel-

A. Company Profile

Formed in 1926, with service between Dallas and Henderson, Texas, ETMF Freight Systems has expanded into 34 states with 102 terminals from which it provides direct service to over 9,000 points throughout the United States. ETMF is one of the 15 largest common carriers in the United States with sales in excess of $200 million. It's trucks travel more than 138 million miles each year to provide service to over 20,000 customers.

ETMF's growth can largely be attributed to its acquisition programs and its commitment to a corporate philosophy of "pride + people + service = profit." Since 1968 ETMF Motor Freight has acquired operating authorities from Valley Copperstate System, Transamerica Freight System, Hemingway Transport, Eastern Express, and Shanahan Motor Lines. These acquisitions enabled ETMF to expand its Southwest and Midwest operation, and include routes between California and the Midwest, and between the Northwest and the Southwest and Southeast. In fact, the company has become a coast-to-coast carrier. Also, in 1971, as an additional service to its customers, the company began its special commodity operation, The Diamond Division. It has since expanded into many special commodity areas. The division now has 66 terminals or agents in 22 states.

Corporate acquisitions, however, do not overshadow the role that ETMF's people and its service orientation have had in its growth profile. The company has over 4,000 employees with an average length of service of 12 years. ETMF's service orientation is reflected in the investment it made in 1973 in an on-line computer system that enables the company to have instantaneous, efficient control of shipments at all times. The system also provides ETMF with the ability to transmit data between the central computer in the corporate office and the terminals.

In 1980, with deregulation of the motor freight industry, ETMF and all other carriers experienced a significant change in their marketing behavior. This change in the legal environment required companies to make a significant commitment to marketing. ETMF responded by allocating $1.2 million to a national advertising program, establishing numerous new terminals in attractive market areas, and developing effective marketing systems for evaluating market areas, establishing long range growth plans, and establishing strategic programs.

Salespeople play a significant role in ETMF's marketing program. They are, therefore, efficiently allocated and managed in each territory. Territory boundaries are based on territorial potential and workload. Particular interest is focused on the size of potential accounts in each territory. Territories will be divided in such a way that each salesperson in a general market area has about the same number of key accounts. Also, the company tries to locate people in a single geographical area. It does not want a salesperson traveling from one end of town to the other each day.

Once salespeople are assigned to territories, they are given a quota of 50 calls per week, including entertainment-oriented calls. Fifteen percent of these calls must be made to new prospects. In order to maximize efficiency and meet quota, each territory is divided into ten sections, based on density of market. Accounts in sections one to five are contacted the first week, and accounts in sections six to ten are contacted the second week. Also, while eight preplan-

ned calls are made each day, salespeople have flexibility to make two unplanned calls. With a routine call plan and an objective division of territories, ETMF maximizes *its coverage of territories, experiences only a minimum amount of discontent from territorial inequities, and effectively controls the call behavior of salespeople.*

oped and submitted to sales management (i.e., once per week).

- A route sheet should be developed and utilized by salespeople when planning calls. This sheet should include these characteristics: (1) be simple to complete; (2) provide all details necessary for effectively following the route; (3) be prepared far enough in advance to provide for appointments and notices to customers; and (4) be circulated to all people who may need to know the salesperson's plans (e.g., service department, credit department, order desk).

- The routing plan should be flexible enough to adjust to unforeseen demands on the salesperson's time. Escape valve days must be provided to allow for call backs, service or complaint calls, or personal emergencies.

Procedure for Routing Salespeople

The first step in sales force routing is to develop a comprehensive list of actual and potential customers. If a firm utilizes appropriate techniques for initially designing territories, such a list should already be available (see previous section on Identifying Market Potential).

After customers are identified, their location must be plotted on a large-scale, detailed map that pictures streets as well as businesses and residential areas. The third step in routing is to identify call time preferences of different types of customers. Generally, customers in certain types of industries will only talk to salespeople at specified times. Fourth, use geographic location and time preferences to cluster customers into trade areas. Finally, through trial and error or with the aid of computer simulation techniques, a schedule should be developed that minimizes time and expense. In some industries, schedules may only be planned a week or two in advance (i.e., when salespeople cannot make regularly spaced calls), while in other cases calls may be scheduled for a year in advance such as with an automobile parts manufacturer with which the authors worked.

Computer Routing. Although trial-and-error procedures can be employed to route salespeople, computer techniques have been developed to aid salespeople and managers in this important activity. One proposed technique uses Bayesian decision theory to quantitatively incorporate travel time, waiting time, probability of a sale, account potential, and profits into a routing model.[10] By considering these factors, the sales manager can calculate the expected value of each customer as follows:

$$\text{Expected Value} = S.V. - (C.G.S. + E)\,P$$
Where:
S.V. = estimated sales volume
C.G.S. = cost of goods sold
E = expense in making the sale
P = probability of purchase[11]

By calculating the expected value of each customer, the sales manager can decide which customers should be contacted and in which order they should be called on.

Assume, for example, that a salesperson has ten prospective customers. Each customer is evaluated to ascertain costs, potential volume, and the likelihood that they will purchase. Potential sales volume and costs are presented in Columns 2–4 of Table 5–4. An evaluation of Column 3 indicates that cost of goods sold is approximately 40 percent for most prospective customers. However, costs associated with selling over $1,500,000 are slightly lower (i.e., 35–37%) because of certain purchasing economies. The expense associated with making the sale (i.e., Column 4) is relatively constant for all sized customers. Taken together, volume and cost evaluation suggest that it is most beneficial to call on large customers. Potential volumes are higher and costs, as a percent of volume, are lower. However, as indicated in Column 5, the probability of selling to larger accounts may, in some cases, be lower. This would reduce the attractiveness of selling to some of the larger volume customers (i.e., customers 005 and 007). At the same time, it increases the priority associated with contacting 001, 002, 006, 008, and 009.

Another computer technique for routing salespeople is an interactive system of call planning designated as CALLPLAN.[12] CALLPLAN incorporates each salesperson's estimate of expected contribution of all possible call policies for each prospect into a mathematical programming structure. From this input data, the computer logically and consistently determines the best time allocation to maximize contribution. Mathematical programming was also used to develop another routing model referred to as SCHEDULE.[13] Utilizing non-linear programming tech-

[10] William Lazer, Richard T. Hise, and Jay A. Smith, "Putting Salesmen in Their Place," *Sales Management Magazine* (March 15, 1970), pp. 29–36.
[11] *Ibid.*, p. 29.
[12] Leonard Lodish, "CALLPLAN: An Interactive Salesman's Call Planning System," *Management Science* (December, 1971), pp. 25–40.
[13] Gary M. Armstrong, "The SCHEDULE Model and the Salesman's Effort Allocation," *California Management Review*, Vol. 18 (Summer, 1976), pp. 43–51.

(1) Customer Code	(2) Sales Volume (000's)	(3) Cost of Goods Sold (000's)	(4) Expense in Making the Sale (000's)	(5) Probabili-ty of Purchase	(2–(3+4)) (5) Expected Value (000's)
001	2,400	888	85	0.3	428
002	800	320	70	0.45	185
003	400	160	65	0.3	53
004	700	280	70	0.6	210
005	1,600	592	80	0.2	186
006	1,200	480	75	0.8	516
007	3,900	1,365	90	0.1	245
008	900	360	70	0.8	376
009	700	280	70	0.95	333
010	1,400	560	80	0.2	152

Table 5–4
Expected Value

niques under uncertainty, the model allocates effort in such a way as to "maximize the probability of achieving a previously specified, acceptable level of return.[14] Although these computer techniques can provide useful information they are complex. It is, therefore, mandatory to either employ a technical staff or utilize an outside consulting firm that is proficient in running such models.

Routing in Specialty or One Call Selling.   To this point, the discussion has focused on salespeople who regularly call on repeat-buying customers. It has also concentrated on the type of selling that presumes a relatively large number of fairly uniform length calls each day. Many sales jobs do not fit such a pattern. For example, an automobile salesperson may find it profitable to call on most buyers once or twice a year—including calls for the purpose of securing leads. Also, an investment counselor might call on a particular type of customer only when an appropriate investment opportunity is available. For these salespeople, routing is a function of unique customer need, and satisfaction of that need is more critical than minimizing time and expense.

A representative of a vacuum cleaner company, the salesperson for an expensive set of encyclopedias, or a person selling home roofing or siding may never intend to make a second call on a prospect that is not sold on the first sales visit. What about scheduling and supervised routing for such salespeople? These represent instances where the salesperson's physical route, as applied to a typical day's work, may be relatively unimportant. Most territories covered by this kind of salesperson are

---

[14] *Ibid*, p. 47.

small enough so that travel time is unimportant. Certain sections of the city or state or certain customer groups may be eliminated from consideration because they are unprofitable. High-spotting may, therefore, be highly desirable. In other words, areas which contain large concentrations of customers will be completely covered—possibly with preliminary screening by telephone.

SUMMARY

Increases in travel costs have made optimum determination of travel routes and territorial boundaries mandatory. In order to design new territories a firm should (1) identify the market potential of each area in the firm's market area (e.g., using S.I.C. method or buying power index method), (2) determine the market size that can optimally be handled by a salesperson, and (3) examine extraneous factors that may affect territory design such as number of key accounts, customer concentration, market support allocated to the area, and strength of competition.

In addition to designing territories, the sales manager is also responsible for helping salespeople determine optimum routes. The first step in accomplishing this task is to develop a list of actual and potential customers. Second, the geographic location of customers is plotted on a map. Third, call time and frequency preferences of customers is identified. Fourth, customers are clustered into trade areas. Finally, utilizing trial and error or simulation techniques, a routing schedule is developed that minimizes time and expense.

QUESTIONS

1. Why is it important to continually review territorial assignments of salespeople?

2. Indicate where some conflicts in strategy and thinking might develop relative to territorial assignments.

3. What are some of the problems associated with overlapping territories?

4. What are the problems associated with the implementation of Walter Semlow's Approach to Territorial Allocation?

5. What steps should be followed by a firm that is assessing and redesigning territorial boundries?

6. What are the objectives of a sound territorial allocation procedure?

7. How does one utilize the SIC method in estimating market potential?

8. What is the most appropriate method of estimating market potential for consumer goods, and why?

9. Identify several techniques for solving territorial size problems.

10. What steps are important in sales force routing?

Case 3–1

Barnes
Fasteners,
Inc.

Mr. John Barnes, President of Barnes Fasteners, Inc., has just finished reviewing his actual and forecasted sales figures for the month of September, for the third quarter, and for the nine months ended September 30th. There are very significant differences in total sales for the entire company compared to forecasted sales, and even more dramatic differences appear when total sales are broken down into regions and product lines. Since Mr. Barnes is president of a publicly held company, he is accountable to shareholders and other interested parties for the performance of the company. He also is responsible for SEC reporting and interim reporting to the company's outside auditing firm.

This is not the first time that Barnes has seen actual results vary from forecasted sales. In fact, actual performance relative to forecasts has recently experienced increasingly larger variances both in dollars and percentages.

Mr. Barnes is very concerned about the company's inability to generate a reliable forecast. It has always been Barnes' policy to use the composite opinion of the sales force in preparing a forecast. He feels that perhaps there are a few regional and/or product line forecasts which are creating a sizable share of the forecasting error. He decided that it is time to set up a meeting with his sales manager, Mr. Fred Parker, and his controller, Ms. Sandra DePalma.

John expressed his concerns to both Fred and Sandra. They both are aware of the problem and have their own interpretation of possible causes and solutions. Fred is of the opinion that the only way to accurately forecast sales is to get the information from the sales force. As Fred points out, "They (the salespeople) know where the action is." He feels that previous forecasting errors were largely the result of new salespeople who were not fully aware of customer desires and territory potential.

Sandra DePalma thinks the sales force composite is not the proper sales forecasting method for a company in the fastener industry. She suggests that other more sophisticated forecasting techniques would drastically reduce the magnitude of the forecasting errors experienced in the past.

Mr. Barnes felt that Parker and DePalma had discussed areas which could potentially contribute to the forecasting variances, but which required further research in order to corroborate or repudiate. Barnes instructed them to prepare reports with substantiating documentation regarding their hypotheses.

After reviewing Mr. Parker's report, which was submitted first, it was readily apparent that forecasts prepared by new salespeople had not been appreciably less accurate than those prepared by veterans. Mr. Barnes now felt that perhaps the sales force composite method of sales forecasting could be improved upon. He anxiously awaited Ms. DePalma's report.

1. Parker's report simply showed that forecasts by new salespeople were not the cause of the variances being experienced. What other possible causes should be considered?

2. What sales forecasting methods should Sandra DePalma present and which method(s) could be recommended as possibly being more suitable for Barnes Fasteners, Inc.?

Case 3–2

Never Fail
Oil
Company

Fujio Yoshino, President of Never Fail Oil Company, feels that the company should depend on a forecast prepared by an outside, capable consultant. One outside consultant, Cliff Baker, has convinced Yoshino that the only worthwhile forecasts are made by causal modeling. This computer method, according to Baker, is the most technically sophisticated forecasting technique available. It is generally referred to as mathematical econometric modeling. A series of equations that relate to the essential functions of the enterprise are tested. Once this is done, the outcome of changing specific variables can be forecast by putting the model through a series of "what if" changes.

Bob Summers, the sales manager, feels that the company is not big enough to afford such a complex and expensive consulting service for forecasting. In fact, Summers goes on to say, "the ultimate decision makers who have a real 'feel' for the marketplace are sales managers and their salespeople." Summers vehemently feels that no computerized, analytical system can replace the problem-finding and problem-solving insights that salespeople and their managers gain from experience.

1. Who is correct in their thinking, the president or the sales manager? Explain your answer.

Case 4–1

Jay Dental
Manufactur-
ing
Company

Joan Rigby, sales manager for the Jay Dental Manufacturing Company, a firm which manufactures high speed drills for dentists, feels for a number of reasons that it would be unfair, and furthermore really impossible, to establish sales quotas for each of her salespeople. Her reasoning is as follows:

(a) Because of the many uncontrollable factors involved, it is difficult to forecast sales and to estimate what can be produced, both of which are basic to setting quotas.

(b) The purchase (as original equipment or for replacement) of high speed drills by dentists can be postponed for a considerable period of time.

(c) A dentist correlates purchases of such equipment with his or her prospective income, which often cannot be projected with any accuracy.

(d) Since dental supply houses act as intermediaries in the purchase and sale of such dental equipment, quota setting is made even more difficult.

(e) Dentists may purchase high speed drills, but it is impossible to determine which manufacturers' drills they will select.

(f) Salespeople are paid a commission on sales out of which they pay their travel expenses.

(g) Salespeople pay very little if any attention to sales quotas, so setting quotas is an exercise in futility.

(h) Rather than a dollar quota, an input activity quota would bring better results.

1. To what extent do you agree or disagree with Joan Rigby and her observations concerning quotas?

2. In those instances where you agree with Joan's reasoning, suggest ways in which the problems of quota setting might be solved.

Case 4–2

J & J
Machine
Tool
Company

J & J Machine Tool Company formerly set sales quotas in the following manner. Total sales for the company were estimated in the sales department. The previous year's sales were used as the basis for this estimate but were modified in accordance with expected changes in general economic and business conditions and the probable effect of such changes on the sales of the company's products. Total estimated sales were then distributed to branch offices in various parts of the country, principally on the basis of past branch sales, but this distribution was modified wherever warranted by known shifts in important economic factors in various geographic regions.

Within each branch office, a complete list was kept of all potential customers, and each customer was assigned to a particular salesperson. At the beginning of the year, each salesperson was required to estimate the amount of sales he or she expected to obtain from each customer on the list. The branch house quota, as handed down from the home sales office, was then distributed to individual salespeople in proportion to their own estimates of expected sales volume. For example, if John Massen, after going over the prospect list, estimated that he would realize sales of $95,000, and if this amount represented 12 percent of the total sales for the branch as estimated by all salespeople, then salesperson Massen was assigned 12 percent of the branch office quota.

After using this method for three years, the company was very much dissatisfied, because it found that the sales actually accomplished by the individual salespeople bore little relationship to the quotas which were assigned at the beginning of the year.

1. What changes would you suggest in this company's methods of setting sales quotas? Why?

2. What additional types of quotas could J & J utilize? What benefits would they realize from implementing an alternative quota plan?

Case 5–1

Servel
Office
Supply
Company[1]

The Servel Office Company manufactured a wide line of office cements, pastes, artists' supplies, stamp pads, ink, ink eradicators, crayons, tempera paints, marking pencils, and ink solvents. During the past four years sales had increased from $1,504,881 to $2,359,337. In December, the president received the final income statement for the company's fiscal year ending November 30. He was extremely disappointed in the net income figure of $23,595 (See Figure 1). The president immediately began an analysis of the company's plans for the following year.

Servel, which had originally specialized in the ink business, was an old and well-established company. With the decline in the sale of conventional writing ink as the result of the ball-point pen, it had expanded into other lines of office supplies. The policy of adding new products was successful, and the fastest-growing items in Servel's line were watercolor paints, rubber cement, stamp pads and stamp-pad inks.

[1]Copyright by Richard D. Irwin, Inc. Published in *Cases in Marketing* by Westfall and Boyd (Homewood, Ill.: Richard D. Irwin, Inc., 1961).

Figure 1
Servel Office
Supply Income
Statement

Net sales	$2,359,337	100.0%
Costs of sales	1,403,805	59.5
Gross margin	955,532	40.5
Commercial expenses		
Shipping and delivery	224,137	9.5
Selling expense	408,165	17.3
Administrative	198,184	8.4
Advertising & promotion	101,451	4.3
Total expenses	931,937	39.5
Net operating income	23,595	1.0

The Servel sales force consisted of twenty salespeople, five manufacturers representatives, and a promotion manager. Sales were made directly to large retail stationers and to wholesale office supply companies. Many customers were both wholesalers and retailers. Institutional and industrial customers were not sold direct; they generally bought from retail stationers. One salesperson handled the major chains and the balance of the sales force worked specific territories. The same salesperson who handled the chain-store business was also responsible for export sales, which were a growing factor accounting for about 6 percent of the company's current sales.

One manufacturer's representative covered the state of Washington, another Oregon, and a third northern California. These were supervised by the salesperson in that territory. Another representative covered Colorado, New Mexico, and Arizona, but he was dropped recently because his volume was too small. The fifth manufacturer's representative covered almost all the rest of the United States. Salespeople from these representatives competed with Servel's own salespeople. Management felt, however, that this competition was good because it forced Servel's salespeople to be more aggressive and it was one way to raise the firm's sales volume quickly.

The president believed that aggressive selling in all territories had resulted in sales growth but that it had also been responsible for higher selling costs, thus reducing net income. Salespeople had been placed in new territories where there was no established volume. The firm had to support these individuals until they developed the market to a profitable level. Such investments could not be capitalized, however, and had to be carried as expenses. He had the controller prepare a study of the sales potential for the company's products by areas. This study (Table 1) substantiated his belief that more effort had to be expended to develop areas in which Servel's present sales were relatively low.

Servel sales had always been low in New York City, for example. This city had been part of two larger territories, but in the previous year Clark and Woodbury were assigned to New York City alone. One of these men, Woodbury, was to concentrate on industrial accounts to be sold directly—a new procedure for Servel. Strand and Stevenson were also new salesmen who were given new territories in which to build up Servel's volume.

In checking selling costs in some of the new areas, the president found that selling costs ran as high as 24 percent of net sales. In the more established territories covered by experienced salespeople, the costs of selling averaged 13 percent

Salesperson	Territory	Share of U.S. Potential %	Annual Servel Sales $	Share of Servel Sales %
Payne	New England and part of New York City	5.4	130,943	7.1
Clark	Part of New York City	4.1	45,641	2.5
Woodbury	Part of New York City	4.1	63,793	3.4
Dillion	Parts of New York, Pennsylvania, W. Virginia, and Maryland	6.4	52,681	2.8
Strand	Delaware, New Jersey, and parts of Pennsylvania and New York	6.7	70,344	3.8
Adams	Virginia, District of Columbia, Tennessee, Kentucky, and parts of W. Virginia, Maryland, and Indiana	6.5	125,915	6.8
Pospisil	N. Carolina, S. Carolina, Georgia, and Florida	6.9	125,840	6.8
Berwick	Ohio	5.7	80,631	4.4
Stevenson	Alabama, Mississippi, Louisiana, and Arkansas	4.7	50,037	2.7
Thomas	Southern Michigan and parts of Indiana	4.3	64,655	3.5
MacRae	N. Dakota, S. Dakota, and parts of Minnesota, Wisconsin, and Michigan	3.7	104,547	5.6
Herbert	Parts of Minnesota, Wisconsin, and parts of Chicago	4.4	81,751	4.4
Finia	Northern Illinois and northwest Indiana	4.7	167,043	9.1
Ragsdale	Part of Chicago	4.0	251,761	13.6
Henderson	Missouri and Iowa	4.8	110,079	5.9
Lewis	Kansas, Nebraska, Oklahoma, Wyoming, Colorado, New Mexico	4.8	69,937	3.7
Miller	Texas	5.6	97,604	5.3
Hinit	Washington, Oregon, Northern California, Montana, Idaho and Northern Nevada	7.4	74,852	4.0
Dashiell	Southern Nevada, Arizona and Southern California	5.8	84,948	4.6
	Total Territories	100.0	1,853,002	100.0
Strother	Chain stores and export		420,550	
Naismith	Promotion man		3,964	
Five manufacturers' representatives			78,126	
House sales *			3,695	
	Total sales		2,359,337	

Table 1
Office Supply
Potential and Servel
Sales

*Sales made by major officers of the company

(see Table 2). The company did not have a uniform sales compensation plan, but believed that the ideal plan would be straight commission and hoped that ultimately all salespeople could be compensated on this basis.

Sales forecasts were prepared by three independent procedures. First, each salesperson was instructed to submit a realistic estimate of next year's sales broken down by fifteen major product groups. This estimate was to reflect current trends in the individual's territory.

The second sales projection was based on a separate estimate for each of the 150 items handled by the company. The president, controller, and sales manager

Table 2
Servel Sales and Selling Expenses by Territory

Salesperson	Sales	Salary and/or Commission	Expenses	Total Selling Cost as of Sales (Percent)	Method of Compensation
Payne	$130,943	$13,094	$3,000	12.3	$250 monthly expense allowance plus 10% of net sales
Clark	45,641	8,645	1,000	21.1	Reimbursed expenses and salary
Woodbury	63,793	15,000	1,500	24.3	Car, reimbursed expenses, and salary
Dillion	52,681	6,720	2,400	17.3	$200 monthly expense allowance plus 12% of net sales[b]
Strand	70,344	8,400	5,500	18.3	Car, reimbursed expenses, and salary
Adams	125,915	12,592	3,000	12.4	$250 monthly expense allowance plus 10% of net sales
Pospisil	125,840	12,584	3,000	12.4	$250 monthly expense allowance plus 10% of net sales
Berwick	80,631	8,063	2,400	13.0	$200 monthly expense allowance plus 10% of net sales[a]
Stevenson	50,037	6,000	5,000	22.0	Car, reimbursed expenses, and salary
Thomas	64,655	9,600	5,000	22.6	Car, reimbursed expenses, and salary
MacRae	104,547	10,454	2,400	12.3	$200 monthly expense allowance plus 10% of net sales
Herbert	81,751	8,200	4,100	15.0	Reimbursed expenses and salary
Finan	167,043	12,000	2,800	8.8	Car, reimbursed expenses, and salary
Ragsdale	251,761	15,500	3,200	7.4	Car, reimbursed expenses, and salary

Salesperson	Sales	Salary and/or Commission	Expenses	Total Selling Cost as of Sales (Percent)	Method of Compensation
Henderson	110,079	11,008	3,000	12.7	$250 monthly expense allowance plus 10% of net sales
Lewis	69,937	8,392	3,000	16.3	$250 monthly expense allowance plus 12% of net sales
Miller	97,604	8,088	5,000	13.4	Car, reimbursed expenses, and salary
Hinit	74,852	9,600	5,600	20.3.	Car, reimbursed expenses, and salary
Dashiell	84,948	11,000	4,300	18.0	Car, reimbursed expenses, and salary
Strother	420,550	28,000	5,800	8.0	Reimbursed expenses and salary
Naismith	3,964	10,000[c]	4,300[b]	360.7[c]	Car, reimbursed expenses, and salary
Five mfr.'s reps.	78,126	8,472	—	10.8	See footnote[a]
House sales	3,695	—	18,000[e]	487.0[e]	
Totals	$2,359,337	$241,412[e]	$93,300[f]	487.0	

[a]Rounded to nearest $100 because final expense reports were not in.
[b]Commission rate was 13 percent part of year.
[c]Naismith was the company promotion manager. While his salary and expenses were properly chargeable to selling expenses in the broadest sense, they could not be compared directly with his own sales, since he spent only a small part of his time in face-to-face selling.
[d]Three representatives were paid commissions of 10 percent; one got 15 percent; and one had a sliding scale of 5 percent on all sales over $10,000.
[e]House sales were made by company officers, whose salaries and expenses were not directly chargeable as selling expense. Travel expenses of $18,000 were not all properly allocated to selling.
[f]The difference between total selling expenses shown here and the total in the operating statement is made up of the sales managers salary and expenses and office sales expenses.

worked on this forecast. In making this projection the historical record was first considered and then modified by knowledge of industry conditions with respect to the specific item. Long-term trends in demand and competitive conditions were considered. For example, heavy sales promotions in the previous year or price cutting that resulted in the dumping of unusually large supplies on the market were factors that would affect sales in the following year.

The third sales projection was made at a roundtable discussion among the president, sales manager, controller, and several of the older, more experienced salespeople. At this conference, sales were forecast for each of the fifteen product groups. Each group was considered as a unit, and dollar volume was estimated for the coming year from data on past sales, current trends, economic conditions, and any other information possessed by the salesmen.

The three sales forecasts for each of the fifteen products groups were then considered and a "best" forecast selected. For example, the forecasts for tempera paints were $290,000, $300,000, and $327,000. Since this was a growing product line, the highest estimate was chosen. The total of the group forecasts was $2,500,000. This total was then broken down by salespeople on the basis of their forecasts and past performances (see Table 3).

Next the controller was instructed to prepare an expense budget based upon this level of sales. All other items of expense were also estimated and a forecast income and expense statement prepared (Figure 2). The president considered these budgets adequate to appraise whether to develop some territories at a high sales cost. Another use for the budgets developed when the president had to

| | | Forecast Selling Costs | |
| | | Salary and/or | |
Salesman	Forecast Sales	Commission	Expenses
Payne	$130,000	$13,000	$3,000
Clark	75,000	11,000	2,500
Woodbury	70,000	16,000	2,500
Dillion	a	a	a
Strand	74,000	8,000	5,500
Adams	135,000	13,000	3,000
Pospisil	135,000	13,500	3,000
Berwick[b]	130,000	9,000	2,400
Stevenson	65,000	6,000	4,200
Thomas	80,000	9,600	4,000
MacRae	108,000	10,800	2,400
Herbert	80,000	8,700	4,000
Finan	182,500	13,000	3,000
Ragsdale	263,000	16,500	3,800
Henderson	125,000	12,500	3,000
Lewis[c]	90,000	9,900	2,400
Miller	90,000	9,000	5,000
Hinit	85,000	10,000	5,600
Dashiell	95,000	11,500	4,000
Strother	450,000	36,000	6,600
Naismith	d	10,000	4,500
Four mfr.'s reps.[e]	75,000	7,500	—
House sales[f]	5,000	b	12,000
Total	$2,542,500	$254,500	$86,400
Less cash discounts	42,500		
Net sales	$2,500,000		

[a]Dillion resigned, that territory was divided between Clark and Berwick.
[b]Berwick's compensation plan was changed, when he got part of Dillion's old territory, to a monthly expense allowance of $200 and a $9000 salary.
[c]Compensation rate changed to $200 monthly expense allowance and 11 percent commission on net sales.
[d]It was planned that Naismith would devote full-time to promotion.
[e]One manufacturer's representative who had covered Colorado, New Mexico, and Arizona was dropped.
[f]House sales would be made by company officers whose salaries could not be charged directly to sales.

Table 3
Forecast of Sales and Selling Costs by Salesperson

decide whether or not to take part in a $38,000 promotional program that had been presented to the company. This program had not been included in the present budget. The program involved a special dealer promotion on paste and the awarding of prizes, including a number of English bicycles to leading salespeople and dealers. The president planned to present it at a sales meeting in order to get the reaction of the entire sales force.

Figure 2

Net sales	$2,359,000	100.0%	$2,500,000	100.0%	$2,600,000	100.0%
Cost of sales	1,389,000	58.9	1,473,300	58.9	1,531,400	58.9
Gross margin	970,000	41.1	1,026,700	41.1	1,068,600	41.1
Shipping and delivery—variable	188,700	8.0	199,800	8.0	208,000	8.0
Shipping and delivery—fixed ...	39,600	1.7	39,600	1.6	39,600	1.5
Total shipping and delivery...	228,300	9.7	239,400	9.6	247,600	9.5
Selling expense—variable[a]	99,100	4.2	104,700	4.2	109,200	4.2
Selling expense—fixed[b]	316,300	13.4	316,300	12.7	316,300	12.2
Total selling expense	415,400	17.6	421,000	16.9	425,500	16.4
Administrative expense	209,000	8.9	209,000	8.4	209,000	8.0
Advertising and promotion......	96,000	4.1	96,000	3.8	96,000	3.7
Total expenses..............	948,700	40.2	965,400	38.7	978,100	37.6
Projected net profit	21,300	0.9	61,300	2.4	90,500	3.5

[a]Variable selling expenses included commissions only.
[b]Fixed selling expenses included salesmen's salaries of five sales clerical people, sales meeting expenses, and miscellaneous other selling expenses.

1. Are Servel's present sales territories equitable and efficient?

2. Should Servel continue to employ the five manufacturers representatives to compete directly with its own salespeople?

3. Would you recommend any changes in Servel's sales compensation and expense plan?

4. Does Servel need to prepare three independent sales forecasts? Why or why not?

5. What value does Servel's projected sales budget (Table 3 and Figure 2) have as a planning and control device?

6. Should Servel participate in the $38,000 promotional campaign? Why or why not?

Case 5–2

Always
Fresh Snack
Company

It's 8:00 a.m., Tuesday morning and Regional Sales Manager, Bill Taylor is about to begin a meeting with his five district sales managers. The purpose of the meeting is to formalize plans to add three new routes to operate out of the Santa Fe Springs, California, distribution center where Bill and his five managers are based. As Bill reviews his notes and waits for the last District Sales Manager, Walt Jenkins, to arrive, let's review some of the background.

Bill Taylor just transferred to this region from managing a region in the Midwest for the last four years. Bill has had a successful nine years with the Always Fresh Snack Company. He started as a route salesman and after three years was promoted to district sales manager; then two years later was promoted to region sales manager. He has always been regarded as a progressive, hard-working, and people-oriented manager. In fact, Bill is so well thought of by Always Fresh that he recently participated in a Field Application Committee workshop with ten other managers to develop company-wide policies and procedures for the addition of new sales routes.

The Always Fresh Snack Company has been in the snack food business for over 40 years. It is the only national snack food company and enjoys a 42 percent share of the flexible bag snack food market. Last year, sales for Always Fresh were $1.4 billion, with a 12-15 percent average sales growth rate for the past five years.

Always Fresh has over 7,000 sales routes throughout the country. Company-operated routes are its only method of distribution. The route salespeople perform the complete distribution function. They load their route truck each day with a complete line of Always Fresh snacks. They deliver them directly to the retailer's store and stock the display. They are also responsible for soliciting inactive accounts on their route, upgrading permanent displays, building special displays during promotional periods, and in general, increasing sales on their route.

The catalyst for Always Fresh's continuous growth is the addition of new sales routes. In fact, last year the firm added over 1,000 new sales routes. The creation of new sales routes is the responsibility of the District Sales Manager. The district sales managers are the company's first line supervisors and manage, on the average, 12 route salespeople. Because of the importance of the route addition process, Always Fresh is assembling a new training program with policies and procedures to assist the district sales manager with this task. Bill Taylor was one of the field managers that assisted the headquarters sales staff with this program. Bill is now going to share an outline of this new program with his district sales managers.

Bill Taylor has been region sales manager at the Santa Fe Springs distribution center for 1½ months. The former region sales manager was in charge for 11 years and recently retired. He had done a good job; however, sales growth during the last few months was somewhat lower than anticipated and salespeople's morale was only fair. Bill was brought in from Kansas City to boost the sagging sales growth and improve morale among the route salespeople.

To gather some background for the impending three route additions, Bill has been arriving at the distribution center at 5:00 a.m. to talk with the route salespeople while they load their truck routes. He wanted to get an idea, first hand, of the general climate regarding route additions. To create a new sales route, accounts are taken from existing routes, route boundaries are changed, and the new route is thereby created. Bill discovered that salespeople felt that the amount of sales volume taken from routes was somewhat arbitrarily determined in the past and sometimes influenced by favoritism. Each District Sales Manager used a somewhat different method for adding new routes. Most salespeople did not like the secrecy that preceded a route addition. They felt that they should be included in the process. Bill's gathering of this information was done with full knowledge and support of his district sales managers. In fact, they often joined Bill in his discussions with the salespeople.

The route salespeople are vitally concerned about adjustments to their routes, because they are paid a commission on their weekly sales. The commission rate is 10 percent of their weekly sales. They also receive a $50 bonus on top of their commission each week. They are guaranteed minimum earnings of $200 per week. The current weekly route average is $3,000, with a range of $2,500-3,700 among the 59 salespeople at the Sante Fe Springs distribution center.

Walt Jenkins just arrived at the meeting, so Bill begins by discussing his findings over the last few weeks. Bill knows that each of the three district sales managers involved in the route additions have begun preliminary planning for their upcoming route additions. He suggests that they might continue by having each of them comment briefly about the method that they have considered using.

Walt Jenkins begins by saying that he might cut each of his 12 routes by $200, to arrive at the $2,400 weekly sales required by the company to start a new route. He thought this was fair and would avoid accusations from the salespeople that he had treated any of them unfairly.

Jack Schilling stated that he preferred to take more volume from the routes that had higher weekly sales, and presented a schedule that he had been working on:

Route No.	Weekly Average Sales (Last 12 Weeks)	Proposed Cut	New Average Sales
762	$3,600	($500)	$3,100
911	$3,400	($400)	$3,000
059	$3,200	($300)	$2,900
138	$3,200	($250)	$2,950
271	$3,000	($200)	$2,800
934	$2,900	($200)	$2,700
907	$2,900	($200)	$2,700
591	$2,800	($100)	$2,700
899	$2,700	($150)	$2,550
115	$2,600	($100)	$2,500
023	$2,500	0	$2,500
662	$2,400	0	$2,400

Frank Alexander said that he believed in getting his salespeople involved in the route addition process. After discussing the matter with his salespeople, they had voluntarily given up specific accounts totaling the necessary $2,400 volume.

1. Can you think of any problems that exist with each of the methods proposed by the three District Sales Managers?

2. Which method do you think may be best?

3. What do you think may be some of the missing elements that Bill Taylor will suggest need to be considered?

Part 3

Organizing and Staffing

6. ORGANIZING THE SALES FORCE

7. RECRUITING AND SELECTING SALESPEOPLE

CASES

Chapter 6 _____

Organizing the Sales Force

After completing this chapter, you will be able to:

- Identify and discuss the elements of organization structure and the rules of structural development.

- Identify alternative organizational patterns and the characteristics, strengths, and weaknesses of each pattern.

- Understand the alternative ways that sales departments can be organized.

A good organization is a group of people who perform a set of clearly delineated tasks in order to accomplish common organizational objectives. The means by which people and resources are brought together to most effectively serve market opportunities is the **organizational structure**. Organizational structure defines tasks to be accomplished, personal interrelationships, and lines of authority and responsibility.

Development of an organizational structure is not a one-time activity. It is dynamic and should change as conditions change. New products are introduced to the market, new territories are cultivated, more sales people are needed to cover territories, computer support becomes necessary, or growth objectives are revised by a new chief executive officer. Each of these changes in the business environment necessitates an examination and possible revision of the organizational structure. If the formal structure is not changed, informal relationships will emerge to accommodate environmental changes. If development of these informal relationships is allowed to continue unchecked, management can easily lose control of the situation.

ELEMENTS OF THE ORGANIZATIONAL STRUCTURE _____

When developing a sales organization, the executive should consider the following factors: (1) authority, (2) responsibility, (3) span of control, and (4) formal and informal organization structure.

Authority _____

Authority is the right of an individual to require the performance of activities by other individuals. As indicated in Figure 6–1, lines of authority (i.e., superior/subordinate relationships) should be clearly defined and extend from the top levels of the organization structure to the lowest level. For example, the president of an organization begins the superior/subordinate relationships that extend to the vice president of marketing, sales manager, and salesperson.

To ensure that important and timely sales information reaches appropriate decision-makers, levels of authority must be minimized. For example, salespeople are often responsible for gathering information which is utilized in forecasting future sales. If the salesperson is five or six levels below the executive who engages in forecasting, there is only a slight chance that the information will reach the appropriate person. This same communication problem can also exist for the sales manager who may report to a district manager, who reports to a regional manager, who reports to a national sales manager, who reports to a marketing director.

Organization theory also suggests that authority to make decisions should be delegated as far down the line as possible. The national sales

Figure 6–1
Principles of Good
Organization

1. There must be clear lines of authority running from the top to the bottom of the organization.

2. No one in the organization should report to more than one line supervisor. Everyone should know to whom he reports, and who reports to him.

3. The responsibility and authority of each supervisor should be clearly defined in writing.

4. Responsibility should always be coupled with corresponding authority.

5. Accountability of higher authority for the acts of its subordinates is absolute.

6. Authority should be delegated as far down the line as possible.

7. The number of levels of authority should be kept at a minimum.

8. The work of every person in the organization should be confined as far as possible to the performance of a single leading function.

9. Line functions should be separated from staff functions.

10. There is a limit to the number of positions that can be coordinated by a single executive.

11. The organization should be flexible.

12. The organization should be kept as simple as possible.

Source: S. Avery Raube, "Principles of Good Organization," in William P. Sexton, *Organization Theories* (Columbus, Ohio: Charles E. Merrill Publishing Company, 1970).

manager, for example, should not have the authority to hire and train new recruits in the Southeastern territory. This should be done by the territorial (i.e., district or regional) manager. Also, the sales manager should not spend 75 percent of his or her time making sales calls. When this occurs the sales manager is no longer performing an appropriate role but is, in reality, a salesperson with an inappropriate title. The local sales manager should recruit, train, motivate, compensate, fire, route, and monitor sales effectiveness in the local area. The national sales manager, on the other hand, should recruit, train, motivate, compensate, fire, and monitor sales effectiveness of each sales manager. By distributing authority appropriately and pushing it down the line, each employee has time to function effectively.

Responsibility

Responsibility means that the individual is accountable for the tasks to which he or she is delegated. According to classical theory, an individual's responsibilities should be consistent with levels of authority. If a regional sales manager, for example, is responsible for the profitability of a territory, the sales manager should have authority to establish policies and make decisions which impact on that territory. Similarly, if territorial decisions do not result in acceptable profits, the sales manager is accountable for not meeting objectives.

Also, although authority can be delegated to lower levels of the organization, responsibility cannot be delegated. If a sales manager is responsible for territorial profits, delegation of certain management activities to a sales supervisor does not absolve the sales manager of the designated responsibility. Likewise, if the regional sales manager's territory is not profitable, the national sales manager must assume ultimate responsibility.

Span of Control

Span of control relates to the number of subordinates that can be efficiently managed by a single supervisor. Although some people suggest that the optimum span of control is five to seven subordinates, the actual number depends on several factors. The following represents a list of factors that may impact on this important decision:

Salesperson's Task. If the salesperson's task can be standardized and simplified, there is little need for personalized management and tight control. Technical salespeople, on the other hand, may need extensive sales aid from a supervisor. Since the supervisor must still perform all management functions as well as provide sales assistance, a narrower span of control is probably in order.

Stage of Territory Development. A new territory may require tighter sales control and, therefore, a narrower span of control than a more mature territory.

Customer Types.   More management control will be necessary when salespeople have a variety of customers to contact. For example, paint salespeople selling to wholesalers, retailers, contractors, painters, and real estate owners will need tighter control than paint salespeople that call only on paint retailers.

Dynamics of Product Development.   If a firm frequently develops and introduces new products, the need for management support and control increases significantly. Promotional programs must be implemented and monitored, new product training sessions must be conducted, and new channels may sometimes be established.

Georgraphical Size of the Territory.   In large, geographically dispersed territories, management time increases significantly. Since sales managers often make sales calls with sales people, the amount of time needed to perform this training/control function is greater in large territories. Span of control should, therefore, be narrower in these territories than in small, geographically concentrated areas.

Duties of the Sales Manager.   Among firms that espouse a narrow concept of management, sales managers are often assigned numerous responsibilities (i.e., selling) other than managing. When this occurs, span of control should be extremely narrow (three or four salespeople).

Determination of an optimum span of control is normally done by subjectively analyzing the above factors as well as monitoring managerial efficiency after the decision is made. If span of control is too tight, cost of management will be higher than additional benefits of such control. If span of control is too broad, the sales manager's time will be consumed by day to day problems, and there will be insufficient time to monitor sales effectiveness, identify problems, and plan future strategies. By experimenting with the ratio of salespeople to managers, firms may find that increased control stimulates profits or that looser control does not negatively impact on direction, motivation, communication, or profits.

Formal and Informal Organization

The **formal organization** is the system of work positions that is recognized by the organizational chart. The **informal organization**, on the other hand, refers to the natural organization of people in response to the social need to associate with others. The informal organization develops through an extended socialization process which results in a system of interpersonal relationships that are not designated by line, staff, or functional charts.

Sales managers must recognize this invisible social structure of working relationships. Wise managers will identify leaders within the informal structure and utilize their influence to accomplish organizational goals. At the same time, sales managers should take a genuine interest in their salespeople, understand their strengths and weaknesses, and help them solve problems. By assuming such an empathetic posture, sales managers can minimize any negative influence the informal organization might otherwise yield.

ORGANIZATIONAL PATTERNS

There are several organizational patterns that are utilized to identify the interrelationships of the sales group with other company units. These are the line structure, line and staff structure, and functional structure. Although other organizational patterns exist such as matrix structures and project-oriented structures, they are normally not used in defining the sales organization and, therefore, are not discussed here.

Line Structure

Line structures are characteristic of small firms that are in the early stages of their life cycle. As indicated in Figure 6–2, line structures have an unambiguous line of authority, responsibility, and communication running from the top to the bottom of the structure. Each person makes decisions and performs functions for his or her operating unit without assistance from any staff members. The sales manager, for example, is responsible for training, forecasting, motivating, compensating, recruiting, and supervising salespeople without any outside assistance.

The primary advantage of the line structure is that lines of authority and responsibility are clear and unambiguous. Since each person only reports to one superior there is less chance of role conflict. In more complex organizational forms salespeople and managers may be expected to accomplish one objective for one person and an incompatible objective for another person. As widely recognized, role conflict can lead to significant mental and physical problems.

Another advantage of the line structure is its low cost. Small firms often experience cash flow problems that can be aggravated by individuals that do not contribute to short-run revenue. Although staff personnel can certainly facilitate long-run growth and development, they may not directly generate short-run revenue. In a small firm where survival may be the prime concern, line personnel must often perform numerous functions in an effort to minimize operating costs.

The primary problem with the line structure is its unresponsiveness to organizational problems and growth opportunities. New product and market opportunities are often overlooked because no one has time to examine and respond to such issues. Also, problems go undetected because there is no monitoring system for identifying existing and potential problems.

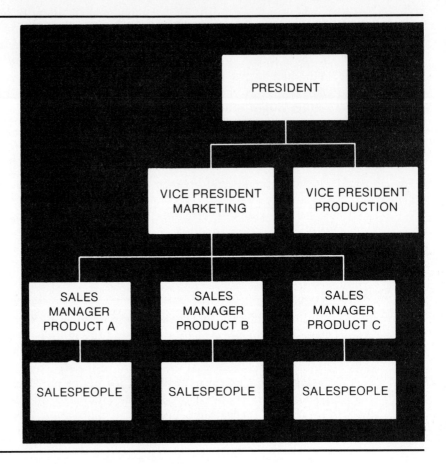

Figure 6–2
Line Structure

Line and Staff Structures

The primary duty of staff personnel is to support line personnel in the accomplishment of objectives. Line personnel are accountable for actual attainment of objectives.

As firms grow and overcome initial cash flow problems, they generally attempt to improve planning efficiency and realize long-run manageable growth. In order to do this, they often employ staff specialists that can provide expertise in specific functional areas. The result of this expansion in personnel is a line and staff organizational structure (see Figure 6–3).

In the sales organization there are several staff positions that effectively support and advise the line sales manager and salespeople. A few of these staff specialists and departments are as follows:

Sales Supervisors. Also referred to as head salespeople, supervisors may engage in the selling function several days a week and work with other salespeople the remainder of the time. As

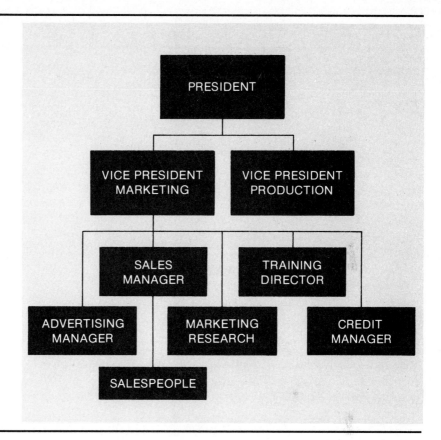

Figure 6–3
Line and Staff
Structure

staff supervisors, their primary responsibility is to improve the selling skills of salespeople

Staff Product Specialists. These specialists work directly with salespeople and provide them with product information. They usually work out of the home office and are used by branch offices to help salespeople in identifying product applications and developments. In industrial firms, product specialists are often referred to as technical engineers.

Staff Functional Specialists. Also employed by the home office, these specialists are distributed to branch offices to develop contests, provide new training programs, and work with individual salespeople.

Sales Correspondents. These individuals are used to write letters to customers and salespeople, develop sales bulletins, and distribute newsletters.

Sales Training Director. Training directors are responsible for

A Company Profile

Founded in Waco, Texas, in 1885, and later headquartered in Dallas in 1922, Dr Pepper has become a major manufacturer of soft drink concentrates and fountain syrups. Dr Pepper sales currently rank second in the Southwest in the soft drink industry. Through such programs as the "Be a Pepper" advertising campaign, the company's goal is to raise its market share in all geographic areas of the United States to the level realized in the Southwest.

Dr Pepper Company markets, distributes, and sells Dr Pepper and Sugar-Free Dr Pepper brands through approximately 500 franchised bottlers in the United States and 12 international markets. Although these franchises are not owned by Dr Pepper, they are supported by the Corporation. The company produces syrup and extract concentrates, and then sells the concentrate to the independent bottlers who convert it into bottled drink by adding sweetners and carbonated water. Dr Pepper also produces fountain syrups that are sold to franchised bottlers, wholesale distributors, and food service accounts such as restaurants. In addition to employing franchised accounts for production and distribution, Dr Pepper also bottles, cans, and distributes its product through nine corporate bottling plants.

Objectives of the company have included increasing market share, improving earnings, and increasing annual dividends to shareholders on a regular basis. During the 1970s and early 1980s, the Dr Pepper Company was extremely successful at meeting these objectives. Not only have sales and market share consistently grown in its highly developed Southwest market, but the company has also experienced substantial gains in its newest markets in the Northeast. Penetration of international markets has

also proceeded according to plans. In 1980, the company realized a 27 percent sales growth in Canada and now markets its product in countries with a combined population of over 300 million. With the acquisition of Canada Dry, Dr Pepper also has potential distribution access to another 91 countries. To help insure accomplishment of corporate plans, the Dr Pepper Company has (1) developed a structure and corporate consciousness that reflects the challenges of the 1980s; (2) continued to test and develop new raw materials that reduce product costs and, at the same time, maintain the company's high quality; (3) expanded its market research and development activities; (4) tightened its control over sales and distribution; and (5) increased its consumer communications through network television advertising.

Dr Pepper's sales organization is organized by function, geographical location, product category, and market. The two primary functional areas, key account and franchise sales, report to a director of sales operations. While key account salespeople work out of the Dallas headquarters and call on major chain and corporate accounts, franchise salespeople are allocated to various geographical areas and serve as the interface between the Dr Pepper Company and the franchise/bottler. Franchise salespeople support bottlers on special promotions, cooperative advertising, and other marketing strategies.

Franchised bottlers employ approximately 10,000 route salespeople who deliver Dr Pepper to retail and vendor accounts. Another 2,000 salespeople operate a presell program in which new and existing accounts are contacted by telephone. Bottlers also employ staff advance salespeople who call *on large accounts within a specified geographic area and merchandisers that support the sales effort by stocking shelves and setting up displays.*

In addition to sales of syrup to bottling operations, Dr Pepper has another market division in its organization that focuses on fountain sales. Also reporting to the director of sales operations, these salespeople make direct account calls on food wholesalers, food service accounts, and franchised bottlers.

By organizing in this manner, Dr Pepper can give maximum support to each geographical area, market, and product, and insure that each sales and marketing function is performed. Major sales functions are performed by key account, franchise salespeople, and merchandisers. Each geographical territory is effectively covered by independent franchised bottlers and company-owned bottling operations. Major markets are also accomodated in the organizational structure with two separate divisions that focus on bottling operations (i.e., call on franchised bottlers) and fountain sales (i.e., call on wholesalers and food service). Finally, each product line also receives separate and distinct attention in the structure. Dr Pepper and Sugar Free Dr Pepper, as well as their newest products, Welch's juices and jellies and Canada Dry's carbonated beverages, each receive independent support from separate marketing groups.

developing a centralized training program as well as actually training and retraining sales people. They may also work directly with salespeople in the field. In addition, some progressive organizations utilize trainers to help management develop better management tools and assist sales managers in the process of evaluating salespeople.

Marketing Research Department. Marketing research departments assist sales by monitoring penetration of markets, identifying potentially productive markets, and measuring the effectiveness of sales programs such as training programs.

The primary advantage of the line and staff organization is the expertise that can be employed in decision-making. Better decisions can be made and growth can be facilitated. In addition, it gives line personnel the time to concentrate on functions directly related to the success of the organization.

The primary problems with the line and staff structure are (1) cost and (2) ambiguity in lines of authority. Often staff specialists attempt to exert authority over line personnel, which may lead to organizational conflict.

Functional Structure

In a line and staff structure, the staff specialists do not have authority over line personnel (i.e., salespeople). In a functional structure, some staff people may be given functional authority. In Figure 6–4, for example, salespeople report to the credit manager as well as the sales manager. The reason credit managers often exercise functional authority over

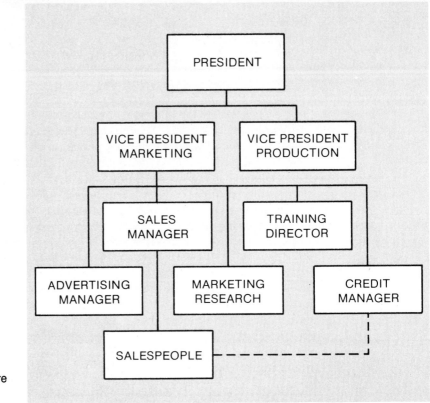

Figure 6–4
Functional Structure

salespeople is to expedite the credit evaluation process. If a direct working relationship is not provided, a salesperson would have to contact the sales manager who, in turn, would have to contact the credit department to get approval on a price concession. Also, the credit department may give salespeople pre-sale advice as well as direct them to potentially profitable accounts. Conversely, the credit department may give salespeople advance notice of potentially poor credit risks.

Taken to the absurd, the salesperson in a functional structure could report to six of seven different staff departments. The primary advantage of such an arrangement is that it expedites performance of staff functions. The disadvantages of the functional structure are as follows: First, the salesperson never knows from whom to take orders (i.e., there is role conflict and demotivation). Second, the sales manager loses control over the salesperson's time. Third, it can lead to confusion as exemplified by the three executives showing up on the same day to travel with a salesperson. Confusion can also result from conflicting orders given salespeople.

ORGANIZING THE SALES FUNCTION

Previous sections of this chapter have focused on factors which impact on the organizing function, rules for organizing, and basic organizational patterns. This section focuses directly on the sales department and the ways in which it can be structured.

Organizing by Functions

Some firms organize the sales group by functions, such as outside sales, inside sales, new account development, and account maintenance. Figure 6-5 illustrates the marketing and sales organization structures that are developed on the basis of functions to be performed. The sales group in this firm is divided according to the inside sales function and outside sales function. Inside salespeople are responsible for handling walk-in traffic as well as telephone solicitation of small accounts. Outside salespeople are responsible for making contact with existing and potential customers, handling customer problems, and providing service assistance.

The primary advantage of a functional division of sales personnel is that it focuses on the accomplishment of critical marketing functions.

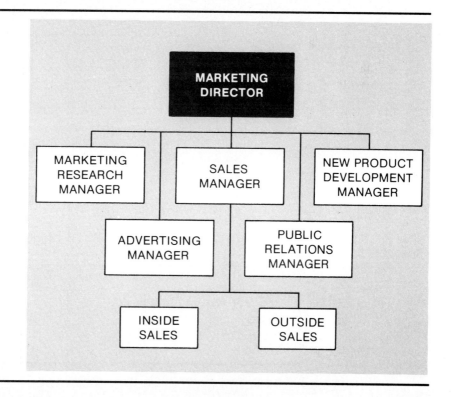

Figure 6-5
Marketing
Organization by
Function

The firm is better able, therefore, to perform functions which are necessary to the accomplishment of marketing objectives. A functional division, however, is not appropriate if the firm has several, unrelated product lines, has numerous types of customer segments, or operates in numerous geographical areas. If these conditions exist, the firm should also divide the sales organization according to product lines, customer characteristics, or geographic regions.

Organizing by Products

When a firm sells various product lines it may decide to have a separate sales force for each line as shown in Figure 6-6. For example, an industrial supplier may divide its sales force into three groups: (1) industrial supply salespeople (i.e., maintenance, repair, and operational items); (2) industrial trucks (i.e., forklifts, power lifts, etc.); and (3) specialty products (i.e., special machine tools). The primary advantage of a product-oriented sales force is that each product line receives individual attention from salespeople. Otherwise, the products that are lower volume, lower profit items may not receive sufficient attention from salespeople.

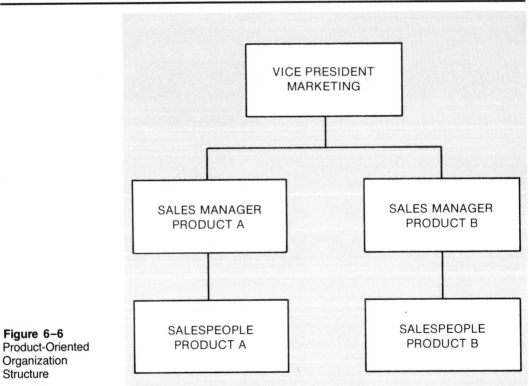

Figure 6-6
Product-Oriented
Organization
Structure

The primary problem associated with a product-oriented organization is duplication of effort. Since a customer might purchase items from each division, several salespeople may spend time calling on and developing the same customer. Not only is this costly to the firm, but many customers do not like taking time to meet with several salespeople from the same firm.

Organizing by Customer-Type

In some cases, firms have different customers with different needs and service demands. A consumer goods firms, for example, may sell to retailers for resale and to institutional customers for use in their oganization. The firm would, therefore, have two sales forces—one that calls on retailers, checks stock on shelves, straightens the stock, and reorders for the retailer, and another sales group that simply calls on institutions and takes orders. An example of a customer-oriented structure is illustrated in Figure 6-7.

Customer-oriented structures are also effective for industrial firms that must apply a component, for example, to a customer's existing or anticipated product design. Because of the sophistication of each customer's technology, it may be necessary to have the application engineers (salespeople) concentrate on a limited number of industries.

The advantages of the customer-oriented structure are suggested by the preceding examples. First, the firm can provide more timely, effi-

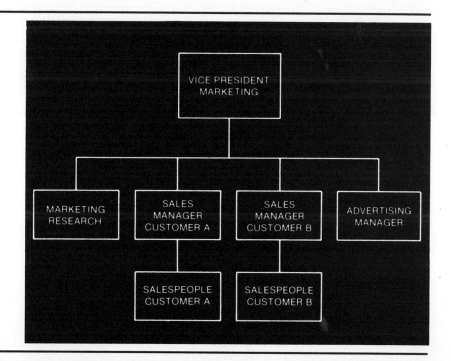

Figure 6–7
Customer-Oriented
Organization
Structure

cient service to customer groups. This is especially true if the firm has a customer group that is critical to the firm's success (i.e., key accounts such as large chain stores). The firm may have a decentralized sales group that calls on small customers and a centralized staff that handles the needs of key accounts. Second, salespeople can develop better insight into the customer's business and, therefore, more effectively satisfy customer needs.

Organizing by Geographic Area

Firms that sell nationally or internationally will normally organize according to regions (See Figure 6-8). Firms that organize into regions can respond to customer needs faster, cover territories more intensively, reduce travel costs and time, and be more sensitive to local conditions and problems. On the other hand, implementation costs associated with having regional mangement and administrative support can be significant.

Organizing by a Combination of Methods

As indicated in the preceding discussion, each basis for organizing has its own unique advantages. Functional structures ensure that all important marketing activities are accomplished. Product-oriented structures emphasize the unique characteristics of each product line. Custom-

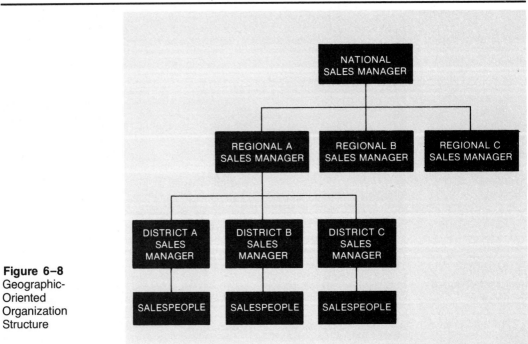

Figure 6–8
Geographic-
Oriented
Organization
Structure

er-oriented structures are responsive to the needs of each customer group. Geographical structures facilitate market coverage and reduce travel costs.

As firms grow and market complexities become more significant, firms often need to realize the benefits associated with several organizational forms. They may, therefore, utilize a structure similar to that shown in Figure 6-9. Many variations, of course, exist. Figure 6-9 illustrates a combination of product, territory, and customer-oriented organization structure.

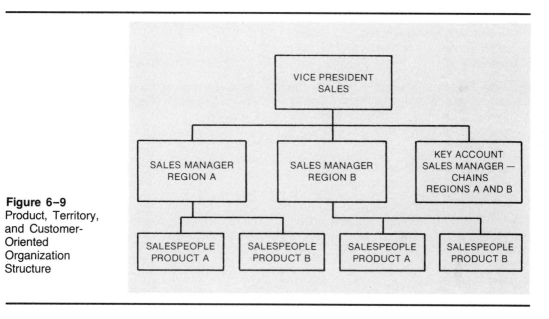

Figure 6-9
Product, Territory, and Customer-Oriented Organization Structure

SUMMARY

A good organization is a group of people who perform a set of unambiguous tasks in order to accomplish common organizational objectives. Organizational structure refers to the manner in which these people are brought together. In general, employees may be organized into a line structure, a line and staff structure, or a functional structure. Also, regardless of which structure is employed for the firm overall, sales departments may be divided according to functions, product lines, geographical areas, market segments or some combination of these. Evaluation of a firm's size, complexity, and scope of operations will normally reveal the appropriate structure for a given situation.

When organizing a sales department into a particular pattern, it is important that firms consider the elements of good organizational design. There must be clear lines of authority. Each person should report to only one supervisor. Responsibility and authority should accompany each other and be defined in writing. Accountability for the acts of subordinates is absolute. The number of levels of authority should be limited and authority should be delegated as far down the line as possible. Optimum span of control should be identified. Finally, the organizational structure should be simple and flexible.

QUESTIONS

1. How does an external market-oriented organization structure differ from an internal-oriented structure?

2. What evidence can you give to support the conclusion that "not enough thought and research has been given to organization structure?"

3. What conditions or circumstances dictate the use of a vertical-oriented sales organization versus a horizontal-oriented sales organization?

4. Many European executives visiting this country have difficulty justifying the large number of staff supportive positions frequently found in U.S. companies. Is this a valid observation?

5. What factors should be considered when developing a sales organization?

6. What are the principles of good organization?

7. Why should levels of authority be minimized?

8. How would one determine an optimal span of control?

9. What are the results of a too tight, or too broad span of control?

10. Identify several organizational patterns. Describe the advantages of each.

11. Identify several ways the sales group can be organized. Describe the advantages of each.

Chapter 7 _____

Recruiting and
Selecting Salespeople

After completing this chapter, you will be able to:

- Identify rules associated with recruiting and selecting salespeople.
- Identify and evaluate alternative sources of potential sales recruits.
- Discuss the procedure for developing a sound recruiting program.
- Evaluate salesperson selection procedures such as screening, interviewing, and testing.
- Discuss the auditing procedure associated with selection.

Salespeople are the cornerstones upon which a significant number of marketing and sales organizations are built. They represent the first line contact with customers and significantly affect firms' images. In many companies the salespeople are given sole responsibility for company growth. In these instances they are truly the most important company resource. Consequently, an appropriate recruitment and selection program is essential for accomplishment of any firm's sales and marketing objectives.

RECRUITING SALESPEOPLE

Finding appropriate salespeople is reported as being one of the major problems experienced by sales executives in every industry. A primary reason for the problem is that selling as a career has not been effectively sold to young people and, therefore, lacks the status and glamour associated with other jobs. In fact, most educational institutions do not include selling in their curricula and educators generally provide little encouragement to students who may have a potential in sales. An even more significant reason for the problem of finding qualified people is the inadequate recruiting and selection procedures employed by some managers. They utilize one source or they do not perceive recruiting as an on-going process.

Firms that expect to maintain a successful program for recruiting qualified salespeople should understand problems associated with recruiting and develop a plan that facilitates the identification of potential candidates. Several steps that can be taken include the following: (1) analyze past records to determine the most effective source for recruiting salespeople; (2) hire students on internship programs and introduce them to the organization's sales function; (3) utilize consultants to find the minorities and females with qualifications to meet present and future sales responsibilities; (4) maintain a training program and a continuous supply of junior sales representatives; and (5) utilize compensation systems and hiring standards that minimize turnover.

Recruiting Sources

Where do firms look for potential sales representatives? Here are a few of the commonly used sources.

Educational Institutions. Most colleges and universities have placement offices that bring prospective employers together with graduating students. It is also possible to directly contact the marketing professors for names of outstanding students that have a potential to excel in sales. Since professors work closely with some students for several years, they gain valuable insight into their potential strengths and weaknesses. The firm can contact the students about possible internships and summer training programs prior to graduation.

Suppliers. One of the best sources of candidates are the major suppliers' salespeople. Since the sales manager has the opportunity to observe the quality of service provided by a supplier's salespeople, more objective recruitment can be made. In most instances information about a salesperson's potential performance can only be gathered through interviews, tests, and vitas.

Present Employees. Companies should give current employees the opportunity to pursue careers in sales and sales management. Since the firm has the opportunity to observe performance, this is another excellent recruiting source. Firms should also query employees for names of friends and relatives that they believe could become good sales representatives.

Business Associates. The sales manager should constantly be alert to business associates who may be able to suggest persons who have a sales aptitude.

Competitors. Although this can be a sensitive issue, competitors' firms often represent a major source of recruits in some industries (i.e., hotel/motel industry). This source is pursued because the salesperson may bring his or her customers to the new company, and costs of training and developing are minimized. On the other hand, these people may be less stable and not willing to conform to company procedures.

Walk-ins.   Most firms receive numerous résumés that are directed at the marketing department or personnel department. Since these people have taken the initiative to sell themselves, they should be given primary consideration.

Employment Agencies.   Since employment agencies are in business to make a profit, they may be more interested in satisfying their own objectives than in satisfying the needs of business firms. They may be long on promises and short on delivery of employment results. If a strong business relationship can be developed with the owner, however, the agency may provide a a better flow of qualified prospects.

Advertising.   The best place to advertise is sales oriented magazines and trade journals. The newspaper should be avoided for most sales jobs because the sales manager will spend an inappropriate amount of time screening unqualified applicants. Also, the sales manager will have little information on which to judge the recruits' capabilities (i.e., vita and interview).

Customers.   This channel should probably not be pursued until a prospective salesperson has already severed a relationship with a customer or the customer consents to the recruitment activity.

Determining the Appropriate Person

Before sales and marketing managers take steps to expand a specific department or sales force, a set of specifications should be developed that identify critical organizational activities. These specifications include the job description and the specification profile. Without these two items it is very difficult, if not impossible, to effectively carry out the function of recruiting as well as selecting, training, controlling, compensating, motivating, and communicating. After the job description and specification profile are developed, the firm must match potential recruits with the needs of the company. Before discussing selection and evaluation, let's look at some specific procedures for developing a job description and specification profile.

Job Description.   Job descriptions are developed for each individual in an organization in order to minimize role ambiguity. Recruits need to know what they are expected to do so that they can focus their efforts on high priority activities as well as appraise their progress toward accomplishment of goals. Also, if allowed to persist, role ambiguity can result in significant demotivation of salespeople.

Steps involved in the preparation of job descriptions include the following:

1 Prepare and distribute a questionnaire that identifies all tasks performed by salespeople and the amount of time devoted to each task.
2 Interview each executive in the marketing organization to identify functions that salespeople should perform.
3 Ask customers to identify services that they need from salespeople.
4 Evaluate study findings, reconcile differences in the various perspectives, and develop a list of relevant activities.
5 Present the job description to salespeople for their discussion and recommendations.
6 Periodically review the job description when market changes, product additions, and corporate changes indicate the need for a revision.[1]

An example of a job description for a salesperson is presented in Figure 7-1.

Specification Profile. After the job description has been developed, a profile of potential recruits must be established. The sales executive must identify the characteristics and the relative importance of each characteristic that should be possessed by potential recruits. In one study of 44 sales executives, it was found that the most important salesperson characteristic is enthusiasm, followed, in order of importance, by organization, amibition, persuasiveness, general sales experience, verbal skill, specific sales experience, recommendations, ability to follow instructions, and sociability.[2]

Although the above characteristics are definitely important, it is important to establish specific characteristics for each selling job. Some jobs such as detail selling for a pharmaceutical company may require young people with high energy levels, while other jobs such as insurance sales may require older, more mature people who can effectively handle pressures associated with such a job. Each firm, therefore, must identify age, education, personality, intelligence, experience, and physical characteristics that are most consistent with their unique selling situation. This can be accomplished by examining the characteristics of other successful salespeople in the industry or by reviewing studies that have been conducted to isolate appropriate selection criteria.

SELECTING SALES PERSONNEL

With the two essential blueprints for establishing a sound selection program, job descriptions and employee specifications, in place, the stage is set for obtaining the facts surrounding a person's background and past performance so that a prediction can be made of future job

---

[1] Adapted from: Charles L. Lapp and Kenneth J. Lacho, Selecting the Salesperson: The Heartbeat of Sales Management," *Louisiana Business Review* (January, 1978), p. 10.
[2] Stan Moss, "What Sales Executives Look For in New Salespeople" *Sales and Marketing Management* (March, 1978), p. 47.

POSITION TITLE:
Salesperson

GENERAL JOB DESCRIPTION:
Salespeople are responsible for selling all of our company's products to our customers. This is primarily accomplished by developing new accounts and maintaining existing accounts. Account development involves identification of customer needs, development of a product to fulfill needs, and the coordination of product testing, plant visits, credit analyses, and new product distribution. Account maintenance involves periodic existing accounts, analysis of production problems, and the reporting of sales information to management.

REPORTS TO:
Director of Sales.

WORK EXPERIENCE:
Previous sales experience in our industry is desirable but not mandatory.

EDUCATION:
A college degree is desirable but not mandatory.

RESPONSIBILITIES:
1. Through systematic prospecting, identify and develop new customers. Approximately 40 to 50 percent of the salesperson's time will be spent developing new accounts.
2. Maintain existing customers by handling customer problems and developing new products. Approximately 40 to 50 percent of the salesperson's time will be devoted to the maintenance of existing accounts.
3. Coordinate and evaluate product testing on existing and new products that are sold to the salesperson's customers.
4. Coordinate and supervise initial production runs for a new product.
5. Aid in the analysis of problems associated with the distribution of products to the salesperson's customers.
6. Analyze the credit status of a potential customer.
7. Provide customers with ideas on the operation and development of their own business.
8. Help dispose of distress product (i.e., produced for a former account, overproduction, not produced according to specifications).
9. Assist in the development of sales plans, forecasts, and marketing plans.
10. Complete all reports on time and in their entirety.
11. Meet specified goals on a continuing basis.
12. Assist in special field assignments.
13. Maintain a high level of goodwill and public relations with all existing and potential customers.

SPECIAL NOTES:
The salesperson must engage in overnight travel to develop and maintain accounts. A salesperson's efforts are rewarded with a salary, commission, bonus, car (or allowance), and company fringe benefits.

Figure 7–1
Job Description

performance. The following useful considerations should be noted:

- Sequence of selection steps and tools will vary among industries and companies.

- A number of selection steps and tools are necessary, as no single selection step or tool is adequate by itself.

- The least costly selection steps and tools should be used first.

This section is designed to suggest an ordered selection process for handling sales applicants, describe several of the tools that are useful in directly eliciting data about the applicant, and provide examples of criteria for evaluating a selection program.

Preliminary Screening

Typically, applicants fall into one of five major categories: (1) those who write unsolicited letters of inquiry; (2) those who answer company newspaper or trade press advertisements; (3) those who call in person; (4) those who are encouraged by someone in the company to make application; (5) those who are recruited from schools or college campuses.

Among people who send letters of inquiry and respond to advertisements, some can be initially screened out by examining qualifications which appear on their résumé. Applicants who are obviously not qualified should be eliminated as quickly as possibly by giving them a brief, courteous, individually typed letter of rejection. Applicants who seem to be qualified should be given a preliminary screening interview.

In the case of applicants who call in person or those who have been encouraged to make application by company employees, it is best to interview them as soon as possible, or set up definite appointments if time does not permit an adequate preliminary screening. As a matter of courtesy and good public relations, all applicants should be given a verbal or written reply. It may prove worthwhile to remember that the manner in which an applicant is rejected can be the basis for winning or losing a potential customer.

The preliminary screening interview should be relatively brief, usually lasting between 15 and 20 minutes. The applicant should be made to feel at ease and every effort should be made by the interviewer to avoid signs of impatience or irritation. Although some firms replace the preliminary interview with a comprehensive application, many sales managers prefer to see a potential recruit before the application is completed.

General Format of the Preliminary Interview. In some firms a standard form or preliminary interview guide is used which helps to keep the interviewer from wasting time with irrelevant questions. The form is designed to elicit a maximum amount of desired information in a minimum period of time. In addition, many of these forms are now tailored to minimize potentially illegal questions under the rulings of the Equal

Employment Opportunity Commission (EEOC).

Beyond normal key points such as educational experience, work experiences, and basic aspirations and goals, the interviewer should ask a series of questions which might uncover areas of future misunderstanding or conflict. Typical examples might include:

How willing are you to relocate?

To what extent are you willing to travel?

What kind of treatment did you receive from your previous employer?

What are your long term financial and employment goals, and how do you propose to attain them?

In addition to ascertaining general background information it is important to identify personal characteristics. Five critical traits identified by McMurray include the following:[3]

- A high level of energy.

- Abounding self-confidence.

- A chronic hunger for money.

- A well-established habit of industry.

- A state of mind that regards each objection, resistance, or obstacle as a challenge.

How to Say No to Applicants . . . Courteously. Any applicant who does not meet the basic requirements set forth in the company selection program should be rejected without delay. This can and should be done in a courteous, yet definite, manner. Figure 7-2 presents several actual examples of how some companies reject applicants.

Handling Qualified Applicants. If the applicant meets all of the desired requirements, the following actions are suggested: (1) briefly explain the job; (2) give the recruit an application form to fill out and return within a specified time; and (3) set up a definite time and date for the *planned* and *patterned* interview. The emphasis on establishing specific time targets provides a sense of urgency and indicates to the applicant that a decision will be reached within a reasonably short period of time. Such a plan should be invaluable in minimizing the amount of time lost by the applicant as well as the company.

The Application Form

The application form still remains as one of the most valuable

---

[3] Robert N. McMurray, "The Mystique of Super-Salesmanship," *Harvard Business Review* (March-April, 1961), p. 117.

Example 1. "The competition for this position was very keen. Had the response not been so great our consideration of your availability might have been more favorable. As it turned out, the only candidates who were able to stay in the running were those with almost 'ideal' qualifications."

Example 2. ". . . although the final selection has not been completed, we are further considering only those applicants whom we feel are best qualified. Please be assured this decision was made only after careful consideration."

Example 3. "We have reviewed your qualifications thoroughly, but at the present time we have no vacancy in which we may use your services."

Example 4. "We are sorry to advise you that, at the present time, we do not have any positions available that might be commensurate with your experience and background."

Example 5. "After carefully considering the information gleaned from your résumé and this interview, we find your background interesting; however, we do not feel your particular qualifications could be utilized to the best mutual advantage in our present opening."

Figure 7–2
Rejection Procedure

Example 6. "We have reviewed your résumé, but regret that we are unable to consider your services at this time. We will, however, keep your file on active status and should a position develop in the near future commensurate with your training and experience, we will contact you."

sources of information in the selection process. It is a fact-finding device which provides a written record of the applicant's background and experience.

Typically, the application form used by most companies will include questions under the following ten major categories:

1. Identification
2. Physical condition
3. Experience
4. Financial condition
5. Military service
6. Education
7. Family condition
8. Outside activities
9. References
10. Applicant's personal statement and signature

The completed application form should be reviewed carefully before proceeding with additional interviews of the applicant. In checking the completed application form, management should look for any potential caution signals such as omitted questions or gaps in the employment record. Since most application forms are designed to provide specific answers to the what, when, how, where, why, and who of the applicant's background, the information which is given should be complete and factual.

Vagueness, excessive exaggerations, and omissions indicate possible danger signals and areas which should be probed during future interviews. Other areas which should be scrutinized are inconsistent and overlapping employment dates, questionable financial position, numerous job changes with no apparent progress, and difficulties with past employers.

What are the advantages of using an application form as a selection tool? The form is: (1) relatively inexpensive when compared to other selection tools; (2) simple and fast to administer; (3) factual information with little, if any, bias; and (4) a signed agreement as to the authenticity of the information. The major disadvantage of the application form, when used without the benefit of a preliminary screening interview, is its inability to identify some of the applicant's personal characteristics.

The Patterned Interview

The patterned interview follows a carefully selected set of questions which are designed to improve interviewing efficiency and eliminate irrelevant questions. It is a probing type of interview in which the interviewer is reminded of specific areas which should be uncovered during the interview process.

Although it insures thoroughness, the patterned interview may lessen the spontaneity of the interview and may reduce the possibility of following, or listening to, important matters mentioned by the candidate. The interviewer may actually become more intent on the questions than the answers. On the other hand, the patterned interview is one of the most valid selection tools when used properly. Studies made in organizations using the patterned interview have shown that it is a method that produces moderate-to-highly-valid results.[4]

Before conducting the interview, the interviewer should formulate an action plan designed to provide complete and factual information. One of the more important preparatory steps is a thorough review of the job description and personal specifications. The next step calls for careful checking of the applicant's file, which should contain a chronological record of everything that has transpired since the original contact with the company. This might include such items as the completed application form, the letter of application, and the results of the preliminary screening interview.

The physical arrangements of the interview room should not be overlooked, particularly in view of the wide divergence of opinion on the best location for an interview. Typically, most interviews are conducted in the interviewer's own office, a company conference room, a hotel or motel room (studio type), a private club or restaurant, or the applicant's home.

---

[4] Herbert J. Chruden and Arthur W. Sherman, *Personnel Management* (6th ed.; Cincinnati: South-Western Publishing, 1980), p. 131.

The interviewer should make notes on areas where further probing is deemed necessary. These would include unanswered questions on the application form, obvious discrepancies, and any points that might need clarification.

The Non-Directive Interview

The non-directive or unpatterned interview allows the interviewer much freedom. The interviewer typically asks broad, general questions and then permits the applicant maximum freedom in answering with little or no interruption. This technique is generally concerned with eliciting feelings and attitudes of the applicant. The main disadvantage of the non-directive or unpatterned interview is that the final evaluation is subject to considerable bias. On the other hand, many interviewers believe that the evaluation process involves the collection and subjective analysis of all available information about an applicant.

After a few opening remarks and a brief exchange of thoughts to serve as an ice-breaker, the applicant should be encouraged to talk about previous work experience. Allowing the applicant to talk about a familiar subject (previous work) normally helps the person to relax in this new, unfamiliar environment.

Once the proper atmosphere has been established, the interviewer should briefly discuss the company and its products or services, followed by a description of the job for which the applicant is being interviewed. Once the interview begins it is critical that the interviewer maintain an objective attitude. Also, the interviewer should keep the interview informal and casual and avoid an argument, criticism, or strong disagreement with the applicant.

Close to the end of the interview the applicant should be asked if there are any additional questions or points which need clarification. The same friendly qualities should be exhibited at the close as were demonstrated at the beginning of the interview. If the applicant's qualifications appear favorable at this point, some word of encouragement may be given without making a definite commitment.

After the interview is over and the applicant has left, it is a good idea to take a few minutes to record information obtained from the discussion. If a summary rating sheet is used, this form should be completed while the interview and the applicant are still fresh in the mind of the interviewer.

Indirect Data Acquisition

Discussion to this point has been confined to methods of acquiring data directly from the applicant. These have included developing a job description and specification profile, conducting the preliminary screening interview, administering the application form, and conducting a patterned interview. This section is designed to examine methods of selection which involve learning about the applicant on a more indirect basis.

Psychological Tests. Although the use of psychological tests has caused considerable controversy among sales managers, most managers now agree that they have a place in the interview process. Specifically, they agree that tests should be used as an aid to judgment, not as an isolated hiring tool.

The primary purpose of the psychological test is to measure attributes and behavior which are not measurable by other selection tools. Although there is some overlap in tests, they can be grouped into five categories: personality, interest, aptitude (potential ability), achievement (or knowledge), and mental ability. In addition, many tests have been specifically developed for persons in selling. As more traits are defined as successful predicators of sales success, there will be an increase in the number of sales-oriented tests.

Problems which directly relate to tests as a selection tool can be summarized as follows:

- Costs associated with analyzing results (i.e., employing an analyst).

- Costs associated with buying or designing a test.

- The problem of acceptance. Many of the people who take psychological tests distrust test validity and reliability and those who administer the test.

- The tendency for sales executives to put too much faith in the results of tests and let them substitute for executive judgment.

- The problem of validity. Validity essentially means that the test measures what it purports to measure. Many tests for salespeople simply do not accurately measure the behavioral characteristics. The mistrust of some people toward test validity is, therefore, justified in some cases.

- The problem of reliability. Reliability relates to the consistency of test results over a period of time. Some problems of reliability have been experienced because applicants' responses are impacted by conditions that are present when the test is administered; i.e., applicant doesn't feel well, no air conditioning, not enough time. Also, as people take tests, they may learn what the prospective employer is looking for and answer based on this expectation. If they take the test at a later date, their answers may change because they do not remember their initial responses.

Those sales managers who have expressed approval on the use of psychological tests as a part of the selection procedure offer these viewpoints. First, tests can serve as an additional tool that checks responses obtained by other selection procedures. Second, tests can be good screening devices which reduce selection error or risk. Third, they help management understand the applicant's needs for training, supervision,

A Company Profile

Briggs-Weaver is a full service industrial distributor with approximately 800 employees in 31 separate locations. The firm inventories more than $17 million of industrial supplies, tools, equipment, machinery, and other materials from over 600 manufacturers. With 300 salespeople in the Southwest, Briggs-Weaver supplies more than $130 million of products to business and industry.

Briggs-Weaver was formed in 1896 when C. H. Briggs and J. C. Weaver joined together to serve the needs of the booming oil industry in Dallas. The firm realized a modest growth until 1964, when it expanded operations and experienced explosive growth as a multi-million dollar, multi-faceted supplier of industry. Briggs-Weaver's success for almost 100 years can largely be attributed to its consistent and dedicated application of its original mission: "to recognize and fulfill the special needs of its customers with the best products and efficient service at realistic prices."

Briggs-Weaver serves the dynamic Southwest industrial community with five separate divisions. The Industrial Supply Division specializes in supplying products for repair, maintenance, and operation. The Capital Equipment Division offers sales, leasing, rental, service, and parts to users of large materials handling equipment such as lift trucks, towing tractors, railcar movers, and personnel carriers. The Machine Tool Division is an organization of specialists that assist customers in selecting appropriate machines for their production requirements. The Special Products Group provides technical knowledge of tooling, materials handling equipment, power transmission products, small machine tools, industrial coatings, and safety supplies. Finally, the Robotics Group supplies a broad assortment of industrial robots.

With its high growth rate, broad diversity of operations, and large sales force, Briggs-Weaver must continuously concentrate on recruiting and selecting high quality salespeople. Even with a turnover rate of less than ten percent, the firm hires 40 to 50 salespeople per year.

Unless it is specifically in need of a seasoned salesperson, Briggs concentrates on finding recruits that can be trained for 2 to 3 years. Trainees work in the warehouse and on inside sales in order to learn Briggs' 600 products and thousands of customers.

When recruiting experienced salespeople, Briggs-Weaver's sales managers search for people that have had a successful career in industrial sales. They maintain and continuously update a file with names of competitive salespeople. Employment agencies and newspapers are seldom utilized to find these experienced people. In most markets, the number of qualified people is so small that the sales managers are normally aware of the top recruits. Also, since the company is one of the largest industrial suppliers in the Southwest with an impressive compensation structure, many experienced industrial salespeople contact Briggs-Weaver to pursue employment possibilities. Also, veteran salespeople who have a desire to grow in a management position are attracted to Briggs-Weaver because of its diverse structure and opportunities for growth in any of its five divisions.

After initially screening new recruits, the candidates are invited to the Briggs-Weaver headquarters to interview as many managers, salespeople, and other employees as possible. Input from all of these people is important in the final selection decision.

Also, management wants each employee to agree to help the selected candidates succeed in their sales positions. After headquarters interviewing is completed, spouses are interviewed to determine how commited they are in supporting the candidate's career. During the time that these interviews are being conducted, references are checked and analyzed.

Finally, Briggs-Weaver sometimes has an industrial psychologist assess the recruit's sales potential. All recruits are also required to take a polygraph test. The polygraph is utilized to verify the validity of information given in interviews and to iden-tify any legal or personal problems that may impact on job performance.

Management outlines all positive and negative aspects of a position with Briggs so that the candidate can make an intelligent decision and avoid any unpleasant surprises later. Managers also attempt to obtain commitments during the interview process. They ask candidates to outline the things that they expect to accomplish while working at Briggs. Recruits are also asked to describe the ideal situation that they would want to exist. This allows management to determine whether the person can be happy working as a salesperson with Briggs-Weaver.

and improvement. Fourth, they point out desirable and undesirable characteristics of the applicant. Fifth, tests can provide an objective analysis and thereby prevent the salesperson's personality from being the critical factor in the selection process. Sixth, applicants are often impressed with the company's desire for objective information as indicated by the use of psychological tests. Finally, in many cases, tests can be invaluable in deciding borderline cases.

It is apparent that sales managers have become more conscious of the possible uses of psychological tests. On the other hand, it also appears that sales and marketing executives have become less susceptable to the extravagant claims that have been made in the past by firms specializing in selling tests or testing services. This would suggest that test are being used more discriminately, and have become one of many tools which make up an effective selection program.

The Applicant's Background. In addition to collecting direct information by administering psychological tests, sales managers should verify all facts that have been provided by the applicant. Typical sources which can be used to verify data include personal references, contact with former employers and associates, a retail credit check, a physical examination and medical report, and a home interview.

Sales managers and personnel specialists have found this procedure advantageous for several reasons. First, it is quick and relatively economical. Second, it often provides information which the applicant prefers to overlook. Third, it serves to verify information supplied by the applicant. Fourth, a third party viewpoint is included in the evaluation. Fifth, the information is obtained free of the influence of the applicant's personality.

Personal References. Personal references which are provided by an applicant may be, and usually are, of little value except for checking a few minor points. Parenthetically, one personnel specialist who is unwilling to completely discount personal references suggests a technique for offsetting the protection usually provided. "Each applicant is required to furnish the names of 12 references. The idea, of course, is that almost anybody can come up with three or four people who will protect him. But 12 is another story. The references are telephoned beginning with the bottom of the list, where protection is likely to be thinnest."[5] It is also a good idea to check references over the telephone and identify the reputation of the person who is providing the reference.

Former Employers. Previous employers and business associates are probably in the best position to provide reliable information on the applicant's personal habits, strengths, and weaknesses. The best method for securing this type of information is a personal visit with the former employer or associate. If a personal visit is impractical, the second best method is to use the telephone. This two-way communication can be invaluable in finding out how a person feels about an applicant from statements, pauses, and tone of voice. The familiar question, "Would you rehire the person?" or "Would you hire the person?" as the case might be, can also provided a wealth of revealing information.

Typically, the areas shown below should be checked during the telephone inquiry: (1) verification of employment dates; (2) duties and responsibilities; (3) beginning and final salary levels; (4) quality and quantity of work; (5) ability to get along with supervisor, associates, and customers; (6) reliability and dependability; (7) reasons for leaving; (8) answers to the question "Would you hire or rehire this person?"; (9) any known financial or domestic problems; (10) moral habits (i.e., drinking or gambling); (11) strong points; and (12) weak points. Also, do not contact just the last employer. Contact should be made with three or four former employers to see if there is a consistent opinion about the recruit.

Retail Credit and Character Reports. Most firms find it advantageous to secure special investigative reports on applicants. These reports not only are designed to check the applicant's credit and general standing in the community, but are also designed to reveal information about employment, education, character traits, health habits, finances, personal reputation, interests, and police record. There are a number of well-known investigating agencies which operate on a nationwide basis, including Retail Credit Company, Hooper-Holmes, and Dun and Bradstreet.

Sometimes there are delays in receiving reports from these agencies, particularly in cases where an applicant has frequently moved. However, it is better to take a little more time and get the most accurate and com-

---

[5] "Improving Sales Recruitment and Selection," *Marketing for Sales Executives* (New York: The Research Institute of America), May, 1972.

prehensive report possible than to make a poor selection because of inconclusive information.

Physical Examinations and Medical Records.   A complete physical examination with a subsequent medical report has become an integral part of comprehensive selection programs. In most cases, the physician is given a briefing on the physical requirements of the salesperson's job.

Recent studies indicate that about one in every ten salespeople is not able to pass a thorough physical examination. The importance of this phase of selection cannot be over-emphasized in view of the substantial amount of physical energy and prolonged periods of tension which most people in sales must be able to endure.

Audit of Selection Practices

According to Al N. Seares, president of Affiliates in Management Services, "The future belongs to those who prepare for it."[6] Yet, sales managers often fail to make proper use of the many sound management practices which are learned during the early stages of development. One example is the **marketing audit** which is defined as "a systematic, critical, and unbiased review and appraisal of the basic objectives and policies of the marketing function and of the organization, methods, procedures, and personnel employed to implement the policies and achieve the objectives."[7]

This well-known marketing aid can assist materially in uncovering weak spots in selection, or any other function, when proper application is made to the problem. An audit should be made periodically to determine if the company selection program is producing desired results. Sales managers should be aware that every person hired represents substantial investment, not only for the company but also for the individual. A sound program frequently can provide the basis for a maximum return on both investments by serving as the vehicle for greater job satisfaction and increased sales and profits. A sample audit is presented in Figure 7–3.

Legal Aspects of Selection

In recent years there has been an increasing amount of legislation, both state and federal, regarding the selection process. The majority of the laws are aimed at tools used in the selection process such as application forms, interviews, and tests.

[6] Al N. Seares is a former Vice President of Remington Rand, Division of Sperry Rand. Mr. Seares also served two separate terms as President of Sales & Marketing Executives-International, is founder of Affiliates in Management services, and developer of The Image Rater System for performance appraisal.

[7] Alfred R. Oxenfeldt, "The Marketing Audit As A Total Evaluation Program," in *Analyzing and Improving Marketing Performance: Marketing Audits in Theory and Practice*, (New York: American Management Association, Management Report No. 32, 1959). p. 26.

(Check the appropriate box as it applies to your selection practice: A—requires primary attention; B—should have secondary attention; C—defer for later study and action; D—this is already done.)

PRACTICE	A	B	C	D	COMMENTS
1. Do we have adequate job descriptions and specification profiles for all sales jobs in our company?	—	—	—	—	
2. Have they been revised within the last year?	—	—	—	—	
3. What sources do you turn to for sales candidates in your company?	—	—	—	—	
4. Have you determined the effectiveness of these sources?	—	—	—	—	
5. What selection techniques are you using for sales candidates?	—	—	—	—	
6. Does each of these techniques make a unique contribution to the selection program?	—	—	—	—	
7. To what extent do you use the information gathered to facilitate training and handling of new salespeople?	—	—	—	—	
8. How closely do you work with your force (e.g., sales supervisors and top management) in connection with selection?	—	—	—	—	
9. Have you found personnel people helpful in selection?	—	—	—	—	
10. How many applicants do you find typically must be screened in order to obtain one acceptable trainee or salesperson?	—	—	—	—	
11. What experience has your company had with tests?	—	—	—	—	
12. Do you use the test results for training and supervision as well as selection?	—	—	—	—	
13. What do we really know about tests as management tools?	—	—	—	—	
14. What are the pitfalls and dangers in using tests?	—	—	—	—	
15. What outside assistance have you found helpful in selecting salespeople?	—	—	—	—	
16. What have you done constructively to cooperate with others in making selling more attractive to potential salespeople?	—	—	—	—	

PRACTICE	A	B	C	D	COMMENTS
17. Have you set up manpower tables to forecast continually your manpower needs?	—	—	—	—	
18. Have you determined what qualities are correctable, somewhat correctable, or not feasibly correctable if lacking in an applicant?	—	—	—	—	
19. Do you have an orientation program for new product lines?	—	—	—	—	
20. Is the salesperson's spouse informed about the mate's responsibilities and relationship with the company?	—	—	—	—	

Figure 7–3
Audit of Selection
Practices

The first laws with substantial impact on employers were the Federal Civil Rights Act, (1964), the Age Discrimination in Employment Act (1968), and the Equal Pay Act (1963). These various acts drastically modified the kinds of questions that could be asked on application forms and during interviews. Most state laws now prohibit questions which pertain to race, color, religion, national origin, or marital status, and although not specifically outlawed by Federal legislation, such questions are looked upon "with extreme disfavor" by the EEOC and the Department of Labor.[8]

An example of questions that can and cannot be asked is presented in Figure 7–4. This Pre-Employment Inquiry Quiz (PIQ) was developed by Robert L. Minter, and has been administered to supervisory personnel responsible for interviewing and screening applicants. Although statistical norms have not yet been established, respondents often obtain less than 50 percent accuracy on the PIQ.

A second area of concern with federal legislation lies with the use of tests. At the time of the passage of the Federal Civil Rights Act, the Congress included provisions to prohibit any discrimination against minorities in the usage of both psychological and mental abilities tests. Subsequently, both the EEOC and the Office of Federal Contact Compliance issued guidelines on testing. These guidelines go into considerable detail on the issues of validating tests, type of criteria, and test utility. For example, unless tests are validated and are the only available hiring procedure, they may constitute discrimination. Also, the EEOC may examine company records to identify evidence of validation and indications of discrimination such as relatively high rejection rates of minority applicants.

---

[8] Wendell L. French, *The Personnel Management Process* (3d ed.; Boston: Houghton Mifflin Company, 1974), p. 269.

Pre-Employment Inquiry	Lawful	Unlawful
(A) Asking the applicant if he has ever worked under another name.		X
(B) Asking the applicant to name his birthplace		X
(C) Asking for the birthplace of the applicant's parents, spouse, or other close relatives.		X
(D) Asking the applicant to submit proof of age by supplying birth certificate or baptismal record.		X
(E) Asking the applicant for his religious affiliation, name of church, parish, or religious holidays observed.		X
(F) Asking the applicant if he is a citizen of the United States	X	
(G) Asking the applicant if he is a naturalized citizen.		X
(H) Asking the applicant for the date when he acquired his citizenship.		X
(I) Asking the applicant is he has ever been arrested for any crime, and to indicate when, and where.	X	
(J) Asking the applicant to indicate what foreign languages he can read, write, or speak fluently.	X	
(K) Asking the applicant how he acquired his ability to read, write, or speak a foreign language.		X
(L) Asking the applicant about his past work experience.	X	
(M) Requesting the applicant to provide names of three relatives other than one's father, husband or wife, or minor-age dependent children.		X
(N) Asking the applicant for his wife's maiden name.		X

Pre-Employment Inquiry	Lawful	Unlawful
(O) Asking for the maiden name of applicant's mother.	_____	X
(P) Asking for the full names of the applicant's brothers and sisters.	_____	X
(Q) Asking the applicant for a list of names of all clubs, societies, and lodges to which he belongs.	_____	X
(R) Asking the applicant to include a photograph with his application for employment.	_____	X
(S) Asking the applicant to supply addresses of relatives such as cousins, uncles, aunts, nephews, grandparents, who can be contacted for references.	_____	X

Figure 7–4
Pre-Employment
Inquiry Quiz (PIQ)

Source: Robert L. Minter, "Human Rights Laws and Pre-Employment Inquires," *Personnel Journal,* Vol. 51 (June, 1972), p. 431.

SUMMARY

The recruiting and selection activities of a company must go hand in hand. The need to have a constant flow of qualified applicants cannot be denied. Such a program can spell the difference between selection under conditions of crisis and uncertainty to selection by effective manpower planning.

In order to identify potential recruits the sales manager should monitor the following sources: educational institutions, suppliers, present employees, business associates, competitors, walk-ins, employment agencies, advertising, and customers. Before effort is expended to identify recruits, however, the firm must have a current description of job functions and a profile of the desired recruit.

Once a recruit is identified, he or she should be screened in a preliminary interview and asked to complete an application form. Details on the application form and references are then checked to determine their validity. The next step in salesperson selection is to conduct in-depth patterned or nondirected interviews of each applicant that survives preliminary screening. Psychological tests may also be administered to provide additional insight into the applicant's strengths and weaknesses.

QUESTIONS

1. Someone in your organization complains that bright college people are not interested in a sales career. This person asked you to overcome this difficulty. How would you proceed?

2. Is it important for salespeople to possess a college degree? Explain your answer.

3. Can the acceptance or rejection of a prospective salesperson be justified because of certain personal biases the interviewer may have about an applicant's appearance, mannerisms, and personality?

4. There are numerous myths concerning the characteristics of effective salespeople. What are some of these myths? Are they justified?

5. Why is it difficult to find good salespeople?

6. How should a job description be prepared? What steps and elements are involved?

7. What are the advantages of using the application form as a selection tool?

8. What advantages does the patterned interview have over the non-directive interview?

9. What problems relate to the use of psychological tests as a selection tool?

10. What is a marketing audit? What are its benefits?

Case 6-1

Johnson Food Company

Early in 1982 Lloyd Johnson, President, was reviewing alternative plans for realizing a higher rate of growth. Johnson Food Company is a ten year old company that specializes in the manufacture of meat and vegetable items for restaurants, hotels, schools, and other institutions. Its meat line includes raw and precooked hamburger patties, chicken fried steak, meat balls, pizza, cutlets, and Mexican food. Its speciality vegetable items are high quality, frozen, breaded products.

During the first eight years of Johnson Food's existence, it realized an annualized growth rate of approximately 35 percent. Lloyd Johnson was able to develop several high quality brokers on the West Coast and in the Southwest that obtained representation for Johnson's products in the four largest and most reputable food distributors in the country. These distributors were able to place their products in several large school districts, including San Diego and Los Angeles. Growth of the school systems and overall growth in the restaurant industry during the 1970's were primarily responsible for the distributor's success.

During the late 1970's and early 1980's, however, Johnson Food Company realized no real growth. In fact, in 1981, it produced the same number of pounds of product as it produced in 1979. This was disconcerting for an entrepreneur such as Johnson who was committed to at least a 25 percent annual growth rate. The fact that the food service market had grown less than one percent during the same period did not seem to impact on Johnson's enthusiasm for growth.

Johnson Food Company's organizational structure reflects the President's desire for control and his orientation toward sales (see Figure 1). The regional salespeople (called sales managers) report directly to the President along with the

Figure 1
Johnson's Organizational Structure

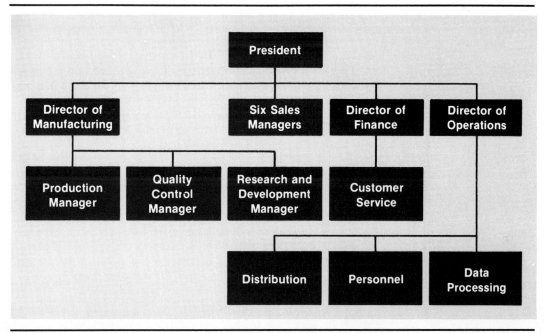

directors of manufacturing, finance, and operations. The sales managers work directly with brokers and distributors in the sale of product. Although sales managers may periodically develop a new customer, their primary efforts are focused on developing and maintaining solid relationships with their distribution network. In fact, commissions are given to brokers even if a sale is made directly to a restaurant without the broker's assistance.

After a number of meetings with department heads and several consultants, Johnson formulated an action plan to help stimulate growth of his company. In general, the plan included the following strategies:

- sell directly to national chain restaurants from Johnson's headquarters—bypassing brokers and distributors.
- identify and develop new products for foodservice.
- plan development of a frozen product for the retail trade (i.e., supermarkets).
- obtain higher penetration of existing markets.

1. Evaluate Johnson's current organizational structure.

2. What changes in the structure will be necessary to implement Johnson's ideas? Develop a new structure.

Case 6–2

Adams Manufacturing Company*

One of the most important questions facing the Corporate Sales Department in 1974 was the organization of Adams' sales force. In its search for ways to make the sales function more productive, the staff group was considering how divisional sales activities could be consolidated to achieve a more effective and efficient personal selling effort.

Adams was a large Chicago food manufacturer with 1973 sales of over $1 billion. Sales had doubled in ten years, and management had set a sales goal of $2 billion for 1983. Five operating divisions were organized around similar product groups. Each division maintained its own sales force (two divisions used brokers), marketing group, and production facilities. Divisional general managers had profit responsibility, and each division was operated as a semiautonomous company. Subject to financial review at the corporate level, divisional general managers were given broad authority in deciding on such things as product line, marketing strategy, and plant investment.

The corporate staff contained several departments charged with coordination and review of divisional activity in each of the functional areas. The Corporate Sales Department coordinated divisional sales efforts in sales force recruiting, sales training, participation in trade conventions, relations with trade associations, and establishing sales policies.

Corporate Sales was responsible for long-range, strategic planning of the sales function at Adams. Under the direction of Jim Little, Vice-President Corporate Sales, the department was engaged in a continuous evaluation of the changing internal and external factors that had an impact on the company's selling effort. An

* Reprinted by permission of John Wiley & Sons, Inc., New York. Published in MARKETING MANAGEMENT, 4th ed. by Kenneth R. Davis (1972).

analysis of these factors had raised several questions about the desirability of maintaining five separate sales forces.

Separate sales forces had been set up in the late 1950's in response to requests from divisional general managers. They had argued that since top management held them accountable for profit goals, they needed control over the tools used to achieve those goals. The tremendous increase in tonnage and proliferation of products in each division supported the argument for divisional sales forces. By 1973, divisional sales forces ranged in size from 150 to 250 people each. Company-wide personal selling costs were about $25 million in that year.

The issue of combining some of the sales functions was first raised at a meeting of the divisional national sales managers in late 1971. Because of the changing trade environment and the rising cost of maintaining an effective sales force, the sales managers agreed it would make sense to consider the idea of consolidating sales activities.

Two distinct types of selling activity had developed at Adams. Retail sales representatives called on retail outlets and performed what Mr. Little termed "light housekeeping duties." The sales representative would check inventory, shelf facings, prices, and in general insure that Adams' products were being displayed in keeping with established policies. When discrepancies were found, they were corrected by the representative or brought to the store management's attention. Little actual selling took place at the retail level. A chain-store manager, in effect, purchased from the regional warehouse operated by the parent company. Seldom did the manager have the authority to purchase directly from a manufacturer.

The actual selling was done by account managers who called on regional offices of the food chain or a wholesale distributor. As the food chain management became more sophisticated, the selling process became more complex. Account managers had to be capable of making a complete presentation on the economic benefits of purchasing a product. This involved an analysis of return on the investment in inventory, profits per foot of shelf space, and the advertising and promotional arrangements that would support the product within the regional market.

Each Adams division divided its sales force into fifteen districts concentrated around population centers. All divisions used the same territorial break-down. In most instances, the Adams sales district closely paralleled the regional territories established by the food chains and wholesalers. A separate district manager and autonomous district headquarters were maintained in each district by each of the five divisions. A division typically employed two to four account managers and seven to sixteen sales representatives in the district, with the exact number being dependent on the district's size. Division No. Three used brokers in all districts and maintained only a district manager. The broker provided the lower-level personnel. Division No. One used this broker arrangement in about one-half the districts. Figure 1 is an organizational chart that is representative of a division's district sales force.

A high turnover rate among sales personnel was the most serious internal problem faced by sales management in every division. While the selling function of account managers demanded increasingly better educated and trained people, management found it difficult to retain good sales representatives who could be promoted to this position. About 10 per cent of the sales force was lost each year, with an attrition rate as high as 25 per cent among sales representatives with less than two years' experience. Most of the sales representatives who left voluntarily were college educated, eager to advance, and judged by superiors to have strong potential for future advancement. Salaries were above the industry average at all levels in the sales organization. The representatives who left characterized their

Figure 1   Current Organization

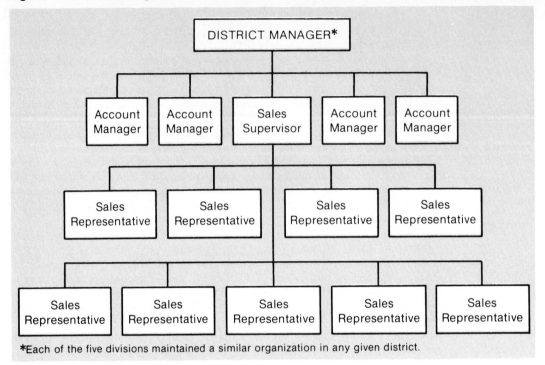

*Each of the five divisions maintained a similar organization in any given district.

Figure 2   Model A

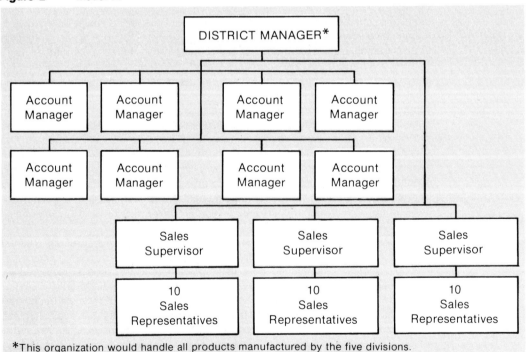

*This organization would handle all products manufactured by the five divisions.

Figure 3 Model B

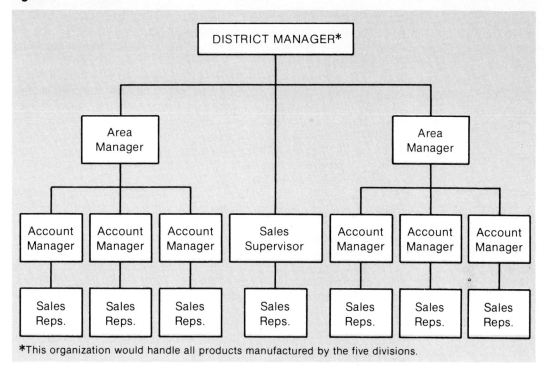

*This organization would handle all products manufactured by the five divisions.

Figure 4 Model C

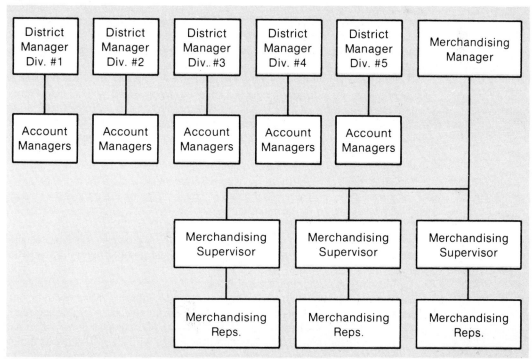

jobs as dull and gave boredom or a lack of challenge as the reason for leaving. The high turnover rate led to increased recruiting and training costs, and an erosion of quality in the field sales forces.

Jim Little felt the prime contributor to the high turnover rate was the fact that all too often a retail sales call was a waste of time. Improved retail management had eliminated many of the discrepancies historically corrected by the manufacturer's sales representative. Retailers simply could not afford sloppy merchandising or out-of-stocks. Often, the sales representative could find nothing wrong, and the sales call was reduced to filling out a rather complicated call report. Mr. Little believed there was still a real need for the retail sales activity but felt something had to be done to redefine and enrich the job.

Jim Little assigned Norman Grant the task of developing several alternative ways of consolidating the sales function. Mr. Grant had considerable experience in both sales and product management. After reviewing the present organization and the external factors affecting the sales force, Mr. Grant drew up three alternative models for consolidating Adams' selling activities.

Model A, shown in Figure 2, provided for complete consolidation of all selling effort under one district manager. Each account manager would sell all of Adams' products to the chain wholesalers and large independent retailers and regional buying offices. Retail activity for each division would be combined, with each sales representative handling all products offered by the five divisions. The retail sales force would be divided into ten-person groups, with a sales supervisor in charge of each group.

With a single district manager instead of the current five, Model A would permit better control over the allocation of resources and selling effort to all of Adams' products. Human resource development would be improved because interdivision transfers above the district level would be facilitated. The Model provided flexibility in the assignment of personnel, with room in account management for the gifted representative with few supervisory skills. On the other hand, individuals who required supervision or who developed supervisory skills could be assigned to the retail sales force.

Several disadvantages were inherent in Model A. There would be a problem of setting priorities as to which products would be emphasized by the sales force. Training the sales force in how to sell the new products each representative would pick up would be a considerable task. The separation of selling functions would make communications more difficult between account managers and merchandising representatives. New procedures for control and evaluation of both groups would have to be designed and implemented.

Model B, shown in Figure 3, focused on customers, with sales representatives reporting directly to the account manager. These retail representatives would be assigned exclusively to the account manager's customers and provide services tailored to the needs of the particular customer. Account managers and retail representatives would handle the full Adams product line. A group of sales representatives would be assigned those miscellaneous retail stores not operated by a major account.

By focusing on customers, Model B would help eliminate trade flow problems. Coordination of the marketing effort between manufacturer, the customer's regional headquarters, and individual retail outlets would be enhanced by organizing along the lines of Model B. However, Model B could lead to some duplication of effort and could possibly prove more expensive than the other alternatives. There was a danger that account managers would concentrate on making quotas and neglect the training of the sales representatives. Assignment of sales representatives to small groups would reduce flexibility in shifting individuals to special projects.

Figure 4 shows Model C, which provided for consolidation of the retail activity only. Separate district and account managers would be retained by each of the divisions. Sales representatives would work across divisional lines, and service products sold by all five divisions.

Norman Grant presented Models A, B, and C to a conference of the national sales managers. In his remarks, Mr. Grant outlined the following broad objectives of a reorganization plan.

1. Recognize change and stay ahead of it.
2. Remain flexible to accommodate all external and internal changes.
3. Decide on the shape and future of our businesses and those of our customers.
4. Increase job satisfaction at all levels. (Reduce turnover.)
5. Increase productivity at all levels.
6. More fully utilize the skills bank the sales department represents.

The sales managers were asked to agree on one Model that would be developed in detail and tested in one Adams district. There was general agreement that something had to be done to meet the changing nature of the selling environment and the sales force turnover problem. Approving the specific changes was another matter. There was a strong reluctance to give up any control over existing sales resources. The sales managers concluded that the extent of consolidation in Models A and B was too large. After considerable discussion, approval was given to go ahead with plans to test Model C. Corporate sales was to select a test district, gather the data necessary to effect reorganization, and present a specific proposal for implementation.

Messrs. Grant and Little decided St. Louis, District No. 11, would be suitable for conducting the test which would take a year to conduct. Mr. Grant prepared a questionnaire to gather data on the number of personnel and compensation, the number and size of stores, average calls per day and call frequency, and the number of brands and sales volume of each in the St. Louis district. National sales managers were asked to complete the questionnaire. Figure 5 shows a tabulation of information extracted from the completed questionnaires. Using this information, together with the data on the number of brands and quantity sold by each division, Mr. Grant determined that a merchandising representative covering all five divisions would be able to average six calls per day. Working from this assumption, he developed the resource requirements and cost figures shown in Figure 6. The cost of operating the proposed merchandising force in District 11 was estimated   at $526,500. When compared to the $1,184,400 currently being spent to support the merchandising representatives and their supervisors, the model indicated a potential savings of $657,900 in District 11.

When first reviewing Norman Grant's analysis, Mr. Little questioned the assumption that each representative would make six calls per day. To be conservative, he felt it would be better to set the call rate at four per day. The number of days per quarter that a representative would make calls could be increased because sales supervisors would assume most in-office functions. By doing this, thirty-nine sales representatives would be necessary in the merchandising force for District 11. The cost of operating the plan would increase $130,500, and the net savings to be realized would be reduced to $527,400. Mr. Little argued that a 29 per cent cut in the sales force at the retail level was more likely to be accepted by the divisions than the 44 per cent cut represented by the thirty-person force. Once

Human Resource Survey—District 11

Job Description	Division 1	2	3*	4	5	Total Adams
DSM	1	1	1	1	1	5
Account manager	4	2	3	4	4	17
Sales supervisor	1	1	3	2	2	9
Comb. sales supervisor	—	—	—	—	—	—
Sales representatives	7	10	16	11	10	54
Secretary	1	1	1	1	1	5
Total	14	15	24	19	18	90

* Broker organization below DSM level.

Financial Castup—District 11
Selling Cost Data (in thousands)—
Sales Representatives and Sales Supers Only

	Division 1	2	3	4	5	Total
Salaries	$114.1	$136.8	$142.5	$226.6	$224.1	$844.1
Sales bonus	6.1	10.7	15.0	28.5	15.5	75.8
Other direct	28.7	41.6	42.5	69.0	80.7	262.5
Expenses	$148.9	$189.1	$200.0	$324.1	$320.3	$1,182.4

Store Classification Comparison—District 11

Store Classification	Progressive Grocer	Division-Supplied Data 1	2	3	4	5
$500—$1MM	723	225	N.A.	499	N.A.	349
$1MM-$2MM	429	461		678		636
$2MM+	295	421		201		385
Total	1,447	1,107	1,209	1,378	1,738	1,370

N.A.—Not Available

Call Frequency and Coverage—District 11

Store Classification	Quarterly Contacts	Number of Stores	Total Calls
$2MM+	13	295	3,835
$1M-$2MM	7	429	3,003
$500-$1M	3	723	2,169
			9,007

Figure 5
District II Data

Merchandising Force

Job Description	Number Authorized	Salary	Total Salaries
Merchandising manager	1	$22,500	$ 22,500
Merchandising supervisor	3	15,000	45,000
Merchandising representative	30	10,500	315,000
Secretary	1	8,000	8,000
	35		390,500
Other direct expense at $4,000 per man			136,000
Total			$526,500

Assumptions for merchandising force
  30 sales representatives
  6 calls per day   Quarterly calls $= 312 \times 30 = 9,360$
  52 days per quarter
  312 calls/man/quarter

Revised assumptions
  39 sales representatives
  4 calls per day   Quarterly calls $= 240 \times 39 = 9,360$
  60 days per quarter
  240 calls/man/quarter

Increased costs under revised assumptions
9 sales representatives $\times$ ($10,500 salary + $4,000 expenses) =
$130,500

National projections of cost savings

District 11's selling costs before reorganization	$1,184,400
District 11's selling costs under new plan	657,000
Savings	$ 527,400

District 11 = 8% national sales volume
$527,400 = 8% of potential savings
$527,400/0.08 = $6,592,500 potential savings

Figure 6
Human Resource
Count Model,
District II

the plan was implemented, further reductions could be made when divisional management could see the successful results. District 11 represented 8 per cent of Adams' national volume. Even with the thirty-nine-person merchandising force, projections of the potential savings on a national basis came to $6.6 million.

The test plan was presented to the national sales managers. In his presentation, Mr. Little listed the following advantages offered by Model C:

1. Every division except Division Four would realize deeper coverage at

the retail level since a total of 1,447 stores would be called on.
2. On the average, retail stores would receive more frequent coverage.
3. By having only one salesperson call on a retail store instead of five, the stature of the sales representative is enhanced. The sales representative becomes more important in the eyes of the store's management.
4. Sales representatives will have greater breadth of responsibility and more varied tasks to perform. Combined with item 3, this will help alleviate the attrition problems.
5. The organization structure is flexible and can be adapted to meet the changing trade environment. New-product lines acquired through acquisition or internal development can be absorbed into the organization without further proliferation of separate sales forces.
6. Cost savings are major.

Mr. Little identified the following risks or weaknesses associated with Model C:
1. Divisions would lose direct control over selling activity at the retail level.
2. The ability of the retail sales representative to handle the entire Adams line was uncertain.
3. The ability to control the salesperson's efforts in terms of setting priorities on which products to emphasize was uncertain.
4. The reporting relationship of the merchandising force had to be determined.
5. The disruption caused by reorganization could be considerable if the transition was not carefully planned.

Divisional sales managers were about evenly divided on accepting the test plan and giving approval for implementation. Two divisions felt the problems of control over the merchandising force and the ability of one salesperson to give adequate attention to all products were too great to risk implementation, even on a trial basis. They pointed out that their sales forces had to be extremely responsive to the special divisional promotional programs. Emphasis shifted from one product or promotion to another almost weekly. Management argued that close coordination between advertising, promotions, and personal selling could only be achieved if marketing management in each division had direct control over the sales force. The meeting ended with a decision not to test the model at the present time.

Mr. Little analyzed the stands taken by each of the sales managers. He felt the divisional sales manager most vocal in opposition was under heavy pressure from his divisional president. The latter man had spent his entire twenty-five-year career within his division. Strong feelings of autonomy had been developed at all levels in the organization. The divisional sales manager had not been in attendance at the preliminary meeting. He had said that when it came time to reach an agreement he would go along with a consolidation plan if the other four sales managers were in agreement. But at the latest meeting, he merely shook his head and said, "No-way, no-way will that plan work." The other sales manager opposed to any form of consolidation argued that since his competition had their own sales forces he needed his also.

The divisions in favor of at least testing the new plan felt that their selling costs were high and they were not getting as effective a selling effort as might result from some form of consolidation. Division Three currently used brokers exclusively. The possibility of gaining some control over an in-house sales force held definite attractions for that division. On the other hand, the national sales manager of this division was reluctant to participate in a test because it would mean terminating the contract with the broker in District 11. The sales manager had urged Mr. Little to conduct the test with only the other divisions, rather than disrupt these brokerage relationships. Another alternative would be to pick a district where the broker was weak to begin with.

Division One used brokers in low-volume districts that added up to 50 per cent of the United States. The idea of being able to sell through an Adams sales representative was appealing to this division also. The issue of testing was less acute here since the district selected was one in which Division One had its own sales force. The fourth division had the strongest sales force, but its top management felt that consolidation offered such attractive cost benefits that it should at least be tested.

Given this opposition from some divisional management, Mr. Little was considering what to do next. He felt that only an actual test of the model would disprove the objections raised. He could go directly to top corporate management with his proposal. The potential savings of $6.6 million would have a powerful effect on gaining endorsement of the plan. If approved by corporate management, there would be sufficient authority behind the plan to get the divisions to accept the test. There were risks in making this end-run move. Real commitment at the divisional level could not be forced. At the same time, further delays and negotiations would probably result in the proposal never seeing the light of day.

A second option would be to modify the model and test plan and present a revised proposal to divisional management. The modified plan would have to contain detail on how the merchandising force could be made responsive to the needs of each division without losing the significant benefits to be gained under the current proposal.

1. Evaluate Model C and the proposed test in the light of internal and external factors affecting the selling effort.

2. Should Mr. Little go directly to corporate management to get approval and authority for implementation? If not, how could the proposed plan be modified to make it more acceptable to divisional management?

Case 7–1

Coleman Industries*

Coleman Industries is recognized as a leader in the production and manufacturing of thermoplastic components for the industrial market. Over 70 percent of all thermoplastic production molds and tools manufactured by Coleman are custom orders. Engineers at Coleman work very closely with salespeople and clients to produce quality precision thermoplastic components and prototype tools, and to do so with a minimum of lead time.

Coleman Industries was founded in 1953 by Wayne Coleman. The company, located in Memphis, Tennessee, was basically a garage-shop operation, manufacturing production molds and production tools for small and medium sized OEMs (original equipment manufacturers) in the Memphis area. Wayne Coleman was indeed a craftsman in his field and it was not long before his sales and customer base had grown significantly.

---

*This case was prepared by Lydia Welch.

In 1971, Mr. Coleman, wanting to retire, sold Coleman Industries to Arbor Industries, an $800 million holding company located in Pittsburgh. Although Coleman remained with the company for six months to insure a smooth management transition, Robert Wilke assumed immediate control as the new president. Mr. Wilke, an engineer himself, was excited that he had been given the opportunity and financial backing to try to expand Coleman Industries to a multi-million dollar subsidiary of Arbor.

By 1981, Coleman Industries reached $44 million in sales. The company takes pride in the fact that many Fortune 500 companies as well as hundreds of smaller OEMs benefit from its unique capabilities and services. Mr. Wilke gives credit for the company's tremendous success to Coleman's 12 person sales force. Ten of the salespeople have strong engineering backgrounds and two have strong sales records in other unrelated industries. The engineering background has always been an industry standard because of the technical complexity of the custom orders. The two sales professionals, however, have been extremely successful.

During the past week, Arbor notified Wilke that the company has authorized his request to hire two additional salespeople for several new markets that Coleman Industries had identified as high potential areas. Wilke immediately notified his national sales manager, Hal Curtis, of the good news and asked him to begin recruiting immediately.

Hal Curtis has been with Coleman for two years, and management has been extremely satisfied with his performance. Sales have increased 35 percent during the past two years utilizing only the 12 visiting salespeople. This was the first time Curtis had been given the opportunity to expand the sales force. He wanted to locate and hire the new salespeople as soon as possible so he could obtain quick sales results from the two new markets.

The markets Coleman was attempting to penetrate were in the Southwest. Curtis contacted three employment agencies in both Dallas and Oklahoma City that specialized in screening candidates with strong sales experience. He also placed a blind newspaper advertisement soliciting qualified applicants in two local newspapers in each city. The advertisement read as follows:

TERRITORIAL SALES MANAGER

National thermoplastics manufacturer seeks innovative and experienced sales manager for Southwest territory. Position requires locating new customers, establishing and maintaining good customer relationships, selling prototype and production tooling, assisting in establishing relationships between company engineers and customer engineers on new tooling projects, and assisting customer service in resolving production related questions and problems. Salary, commission, and bonus. Car allowance. Travel required. Only serious candidates need apply. Please send resume and salary history to:

P.O. Box 88513
Pittsburgh, PA 19123

After reviewing the qualifications of 60 people responding to the newspaper ad and 10 people who were recommended by the agencies, Curtis decided to interview 24 of the applicants. He spent approximately three days each in Dallas and Oklahoma interviewing the sales applicants. He screened the recruits in terms of their technical skills, aggressiveness, enthusiasm, and interpersonal skills. At the end of the week he had eliminated all but 5 candidates, one of which was recruited by one of the agencies. After asking for and checking references of the 5 candidates, the sales manager requested that each candidate visit the plant and interview with a selected group of company executives.

Upon completion of these one-day sessions, Curtis then began receiving input from people who had interviewed the recruits. Much of the input contradicted the sales manager's feelings on the sales potential of each candidate. While many of the company executives held on to tradition by recommending the technically-oriented candidates, Curtis felt those candidates with strong sales backgrounds could be trained and subsequently would produce more than the other recruits. His rationale for supporting the sales-oriented people was that their interpersonal skills would far outweigh any deficiencies in technical expertise.

Because of the differing points of view between Curtis, Wilke, and other company executives, Hal Curtis arranged a meeting in an attempt to resolve the disagreement.

1. Evaluate the recruiting and selection methods employed by Hal Curtis to locate and screen the sales applicants.

2. What other recruiting methods might have been used?

3. What issues should be discussed and evaluated during the upcoming meeting between Mr. Wilke, Mr. Curtis, and other company executives?

Case 7–2

Ag Chemical Company

Tom Brown, President of Ag Chemical Company, has been concerned that his company has not been obtaining a sufficient number of salespeople. The market for Ag Chemicals has been expanding. The sales for Ag Chemicals have increased but the company has been losing market share in its major market areas of Illinois, Indiana, Minnesota, Wisconsin, Iowa, Nebraska, Missouri, and the Dakotas.

During the previous year Mr. Brown has on at least eight occasions in person and twice by memorandum encouraged Michelle Snow, the sales manager, to propose a program for recruiting and selecting salespeople. Either Snow did not comprehend the urgency of the matter or deliberately ignored Mr. Brown, feeling it was not important since sales were on the increase.

In a special office conference, Brown called on Snow. Brown told Snow, "For over a year I have been asking you to develop some productive methods of recruiting and selecting salespeople so we can take advantage of existing profits and market growth. You have ignored me as long as I can allow. It has reached the point that you either have a program of recruitment and selection, or we are going to have a new sales manager. Do you understand?"

Michelle replied, "Yes, I understand. I didn't think you were serious until today."

Michelle left the president's office more than a bit shaken. This was her fourth sales manager's job in five years and she just could not afford to make another job change. Michelle spent the week studying all the materials she could find on recruiting and selection. She called some friends who were sales managers, but they did not seem to be of any assistance.

In desperation, Michelle began reviewing some back issues of *Agri-Marketing* in hopes of finding some helpful suggestions. She found several articles discussing summer internships. This approach excited Michelle, and she thought Mr. Brown, being a graduate of an agricultural college, would be impressed with this approach. She immediately launched headlong into implementing a summer internship program. Michelle felt this program would give the company a pool of applicants and relieve it of finding people to work during May, June, and July, a period in which extra help always had to be hired. Michelle felt students between their junior and senior years have serious thoughts about specific career choices and are close enough to graduation to be strongly influenced by a favorable summer work experience.

Michelle proposed that the programs start in April by recruiting summer interns from a few colleges and high schools where the company is likely to be known. The program was outlined as follows and sent to selected schools.

SUMMER INTERNSHIP*

ORIENTATION (LECTURE)	Overview of the company, its products, its people, its customers. Administrative staff and their functions.
SALES TECHNIQUES (LECTURE)	Sales Manager
ON-THE-JOB TRAINING	Line Manager

*Compensation will be $600-$800 per month plus expenses depending on experience.

Michelle implemented the program. Five students from five different high schools and six students from three colleges in Iowa participated.

After the summer program was over Mr. Brown visited one of the colleges from which one of the summer interns, Brent James, had come. He ran into Brent on the campus and naturally asked him what he thought of his summer experience. Brent, not realizing Mr. Brown was President of the Ag Chemical Company really told him just how he felt about it. The complaints went on and on. Brent's major complaints, however, that he related to Mr. Brown were:

(1) He did not really learn much about the company working as a laborer in the warehouse where he had spent most of his time.

(2) He did not like being put on an equal basis with high school students.

(3) The few lecture sessions he attended were boring and poorly prepared.

(4) The pay was not nearly as much as he could have made as a construction worker.

1. If you were Mr. Brown what would you have said to Michelle Snow after your campus visit?

2. If you were Snow, how would you have replied?

3. Was the internship program an effective solution? Were there alternatives? Explain.

Part 4

Developing and Maintaining Salespeople

Chapter 8 _____

Training New
Recruits

After completing this chapter, you will be able to:

- Identify the importance and benefits of an effective training program.

- Identify appropriate training objectives and a methodology for developing objectives.

- Explain the administrative aspects of training: who should train; where should training take place; when should training take place, and; how should training be carried out.

- Identify all methods for training new recruits.

As competition for markets continues to become more intense, as products become more complex and sophisticated, and as young people become more sensitive to the value of education, training becomes a more critical element in the sales force development program. Today, sales managers must be more sensitive to the needs of trainees and provide them with the tools necessary to meet sales challenges. Similar to other professionals such as athletes, salespeople must receive the most up-to-date techniques for accomplishing their assigned tasks. As better, more effective techniques become available they must then be retrained to meet new challenges. This chapter focuses on contemporary methods of training and the importance of initial training.

INCREASED IMPORTANCE OF TRAINING SALESPEOPLE _____

Regardless of how much sales ability an individual may possess when hired as a new member of the sales force, both initial and continued training will be required. Initial training is important because the new salesperson must be acquainted with company objectives, production capabilities, operating policies, market opportunities, product characteristics, and effective selling techniques. Also, it is important that new recruits develop good selling skills and positive attitudes early in their careers. Proper training and appropriate techniques can help insure immediate success and, therefore, higher-level motivation and a positive attitude.

Since positive attitudes deteriorate, new technologies replace familiar product lines, bad habits develop, and new sales approaches make traditional techniques obsolete, continuous retraining is also necessary. Although experience is an important teacher, it can also serve as an obstruction to long-run development. Salespeople that never evaluate their sales techniques or are insensitive to new sales and product ideas can soon find their skills obsolete and ineffective. They become like the salesman who claimed he had ten years of experience, when, in fact, he had only one year of experience ten times over again. The next chapter extensively covers continuous training.

BENEFITS OF TRAINING

The benefits of a sound training program should accrue to both the salesperson and the company. As a result of training, the salesperson should (1) become more quickly indoctrinated to market conditions, (2) better understand the needs and idiosyncrasies of specific customers, (3) have more confidence in making a presentation and handling objections, (4) realize a higher close rate, (5) be more aware of competitors and the strengths and weaknesses of their product line, and (6) unequivocally believe in and support his or her company. In other words, the training program places salespeople in a better position to meet competition and solve specific customer problems.

Also, overall company marketing programs are more effective when salespeople are trained because they will know how to incorporate company programs into their sales program. The synergistic effect of such a total balanced marketing program should be improved sales volume, improved morale, reduced turnover, and lowered selling costs. Such results, however, necessitate both effective and efficient training based on a careful definition of objectives to be attained and periodic review of progress toward their accomplishment.

COST OF TRAINING

The cost of training a salesperson has increased substantially during the past several years. As indicated in Table 8-1, the cost of training an industrial products salesperson rose from $13,941 in 1977 to $21,017 in 1981. For consumer products companies, average training costs per salesperson increased from $10,181 in 1977 to $14,291 in 1981. Because of these substantial increases in cost, it is even more critical for firms to maximize gains from their sales force training and development. They must precisely identify objectives to be accomplished, utilize the most effective training techniques, and monitor the extent to which objectives are accomplished. Remaining sections of this chapter deal with these important topics.

	Training Cost (Including Salary)				
Type of Company	1977	1978	1979	1980	1981
Industrial Products	$13,941	$15,479	$19,025	$20,093	$21,017
Consumer Products	10,181	11,338	13,173	13,625	14,291
Services	8,460	8,823	9,918	12,864	12,772

Table 8-1
Average Cost of
Sales Training Per
Salesperson

Sources: Sales and Management Survey, *Sales and Marketing Management,* (February 27, 1978), p. 72; (February 26, 1979), p. 66; (February 25, 1980), p. 68; (February 22, 1982), p. 82.

OBJECTIVES OF TRAINING

Within any organization identification of training objectives is vital to the success of the sales training program. Objectives not only help the firm coordinate its sales training with other training activities and goals, but also provide a means for evaluating the training program and guiding in the development of new training policies and procedures. These objectives should be *meaningful* and *measurable,* and should specifically state what is to be accomplished. Examples of frequently used objectives which are far too vague to have any real meaning are: improving sales volume, building profits, and increasing return on investment.

Determining Specific Objectives

Before a list of meaningful and specific objectives is presented, several rules for arriving at these objectives must be understood. First, in order to insure that objectives are meaningful the sales manager should consider the viewpoints of management, customers, and the sales force. These groups will be concerned with the impact of training on both their jobs and attainment of their personal goals. For example, sales management will most likely be concerned with the attainment of increased sales volume and profit, whereas the sales force will be concerned with training as it relates to personal needs, increased earnings, promotional opportunities, security, and satisfaction. Customers, on the other hand, expect training to provide salespeople with the tools necessary to satisfy their need for assistance and product information.[1] If the training program is to be successful, all of these viewpoints must be incorporated into training objectives.

Second, the sales manager must analyze the characteristics of the sales function and identify which tasks, activities, and behaviors are critical to successful performance of the job. It is possible that individu-

---

[1] *Duns Review and Modern Industry,* Vol. 81 (December, 1963), pp. 353–354.

alized training will be necessary to fit the needs of each salesperson as well as satisfy the requirements of different customer groups.

Third, it is important to analyze the capabilities of each salesperson in order to determine their specific training needs.[2] For example, if a job requires extensive technical knowledge of the product, training needs of a recent college graduate will be different than the needs of a mechanical engineer. Although both individuals will require training, levels of intensity may vary significantly.

Objectives

After an evaluation of customer, company, and sales force needs is completed, the sales manager is ready to establish specific training objectives. Although specific content of the training program will vary from company to company and salesperson to salesperson (see Figure 8–1), most programs will provide information in the following categories:

Company Policies, Procedures, and Practices. Both experienced and inexperienced salespeople should have a thorough understanding of company objectives and policies, organizational structure and lines of authority, company sales policies and procedures, and executive business philosophy and direction.

Product Knowledge. The objective here is to inform new salespeople of product features, performance advantages, customer benefits, terms of sale, advertising and promotional programs, and information on how products are produced. Not only will this information provide a valuable data bank for the salesperson, but it should also help the sales force feel more comfortable in its sales role.

Characteristics of Customers and Competitors. New members of the sales force should be introduced to the different types of customers, their needs, buying motives, and buying habits. They should also be provided information on competitors' products, policies, services, competitive advantages, warranties, and credit policies.

Market Information and Analysis. Companies requiring their salespeople to participate in planning and forecasting activities should instruct the sales force in basic market analysis techniques. Salespeople should also be taught how to identify and take advantage of new market opportuntities and new product applications.

Selling Techniques. Another objective of training is to teach salespeople how to (1) make an effective sales presentation, (2) meet and overcome objections, (3) prospect for new customers, (4) close sales, (5) plan sales activities, (6) quote prices, (7) make

---

[2] *Ibid.*, pp. 356–357.

demonstrations, and (8) follow-up on sales. Firms should develop a separate manual which details how to handle each activity. Specific presentations and closes should be included. Common objections and words to use in order to overcome such problems should also be detailed.

Field Responsibilities and Procedures. Salespeople should know that they are expected to divide their time between active accounts and potential accounts. They should also know how to use their expense account, prepare other forms, and route trips most effectively.

1. How to establish territory potentials.
2. How to prospect.
3. How to route salespeople and schedule their time.
4. How to appraise salespeople and determine the best way to motivate them.
5. How to provide necessary inside training.
6. How to provide necessary field training.
7. How to make the approach in the field.
8. How to take the prospect's measure.
9. How to prepare the dossier on each salesperson.
10. How to determine the personality type and buying motives of the prospect.
11. How to prepare and make the selling presentation.
12. How to measure the prospect's level of interest during the presentation.
13. How to anticipate the prospect's objections and prepare answers for them.
14. How to ask for an order.
15. How to follow up after an order.

Figure 8–1
Elements of Sales Training

ADMINISTRATION OF THE TRAINING PROGRAM

Who should conduct the training program? Where should training take place? When should training take place? How should training be carried out? These are administrative questions the sales manager must answer.

Who Should Train

One of the most important decisions in the development and administration of the training program is the selection of an instructor. Now only will this person be responsible for imparting knowledge to salespeople but will also serve as an example for future activities and performance. If the trainer does not take certain aspects of the training pro-

A Company Profile

Xerox Corporation was formed in 1906 as Haloid Company, a photographic paper supplier. With its markets maturing and growth declining in the 1940's, Haloid Corporation contracted with Battelle Institute to develop and market a photographic reproduction machine which was based on the process of xerography. After introducing the slow, inconvenient Xerox copier in the late 1940's and Copyflo in 1955, Haloid began development of a fast, inexpensive, and high quality copy machine. In 1958 the company changed its name to Haloid Xerox, and in 1961 became Xerox Corporation. In 1960, Haloid Xerox introduced the 914 copier, the first machine to utilize bond paper. The fact that the 914 provided reproductions on bond paper gave it a significant competitive advantage over other machines that required a special, treated paper.

In addition to reprographics, Xerox is involved in publishing magazines, books, and education material. Xerox also markets paper supplies, graphic products, reproduction centers, Cheshire labeling products, and electronic communication and computer products. Most people agree that Xerox's development and acquisition of a diversity of contemporary technologies placed it in a prime position to dominate the "office of the future" market in the early 1980's.

Although Xerox is most well known for its leadership in the duplicator industry, it is also perceived to have one of the most progressive sales training programs in the country. The firm has developed in-house training programs that are utilized to train salespeople in both Xerox and other industrial organizations. We concentrate here on detailing the training program for salespeople that are employed in the office prod-

ucts division of Xerox (i.e., paper, supplies, word processors, computers, facsimile.)

New recruits initially go through a six to eight week preschool in a branch office. During the preschool, trainees study all aspects of the company: its history, growth, philosophy, present market status, and future direction. Trainees also engage in extensive product training so that they are familiar with each product that they will sell. In addition, the trainee works with salespeople in the field and with marketing support.

After the preschool in the branch, sales trainees then travel to Xerox's Training Center in Leesburg, Virginia; a highly sophisticated facility with the most contemporary and sophisticated educational aids and instructors. Trainees live in on-campus dormatories and attend classes for three weeks. During the first week, they learn how to identify and satisfy the needs of customers. They learn how to collect pertinent customer information, ask appropriate questions, and match needs to product. During the second week trainees concentrate on competitive analysis. They are shown competitive products and the differences between the various alternatives. They also focus attention on sales strategies that can be employed to give the Xerox salesperson an advantage over competitive salespeople. Finally, week three focuses on territory management. Trainees learn how to identify qualified prospects, effectively route their activities, manage their time, and develop proposals.

Xerox has also developed a MAR School for salespeople that graduate from the basic sales school. Also conducted at the Leesburg facility, the MAR School is designed to move trainees closer to becoming a major account representative (i.e., MAR). The emphasis in this school is on team selling, and maximizing productivity. They study cases and engage in practice calls.

After classroom training is concluded, the trainees graduate to designated territories. They work in and help support an account representative's territory for 3 to 12 months before moving to their own territory as a major account representative (MAR). Training does not end with appointment to a territory. Xerox has a continuous training program that is designed to maintain the skills and knowledge of each account representative. Every quarter, regional trainers go to field offices to teach salespeople new sales skills and present new technologies and products. In addition, the marketing support group develops and disseminates video cassette programs, workbooks, and exercises.

Xerox continuously practices a policy of development, testing, implementation, evaluation, and redevelopment. The company frequently adds new programs so that salespeople are equipped to meet the challenges of a technologically sophisticated industry. Also, every three or four years the company changes the training program to insure that it meets state of the art developments in education. Xerox's orientation toward high quality education is one of the primary reasons Xerox continues to meet the challenges of competition and maintains a dominant position in a number of industries.

gram seriously, there is a good chance that the trainees will also deemphasize the same areas of sales.

As indicated in Table 8–2, in small and medium-sized firms the sales manager is primarily responsible for administering the training program. Although larger firms frequently utilize the services of a training director, 46 percent still utilize the services of sales management. Other people involved in training include product managers, personnel mangers, consultants, and other line executives.

Table 8–2
Personnel Involved
in Training
Administration

| Personnel | Size of Sales Force | | | |
	Under 10	10–25	26–50	Over 50
Sales Management	89%	60%	45%	46%
Training or Development	0%	10%	18%	70%
Executive	33%	20%	27%	2%
Other	10%	10%	18%	8%

Source: *Training and Equiping Salesmen*, "Dartnell Survey of Sales Training Practices," Dartnell File 5-2, p. 2.

The primary reasons firms prefer to use sales management in program administration are as follows: (1) the programs are more credible to trainees since the manager has actually worked in the field; (2) on the job training techniques can more easily be applied; (3) costs associated with employing a trainer or consultant are eliminated (particularly significant for smaller firms). On the other hand, sales managers are not necessarily good instructors and may not have sufficient time to devote to this critical function. Also, sales managers often overemphasize their own experience and ignore contemporary sales techniques. While utilization of sales trainers and outside consultants overcome problems associated with sales managers as trainers, the resultant program loses the realism which is added by the manager.

Where to Train

As indicated in Table 8–3, training may take place at the home office, a field office, regional office, plant location, central training facility, or a noncompany site. Although there are numerous potential training sites, the firm must select the location(s) which is consistent with objectives to be accomplished. When company policies and product information are being emphasized, for example, training can appropriately be held in the home office, a central facility, or the plant. When sales procedures and customer characteristics are being stressed, training should take place in the field.

When to Train

Training should be a continuous process. In order to teach new salespeople initial skills, give them important market, product, and company information, and give them that vital, initial motivation, it is

Table 8–3
Sites Most Frequently Used for Sales Training

Location	% of Companies Conducting Training at This Location			Median Length of Training Time at This Location		
	Industrial Products	Consumer Products	Services	Industrial Products	Consumer Products	Services
Home Office	71%	33%	95%	8 wks	8 wks	4 wks
Field Office	57	83	67	11 wks	6 wks	5 wks
Regional Office	50	50	50	8 wks	2 wks	4 wks
Plant Locations	36	8	0	2 wks	1 wk	0 wks
Central Training Facility (away from home office)	14	33	17	3 wks	2 wks	1 wk
Noncompany Site (hotel, restaurant, club)	7	8	17	1 wk	1 wk	2 wks

Source: "Special Section on Sales Meetings and Sales Training," *Sales and Marketing Management* (February 22, 1982), p. 82.

mandatory that new salespeople be trained extensively before making a call. Experienced salespeople who are changing jobs, also need retraining in order to orient them to new markets and effective selling techniques for new customers. Also, bad habits which are developed need to be dealt with and eliminated. Finally, all salespeople need to be continuously trained on new product technologies and innovative sales techniques.

It is also important to remember that training should take place before new outside salespeople are actually needed. In other words, firms should be developing new recruits before a territory opens. When a territory becomes available the company can then fill the position with a competent salesperson. Therefore, the firm does not experience lost sales, inadequate service, and competitive pressures from not having the territory covered or from having an inexperienced salesperson in the territory. Exxon Company, for example, continuously trains new salespeople at a central training school. Graduates of the school are assigned to a district sales office in order to receive field training from an experienced salesperson and/or supervisor.

Interrelated with the problem of when to train is the problem of how long to train. As indicated in Table 8–4, training programs were longer in 1978 than in 1975. In fact, among industrial goods firms the median length of training programs has nearly doubled since 1975, and for consumer goods firms the median length of training has almost quadrupled.

How to Train: Nonparticipative Methods

Sales training can be carried out in a variety of ways, utilizing numerous techniques and methods of instruction. These can generally be categorized as participative and nonparticipative depending upon the role played by the trainee in training. Figure 8–2 categorizes training methods as participative or nonparticipative.

As the title suggests, nonparticipative training does not give the salesperson an opportunity to participate except as a listener. There is typically a one-way flow of communications with little, if any, feedback.

Participative	**Nonparticipative**
Role Playing	Lecture
Case Study	Audio-Visual
Discussion	Demonstration
Panel	Sales Bulletin
Workshop	Sales Manual
Brainstorming	
On-the-Job Training	
Programmed Instruction	

Figure 8–2
Training Methods

Time Period	Industrial Products		
	1975	1978	1981
0 to 6 wks	17%	16%	35%
Over 6 wks to 3 mo.	33	9	17
Over 3 mos. to 6 mo.	17	42	30
Over 6 mo. to 12 mo.	33	33	12
Over 12 mo.	—	—	6
Median Training Period	12wk	24wk	23wk
	Consumer Products		
	1975	1978	1981
0 to 6 wks	54%	25%	43%
Over 6 wks to 3 mo.	13	16	7
Over 3 mos. to 6 mo.	20	42	36
Over 6 mo. to 12 mo.	13	9	14
Over 12 mo.	—	8	—
Median Training Period	5.5wk	16wk	20wk
	Services		
	1975	1978	1981
0 to 6 wks	48%	36%	33%
Over 6 wks to 3 mo.	26	28	33
Over 3 mos. to 6 mo.	18	27	17
Over 6 mo. to 12 mo.	4	9	17
Over 12 mo.	4	—	—
Median Training Period	7wk	8wk	12wk

Table 8–4
Length of Training
Period for New
Salespeople

Source: "Special Section on Sales Meetings and Sales Training," *Sales and Marketing Management* (February 21, 1977), p. 90; (February 26, 1979), p. 66; (February 22, 1982), p. 82.

The salesperson is expected to read or listen to the training message, understand its contents, and be prepared to use the information to assist in meeting personal and territory objectives. Such methods include lectures, use of audio-visual presentations, demonstrations, sales bulletins, and sales manuals.

Lecture. The lecture is a nonparticipative method of instruction which relies on a formal presentation on a specific subject area by a person who is preceived to be an expert on the relevant subject. The lecture is primarily used to transfer large amounts of company and product information to salespeople quickly.

The primary disadvantages of lecture are that salespeople do not actually experience what is being taught, retention of material is limited, and individual needs are not met. Therefore, lecture should only be used to transfer simple information or used in conjunction with other training techniques.

Audio-Visual   Audio-visual equipment can be used in both participative and nonparticipative training programs. A nonparticipative application involves the supplemental use of audio-visuals in lectures and demonstrations. When used in such programs, audio-visuals make the program more interesting and facilitate learning. Also, people are conditioned to learn by way of audio-visual through their extensive exposure to television.

In a participative sense, audio-visual equipment, cassettes, and computer equipment can all be used to help the salesperson learn through self-instruction. The primary advantage of such equipment is that salespeople can learn at their own pace depending on their personal capabilities. For example, Inland Steel Co. used audio-visual equipment simultaneously with role playing. A salesperson could act out a situation, record it on a machine, then replay the performance instantaneously to identify problems.[3]

Demonstrations.   Demonstrations are utilized to dramatize certain information about a product, service, or sales technique, Often-times they support a lecture or film by emphasizing a key point. Thom Norman, a nationally known expert on telephone techniques, uses such a procedure when training salespeople in telephone prospecting. In addition to explaining the theory of prospecting, Mr. Norman also makes calls and sets appointments for the trainees. After they have actually experienced how effective the technique can be, their resistance to the telephone is usually reduced.

Sales Bulletins   One of the most familiar training devices is the printed bulletin or memo which is usually sent from headquarters to the field sales force. Bulletins can cover a specific subject area, provide recognition for outstanding performance, or serve as a motivator by indicating progress toward stated personal, territory, district, or company goals.

Sales bulletins may range from a short, one-page, one-idea communication to a multi-page printed newsletter. In fact, there are several companies which specialize in selling a packaged newsletter service. These newsletters are designed to provide a constant flow of new ideas to the sales force and are frequently credited for helping salespeople get out of sales slumps.

Sales Manuals.   Different than sales bulletins, sales manuals are more like a reference tool which serves as a major source of information for

---

[3] "AV Plays A Leading Role, *Sales Management*, Vol. 115 (August 4, 1975), p. 55.

every member of the sales force. They are frequently bound in a three-ring binder so that additions, changes, or deletions can be made rapidly.

The sales manual usually provides a wealth of information for new and old salespeople. It provides background information on the company, its management, products, and markets. In addition, it should also include a copy of a salesperson's job description, various sales policies, procedures and rules, available training programs, and information on compensation, fringe benefits and anything else which might lessen the possibility of any future misunderstanding between the salesperson, the company, the supervisor, or customers. Figure 8–3 lists other topics that may be included in manuals.

In addition to being a policy manual, the sales manual facilitates the training program. Particularly for firms which use on-the-job training, the sales manual can supplement participative training. APECO Corp., for example, would initially train recruits for 90 days.[4] The district manager would give the recruit on-the-job training during the day and then the recruit would study the manual on sales techniques at night. This procedure eliminates the need for expensive and time-consuming seminars to present company, market, and product information and makes on-the-job training more effective.

How to Train: Participative Methods

Participative training methods actively involve salespeople in the training procedure. Since retention is greater when people read, discuss, and participate in the development of an idea than when they are simply presented the idea, the participative method is considered to be an effective learning tool. Participative methods which will be discussed in this section include role playing, case study, panels, workshops, brainstorming, on-the-job-training, and programmed instruction.

Role Playing. Developing real life sales situations and having them enacted by salespeople before an observing peer group offers a valuable learning experience for the participants and observers. The procedure involves (1) identification of an aspect of selling which needs study, (2) appointment of a buyer and seller or team of buyers and salespeople, (3) development of sales strategy, (4) enactment of the selling situation in front of other salespeople, and (5) critique of the sales situation. For example, Inland Steel Co. used role playing to identify techniques for converting past customers into actual customers.[5] Since their customers no longer used Inland as a supplier, there were obviously objections to some aspects of Inland's operation. Inland's trainers, therefore, created a situation where the sales manager acted as a purchasing agent and three

[4] "For APECO Training is a Confidence Game," *Sales Management*, Vol. 104 (May 1, 1970), p. 59.
[5] Don Korn, "Don't Call Inland's Salesmen Run-of-the-Mill," *Sales Management*, Vol. 109 (November 13, 1972), pp. 26–27.

Figure 8–3.
Suggested Tab Titles for Sales Manuals

COMPANY
History
Organization
Policies
Objectives
Executive Personnel Roster

PRODUCTS
Construction
Sales Features
Repeat-Order Potential
Engineering Data
Spec Sheets

CUSTOMERS
Type of Industry
Products
Order Potential
Buying Influence by Job Title
Special Problems

PROSPECTS
Needs—Approaches
Follow-ups—Products
Type of Industry
Order Potential

HOW TO SELL
Timing—Appearance
Arguments—Follow-ups
Letters Between Calls
Telephone Contacts
Presentations
How to Write Specifications

MARKET POTENTIAL
Sales by Industry
Sales by Areas
Sales by Seasons
General Data
Government Reference Material

PRODUCT APPLICATIONS
Demonstrations
Standard Uses
Special Uses
Tie-ins with Other Products
Job Analysis
Case Histories
Job Photos
Testimonials

DISTRIBUTION
Policy
Areas—Channels
Outlets—Statistics

PRICING
Policy—Discounts
Credit Requirements
Terms—Finance Plans
Shipping (Local Rates)

SALES OPERATION
Commission Arrangements
House Accounts
Guarantees
Franchises
Mutliple-Line Dealerships
Quotas
Service Policy
Home-Office Help
Incentive Programs
Special Problems

COMPETITION
Position in Industry
Policies—Reputation
Product Advantages
Product Disadvantages
General Strengths
General Weaknesses

PROMOTIONS
National Advertising
Schedules
Co-op Advertising
Direct Mail—Ad Mats
Radio Continuity
TV Spots or Programs
Merchandising—Premium Material
Signs, Banners, Trademarks
Point-of-Sale Helps
House Organs—Bulletins
Pattern Sales Letters
Trade Shows
Public Relations Program

GENERAL
Sales Training
Trade Associations
Trade Practices
Glossary of Trade Terms

Source: *How to Develop a Good Sales Manual* (Milwaukee: The Heinn Company) Undated.

salespeople acted out their role as a team of Inland salespeople. After objections were presented and handled, an audio-visual tape of the incident was played and evaluated for weaknesses and potential solutions.

There are several variations of traditional role playing:

Spontaneity Exercise. The roles are unstructured. No pre-role coaching is provided.

Stop-Action Techniques. The sales manager stops the interview to make observations and critique a statement or action.

Doubling. Another person sits with the buyer or seller and interjects comments about what is being observed. The other member can take the comment into consideration and revise the presentation.

Mirroring. An observer imitates the behavior of a buyer or seller in order to emphasize strengths or weaknesses.

Multiple Role Playing. Teams of buyers and sellers are used instead of just one buyer and one seller (i.e., Inland Steel example).[6]

In order for role playing to be effective, the following rules should be used to guide the session:[7] (1) Is should be designed to study and discuss a selling situation and not to evaluate salesperson performance; (2) Participant roles should be carefully studied and prepared (except when conducting a spontaneity exercise); (3) The episodes should be kept short enough to get everyone involved as a salesperson, buyer, and observer; (4) The salesperson should be given freedom to handle critiques without too much management interference; (5) Observers should not be allowed to nitpick; (6) The session leader should not just point out what is wrong with the performance; he or she should also discuss what is done right; (7) The buyer should be told under what circumstances he or she will buy, will put the salesman off, or will turn the salesman down.

If properly conducted, role playing has several significant advantages. Role playing gives the salesperson practice at selling before a customer is contacted. It also gives salespeople the opportunity to share ideas and experiences. It identifies critical weaknesses in sales techniques. It facilitates retention and learning by actually engaging the trainee in a situation and allowing him or her to study the performance. Role playing forces salespeople to put themselves in the prospect's position and, therefore, helps them understand the prospect's viewpoint. On the other hand, criticism in front of one's peers can demotivate. It is, therefore, mandatory to point out strengths and provide help, not unwarranted criticism. Also, some salespeople will not perform well in

---

[6] "Role-Playing Revisited—Its Still a Vital Sales Training Tool," *Research Institute Marketing for Sales Executives*, Vol. 3 (June 9, 1977), pp. 1–3.

[7] "Motivating and Training Salesmen to Close," *Sales Management*, Vol. 106 (June 1, 1971), pp. 26-27.

front of a group. Therefore, other training approaches should be used to supplement role playing.

Case Study. Firms that employ the case study method of training require salespeople to read a hypothetical or actual case history, devise a solution to the case, and discuss their solution with other salespeople. Not only does the method give salespeople the opportunity to study actual situations, it also teaches them to think objectively and systematically. In addition, it promotes interaction and a sharing of ideas among members of the sales force.

One approach, referred to as Sales Impact, developed by Palmer/Paulsen Associates, utilizes cases to study 26 different areas of sales.[8] Salespeople study a case related to one of the 26 topics. Each writes a brief opinion of the case, then distributes the analysis to other salespeople for discussion. The case study method is complemented with a sports-related contest (baseball, football, or golf). Salespeople can earn runs, yards, or strokes for "submitting case studies on time, writing the best answer for a region or for the whole sales force, making their quotas, exceeding their quotas, or achieving top monthly sales volume."[9]

Discussion. The discussion method involves the interaction of groups of salespeople under the guidance of a group leader. Discussion can be unstructured, structured around a specific aspect of the sales function, or structured around a case. Similar to the case method, the discussion technique is advantageous because it gives salespeople the opportunity to learn from other salespeople. However, there are several variations which can be used to attack specific sales problems.

Panel. Panels consist of several persons who are considered experts on a particular subject. After an initial presentation by panel members, questions and/or discussion is encouraged. Not only do salespeople benefit from interaction with other salespeople, they benefit from ideas presented by people outside of their organization.

Workshop. Workshops bring together elements of many participative and nonparticipative training programs. They are usually conducted by one to four sales experts and are several days in duration. Salespeople attending workshops have opportunities to exchange ideas with people who have unrelated experiences.

Brainstorming. A brainstorming session is a discussion designed to generate unique ideas in order to solve a problem. For example, a sales group may have trouble overcoming a common customer objection. In order to develop new approaches to solving the problem, eight or ten salespeople and sales managers may be organized to identify potential solutions. Brainstorming sessions

---

[8] "Playing Impact's Game: Third Down, Man on Second," *Sales Management*, Vol. 108 (May 1, 1973), p. 48.
[9] *Ibid.*

are most effective if several key principles are followed:

- Encourage the free flow of ideas. Do not criticize or evaluate ideas.

- Initially accept all ideas irregardless of their feasibility.

- Generate as many ideas as possible.

- Add to or expand upon ideas.

On-the-Job-Training.   On-the-job-training gives the trainee the benefit of learning skills in a real-world environment. Generally, on-the-job-training is conducted by a senior salesperson, sales supervisor, or sales manager. A trainee is assigned to one of these individuals and they plan their work and make calls together. For the first few weeks, the trainee usually studies a sales manual and observes the sales procedure of the trainer. After this initial orientation the trainee normally takes the lead in making presentations while the trainer observes. Immediately after a call, the trainer and trainee will often engage in a "curb conference". The trainer will ask some of the following questions in such a conference:

- When, during the presentation, do you think the prospect had enough information with which to make a decision?

- Could you have closed earlier? When?

- In what other ways could you have asked for the order?

- Can you think of other reasons you could have used to encourage the customer to buy?

- Could anyone else in the firm have helped you get the order?"[10]

In addition to giving salespeople actual field experience, on-the-job training gives the trainer more information with which to assess the recruit's ability. On the other hand, it is time-consuming for the trainer and expensive for the firm since each recruit is trained individually.

Programmed Instruction.   Used primarily to teach trainees product, market, and company information, programmed instruction involves the presentation of sequenced information on a computer terminal or in a manual. Upon receipt of information, the trainee is asked to respond to a question about the information. If the response is not correct, the trainee receives additional information and is asked the question again.

Merrill-National Laboratories' 554 salespeople use a Control Data

---

[10] Homer Smith, "Training Can Help—Up to a Point," *Sales and Marketing Management*, Vol. 118 (June 13, 1977).

computer system (PLATO) to learn product information.[11] Through a question/answer type program, salespeople learn about new products in 1½ days instead of the four days which were required with training seminars.

There are several advantages to programmed instruction: salespeople can learn at their own pace; travel time and expenses related to seminars are eliminated; more time can be devoted to selling; and it is an effective learning technique. The primary problem associated with such systems is the cost of development and implementation.

SUMMARY

Initial training of new recruits is possibly the most important activity of sales managers in terms of developing and motivating salespeople. It improves their chance of success, reduces customer-oriented problems, and, therefore, makes salespeople more productive and confident. The program should focus on teaching the salesperson about company policies, product characteristics, customer characteristics, market innovations, selling techniques, and field responsibilities.

Initial training is administered by either the sales manager, a professional training consultant, a sales supervisor, or a training director. Other company personnel such as the personnel director, product manager, and line executives also help in the implementation of training programs. Normally, such programs either take place in the field, at the home office, or at a training center.

Training methods employed for new recruits include lecture, audio-visual, demonstration, sales bulletin, sales manual, role playing, case study, discussion, on-the-job training, and programmed instruction.

QUESTIONS

1. What should be provided to the new salesperson during initial training?

2. If inititial training is strong, what is the need for later training?

3. Discuss the major benefits of a sound training program.

4. What accounts for the high cost of salesperson training?

5. How are specific objectives determined?

6. What attributes are desirable of the training instructor? Why are sales managers often preferred?

7. Are there advantages to nonparticipative training?

8. How could sales trainees be made to feel more comfortable when involved in participative training methods?

9. Discuss possible combinations of participative training methods.

10. Why is on-the-job training worth the expense?

11. Discuss the merits of programmed instruction.

---

[11] "Plato's Wisdom," *Sales and Marketing Management*, Vol. 120 (June, 1978), p. 19.

Chapter 9 _____

Continuous Training
and Retraining

After completing this chapter, you will be able to:

- Define continuous training and retraining.

- Identify appropriate methods and procedures for developing continuous training programs.

- Discuss methods for evaluating the effectiveness of training programs.

Learning is a continuous, never-ending process. Although some learning and personal development will take place in the field, a salesperson's skills may deteriorate and bad selling habits may replace effective techniques. Also, unless salespeople are continuously reviewing the results of sales research, new information and technologies may not be used to refine and improve sales procedures.

It is the responsibility of both the salesperson and sales manager to insure that skills do not deteriorate, that new techniques are used, and that new sales information is learned. This is accomplished through continuous training, re-training, and evaluation and redevelopment of the training program.

Continuous training is the process of refining and developing skills learned during initial training. **Retraining** involves teaching new sales techniques and new product information to experienced salespeople.

Not only does this chapter examine the procedures of continuous training and retraining, it also examines methods of insuring that these training efforts are effective.

CONTINUOUS TRAINING

The objectives of continuous training are to (1) insure that techniques presented during initial training are utilized effectively, (2) provide additional training which was not available during initial training, (3) instruct salespeople on how to implement a program of self instruction, and (4) identify salesperson weaknesses in order to assess future training needs. These objectives can be accomplished by implementing any of the following techniques:[1]

- On-the-job Coaching.

- Counseling.

- Courses for Self-Instruction.

- Workshops, Clinics, and Seminars.

- University Instruction.

- Observe Senior Salesmen in Action.

- Sales Meetings.

- Films on Sales Skills.

- Review of journals and newspapers on business (i.e., *Business Week, Forbes,* etc.); marketing (i.e., *Sales and Marketing Management, Journal of Marketing*), news; (i.e., *Time, Newsweek,* etc.); and customers' industries (i.e., trade journals).

Since self-instructional methods, workshops, sales meetings, and other related methods were discussed in the previous chapter, they will not be reviewed here. This chapter, therefore, primarily focuses on coaching and counseling.

On-The-Job Coaching

Coaching is a continuous process of helping salespeople acquire more knowledge, improve sales techniques, and develop self-improvement programs. Coaching is carried out in the field by the sales manager or sales supervisor and may simply be a casual suggestion or it may be a significant part of the formal performance review. Regardless of the complexity or formality of coaching, it is the heart of the supervisory process of getting things done on a cooperative basis.

Determine the Salesperson's Individual Needs.   If the goal of coaching is to help salespeople satisfy their individual needs, then these needs must initially be identified and continuously monitored by the sales manager. These needs may include security, job satisfaction, recognition, adequate compensation, rapid promotion, power, and excellence in a specialization. Different salespeople have different needs and ambitions and the type of coaching should reflect those needs. For example, if a salesperson is only interested in financial rewards, then the manager should emphasize the amount of money which could be made by utilizing a particular selling technique. For a salesperson interested in moving

---

[1] Adapted from: Homer Smith, "A Checklist for Upgrading The Sales Force," *Sales and Marketing Management* (August 9, 1976), p. 44.

into sales management, the supervisor should indicate the path to management — through complete understanding and application of effective sales techniques.

Plan the Coaching Session.   Prior to working with the salesperson in the field, the sales supervisor should become completely familiar with the salesperson's performance and development. The supervisor should: study the salesperson's call frequency, sales performance, profit contribution, and closing rate; track the salesperson's progress toward accomplishment of objectives; review notes of the last coaching session to identify what the salesperson is supposed to be working on; develop a plan for the upcoming coaching session; and review the plan with the salesperson prior to the session.

Be Specific in Performance Analysis.   Oftentimes the sales manager will review the salesperson's call effectiveness in general terms with no specific identification of problems. For example, the sales manager may say, "Your close is not as strong as it should be. Work on it!" Instead of making such an open-ended response, the manager should specifically identify the problem. For example, he could say, "When you make a closing statement you should not say another word until the client speaks." Then relate a story to the salesperson in which one of the senior sales representatives sat in silence waiting for a client to respond to a closing question for 10 minutes.

Look for Specific Causes of Good or Poor Performance.   Examine the sales call critically and evaluate the preapproach, approach, presentation, handling of objections, and close. Make notes of both positive and negative aspects of the performance. Then relate both areas to the salesperson. Also identify why one call was successful and another call was unsuccessful. In addition, probe for personal information which may explain changes in performance.

Make Coaching a Two-Way Process.   Coaching may best be thought of as a shared problem-solving process. The supervisor and salesperson should attempt to jointly and realistically identify results which have been achieved and problems which still persist. Tactics and strategies for improving performance should be discussed in an atmosphere of mutual respect. Such discussions stimulate creative problem solving and help in the identification of possible causes of and solutions to problems in a salesperson's handling of a customer.

Provide for Self-Correction.   The more salespeople can correct problems through self-improvement programs, the more time the manager will have to improve the total operation. The sales manager can provide salespeople with written material which deals with specifically identified problems. The company can financially support self-instructional programs, cassette programs, seminars, and workshops. Homelite, for example, sends tapes on new ideas, sales tips, and company news every two months to field sales representatives.[2]

Self-instructional programs are effective, however, only when specific problems are identified and defined. Such programs, therefore, do not eliminate the need for effective coaching; they simply supplement coaching and help the sales manager improve productivity.

Maintain a Field Coaching Log. Success at field coaching is primarily dependent on the quality of planning and analysis performed by the sales supervisor. The supervisor must specifically plan the session, carefully observe the salesperson's performance, and relate observations to the salesperson. To accomplish these objectives the supervisor must maintain notes on each activity. At the end of a session, notes can be used not only to evaluate performance, but to serve as the basis for subsequent coaching sessions.

One field coaching log which was developed by Research Institute of America from information provided by Porter Henry and Company, is presented in Figure 9–1.

Counseling

Counseling is a technique for identifying and solving a salesperson's business or personal problems through face-to-face communication. While the objective of coaching is to analyze and improve sales techniques, the objective of counseling is to examine and solve any problem that may impact on performance. Through meetings with a salesperson, the sales manager may attempt to uncover financial problems. The manager may then help the salesperson develop a plan of action to resolve the problem. The plan may involve meetings with other company personnel or treatment from a physician or other specialist. The sales manager's role as counselor is to be an understanding friend and help the salesperson develop a plan. Actual implementation of the plan must be initiated by the employee.

Advantages and Disadvantages. There are several significant advantages of counseling. First, similar to other training techniques, counseling is an effective motivational tool. It is an attempt to better understand the unique needs, motivations, and problems of each salesperson. With an understanding of each salesperson's needs, the manager is in a better position to improve productivity through motivational programs. Second, counseling can help reduce turnover. Many personal problems that go undetected during normal business operations oftentimes result in a salesperson's dismissal or resignation. If these problems can be identi-

---

[2]"How Homelite Trains to Reach New Markets," *Sales Management*, Vol. 108 (May 1, 1972), p. 35.

SALES REP'S NAME / DATE / FIELD CALL LOG

1. PLANNING:	Review the rep's records—volume, calls, correspondence, last coaching notes, any physical evidence of activity—to measure progress. Set new goals for visit—in line with rep's established development plan, specific weaknesses to study, strengths to stress, etc.	NOTES:
2. PRE-CALL BRIEFING:	Discuss which accounts will be called on. Review status of accounts. Discuss presentation strategy and goal for each call. Define the roles each of you will play during call.	NOTES:
3. MAKING THE CALL:	Observe verbal and non verbal elements: Is rep sticking to his/her objective? Best/Worst point of the call. Keep in mind the curbstone conference that will follow: What to stress there?	NOTES:
4. CURBSTONE:	Make it immediate and informal and short wherever possible. Concentrate on one or two priority points—reinforce as often as you criticize. Let the rep do most of the analyzing and setting next objectives.	NOTES:
5. WRAP-UP:	Not necessary to "curbstone conference" after every call, but it is important to review the day or total time period spent with rep. Get commitment from him/her on follow-up objectives. Set up a follow-up phone call, memo, whatever, for interim before the next coaching session	NOTES:

Figure 9–1
Field Coaching Log

Source: Research Institute of America, *Research Institute Marketing for Sales Executives*, Vol. 4 (July 6, 1979), p. 6.

fied and dealt with, turnover may be reduced substantially. Third, counseling can help salespeople understand themselves better. By listening and asking questions, a trained counselor can give salespeople valuable insight into their behaviors, values, and attitudes. This information can then be used by the salesperson and sales manager to develop a program of self-improvement.

The primary disadvantage of counseling is that the sales manager may become an emotional crutch for the salespeople.[3] Salespeople may take advantage of the manager's willingness to listen. Rather than performing duties associated with being a sales manager, the manager becomes a sounding board for employee problems.

Rules. In order to maximize benefits and avoid weaknesses associated with counseling, sales managers should follow the following rules.[4]

- Dig deeply to uncover the real reasons for poor performance.

- Even though counseling involves friendship and understanding, maintain a superior/subordinate relationship.

- Show the salesperson how he or she can benefit by changing an attitude. Indicate why performance is being hurt and how it will improve with changes in attitude and behavior.

- Make sure counseling is continuous. Although formal sessions are important, impromptu meetings can be helpful for spotting problems before they become too significant.

- Do not interrupt counseling sessions.

- Point out the person's strengths before questioning about weaknesses. Make sure the session is designed to help and to provide direction; not designed to criticize.

RETRAINING

As was indicated previously, retraining is utilized to instruct experienced salespeople on new sales techniques and new product information. Retraining is also used to develop salespeople into management personnel. Homelite, for example, implemented a program in 1972 to increase 160 salespersons' and 7,500 dealers' product knowledge, sales skills, motivation, and job satisfaction.[5] It was done because Homelite was entering the lawn and garden business, chain saw competition was increasing, and new management personnel was needed.

Retraining is critical for the long run success and personal growth of salespeople and managers. Technologies are continuously developing and making product knowledge obsolete. The state of the art in sales is also rapidly developing to provide salespeople with more tools to effi-

---

[3]"Counseling the Salesman," *Effective Leadership of Salesmen,* Marketing Manpower Development, Inc. (1965), p. 4.

[4]*Ibid*., pp. 3-19.

[5] "How Homelite Trains to Reach New Markets," *loc. cit.*

ciently accomplish assigned tasks. Buyers are becoming more sophisticated and demand a salesperson that can help satisfy their needs and provide fresh, new ideas. In other words, the entire selling environment is continuously changing and salespeople must change in order to avoid their own obsolescence.

When to Retrain

Retraining can take place anytime after initial training. Sterling Drug Company conducts retraining after salespeople have been on the job for only three months. Kellogg Co. holds retraining every two or three months in order to ensure that salespeople understand new products and new sales techniques.[6] Specifically, retraining is necessary whenever there is:

- A change in the salesperson's job requirements (e.g., territory changes).
- A change in customer markets and customer requirements.
- Development of new products or services.[7]
- Development of new sales techniques (i.e., change in the state of the art).
- An apparent deterioration of sales skills. An analysis of the field evaluation report suggests areas which need improvement. Such an evaluation report is shown in Figure 9–2.

Where to Retrain

Similar to initial training, retraining takes place in the field, at the home office, at field offices, at a training facility, or at any other convenient location. With retraining, however, the fact that the trainee is an experienced salesperson should be considered. Studies have shown that experienced salespeople may resist training efforts, and learning may be less effective than with new recruits.[8] Therefore, it may be advisable to utilize a training facility that has the most up-to-date teaching aids. Armour-Dial's training facility, for example, includes a simulated super market which can be used to teach retail management.[9] Although not all firms can afford modern training facilities, the site should be away from interruptions of a field office.

---

[6] "Training to Reach New Heights," *Sales and Marketing Management*, Vol. 117 (August 9, 1976), p. 43.

[7] Homer Smith, "To Make Training Click, Train by Objectives," *Sales and Marketing Management*, Vol. 117 (August 9, 1976), p. 44.

[8] John Withey, "Training the Older Salesman," *Sales Management*, Vol. 115 (August 4, 1975), p. 93.

[9] "Sales Training Centers-Educational Wonderlands," *Sales Management*, Vol. 104 (June 1, 1970), p. 58.

CONFIDENTIAL

Field Evaluation & Career Development Report

4 Superior
3 Excellent
2 Average
1 Satisfactory
Date_____ 0 Needs Improvement

Salesperson_____ Regional Manager_____

Date Report Discussed With Salesperson_____

	0	1	2	3	4
1. Sales Profile					
Knowledge of product					
Product line representation and stock balance					
Opening new accounts and follow-up of leads					
Knowledge of advertising and sales promotion procedures					
Sales conference preparation and participation					
Creative selling techniques					
Ability to meet assigned goals					
2. Time & Territory Management					
Account analysis					
Work load analysis					
Allocating time for maximum productivity					
Customer sales planning					
Territory coverage					
Territorial control					
3. Customer Relations					
Familiar with all company policies and procedures					
Creates confidence with accounts					
Handles complaints locally where possible					
Rapport with customers					
Control of credit problems					
4. Personal Traits					
Appearance					
Reliability					
Attitudes—job and company					
5. Growth Development					
Potential for advancement					
Motivational level					
Desire for advancement					

Figure 9–2
Report to identify
Need for Retraining

Source: Clark Lambert "In Upgrading, Good is Better, Better is Best," *Sales and Marketing Management,* Vol. 117 (August 9, 1976), p. 47.

A Company Profile

The Minnesota Mining and Manufacturing Company, or 3M Company, began operations in 1902 producing sandpaper. Today the company offers about 45 diversified product lines including many thousand individual items which they manufacture and sell. Although 3M is probably best known for its widely-used "Scotch" brand tape, the company also offers products as diverse as the reflective material used on license plates and "Vistar", an herbicide which can be sprayed over soybeans to prevent johnson grass.

Product groups include abrasives, adhesives, chemicals, business products, consumer products, health care products and services, photo and graphic arts, recording materials, tapes and allied products, and traffic control safety systems and advertising services. In order to manufacture such a wide range of products, 3M owns and operates approximately 130 manufacturing facilities throughout the world.

Between 1970 and 1980, 3M tripled its sales volume from less than $2 billion to $6 billion. Its continued orientation toward growth is reflected in both its research and employee recruiting programs. In 1981, 3M allocated over $300 million to support a research and development program that was commissioned to develop technologies and products which offer superiority, quality, and value. Employee recruiting and selection policies are also instrumental in its growth. Instead of recruiting trainees, 3M seeks out and hires people that can bring experience to the sales and marketing effort. In fact, only about 10 to 12 percent of 3M's employees are recruited from college campuses.

In addition to recruiting and supporting the appropriate salespeople, 3M also attempts to motivate its people through challenging assignments and thorough training. Training is on-going and individually tailored to each person's requirements. In addition to on-the-job training with managers and trainers, new salespeople receive basic selling skills training within their first six to eight weeks with the company. Conducted in 3M's St. Paul, Minnesota training facility, sales skills training employs the utilization of audio/visual presentations, role playing, and critiquing.

Also during the initial six to eight weeks, a sales trainer works with sales representatives in the field to help them understand the unique characteristics of territories and products. These trainers are sales representatives who have demonstrated outstanding sales and communication skills, and have continuously met performance standards. Oftentimes the trainer's position is utilized as a steppingstone for someone who wants to move into a management position.

Training does not stop for sales representatives after the eight weeks. With a company philosophy of growth through the development of new and improved technologies, salespeople must be readied for new assignments, territories, products, and advancement on a continuous basis. Periodically, salespeople are sent back to St. Paul for advanced selling skills workshops. Seminars or workshops on selling skills and motivational types of presentations are also given in the branch offices.

The type of continuous training that is offered to sales representatives may vary from one division to another. Training clinics which may be conducted for sales representatives of one product line or in one area of the country, may not necessarily be offered on a company-wide-basis.

Regardless of the program, division, or product line, managers play a significant role in the continuous training and development of the sales force. A majority of the time is spent in the field by sales managers, allowing them to monitor the progress of their salespeople and helping them with problem-solving and decision-making activities.

Managers operate with a Management by Objectives philosophy, assisting sales representatives with setting goals and objectives, and helping them outline a plan to accomplish those goals. This close interaction a manager has with the sales representatives allows the manager to identify trouble areas where a sales representative needs special attention or training. If additional product knowledge is needed, the manager can arrange a special training session for the employee. Sometimes detailed classroom instruction is needed for products which are highly technical in nature, such as microelectronic components or surgical implants. If selling skills need improvement, the manager can choose from a number of options. The individual can be assigned a trainer, sent to a clinic or seminar in a branch office or outside of the company, or sent back to St. Paul for additional training.

Sometimes the salesperson may simply be a mismatch for a particular product line with respect to the type of industry or clientele involved. For example, selling a large office machine may require more extensive contact and follow up with each customer than selling small business supplies such as Scotch brand Magic Mending tape. In such instances, a manager can arrange to move an employee into an area where he or she may operate more efficiently. In 1981, 3M had a low turnover rate in its sales force. Much of this can be attributed to:

1) attracting the right people to join the company,

2) the training philosophy,

3) the fact that the company challenges employees with new assignments, and

4) the company's long-term objective of growing 10 percent annually in real terms (in addition to inflation) creates personal growth opportunities through expansion.

Who to Retrain

All salespeople should be retrained. Retraining should accompany changes in technology, product lines, organization skills, or customer markets. Analysis of these organizational, environmental, and personnel changes will indicate who should be retrained. Retraining should not simply be a function of seniority. Although some salespeople will need retraining at the end of one year, some will not. In fact, one study indicated that interchange of ideas is facilitated if salespeople with diverse amounts of experience are retrained together.[10] Conducting a training session with salespeople who all have one year of experience contributes much less to the learning process.

How to Retrain

Retraining can employ any of the techniques discussed in the chap-

[10] Withey, *op. cit.*

ter on initial training. With retraining, however, it is even more critical that techniques be interesting, innovative, and effective. Seasoned salespeople may be asking themselves the following questions prior to and during retraining sessions:

- Will this mean more work?

- Will the extra effort be worth the added benefit?

- Am I better off using techniques that have proved effective in the past?

- Does the trainer know more than I do?[11]

Because of these hidden objections, it is necessary that the trainer initially sell the sales group on the idea of retraining, handle their objectives during the presentation, and ask them for their ideas whenever new approaches are presented. Let the salespeople develop ideas with the trainer simply guiding and directing the session.[12] In other words, retraining involves much more discussion and interchange of ideas than initial training.

EVALUATION OF TRAINING

Evaluation of sales training is extremely important not only because of the expense involved in training, but also because of the direct effect it has on salesperson performance, productivity, and turnover. All training methods, new and old, should, therefore, be evaluated to determine the extent to which they contribute to expeditious learning and depth of understanding. Also, management should constantly be questioning the program to determine if any errors are being made—see Figure 9-3 for a list of common sales training errors.

The general procedure for evaluating training effectiveness includes the following:

- Identify training objectives.

- Determine method for measuring the extent to which a procedure contributes to objectives.

- Measure contribution of objectives.

Training Objectives

Most training programs are designed to (1) improve selling skills, (2) teach product, company, competitive, and market information, (3) build confidence, and (4) improve productivity in terms of profit contribution.

---

[11] "Ferret Out Hidden Objections and Sell Benefits to Make Sales Training More Effective," *Research Institute Marketing for Sales Executives*, Vol. 4 (March 2, 1978), p. 5.
[12] *Ibid.*

1. Training often fails to keep pace with changing needs of salespeople.
2. In orientation training, course content often makes no allowance for obvious information that a recruit may already know.
3. Management relies too much on on-the-job training.
4. Planners too often rely on what they find to be the easiest training format—sales lecture.
5. There may be too much entertainment and not enough hard training.
6. Visual aids lack imagination.
7. Training may emphasize too much theory and inspiration and be weak on specific information for immediate use.
8. Salespeople sense a lack of management support.
9. Training is too often left to outside specialists.
10. Too little emphasis on buyer psychology.
11. Training budgets are inadequate.
12. Training is more company oriented than customer oriented.

Figure 9–3
Common Sales
Training Errors

Source: *Sales Manager's Bulletin*, National Sales Development Institute, No. 897 (May 30, 1976), pp. 10–11.

By defining objectives and consistently measuring the extent to which programs satisfy objectives, the firm can monitor the effectiveness of alternative training programs. If a new program is implemented, the firm can then objectively determine if it is better than preceding programs. Without such identification of objectives, effectiveness is subjectively determined by the sales manager. Sales manager bias or a change in sales managers will make consistent monitoring of effectiveness impossible.

Measuring Effectiveness

In addition to subjectively screening common errors in training, there are several methods for evaluating a program's effectiveness. They include opinion surveys, experimental evaluation, and written exams.

Opinion Survey.   Opinions should be sought from trainees and training supervisors. Although effectiveness of a program cannot specifically be calculated from an opinion survey, problems which may impact on effectiveness can be identified. Specifically, opinion surveys should be designed to determine attitudes of trainees and supervisors toward the method of instruction, knowledge and competence of the instructor, content of the program, length of training, training facilities, and training material. Trainees should also be asked to recommend possible changes in the training format and indicate the most helpful and most useless aspects of the program.

Responses to opinion surveys should be anonymous. Questionnaires should be completed at the end of each program and approximately six months after conclusion of the program. Table 9-1 presents a sample questionnaire which can be utilized upon conclusion of the program. Six months after conclusion of the program, management should administer another questionnaire which attempts to identify material that should have been included in the program in order to help salespeople handle their jobs more effectively. Management should wait six months so that salespeople will be in a better position to evaluate actual program content. Prior to this time they will not know enough about their job requirements to effectively assess program content.

Experimentation.   The best and possibly only method for quantitatively assessing training effectiveness is experimentation. Primarily utilized to measure effectiveness of retraining programs, experimentation attempts to identify cause and effect relationships. For example, a company may want to determine the extent to which a self-instruction cassette program affects sales volume. In order to show the effectiveness of the program the company would select two groups of salespeople. One group, the experimental group, would receive the cassette program and be required to use it during a designated week. Another group, the control group, would not receive the cassette program. Effectiveness of the program would be equal to change in the experimental group's sales volume minus change in the control group's sales volume. The control group is used to measure changes in sales volume which is attributed to factors other than the cassette training program (i.e., weather changes, economic changes, competitive changes, promotional changes, etc.). Figure 9-4 illustrates how effectiveness of such a program is measured.

Other experimental designs can be used to measure the effectiveness of numerous sales training programs. For example, experimentation could be used to determine which training method is most effective. Three groups could be employed—one experimental group would receive a cassette program, another experimental group would receive on-the-job training, and a control group would receive no training. Changes in sales for the three groups could be used to measure relative effectiveness of the programs.

Figure 9-4
Experimental
Design to Measure
the Effectiveness of
a Self-Instructional
Cassette Program

Experimental Group	Control Group
Measure Sales Volume (X_1)	Measure Sales Volume (Y_1)
Implement Cassette Program	No Cassette Program
Measure Sales Volume (X_2)	Measure Sales Volume (Y_2)
Determine Program Effectiveness $(X_2 - X_1) - (Y_2 - Y_1)$	

Table 9–1
Training Program Opinion Survey

A. How satisfied were you with:

	Very Satisfied	Satisfied	Indifferent	Dissatisfied	Very Dissatisfied
1. Opportunity for Personal Interaction With Other Participants	◡	◡	◡	◡	◡
2. Opportunity for Person Interaction with trainer(s)	◡	◡	◡	◡	◡
3. Meeting Room: Seating Arrangement	◡	◡	◡	◡	◡
4. Meeting Room: Seating Comfort	◡	◡	◡	◡	◡
5. Meeting Room: Lighting	◡	◡	◡	◡	◡
6. Meeting Room: Sound Equipment	◡	◡	◡	◡	◡
7. Length of the Training Program	◡	◡	◡	◡	◡
8. Workbooks and other Training Material	◡	◡	◡	◡	◡
9. Organization of the Training Program	◡	◡	◡	◡	◡

Comments: If you are dissatisfied with any aspect of the program, why?

B. Rate each trainer and speaker:

SPEAKER (Name)	Knowledge of Subject				Ability to Communicate				Overall Training Ability			
	Excellent	Good	Fair	Poor	Excellent	Good	Fair	Poor	Excellent	Good	Fair	Poor
	◡	◡	◡	◡	◡	◡	◡	◡	◡	◡	◡	◡
	◡	◡	◡	◡	◡	◡	◡	◡	◡	◡	◡	◡
	◡	◡	◡	◡	◡	◡	◡	◡	◡	◡	◡	◡

COMMENTS: _____

C. What is your opinion of training methods employed in the program. First, check the methods used. Second, for those methods checked, indicate your attitude toward the extent of their use.

Regardless of the specific experimental technique used or program studied, the following steps in experimentation must be employed:

1. Identify specific training programs to be studied.
2. Formulate a hypotheses about the effectiveness of the programs.
3. Construct an appropriate experimental design.
4. Formulate made-up results to insure that the problem can be solved with the design.
5. Check to make sure that results can be handled with appropriate statistical procedures.
6. Perform the experiment.
7. Apply statistical procedures.
8. Draw conclusions about the validity of the study and the effectiveness of training programs.[13]

This discussion is not designed to train one how to employ experimentation. There are numerous designs and procedures each having their own set of problems. At this point, simply understand the general procedure of experimentation and the fact that it is the best method for measuring effectiveness.

Written Exams.   Written exams are effective for measuring the extent to which product, market, company, and competitor information is learned. After training sessions which deal with these topics have been completed, an exam should be administered to each trainee. Scores can be used to determine how effective the sessions were at transfering this knowledge and to identify which salespeople need additional training. Composite scores can be maintained and studied over time to determine acceptable and unacceptable ranges of scores.

SUMMARY

Continuous training refers to the process of refining and developing new skills. Retraining involves teaching new sales techniques and new product information to experienced salespeople. Both procedures are a vital aspect of personal development and should be an integral part of any sales management program.

The objectives of continuous training are accomplished with on-the-job coaching, counseling, courses for self-instruction, workshops, university instruction, observation of senior salespeople, sales meetings, films, and journal articles. Although all of the techniques may be helpful, on-the-job coaching and counseling are the most effective. Coaching is carried out in the field by the sales manager and may be as simple as a casual suggestion, or it may be a significant part of formal performance review. Counseling involves meeting with salespeople to examine and solve any problems that may impact on performance.

Retraining is designed to instruct experienced salespeople on new techniques and product information. Although techniques and

[13]Adapted from Thomas C. Kinnear and James R. Taylor, *Marketing Research: An Applied Approach* (New York: McGraw-Hill Book Company, 1979).

procedures utilized in retraining are similar to initial training, retraining concentrates more on the interchange of ideas and salesperson input.

During and after implementation of the training program, program effectiveness should be evaluated. The major methods for measuring the effectiveness of training programs include opinion surveys, experimentation, and written exams.

QUESTIONS

1. Why should coaching be a two-way process?

2. How would retraining techniques differ from a salesperson's initial training?

3. Why are coaching and counseling more effective than other methods of continuous training?

4. What methods could be used to evaluate the effectiveness of the training program?

5. What are the objectives of continuous training?

6. In order to have effective on-the-job coaching, what should the sales supervisor do prior to working with the salesperson in the field?

7. Define "counseling" and discuss the advantages and disadvantages of counseling.

8. When is the best time for retraining to take place?

9. List the general procedure for evaluating training effectiveness.

10. What elements should be included in a coaching log?

Chapter 10 _____

Sales Force
Evaluation

After completing this chapter, you will be able to:

- Define performance evaluation and identify its importance to the sales organization.

- Identify the procedure for evaluating the performance of salespeople.

- Illustrate the utilization of quantitative and qualitative factors in the performance review process.

- Identify rules and procedures for effectively conducting an appraisal interview.

- Identify and illustrate procedures for evaluating organizational sales effort.

Managerial effectiveness is largely contingent upon one's ability to identify problems and make timely adjustments in strategy. In the sales organization, most potential problems are associated with personal sales activity. In order to operate effectively as a sales manager, therefore, one must utilize a system which monitors sales performance and alerts management of potential problem areas. In other words, the firm should have a **sales control mechanism** (i.e., a system for evaluating sales performance). As indicated in one study of salesperson effectiveness, salespeople should be "evaluated on their performance . . . and should be furnished constant feedback on how well they are meeting the organization's expectations."[1]

SALES FORCE EVALUATION DEFINED
_____

Performance evaluation involves a quantitative and qualitative assessment of deviations from performance standards with a view toward development of programs for improvement of salespeople. As indicated by the definitions, the sales manager first develops perform-

---

[1] Charles M. Futrell, John E. Swan, and John T. Todd, "Job Performance Related to Management Control Systems for Pharmaceutical Salesmen," *Journal of Marketing Research*, Vol. XIII (February, 1976), p. 31.

ance standards. The manager then allocates and directs salespeople toward accomplishment of standards. Both during and after implementation of the sales plan, the sales manager analyzes actual results relative to planned performance. Deviations from the plan are then accounted for in strategy development.

IMPORTANCE OF PERFORMANCE REVIEW

Studies have consistently shown that 50 to 75 percent of business firms have formal systems for evaluating employees.[2] Firms that conscientiously maintain performance control procedures will realize benefits that are associated with this significant management function. First, salesperson problems can be quickly identified and monitored. Second, performance review can be one of the firm's most effective motivational tools. If the sales manager monitors performance, problems can be identified and corrected before motivation is adversely affected. Third, deviations from performance goals can aid in development and administration of a compensation plan. Fourth, performance appraisal can help the sales manager identify appropriate training programs for various salespeople. Fifth, objective review can be utilized to justify the promotion or termination of salespeople. Unfortunately, some firms do not realize the full benefits of performance review because of flaws in their review procedure. Figure 10–1 lists some of the mistakes commonly associated with performance review.

PROCEDURE FOR EVALUATING PERFORMANCE

An objective and precise procedure for evaluating performance should be established by management to insure that each salesperson is evaluated on merit and not favoritism. The procedure should also insure that each salesperson is evaluated by the same methods and criteria as every other salesperson. See Figure 10–2 for a summary of rules of performance evaluation.

The following represents an outline of steps designed to obtain an objective appraisal of salesperson performance.

1. Precisely define each salesperson's duties and responsibilities. Before salespeople can legitimately be evaluated, they must understand what is expected by management. They must be aware of their duties and responsibilities as well as the function and scope of their job.
2. Clearly define corporate and territorial sales objectives. Corporate objectives serve as a basis for evaluating overall company performance while territorial goals are utilized to evaluate regional, district,

---

[2] Kenneth J. Lacho, G. Kent Stearns, and Maurice F. Villere, "Employee Performance Appraisal Practices in New Orleans," *Louisiana Business Survey*, Vol. 10 (January, 1979), pp. 2–3.

Figure 10–1
Common Mistakes
in Performance
Review

1. Putting too much emphasis on criticizing for poor performance rather than focusing attention on programs to improve future performance.
2. Selecting measurement standards that are not related to the corresponding activity.
3. Failing to be objective in the assessment of performance.
4. Giving a good or bad rating on factors that are not controllable by the salesperson.
5. Allowing length of service to effect assessment of performance.
6. Letting the influence of previous ratings impact on current rating.
7. Failing to recognize that even an excellent salesperson can improve certain areas of performance.
8. Allowing personal feelings about a salesperson's attitude and work habits to affect objective assessment of performance.
9. Expecting too much from the appraisal program. Salesperson development requires long term program implementation.
10. Selecting too few or too many factors upon which to evaluate performance. Evaluation of too many factors complicates evaluation and reduces the influence of critical factors.

Source: Adapted from: Charles L. Lapp and Jack Dauner, *How to Plan an Evaluation Program,* Part Two (A Special Dartnell Sales and Marketing Feature), p. 8.

Figure 10–2
Rules of
Performance
Evaluation

1. Every superior should formally and informally evaluate performance of subordinates.
2. Evaluation of a salesperson's performance can serve as a basis for promotion.
3. Standards must be established in order to effectively measure performance.
4. Avoid pseudo-psychological methods of evaluating the performance of salespeople.
5. Do not allow personal biases to replace objective evaluation when assessing performance.
6. Make sure that differences in territory characteristics are reflected in the evaluation procedure.
7. Maintain a file of critical performance indices that are observed during day-to-day evaluation.
8. Evaluation should be an on-going process. Interpersonal reviews should take place semi-annually or annually.
9. Performance evaluation should serve as the basis for program development.
10. An appraisal interview should be conducted individually with each salesperson. Two-way communication should be encouraged during the interview.
11. Salespeople should be trained to welcome evaluations as an opportunity to learn and improve.

Source: Adapted from: Charles L. Lapp and Jack Dauner, *How to Plan an Evaluation Program,* Part Two (Dartnell), pp. 8–9.

and salesperson performance. Examples of these goals may include the following: increase total dollar sales volume by 12 percent; increase number of new accounts by 5 percent; increase average sales per call by 10 percent. Management should also establish other quantitative objectives for the sales force that relate to performance.

3. Identify qualitative objectives that salespeople are expected to achieve during a specified time period. Such qualitative objectives might include: increase the number of sales calls per day by developing more efficient routing plans; develop more effective methods of planning and preparing for sales calls; make better use of sales aids furnished by the company.

4. Measure performance. Measurement of quantitative performance can be facilitated with evaluation forms and reports. For qualitative factors, a rating scale for each factor must be established.

5. Compare actual performance to objectives.

6. Develop programs to correct performance problems.

Please see Appendix A for an example of a performance evaluation and Appendix B for an example of a coaching log for performance evaluations.

PERFORMANCE CRITERIA

Figure 10–3 outlines the primary criteria that can be utilized to evaluate salesperson performance. These standards for control are divided into two catagories, quantitative criteria and qualitative criteria.

Quantitative Criteria

Quantitative performance standards provide management with an effective tool for quickly responding to the needs of salespeople. When sales volume or profits do not meet anticipated levels, the sales manager can review quantitative indicators to identify reasons for suboptimum performance. Development of new business may be off, the number of lost accounts may be too high, expenses as a percent of sales may be too high, the number of calls necessary to make a sale may be too high, or any number of other factors may contribute to the problem. Once the problem is pinpointed, the sales manager can then focus attention on the precise activity and attempt to develop a corrective program.

As indicated in Table 10–1 on page 225, John Jones has continued to develop new business. Although his sales have grown, there is also an indication that Jones has lost some accounts that are more profitable than the new accounts. Specifically, his sales have increased by $60,000 while his expenses have increased by $50,000 and profit has only increased by $10,000. He has developed five new customers and lost five existing customers. This has resulted in a decline in "net profit as a percent of sales" from 12.6 percent to 8 percent.

While reporting procedures and performance criteria are established

Quantitative Criteria

Dollar Sales Volume . . . . Unit sales volume as a percent of
number of sales calls.
Unit Sales Volume . . . . Expenses as a percent of sales.
Sales by Product . . . . Travel time to selling time.
Sales by Customer Class . . . . Cost per sale.
Sales Volume as a Percent of
Market Potential . . . . Gross margin by product.
Sales Volume as a Percent of
Quota . . . . Gross margin by customer class.
Number of New Accounts and   Change from previous years' sales
Number of Lost Accounts . . . . volume and gross profit.
Number of Cancelled Orders . . . . . Number of customer complaints.

Qualitative Criteria

Knowledge of product characteristics and application.
Knowledge of price structure, competitive prices, distribution, network,
promotional programs, and company philosophy.
Ability to prospect, make a presentation, handle objections, and close.
Ability to handle customer complaints and problems.
Use of sales aids.
Skill in using the telephone.
Utilization of written correspondence.
Personal characteristics such as appearance, independence, ability to
assume responsibility, aggressiveness, initiative, listening habits, verbal
communications, sincerity, enthusiasm, health, self-confidence, and
family life.

Figure 10–3
Performance
Criteria

by the national sales manager and staff, quantitative information on salesperson performance is normally gathered, organized, and evaluated by the first-line sales manager. Summary data on sales volume, gross margin, and sales expenses are then submitted to higher level sales managers for their evaluation and review.

Gathering of quantitative information is facilitated by the utilization of activity reports. Although there are numerous reports that can be utilized by management, three reports will generally provide most of the information needed by management (See Figure 10–4 on page 226 for a nomprehensive list of possible reports). First, the Call Report shows the name, location, and classification of each company contacted by the salesperson. It also shows the details of any conversation, the results of an interview, and notations concerning future steps to be taken. It may also specify the time of each call. This report gives the sales manager insight into the salesperson's ability to route calls, effectively manage time, and develop account priorities.

A second common report is the Expense Report. It details all expenses associated with sales activity and serves as the basis for expense reimbursement and expense-to-sales evaluation. It also aids in

	Past Years	Past Years—Year-to-Date
Total Sales	$250,000	$190,000
Product A	$150,000	$110,000
Product B	$100,000	$ 80,000
Customer A	$140,000	$100,000
Customer B	$110,000	$ 90,000
Number of orders	200	190
Sales per order	$ 1,250	$ 1,000
Total quota	$400,000	$350,000
Sales as a percent of quota	62.5%	54.2%
Market potential	$1,000,000	$950,000
Sales as a percent of market potential	25%	20%
Gross profit	$ 50,000	$ 40,000
Gross profit as a percent of sales	20%	21%
Total expenses	$200,000	$150,000
Expenses as a percent of sales	80%	78.9%
Net profit	$ 20,000	$ 24,000
Net profit as a percent of sales	8%	12.6%
Number of new accounts	20	15
Number of lost accounts	10	5
Number of cancelled orders	40	30

Table 10–1
Analysis of
Performance: John
Jones

the assessment of each salesperson's contribution to profit. Some accounts may contribute more to expenses than sales and, therefore, be unprofitable. These accounts should possibly be eliminated.

Finally, the Itinerary and Hotel/Motel Routing Report shows evidence of call planning for a given period and informs management where the person can be reached at various times of the day. Many companies require both a daily and weekly itinerary routing report.

Qualitative Criteria

Qualitative factors are continuously evaluated in order to identify reasons for suboptimum performance. While quantitative factors may indicate problem areas, qualitative factors suggest ways that problems can be alleviated. A salesperson may have family problems, lack of confidence, or little imagination relative to product applications. There are numerous factors that can be monitored and improved upon if the sales manager takes a sincere interest in the needs of his or her salespeople.

In addition to the identification of ways in which salespeople may improve, qualitative analysis forces management to be truly interested in the sales force as individuals with unique desires, needs, and problems. The sales manager develops a better understanding of the

Call Report — Shows name, address, and classification of prospects and customers.

Expense Report — Details all selling expenses.

Itinerary and Hotel/Motel Routing Report — Daily and weekly call and travel plan.

Credit Information Report — Credit information on new customer or potential customer.

First Contact Qualifying Report — Details company name, address, type of business, types of products used, name of buyer and influential decision makers, present source of supply, and special hours for interviews.

Lost Order and/or Customer Report — Name of lost customer, why customer was lost, and name of new supplier.

Competitive Activity Report — New products in the market, promotional campaigns of competitors, changes in competitors' personnel and programs.

General Economic Report — Changes in market place affecting product demand, customer purchasing power, and customer credit needs.

Special Event Report — Results and costs of trade shows, fairs, conventions, etc.

Figure 10–4
Alternative Sales
Reports

Product Specification Report — Details customer specifications for raw materials or special formula (i.e., chemical, plastics, paper, and food industries).

Customer Complaint Report — Nature of and reasons for complaints.

unique motivations of each salesperson and, therefore, is in a better position to develop effective, personalized incentive programs.

Qualitative analysis should be performed at least once a year for senior salespeople and once every six months for new recruits. It should be a formal, individualized review performed at a location away from office interruptions. The evaluation should be performed by the first line sales manager that works with the salespeople and should focus on programs for improvement rather than salesperson problems. Additional information on the appraisal interview follows in a separate section.

In order to insure consistency and completeness in the evaluation of each salesperson, a formal questionnaire should be developed and utilized. The questionnaire should include questions which measure the sales manager's attitude toward each important performance attribute of salespeople. For example, relative to enthusiasm, the sales manager may use the following four point rating scale:

( ) Extremely enthusiastic.
( ) Somewhat enthusiastic.
( ) Lacks enthusiasm—may be apparent to customer.
( ) Extremely unenthusiastic—definitely apparent to customer.
COMMENTS: _____
ACTION TO BE TAKEN: _____

A similarly designed scale should also be used for other factors such as dress, prospecting skills, closing techniques, and ability to handle complaints. In addition to rating each salesperson on these factors, the sales manager should also make comments about deficiencies and strengths, and suggest possible reasons for problems. There should also be a section for development of an action plan as suggested by the findings. Some firms also provide a space to put the previous year's score and past recommendations for improvement.

Appraisal Interview

In addition to being responsible for quantitatively and qualitatively evaluating salesperson performance, the sales manager must also personally communicate the results of this evaluation to each salesperson. The interpersonal communication of performance data is referred to as the **appraisal interview**. The primary objectives of the interview are to strengthen the association between each salesperson and the sales manager, to better understand reasons underlying each salesperson's performance, and to outline a personal improvement plan for each salesperson.

An appraisal interview should be conducted every time salespeople are evaluated. A separate two to four hour interview should be conducted for each salesperson. In preparing for each interview the sales manager should select a remote location, allow enough time to complete the appraisal, and develop an understanding of the salesperson's strengths, weaknesses, and potential for improvement. The sales manager should also develop an action plan and a time schedule for implementing the plan. In fact, the interview should be positive in nature. It should emphasize the salesperson's strengths and focus on programs for improving weaknesses. Other suggestions for the appraisal interview are presented in Figure 10–5.

1. Prepare an agenda, study the salesperson's problems and strengths, set interview objectives, and listen carefully to salesperson's ideas.
2. Be emphatic and understanding—do not pass judgment prematurely.
3. Emphasize that it is a learning session.
4. Frequently summarize ideas discussed in the meeting.
5. Try to get the salesperson to understand weaknesses and agree that action needs to be taken.
6. Allow flexibility in the action plan so that the salesperson can help in its development.
7. Do not lecture or attack the salesperson—facilitate understanding.
8. Let the salesperson help establish priorities and a plan of action.
9. Monitor the salesperson's activities after the interview to insure implementation of the action plan.

Figure 10–5
The Appraisal Interview

A Company Profile

Zoecon Industries was formed in 1948 by two DuPont chemists who wanted to supply ranchers and feed lots with high quality, state-of-the-art, non-crop pest control products. From its beginning as a small, garage operation, Zoecon has grown into a $50 million wholly-owned subsidiary of Occidental Petroleum. The company's growth has not only been impressive, but it has been manageable, with a two-fold expansion in sales volume every three or four years.

A significant portion of Zoecon's growth can be attributed to the identification and penetration of high potential market segments. After identifying markets, the company has developed products that require similar technologies to the ones employed to meet the needs of large animal markets. This strategy has resulted in the establishment of three divisions: large animal sales, specialty pet sales, and consumer sales.

Zoecon's Large Animal Division, Star Bar, dominates the non-crop pest control industry with approximately 50 to 80 percent share of the market. The division employs eight salespeople and two distribution channels. Three of the salespeople call on distributors that sell directly to feedlots, and five of the salespeople call on distributors that sell to dealers who service ranchers.

Zoecon's Specialty Pet Division focuses on the veterinarian and pet shop markets. Five salespeople are employed to service distributors who sell directly to veterinarians, and five salespeople call on distributors who supply pet shops.

The Consumer Division consists of five salespeople who sell to mass market retailers through brokers and distributors, and one national accounts salesperson who devel-

ops co-manufacturing arrangements with other non-crop pest control product manufacturers.

Since Zoecon's channels of distribution consist of distributors, the primary focus of the company's sales and marketing programs is to support these important intermediaries. In fact, it targets promotions, conducts contests, and focuses sales effort on the distributors' salespeople. They are Zoecon's primary customers, and are considered in most of the company's marketing decisions.

In order to maintain an awareness of the productivity of its marketing employees, Zoecon employs an annual performance evaluation of its salespeople and managers. The objectives of performance review are to (1) establish performance goals for the following year, (2) identify activities that may help the salesperson's chances of being promoted and (3) discuss ideas about the company and where the company is going. Overall, Zoecon is genuinely sensitive to motivational implications of performance review. The review is, therefore, not only designed to measure achievement of goals, but also to help salespeople improve performance and, hence, succeed.

Performance review begins with the development of a job description which details activities salespeople are expected to perform. The second step in assessing performance is to establish financial and nonfinancial objectives for each salesperson. Financial objectives utilized by management to assess performance are sales by distributor, package size, product, and month. Actual sales are then compared to target sales to arrive at a quantitative performance index.

Nonfinancial objectives relate to such factors as organization, quantity of work, quality of work, dependability, working relationship with peers, forecasting accuracy, product and distribution knowledge, ability to transfer knowledge to others, ability to identify problems and opportunities, initiative, and listening skills. The rating scale utilized to evaluate the extent to which salespeople meet performance indices is as follows: (1) distinguished performance, (2) superior performance, (3) good performance, (4) needs development, and (5) unacceptable performance.

The next step in performance review is completion of the performance rating form. The form is completed by both the salesperson and the salesperson's immediate supervisor. By having both people fill it out, any discrepancies in perception can be identified and discussed. If the salesperson and sales manager cannot resolve the conflict, a third party may intervene.

Finally, the financial and nonfinancial indices are weighted evenly, and an overall performance index is calculated. For example, if a salesperson receives a "superior" rating on financial objectives and a "needs development" rating on nonfinancial objectives, the overall rating is "good". If the supervisor identifies areas that need improvement, he or she will then develop a plan for correcting the situation. This evaluation system is an important aspect of Zoecon's plan to maintain dominance in some markets and become a leader in new, fast-growing markets.

EVALUATING TOTAL SALES PERFORMANCE

Performance review of each salesperson is normally organized and implemented by sales managers at the local or regional level. Each salesperson is evaluated in order to identify strengths, weaknesses, and potential programs for improving performance. The objective of an evaluation of the total sales organization is similar to the review of individual salespeople. The firm's performance is analyzed to identify weaknesses and strengths with a view toward development of programs for improving the firm's status. In fact, overall performance can be envisioned as a composite of the performance of individual salespeople. The most common indicators used for evaluating corporate sales performance are total sales volume, sales by territory, sales by product, sales by customer category, and gross margin.

Total Sales Volume

The most common basis for evaluating performance of the sales organization is total sales volume. Although it is not the most accurate measure of performance, it is an excellent indicator of existing and potential problems. An actual sales volume that is lower than expectations is symptomatic of a problem in the organization. It tells management to examine various operating divisions in order to locate problems that are reflected in the inadequate sales reading.

Table 10–2 shows performance evaluation by sales volume. Sales volume is compared to the sales objective to identify the extent to which the firm is realizing expectations. Volume is also compared to total industry volume to identify the firm's market share. Yearly trends are also identified in order to give additional meaning to current sales levels. The firm depicted in Table 10–2 has realized fairly steady growth and has normally met sales objectives. In 1982, however, company productivity has declined while industry potential is increasing.

	Sales Volume ($Million)	Sales Objective ($Million)	Sales/ Objective	Industry Volume ($Million)	Market Share
Year to Date (1982)	2.0	2.8	71.4%	29	6.9%
Year to Date (1981)	2.2	2.3	95.7	26	8.5
1981	6.5	6.4	101.6	68	9.6
1980	5.9	5.7	103.5	65	9.1
1979	4.9	4.2	116.7	52	9.4
1978	3.5	3.6	97.2	40	8.8
1977	3.0	3.0	100.0	31	9.7

Table 10–2
XYZ Company Performance: by Sales Volume

The weakness associated with performance evaluation by sales volume is illustrated in the example of XYZ Company. Although problems began to emerge in 1982, it is impossible to specifically identify the source of the problem with aggregate sales figures. In order to more precisely isolate specific problems, additional sales analysis should be performed by territory, product, and customer category.

Sales by Territory

Analysis of sales territory enables the national sales manager to identify problems with the sales volume of each geographic area and, in some cases, reasons for the problems. An evaluation of three territories is presented in Table 10–3. Although significant problems are evident in territory A, there are also problems developing in territories B and C. In territory A market share declined from 8.3 percent during the first four months of 1981 to 5.9 percent during the first four months of 1982. Also, total industry volume declined from $9.6 million to $8.5 million.

Although market share in territories B and C also declined during the same periods, total industry volume increased slightly. This territorial analysis initially suggests that 2 problems may exist. First, the company's overall marketing program is not keeping pace with competitive programs. Marketing problems are particularly evident in territory A. Second, some products may be in the saturation or early decline stage of the product life cycle. Industry volume in territory A has already reached the saturation point and territories B and C may be saturated in the next

Territory A	Sales Volume ($Million)	Sales Objective ($Million)	Sales/ Objective	Industry Volume ($Million)	Market Share
Year to Date (1982)	.5	1.0	50.0%	8.5	5.9%
Year to Date (1981)	.8	.8	100.0	9.6	8.3
1981	2.1	2.0	105.0	22.4	9.4
1980	1.9	1.7	111.8	22.2	8.6
Territory B					
Year to Date (1982)	.7	.9	77.8%	10.2	6.9%
Year to Date (1981)	.7	.8	87.5	8.3	8.4
1981	2.2	2.3	95.7	22.7	9.7
1980	2.0	1.9	105.3	21.4	9.3
Territory C					
Year to Date (1982)	.8	.9	88.9%	10.3	7.8%
Year to Date (1981)	.7	.6	116.7	8.1	8.6
1981	2.2	2.1	104.8	22.9	9.6
1980	2.0	2.1	95.2	21.4	9.3

Table 10-3
XYZ Company
Performance: by
Territory

year or two. In order to further identify specific problems, the XYZ Company may find it helpful to analyze sales performance by product.

Sales By Product

As evidenced by the preceding discussion, corporate sales performance evaluation goes from a general (aggregate) appraisal to a more specific analysis. The XYZ Company obviously has some problems with their marketing programs, as shown by total sales figures, and possibly has some problems with the market potential of their product lines.

The sales analysis by product that is presented in Table 10-4 provides XYZ Company with some insight into this problem. Market share for product line A has declined from 8.6 percent to 6.2 percent and market share for product line B has declined from 8.3 percent to 7.5 percent, thus lending further support to the theory that marketing programs are inadequate. Also, industry sales volume of product A declined from $14 million during the first four months of 1981 to $13 million during the first four months of 1982, thus indicating that product A may well be in the late maturity or early decline stage of the product life cycle.

Product Line A	Sales Volume ($Million)	Sales Objec- tives ($Million)	Sales/ Objective	Industry Volume ($Million)	Market Share
Year to Date (1982)	.8	1.5	53.3%	13	6.2%
Year to Date (1981)	1.2	1.3	92.3	14	8.6
1981	3.5	3.6	97.2	37	9.5
1980	3.3	3.0	110.0	36	9.2
Product Line B					
Year to Date (1982)	1.2	1.3	92.3%	16	7.5%
Year to Date (1981)	1.0	1.0	100.0	12	8.3
1981	3.0	2.8	107.1	31	9.7
1980	2.6	2.7	96.3	29	9.0

Table 10–4
XYZ Company
Performance: by
Product Line

Sales by Customer

Additional analysis can be performed to identify sales problems associated with customer groups. Customers may be divided and analyzed according to standard industrial classification, key account status, number of employees, or any number of other critera. After customers are classified, analysis proceeds as was illustrated in the preceding sections on territory analysis and product analysis.

Evaluation of sales by customer provides insight into the effectiveness of resource allocation programs. If sales management exercises little control over the allocation of salespeople to individual customers and customer categories, it is possible that some customers may be neglected. Salespeople oftentimes utilize very unscientific criteria for establishing a call plan (i.e., they may only call on customers with which they are familiar). It is the sales manager's responsibility to monitor penetration of each customer category and redirect sales effort when sales potential is not being realized.

One final word of caution is in order. Our discussion has focused on the firm's *dollar sales* figure, whether by territory, product, or customer. In times of rising prices, rising dollar sales figures may be misleading, for *unit sales* may actually be falling. Therefore, it is up to the sales manager to monitor unit sales as well as dollar sales. Such information can be invaluable to production and marketing planning.

Distribution Cost Analysis

In addition to evaluating revenue information, the sales manager should also examine attendant costs. Although a territory, product, or customer may generate significant sales volume, revenue gains may be more than offset by excessive sales and maintenance costs. These costs should be evaulated for each market segment and product to determine the extent to which sales efforts contribute to profits or losses. If costs associated with selling more are high enough, it is possible that a firm could sell itself into bankruptcy.

Specific questions that can be answered with distribution cost analysis are as follows:

1. How much money does it cost to sell a specific product or product group?
2. How much does it cost to sell to customers located in each territory?
3. How much does it cost to sell commercial accounts and industrial accounts?
4. How much are territory costs of each salesperson?
5. How much does it cost to sell one order size as contrasted to other order sizes?

Distribution cost analysis enables one to make an assessment of the profitability of areas, customers, products, and orders. A firm may realize an annual profit but have several unprofitable customers. Large customers, for example, may demand excessive price discounts on large orders or may require numerous, costly support services such as special displays, advertising allowances, and frequent contact with salespeople. In other instances, small customers may be unprofitable because too much advertising and sales effort are concentrated on securing and maintaining their business. In one case it was determined that 54 percent of salesperson time was spent on customers that accounted for 8 percent of total sales. Also, 44 percent of the orders obtained from these small customers were made at a loss. The firm should either raise prices on small orders, only handle such orders over the telephone, or let competitors have the accounts.

Basis for Distributing Costs.   There are numerous ways that costs can be divided and analyzed. Some firms simply divide costs into two groups: (1) costs associated with obtaining orders, and (2) costs associated with filling orders. Other firms utilize a more detailed breakdown of costs into the following categories:

- Direct selling expenses (i.e., compensation and travel expenses of salespeople).

- Advertising and sales promotion expense.

- Delivery expense.

- Warehousing and handling expense.

- Credit and collection expense.

- Financial expense.

- General distribution expense (administrative expenses not included in other categories).

A breakdown of costs and methods for allocating costs are presented in Figure 10–6.

Figure 10–6
Distribution Costs
and Bases of
Allocation

Functional Cost Group	Basis of Allocation
Outside Selling:	
Personnel Cost (consumers, etc.)	Dollar sales
Travel and auto costs	Call- miles
Sales Supervision	Calls
Sales Call Reports	
Sales Records (order review, traffic, postage, and stationery for invoices)	
Accounts receivable posting	Orders
Invoice Typing (personnel costs, etc.)	Orders × 3 plus invoice lines
Credit Authorization	
Credit manager, etc.	Per customer
Bad Debts	Direct
Collection	Direct
Accounts Receivable — Interest on borrowed funds	Average Balance
Advertising	Direct
Finished goods storage	
(Interest on borrowed funds)	Average inventory value
(Space costs)	Space - sq. ft.
Packing - (supplies)	Direct
Packing, Trucking, Supervision	No. of units sold × handling unit

Source: Adapted from Longman and Schiff, *Practical Distribution Cost Analysis* (Homewood, Ill.: Richard D. Irwin, Inc., 1955).

As indicated previously, each cost can also be allocated to various territories, products, and customer groups. Table 10–5 shows a distribution of costs to XYZ Company's two product lines. When comparing these costs to revenue, the firm can determine which products contribute to profit. Although product A does not contribute to profit, the decision to drop the product cannot be automatically determined from the financial data. There are several reasons why a firm may decide to keep an unprofitable product. First, it may be needed to complete a line. Since many customers like to buy all of their requirements from one supplier, a company may carry unprofitable products in order to sell their profitable items. Second, the product may be needed simply

	Product A	Product B
Revenue	$3,500,000	$3,000,000
Cost of Goods Sold	−2,700,000	−1,300,000
Gross Margin	$ 800,000	$1,700,000
Expenses:		
Direct Labor	50,000	70,000
Sales Commissions	350,000	300,000
Administrative Expense	80,000	65,000
Advertising	20,000	19,000
Packaging	50,000	-0-
Misc. Selling Expense	100,000	95,000
Allocated Overhead	150,000	150,000
Total Expenses	$ 800,000	$ 699,000
Contribution to Profit	-0-	1,001,000

Table 10–5
Cost Analysis for
XYZ Company (By
product line)

because competition has a similar product available. Third, the unprofitable item may be contributing to overhead and hence justify its retention.

Obtaining Salesperson Support. Although the financial division will actually collect and analyze cost information, salespeople and sales management are responsible for controlling selling costs. The firm must, therefore, educate sales personnel on the importance of controlling costs, set cost limits for various selling activities, and establish a compensation system that rewards people for profit contribution rather than sales volume.

SUMMARY

The sales manager is primarily responsible for evaluating performance of the sales force. Evaluation of salespeople is accomplished through both a quantitative and qualitative performance review. Quantitative review involves an analysis of each salesperson's sales volume, gross margin, expenses, and change in performance. The sales manager may also examine sales volume and gross margin by product, by customer, and as a percent of market potential. Qualitative criteria for measuring performance include the salesperson's (1) knowledge of product characteristics, product applications, price structure, competitive practices, distribution program, and promotional program, (2) ability to sell, (3) ability to handle complaints, and (4) use of sales aids.

The sales manager is also responsible for evaluating performance of the sales organization. Evaluation criteria for appraising the overall health of the sales group include total sales volume, sales by territory, sales by customer, sales by product, and profit contribution.

QUESTIONS

1. What benefits result from performance review of salespeople?

2. How is the definition of corporate and territorial objectives of use in performance evaluation?

3. Qualitative factors are difficult to evaluate without bias; emphasis must be placed on evaluation of quantitative performance criteria. Support your opinion of the statement.

4. How can the sales manager insure that the appraisal interview will be positive in nature?

5. What benefit is evaluation of sales by customer?

6. What could result from the lack of distribution cost analysis?

7. Is there justification for continuing to carry an unprofitable product?

8. Should results from a salesperson's performance evaluation be used as a basis for promotion?

9. How can information from alternative sales reports be used by management in performance review?

10. Which figures should be analyzed in the evaluation of corporate sales performance?

APPENDIX A
Targets for Year and Performance Evaluation

		VOLUME	MARGIN
Dollar Sales Volume and Margin by Period	P-1	$ _____	$ _____
	P-2	_____	_____
	P-3	_____	_____
	P-4	_____	_____

	VOLUME	MARGIN
Dollar Sales Volume and Margin by Market	$ _____	$ _____
Markets		
_____	_____	_____
_____	_____	_____
_____	_____	_____
_____	_____	_____

	VOLUME	MARGIN
Dollar Sales by Product	$ _____	$ _____
Products		
_____	_____	_____
_____	_____	_____
_____	_____	_____
_____	_____	_____
_____	_____	_____

		VOLUME	MARGIN
Total Sales Volume and Margin by Period	P-1	$ _____	$ _____
(New Customers)	P-2	_____	_____
	P-3	_____	_____
	P-4	_____	_____
Number of New Accounts		_____	_____

PART I: EVALUATION QUESTIONS

Product Knowledge (Characteristics):
4 — Extremely knowledgeable of product characteristics—Can handle all customer questions and problems.
3 — Knowledgeable of most product areas—sometimes not sure of product problems and characteristics.
2 — Has some problem with product characteristics.
1 — Unable to handle product-oriented questions and problems.

New Product Applications (Identifying New Product Areas):
4 — Keenly aware of product application—always looking for new product possibilities for existing customers.
3 — Somewhat aware of new product applications.

2 — Not very aware of new product applications; for the most part stays with existing product lines and applications.

1 — Not at all sensitive to new product applications—sticks with existing products.

Knowledge of Price Structure and Methods:

4 — Completely confident in development of adequate price. Totally understands what the role of price is and should be.

3 — For the most part is confident and understands pricing procedure but periodically shows signs of inadequate confidence and misuses price.

2 — Is not real confident in techniques for handling pricing problems— needs assistance.

1 — Totally lacks confidence in pricing—does not understand its role in selling.

Knowledge of Competitors and Their Programs:

4 — Has a complete understanding of direct and indirect competitors' programs, prices, philosophies, product characteristics, customer bases, strengths and weaknesses.

3 — Has a general understanding of competition but does not have understanding of the specifics.

2 — Not a real good understanding of competition.

1 — Inadequate understanding—unaware of some competitors and their programs.

Understanding and Application of Company's Business Philosophy:

4 — Understands our business orientation and applies it in daily activities.

3 — Understands the philosophy but periodically misapplies the concepts.

2 — Does not completely understand nor apply philosophical concepts of our company. However, there is some understanding.

1 — No understanding or application of business concepts.

Identification of Potential Prospects:

4 — Consistently looking for and developing potential customers.

3 — Generally looks for new prospects but is limited in use of potential sources.

2 — Not very effective at finding new prospects.

1 — Not at all effective at developing new prospect lists.

Knowledge of Prospective Prospect:

4 — Completely briefed on potential customer's business before making contact.

3 — Aware of most aspects of potential customer's business.

2 — Not very aware of customer's business.

1 — Needs significantly more info on potential customers.

Ability to Make a Presentation:

4 — Presentations always meet standards of an effective presentation. There is no apparent need for improvement.

3 — Periodically there are problems with his ability to make a presentation. Only slight improvement is necessary.

2 — Ability to make a presentation is not very good. Several areas need improving.

1 — Presentations are not acceptable. There are numerous problems that must be worked out.

Ability to Handle Objections:

4 — Excellent technique and positive customer response to objection handling.

3 — Good technique but sometimes experiences problems with overcoming objections.

2 — Has problems with technique as well as ability to handle and overcome objections.

1 — Does not attempt to handle most objections and either has poor technique or exhibits no technique.

Ability to Close:

4 — Excellent closer—timing and technique is near perfect.

3 — Good closer but periodically does not identify appropriate times to close.

2 — Technique and timing needs some improvement. Misses or does not effectively take advantage of opportunities.

1 — Needs significant improvement.

Handle Customer Complaints:

4 — Always sensitive to customer problems and effectively neutralizes complaints.

3 — Usually is sensitive to customer problems.

2 — Sometimes handles complaints effectively.

1 — Seldom handles complaints effectively.

Use of Sales Aids:

4 — Innovatively utilizes sales aids to present ideas to customers.

3 — Uses standard sales aids but adds nothing unique to presentations.

2 — Does not always use company sales aids.

1 — Seldom, if ever, utilizes sales aids.

Skill in Utilizing the Telephone:

4 — Has excellent telephone skills.

3 — Has good telephone skills but could use some improvement.

2 — Fair telephone skills but needs major help in several areas.

1 — Poor telephone skills—needs extensive training in the area.

Utilization of Written Correspondence:

4 — Excellent writing skills plus uses correspondence at appropriate times.

3 — Good writing skills and usually uses written correspondence at appropriate times (could use help in one of the areas though).

2 — Fair writing skills and does not take advantage of opportunities for corresponderce (both areas need some help).

1 — Needs significant amount of help in writing memos and letters.

Appearance:
4 — Always dresses professionally—looks like the successful salesperson that the client wants to deal with.
3 — Appearance is good.
2 — Appearance fair.
1 — Poor appearance.

Organization:
4 — Excellent.
3 — Good.
2 — Fair.
1 — Poor.

Reporting:
4 — Always submits reports on time.
3 — Usually submits reports on time.
2 — Seldom submits reports on time.
1 — Never submits reports on time.

Aggressive:
4 — Always asserts himself well in identifying as well as developing new accounts.
3 — Usually asserts himself.
2 — Seldom assertive.
1 — Never assertive.

Listening Habits:
4 — Always listening well and accurately interprets verbal communication.
3 — Normally listens but sometimes misinterprets relatively simple communication.
2 — Frequently does not listen and understand verbal communication.
1 — Poor listener—needs help.

Responsibility:
4 — Extremely responsible for managing existing and new accounts.
3 — Somewhat responsible.
2 — Not very responsible.
1 — Not at all responsible—irresponsible.

Verbal Communication:
4 — Excellent verbal skills—extremely articulate.
3 — Good verbal skills; sometimes has trouble developing thoughts.
2 — Fair verbal skills.
1 — Poor verbal skills.

Sincerity:
4 — Always appears to be sincere and genuine.
3 — Sometimes comes across as being insincere.
2 — Often is perceived as being insincere with customer.
1 — His obvious insincerity is easy to detect and creates a credibility problem with customers.

Enthusiasm:
4 — Extremely enthusiastic; gets others excited with his enthusiasm.
3 — Somewhat enthusiastic.
2 — Not very enthusiastic.
1 — Not at all enthusiastic.

Organization:
4 — Extremely organized in all aspects of work situation.
3 — Lacks some organization in a few areas of his work.
2 — Not too organized—needs periodic help in organizing himself.
1 — Not at all organized—always needs help in organizing himself.

Self-Confidence:
4 — Self-confident in all selling or management activity.
3 — Generally self-confident but exhibits some uncertainty.
2 — Not very self-confident. In fact, is sometimes negative about his abilities.
1 — Poor self-confidence—extremely negative about personal abilities.

PART II: ACTION PLAN FOR IMPROVEMENT

Areas Requiring Improvement	Person Responsible	Action Plan	When Accomplished?

PART III: SALES PERSON'S FUTURE ASPIRATIONS:

_____

_____

_____

_____

APPENDIX B
Coaching Log—In Field Analysis of Performance

Salesperson: _____ Customer: _____

Date: _____ Location: _____

PRE-CARE PLANNING	YES	NO	NOT APPLICABLE
● Has information about customer before call?	____	____	____
● Appointment made in advance?	____	____	____
● Understands objectives of the call?	____	____	____

Comments: _____
_____
_____
_____
_____

PRESENTATION	YES	NO	NOT APPLICABLE
● Concise and to the point?	____	____	____
● Restates important ideas that were not understood by customer?	____	____	____
● Preapproach-general discussion about things the customer is interested in?	____	____	____
● Identifies customer's procedures and general attitudes toward our concept before making presentation?	____	____	____
● Maintains control of the interview through questioning; changing focus on conversation, etc?	____	____	____
● Attends to nonverbal signals?	____	____	____
● Adjusts speed of presentation to client's listening habits and abilities?	____	____	____
● Told the customer why he should buy our products?	____	____	____

	YES	NO	NOT APPLICABLE
• Showed a sincere interest in the customer?	___	___	___
• Used customer's name before making important points?	___	___	___
• Was the presentation a two-way communication? Did salesperson allow the customer time to talk?	___	___	___
• Watch the prospect for clues?	___	___	___
• Persistent?	___	___	___
• Enthusiastic?	___	___	___
• Dramatizes the sales calls?	___	___	___
• Remembers names of other people in the organization and uses them?	___	___	___

Comments: _____

_____

_____

_____

_____

HANDLING OBJECTIONS	YES	NO	NOT APPLICABLE
• Restates the customer's objection to make sure that he or she understands what it is? Also, asks the potential buyer for agreement that there is understanding?	___	___	___
• Agrees with the person in part? In other words, indicates that he or she understands the customer's concern. "That's a good question." "That's why I want to give you a demonstration."	___	___	___
• Welcomes the objection?	___	___	___
• Listens carefully to the objection?	___	___	___

- Understands the "real" objection? ⎯⎯⎯ ⎯⎯⎯ ⎯⎯⎯

- Gets the customer talking about the objection before handling it? In other words, did the salesperson get the customer to restate and reexplain? ⎯⎯⎯ ⎯⎯⎯ ⎯⎯⎯

- Specifically answers the objection? ⎯⎯⎯ ⎯⎯⎯ ⎯⎯⎯

- Relates 3rd party experiences? "Other customers that had a similar question bought anyway, and love it." ⎯⎯⎯ ⎯⎯⎯ ⎯⎯⎯

- Questions the customer to try and uncover hidden objections? Or maybe try an experimental close to see if there are any objections? ⎯⎯⎯ ⎯⎯⎯ ⎯⎯⎯

Comments: _____
_____
_____
_____
_____

CLOSING	YES	NO	NOT APPLICABLE
• Did the salesperson observe physical signals that the customer is ready to buy? (i.e., relaxes with thought, takes more time to inspect and think about the item, makes a positive statement about the product, starts asking an inordinate number of questions)?	⎯⎯⎯	⎯⎯⎯	⎯⎯⎯
• Quiet after the closing statement?	⎯⎯⎯	⎯⎯⎯	⎯⎯⎯
• Observe facial expressions?	⎯⎯⎯	⎯⎯⎯	⎯⎯⎯
• Get step-by-step agreement to various points about the company and the product?	⎯⎯⎯	⎯⎯⎯	⎯⎯⎯
• Summarize sales points frequently?	⎯⎯⎯	⎯⎯⎯	⎯⎯⎯

- Ask for the order?   _____ _____ _____

- Make trial closes at these
  stages:
    a. after strong demonstration?   _____ _____ _____
    b. after getting agreement on a
       minor point?   _____ _____ _____
    c. after overcoming an obstacle
       when he or she gets a
       buying signal?   _____ _____ _____

- Thank the buyer?   _____ _____ _____

Comments: _____

_____

_____

_____

_____

HANDLING COMPLAINTS	YES	NO	NOT APPLICABLE
• Restate the complaint in own words? Let customer know you understand?	_____	_____	_____
• Ask questions to get as much information about the complaint as possible?	_____	_____	_____
• Inflates the importance almost to the point of exaggeration?	_____	_____	_____
• After the complaint is handled, see if there was some other problem that led to the objection? (if the complaint did not seem to be significant)	_____	_____	_____
• Agree with the customer?	_____	_____	_____
• Accept responsibility for the error?	_____	_____	_____
• Follow up to make sure that everything is o.k.?	_____	_____	_____

Comments: _____

_____

_____

_____

_____

MANAGING THE TERRITORY	YES	NO	NOT APPLICABLE
• Routing calls; call on other potential accounts while in a particular geographical area?	_____	_____	_____
• Time spent on lunches, travel, waiting are productive?	_____	_____	_____
• Time wasted on prolonging interviews?	_____	_____	_____
• Call on preferred customer too much?	_____	_____	_____
• Spend too much time with people that can't help accomplish sales objectives?	_____	_____	_____
• Consistent and systematic follow up on prospects?	_____	_____	_____

Comments: _____
_____
_____
_____
_____

APPEARANCE AND ATTITUDE	YES	NO	NOT APPLICABLE
• Cheerful?	_____	_____	_____
• Confident?	_____	_____	_____
• Alert?	_____	_____	_____
• Have any nervous habits? (scratching head, rubbing nose, etc.)	_____	_____	_____
• Clothes in style and harmony?	_____	_____	_____
• Relaxed?	_____	_____	_____

Comments: _____
_____
_____
_____
_____

FOLLOW-UP-2nd CALL	YES	NO	NOT APPLICABLE
• Summarize the details for the last call? (what is being sold,			

how you came to the
customer, what has happened
since the last sales call?) _____ _____ _____

● Did the salesperson make a
comment about the last call or
answer a question that the
client raised? _____ _____ _____

● Jot down a few notes after the
1st call to use on the 2nd call? _____ _____ _____

● Adds significantly new
information that specifically
pinpoints needs? _____ _____ _____
Comments: _____
_____
_____
_____
_____
_____

OTHER	YES	NO	NOT APPLICABLE
● Tells the customer about our satisfied customers? (i.e., delivers the benefits offered)	_____	_____	_____
● A good listener?	_____	_____	_____
● Avoids talking about himself (herself) and his (or her) problems?	_____	_____	_____
● Tactful?	_____	_____	_____
● Sends cards on birthdays, anniversaries, etc.?	_____	_____	_____
● Accepts responsibility for his success or blames prospects, employees, etc.?	_____	_____	_____
● Solves problems immediately?	_____	_____	_____
● Avoids questions that may receive negative response?	_____	_____	_____
● Utilizes confidence-building questions?	_____	_____	_____
● Demonstrates the benefits in addition to telling the customer about them?	_____	_____	_____

● Completes call on time? _____ _____ _____

Comments: _____

_____

_____

_____

SPECIFIC POINTS TO COVER WITH SALESPERSON:

_____

_____

_____

_____

_____

_____

Case 8-1

Collins
Pharmaceu-
tical
Company

The Collins Pharmaceutical Company located in Chicago, Illinois, is an ethical drug manufacturer (prescription drugs) that distributes nationwide. Because of the introduction of six new products Collins has grown at an annualized rate of 40 percent during the past five years.

Medical sales representatives, sometimes referred to as detail men, call on approximately six physicians each day to persuade them to prescribe Collins' products for patients. Although competition for the physicians' attention is intense, Collins has been successful at building a strong image in the marketplace and, therefore, exerts significant influence over physicians. Collins' primary competitive advantages are consistent product quality and reliability in delivery.

Collins' organizational structure is as follows:

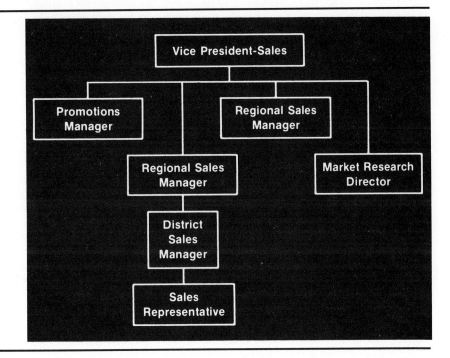

Figure 1
Collins'
Organizational
Structure

The company has 140 salespeople in 16 districts. New recruits are trained at the district level by their manager. The managers give them two weeks of exercises to complete on Collins' various products. The recruits then spend a week in the field with salespeople who teach them how to deal with physicians and how to route sales effort in order to maximize productivity. After the three-week sales training program, the new salespeople are assigned a territory.

During the past two years, turnover in the sales force has increased from seven percent per year to eleven percent. Recruiting standards have not changed. The Company still looks for people between 25 and 32 years of age that are enthusiastic, stable, and have high moral character. Also, a college degree is preferred.

1. What changes do you recommend to help Collins reduce turnover?

2. Evaluate the company's training program.

Case 8–2

Computer Software Company

Computer Software Company is a young corporation which has experienced tremendous growth in the past five years. The company develops high quality software packages for the accounting applications of General Ledger, Accounts Payable, and Fixed Assets Systems. It also markets system software products such as Tape Management, Disk Management, and Data Systems. Its major markets are banking institutions and commercial businesses specializing in manufacturing, retailing, medical, and transportation industries. Computer Software Company has at least five or six major competitors in the software field, all of which offer excellent software products and have fine reputations in the industry.

The size of the sales force has more than doubled in the past five years. Stephen Searl, national sales manager for the Computer Software Company, has been studying the sales statistics for each salesperson, including total number of sales calls made, duration of sales calls, number of calls per prospective client, and number of successful and unsuccessful contacts. After analyzing the statistics, Mr. Searl is concerned about the performance and effectiveness of the newer salespeople. Even after extensive product training and long periods in the field, the newer salespeople are less successful in selling the product than the salespeople who have been with the company since its earliest years.

When Computer Software was a relative small company, it recruited primarily experienced technical salespeople from other companies. Management thought it was too expensive and time consuming to train and develop inexperienced sales recruits. As the company began to develop markets and significantly expand its product line, training and retraining of all salespeople, including experienced people, became a necessity.

With the implementation of initial and continuous training programs came a change in Computer Software's recruiting orientation. While the company traditionally hired experienced sales representatives, it began to recruit and hire inexperienced people with a seemingly high potential for success. Stephen Searl believed that this approach to recruiting and employee development would improve the quality of the company's people and reduce the risks associated with turnover of veteran sales representatives.

Most of the new salespeople were recruited from several Midwestern universities and through local newspaper advertisements. After the personnel department preliminarily screens candidates, Stephen Searl conducts extensive, patterned interviews to determine their communication skills and technical capabilities. Candidates that pass the patterned interview subsequently visit with the President of Computer Software, Patricia Campbell. Insight she gains from this unstructured conversation is relayed to Searl. He conducts a final interview with each candidate and makes a decision within two to three days.

During their first week of employment, trainees receive a company orientation which is conducted by various department managers. The trainees are briefed on the company's philosophy, policies, procedures, customers, marketing programs, distribution structure, and products. After the initial orientations, the administrative marketing assistant utilizes a three-week, self-administered video training program to educate salespeople on product features and competitive advantages of the company's product line. This is followed by a two to four month on-the-job training program that is coordinated by the National Sales Manager and conducted by senior salespeople. When Searl and the senior salesperson believe that the recruit is ready to competently develop and maintain accounts, a territory is assigned to the new person.

1. What are some possible reasons for problems with new recruits?

2. How would you approach diagnosing the problem?

3. What recommendations would you make to help remedy the problem?

Case 9-1

Kalo
Laborato-
ries*

In early 1981 Stephen Young, manager of personnel development, Kalo Laboratories, began planning the fall Sales Executive Seminar (SES) for district sales managers. This was to kick off a new program of continuous training for district managers. In Young's opinion, training sales managers was Kalo's main problem. Doris Baily, recently promoted from district sales manager, was to assist in setting up the SES and in conducting it. Young awaited Baily's arrival at the home office so that the fall program's planning could begin.

Kalo Laboratories of Trenton, New Jersey, produces ethical drugs and certain pharmaceuticals. It is a subsidiary of Standard Products Company, a large conglomerate, whose 1980 sales exceeded $400 million, with Kalo accounting for $80 million. Kalo has four sales divisions: (1) hospital, (2) pediatric, (3) physician, and (4) government.

There are three groups of Kalo salespeople: (1) "detail men" who call exclusively on either physicians or pediatricians, explain product features and uses, and urge the prescribing of Kalo products, (2) salespeople who call on hospitals, perform "detail" tasks, and write orders, and (3) individuals who visit veterans' hospitals, military medical facilities, and large government installations, and who are skilled in negotiating and bidding on large contracts.

Each of sixty district managers supervise from 8 to 12 of Kalo's 650 sales representatives. Each district manager reports to one of twelve regional managers. The company adhers to a promotion-from-within policy, and all district managers have prior experience in ethical drug and pharmaceutical sales. The sales organization manual outlines district managers' duties in seven areas:

1. *Office Procedures:*
   General reports, correspondence, inventory of supplies, and supervision of office personnel.
2. *Field Supervision:*
   Improvement, training, evaluation, demonstration, assistance, and personal supervision of the field sales force.
3. *Personnel Improvements:*
   Determination of need and organization of a personal improvement plan for each salesman. Relate to appraisal and evaluation.

---

*Reprinted by permission from Richard R. Still, and Clyde E. Harris, Jr., CASES IN MARKETING: Decisions, Policies, Strategies, 1977, Prentice-Hall, Inc., Englewood Cliffs, N.J.

4. *District Progress:*
   Accountable for territorial profit and service.
5. *Reporting Function:*
   Preparation of general and specific reports and communication with the regional manager and the home office.
6. *Personnel Selection:*
   Recruiting, screening, interviewing, and assisting the regional manager in the final selection of applicants.
7. *Special Duties:*
   Conducting sales meetings, attending annual SES, terminations, policing expense accounts, and other special assignments.

Early in 1980 Kalo adopted a new sales-training philosophy stressing customer orientation, the buyer-seller communication process, and advanced selling methods. Implementing this new philosophy involved using the latest developments in individualized training and participation techniques. Therefore, a new personnel center, complete with modern conference rooms and equipped with the latest and most advanced audio-visual equipment, was built in Trenton. All salespeople received training there before assignment to sales districts. Young gave his evaluation of the results thus far achieved by saying: "I believe the initial sales training program is good, but our continuous training is suffering a breakdown as our district managers still stick to outdated techniques and continue to emphasize a product-oriented approach. We must do a better job of training the trainer." He believes they should coordinate and conduct on-the-job sales training continuously rather than sporadically. Young also voiced concern for the district managers' performance in field supervision and personnel improvement.

The district manager training program consists of intensive study of the sales organization manual, exposure to topics covered by past seminars, case studies, problem solving, and general discussion. The annual SES constitutes the only continuous training program for district managers. In December, 1980, Young asked Jerry Chambers, a district manager from the southeastern region, to appraise the current state of district manager training and to submit a proposal for its improvement (see Figure 1). No decision on this proposal had been reached by early 1981, since Young was awaiting Baily's arrival. The forthcoming SES included a computerized marketing game emphasizing bidding, pricing, budgeting, and certain aspects of marketing. Young wondered if this game should be replaced with a different type of program. He faces the twofold problem of training both new and old district managers and of organizing the SES.

Figure 1
Proposal

FROM	J.L. Chambers	DATE	December 18, 1980
TO	S.J. Young	SUBJECT	Proposal: New and Senior District Manager Training

PROPOSAL: *New and Senior District Manager Training*
I.   Objective—The implementation of this program will minimize the maturation time of the early appointed District Manager, as well as maximize the managerial capabilities of Senior District Managers.
II.   Procedure—
      A.   Field Contact—Rather than a formal introductory

meeting, the new District Manager will meet personnel through visiting their respective territories. Since
this contact will be made prior to a review of personnel records or Regional Manager counseling on this
subject, the new District Manager will not have
preconceived opinions of salespeople's capabilities.
The resultant atmosphere will be conducive to open,
candid discussion allowing both parties to meet on
common ground.

B.   Orientation with Regional Manager—After completing
the above step, a thorough personnel discussion will
also be reviewed at this time. Selected confrontations
will then be shown the new District Manager.
Because the District Manager will view his or her
knowledge inadequate to handle the situations depicted, he or she will be motivated to search out the necessary information. Based on the recognition of those
areas that require primary effort, the District Manager
will outline a course of study with the Regional Manager which will be encompassed by the seven categories enumerated below. Case histories from former
seminars and tape recorded discussions of those topics listed below the categories mentioned will provide
a reservoir of applicable information.

1.   Office Organization — Procedures
     a.   Value of Basic Organization.
     b.   Preparation for Field Contact.
     c.   Report Evaluation.
2.   Field Supervision
     a.   Training New People.
     b.   The Hospital Sales Representative — Hospi-
          tal Penetration.
     c.   Personnel Evaluation Techniques.
     d.   Capturing Government Business.
     e.   Drug & Wholesale Working.
     f.   The Pediatric Salesperson.
3.   Personnel Improvement
     a.   Understanding Man — Application of Drive
          Patterns & Motivational Interviews.
     b.   Motivation of Senior Salespeople.
     c.   Counseling Techniques.
4.   District Progress
     a.   Gathering Distribution Data — Territory Con-
          struction Procedures — Pool Allocations.
5.   Reporting
     a.   Written Communication Techniques.
     b.   Field Contact Report Construction.
6.   Personnel Selection
     a.   Applicant Screening — Sources of Candi-
          dates — Interviewing the Applicant.
7.   Special Duties
     a.   Organization of District Meetings.

The Regional Manager orientation session will require approximately two weeks. Upon completion, the Regional Manager will contact other District Managers of the region and arrange for a one-day introductory visit, with each manager, for the new District Manager.

C.   *Personnel Central*

1. *The New District Manager* — The new District Manager will participate in a two-week training period in Trenton. The new District Manager will occupy the District Office, which has been established at Personnel Central. Since this office has been organized to be representative of a typical district office, the District Manager will have an opportunity to become acquainted with systems and procedures applicable to the new position. Upon entering training, the District Manager will be requested to bring personnel files relative to each salesperson.

   These records will be valuable in conducting routine district business while in training, as well as providing search material for confrontation assignments. Training will proceed in accordance with the steps enumerated below.

   a. *Video Confrontations*—Two video confrontations will be completed on primary district problems. Through telephone contact with the Regional Manager, the District Manager counselor will explore specifics required for role play setting. On completion, the counselor will suggest search of similar case histories, confrontation, and a review of personnel records involved before rescheduling further tryout.

   b. *Sensitivity Training*—The District Manager will participate in sensitivity training through being assigned two salespeople upon their entering the course. The District Manager will occupy the third chair, counsel the people assigned and, in turn, discuss all progress with the District Manager counselor.

   c. *Recruiting, Screening, Hiring*—The District Manager will be required to complete confrontations as well as select four (4) candidates for hiring. Basis for selection of personnel will be discussed with District Manager counselor.

   d. Time remaining, the District Manager will complete selected confrontations as suggested by the Regional Manager during the phone call previously mentioned, or through selection by the District Manager counselor.

e. The District Manager will complete the confrontations mentioned in (a) above and accept as his Back Home Commitment the completion of these confrontations with the personnel involved.

2. *The Senior District Manager.* The senior District Manager will complete steps (a), (b), (d) and (e) as listed under New District Manager training. The exception will be that the Senior District Manager need only bring those records pertaining to the personnel that form the basis for confrontations listed under (a) above.

Since emphasis will be devoted to primary areas of weakness, the District Manager counselor should thoroughly discuss these with the Regional Manager prior to commencement of training. Concentration in these areas can then be implemented as outlined in (d) above. Senior District Manager training should require one (1) week.

III. *Materials Required*—As stated in II.B., Confrontation Capsules, selected case histories from former seminars, and the seventeen (17) taped topics listed under subheadings 1-7 will require duplication and distribution to the Regional Managers. As well, each Regional Manager will require one Fairchild projector.

While the majority of our Regional Managers currently have facilities to implement Regional Personnel, those that do not will be required to secure adequate additional office space.

IV. *Implementation*—Implementation of this program depends upon several factors. First, a District Manager counselor must be appointed to fulfill this new responsibility in Personnel Central. Second, as stated, Regional office facilities must be approved and secured by those that currently do not have such space available. Finally, reproduction of those materials noted will have to be accomplished.

It is anticipated that all three requirements mentioned can be accomplished in order to institute this program by January 15, 1980. At that time, it is recommended that a continual rotation schedule be developed that will allow simultaneous training of four (4) District Managers. Since Personnel Regional will be instituted coincident with this date, the Regional Manager will then have adequate decentralized training aids to augment the proposed central program.

V. *Conclusion*—The need for formalized managerial training has long been recognized. Implementation of this program not only fulfills current requirements, but offers an excellent base for future meaningful expansion in areas helpful in maximizing managerial skills. It is felt that an early decision to implement this program, by the date suggested, will further insure our continued progress in the years ahead.

1. Should Chambers's proposal have been accepted and implemented?

2. What further recommendations for training the district sales managers would you have made?

Case 9–2

Ron Morgan

Within a few weeks after he received his initial field training, Ron Morgan made his presence felt in the Springfield territory. He was a dynamic young man of 24 years who grasped product information exceedingly well and appeared to have a convincing manner in conveying his thoughts to the physicians upon whom he called.

Enthusiasm was second nature to Ron. Hours and long trips never bothered him. He thought nothing of working Saturdays, and often spent evenings visiting with interns and residents in many hospitals.

Ron was employed by Spartan Laboratories in January, 1980. Prior to his employment by Spartan, he worked on an assembly line in his uncle's plant which manufactured components for air conditioners. His uncle had developed a prosperous and growing business over the years, and offered Ron a permanent job after his graduation from college in June, 1979. Ron felt that he wanted to succeed on his own merits without the benefit of family connections, although he knew that his uncle's business offered him security and rapid future progress.

At the end of his first year with Spartan Laboratories, Ron had exceeded all expectations of Victor Sherwood, his district manager. Vic was convinced by this time that he hired a real gem, and hoped Ron would continue to be a top producer. Ron was top man in his district and third man in the country at the end of 1982.

Vic Sherwood praised Ron on his accomplishments, but was careful not to over encourage him. Vic realized that Ron was ambitious, but young, and it sometimes puzzled him just how he could keep Ron productive over the next few years. There was no doubt in Vic's mind that Ron had potential for growth in the organization, but Spartan management was not inclined toward promoting salespeople until they had at least five to eight years experience in the field carrying a bag.

The year 1981 was another record-breaking year for Ron. He again led his district and was top man in the country. Although he never pressed the issue, on occasion Ron did speak to Vic about the future. Vic tried to be noncommital without evading the issue, and assured Ron that practice will bring its rewards.

The early months of 1982 were met with rough competition by Spartan. One of their major products was competing with a new, dramatically different, and superior compound developed and marketed by a leading manufacturer. While sales were slipping badly in many territories throughout the country, Ron was holding his own and was meeting 1981 sales figures.

In June, 1982, Stanley Hoffman, Spartan Sales Manager, resigned. On July 1, the president of the company announced the appointment of Victor Sherwood as Sales Manager. One of the first problems which faced Victor was the appointment of a successor. He naturally thought of Ron, but realizing his youth and relatively short experience in the field, Vic gave more serious consideration to Jim Bradley, a salesperson who had joined Spartan nine years before. Jim was thirty-six years old, had a very successful career with Spartan, and was highly respected by his fellow salespeople.

When Ron arrived home on the evening of August 1, as usual he opened his mail as soon as he arrived. His wife stood nearby and noticed him turn pale as he read of Jim Bradley's appointment to the position of Northeast District Manager.

Sales volume in the Springfield territory showed a noticeable drop during the next several months. By the end of the year, Ron's sales position was nearer the bottom than the top of his district. Victor Sherwood was well aware of Ron's performance. During what appeared to be an unplanned visit to Springfield early in 1983, Vic telephoned Ron one evening, asking him to meet him at the hotel the next morning. Ordinarily in the years before when Vic would call him upon arriving in town the evening before, Ron would immediately drive downtown and return home with Vic. Not this time.

The next day Vic made a number of calls with Ron and noticed a discouraged, almost demoralized attitude. Late in the afternoon, Vic asked Ron if he and his wife, Ruth, would join him for dinner. Ron said he would, but his wife wasn't feeling well. After a couple of cocktails, Vic brought up the subject of Ron's sales performance since the previous September. Ron had little to offer in explanation, but did admit that the disappointment of not being selected for the job Vic left to become Sales Manager had an effect on his performance.

Following his visit with Ron, Vic wrote to him[1] (and to Jim Bradley)[2] restating parts of his conversation during dinner a few nights before. Vic wondered just how he and Jim could reinstill what appeared to be lost enthusiasm, drive, and ambition into Ron Morgan.

1. How could Vic Sherwood have handled the situation differently? Ron Morgan?

2. What can Vic do to recapture Ron's lost enthusiasm and help him return to being a top producer?

3. Can Jim Bradley be of any assistance to Vic in this situation? Explain your answer.

Appendix A

SPARTAN LABORATORIES		INTER-OFFICE MEMO
TO: Mr. Ron Morgan	DATE:	January 29, 1983
FROM: Victor Sherwood	COPIES:	Mr. Bradley
SUBJECT: Territorial Operation		

During my visit to Springfield a few days ago, we had the opportunity to discuss together various phases of your territorial performance covering the past several months. As I mentioned to you then, Ron, I have been extremely disappointed in your sales picture and in your daily call average of only four physicians.

Quite frankly, Ron, this situation cannot continue! Although economic conditions may control sales figures to some extent, the very least we can expect is a definite improvement and upward turn in physician calls. I cannot justify any excuse for one, two, or three physician calls, repeatedly day after day. Certainly you must be concerned about this matter, but it appears to me that little effort has been extended on your part to improve your territorial performance.

As you are aware, we are striving to attain an over-all average of seven physician calls per day, plus other calls to total thirteen. We are very close to that average and several representatives are surpassing it with little or no difficulty.

---

[1]See Appendix A.
[2]See Appendix B.

Adapted with permission from MANAGEMENT OF THE SALES FORCE, William J. Stanton and Richard H. Buskirk, 5th ed.; Richard D. Irwin, Inc., 1978.

I suggest you give this entire matter serious thought during the next few days, Ron, and then let me know how you plan to improve your sales and increase physician coverage in your territory in the future.

I will await your reply.

Best regards

Victor Sherwood

Appendix B

SPARTAN LABORATORIES   INTER-OFFICE MEMO

TO: Mr. Jim Bradley   DATE: January 29, 1983
FROM: Victor Sherwood   COPIES:
SUBJECT: Personnel Report—Mr.
          Ron Morgan

During my field visit this week with Mr. Morgan, I once again had the opportunity to discuss and completely review with him his territorial performance covering the past several months.

I pointed out to Ron that he has never had a better opportunity than now to prove his true value to Spartan. If he were to pull himself out of his present position and work his territory up to where it would place him among the top territories by the end of the year, he could prove to us that he has the potential we believe he has. I also mentioned the possibility of a salary increase in July as an expression of our sincerity and confidence in his abilities. He honestly does not want to be considered for an increase at this time, because in his own words he "doesn't deserve one." He further stated that when his territory was showing progress he was adequately compensated in salary increases and would not consider it proper to receive an increase this July.

It is only natural that the thought comes to mind there may be a possibility that Ron would leave Spartan to join his uncle's company. Upon discussing this subject with him, this move appears unlikely—but could still be possible through family pressure. It appears as though Ron would not be especially happy working under his brother-in-law, a vice president. The only way that Ron would consider going with this firm would be if his uncle does not retire as he plans so he might in some way lean upon him for guidance.

It is my hope that Ron is sincere in his desire to pull his territory up during the next six months and that he will continue to work for Spartan Laboratories.

Vic Sherwood

Case 10–1

Baine-
Hausley
Publishing
Company

Baine-Hausley Publishing Company is a 35 year old company specializing in childrens' books. It grew at an annualized rate of 20 percent between 1948 and 1968 on the strength of several best selling titles and the baby boom that followed World War II. During the first fifteen years of Baine-Hausley's existence, it sold primarily through book agents that called on distributors and retailers. James Hausley, a Vice President and partner, directed the marketing effort and sold directly to the multiunit book stores and department store chains. Agents handled the other markets.

In 1980, after 12 years of erratic sales and profits, Baine and Hausley decided to sell the business and retire. They located a magazine publisher, Oren-Kensington Unlimited, that was interested in diversifying into the children's market and, therefore, agreed to an attractive acquisition. Although the magazine publisher wanted the Baine-Hausley division to remain autonomous, it did want to gain some control over the company's operations. Therefore, the publisher appointed Harry Campbell as president and chief executive officer of the company. After successfully turning a drug company and soft drink company around through development of innovative and aggressive advertising and promotional programs, Campbell was recruited to Oren-Kensington as its vice president of marketing. He was appointed to the Baine-Hausley division to develop it into the largest publisher of childrens' books in the country.

After evaluating the company's current condition, Campbell decided that some immediate changes were necessary to support future growth. First, he hired Peggy Koehler as vice president of finance. In addition to being an outstanding financial analyst, Ms. Koehler was also an expert in acquisitions and mergers. Campbell was confident that she could reorganize the department, clear up problems the company had been experiencing with bad debts, and give direction to Baine-Hausley's growth program.

The other major change Campbell made during his first two months as president was to hire a director of sales, Hal Curtis, who could develop a direct sales force and slowly eliminate marginal agents in the Southeast and Atlantic Coast. Campbell wanted to eventually replace agents in all major markets with a direct sales force.

After two years with Baine-Hausley, Curtis felt like it was time to visit with Campbell about a problem that he had attempted to resolve for the past eight months. He no longer had the time or patience to tolerate the tight credit policies and credit approval delays that his salespeople were experiencing with Koehler's department. His salespeople were paid a straight commission on sales volume and were becoming dissatisfied with the company's insensitivity to their financial needs. Also, since performance evaluation was based completely on sales volume, many of the salespeople believed that they were receiving rating scores that were unjustly determined. Curtis shared their concern, but had to conform to policies that specified how salespeople would be compensated and evaluated.

After visiting with Leslie Sands, Campbell's secretary, and setting up a date for the weekend, Harry opened the door. "Hal, glad you are here. Let's go into my office and talk."

"Harry," Hal said, "I've about had it with Peggy Koehler. Everytime one of my salespeople submits an order all she thinks is important is a thorough credit check. Sometimes that takes weeks, and in the meantime I lose many potential customers (both new and repeat). She just doesn't realize that without sales there wouldn't be a company. Not only does she drag her feet, she will not allow any accounts a few extra days to pay the invoice. I spend half of my time begging her to hurry or to extend the payment period. What gives her the right to be so high and mighty?" Harry had no sooner finished attempting to appease Curtis when Koehler came into his office.

"Harry," Koehler said, "I overheard you and Mr. Curtis talking, and I feel I should have a few minutes to explain my side. Mr. Curtis has absolutely no understanding of finance, and furthermore he is not the least bit interested in learning more about it. All he wants to do is sell to anybody, on whatever terms they want, just so he and his salespeople get a larger commission and bonus. Maybe you can make him understand that from a controller's point of view, I want to be able to accept every order as long as the customers prove credit worthy and the payment terms are reasonable. You know yourself, Harry, we can't afford bad debts with our profit structure as it is. Also, with the cost of money these days, we certainly can't afford to carry our customers for 60 to 90 days."

About that time, Leslie opened the door and handed Mr. Levy a message.

"Anyway," Koehler continued, "how can I get through to Curtis the importance of running a tight financial company?" "Hal," Mr. Campbell said, "don't you think you could give Peggy some time to look at what she has been talking about?"

"Certainly I am willing to continue to try to find a solution to this problem," Hal said. "But, I don't know what can be done. All I know is that Peggy Koehler is jeopardizing attainment of my sales forecast. I just wanted you to be aware, Harry, that some areas in this company are directly interfering with sales—this company's most important function." Hal Curtis brushed by Mr. Campbell, Ms. Koehler, and Miss Sands and left the office.

Harry Campbell had been in advertising for 20 years and had neither selling nor financial experience. He had relied heavily on Curtis and Koehler in managing the company. He knew something must be done quickly before the situation got worse. Campbell felt both people had valid points. He also knew from past experience that sales and finance oftentimes had conflicting objectives. He wondered what could be done to show Koehler and Curtis that they were both working for the same company toward the same objectives.

1. What should Campbell do to change the conflict between Curtis and Campbell?

2. What factors have contributed to the conflict?

3. What could Curtis and Koehler do to minimize their problems?

Case 10–2

World Data
System

World Data System was formed in 1973 to help solve the ever increasing challenge of communications security. Governments, military groups, and industrial organizations communicate confidential information daily by way of telephone, telegraph, radio, facsimile, telex, computer, and communicating word processor.

Because of the relative ease of capturing unsecured transmissions, it became apparent that military groups were unknowingly giving away top secret information, and corporations were allowing competitors to have access to research and development breakthroughs, market studies, financial data, new product information, production plans, and pricing strategies. World Data System, therefore, developed encryption devices that scramble messages into an unintelligable form as the message leaves the communication device (i.e., telephone, radio, telex, computer terminal etc.). When the message reaches its destination another encryption unit that is synchronized with the unit at the sender's location unscrambles the message so that the receiving party understands it. Without the receiving unit the transmission would be garbled and unrecognizable.

Being an internationally oriented company, World Data System has organized to most effectively satisfy the needs of its distant markets. International salespeople are organized into geographical territories, with each one responsible for a continent or part of a continent. For example, there is a salesperson who is responsible for managing the South American market. A total of six salespeople handle corporate marketing activities in these worldwide markets. The day to day sales activity and client development is handled by dealers that have been established in each country. World Data System domestic sales are handled by three sales people, each of which is responsible for one of three major markets: the federal government, companies west of the Mississippi River, and companies east of the Mississippi River.

The company can be characterized as a company that is evolving from a high growth, entrepreneural company to a professionally managed organization with a planned growth pattern. During the transition it became apparent that one of the primary keys to success was maintenance of a system for evaluating salesperson performance. The Vice President of Marketing, Jack Jones, developed a program in 1982 to effect changes that would help give management a handle on performance.

The system of performance evaluation was implemented to help Jones identify weaknesses of salespeople and develop programs of improvement. During World Data System's early growth years, salespeople were evaluated for annual sales volume only and were generally not accountable for attainment of sales objectives. The revised evaluation system includes (1) a quarterly and annual review, (2) a comprehensive assessment of both sales and profit by market and product, and (3) a subjective assessment of prospecting and closing skills. Jones would travel with each salesperson every three months to evaluate these subjective factors. At the beginning of the year salespeople set dollar sales volume and profit goals by quarter, market, and product. They also established goals for developing new accounts. Each quarter salespeople are evaluated on the following factors: sales by product, sales by market, and quota attainment. At the end of the year they were evaluated on each quantitative factor as well as the subjective factors.

1. Evaluate Jones' performance evaluation system.

2. Establish a format for an expanded evaluation program.

3. In view of World Data System's position in their life cycle what additional programs should they implement?

Part 5

Motivational Aspects of Sales Management

11. COMMUNICATION SYSTEMS

12. MOTIVATING SALESPEOPLE

13. COMPENSATION OF SALESPEOPLE

CASES

Chapter 11 _____

Communication Systems

After completing this chapter, you will be able to:

- Identify the importance of effective communication in sales force management.

- Detail the elements and procedure associated with effective interpersonal communication.

- Identify and discuss problems which distort and interfere with effective communication.

- Emphasize the importance of two-way communication.

- Identify various tools that may facilitate communication among salespeople, sales managers, customers, and suppliers.

Sales managers and salespeople are continuously confronted with problems which are brought on by both internal and external changes in the environment in which they operate. Managers must match characteristics of applicants to the company's unique personnel demands, effectively train salespeople, allocate salespeople to alternative territories, anticipate and satisfy consumer needs, motivate salespeople to excellence, develop and control salesperson compensation plans, and evaluate sales force performance. Meanwhile, salespeople must identify the needs of customers, communicate ideas to the customer to satisfy those needs, and inform developers of new products of changes in customer requirements. In other words, sales managers and salespeople are problem solvers, and their decision-making effectiveness is largely contingent upon their ability to identify and resolve these problems.

Initiation of the problem solving process begins with an awareness that something has deviated from the normal or expected. For example, a company's premier salesperson's fourth quarter sales are only 50 percent of his or her average production. If the firm has no information on specific aspects of the salesperson's performance, then identification and resolution of this person's problem may be impossible. If, on the other hand, the sales manager has collected information from within and outside the company on the salesperson's profitability, call frequency, average number of new accounts, average sales to existing accounts, and closing rate, as well as changes in the size and characteristics of the salesperson's territory, identification of the *real* problem is highly probable.

The point is that effective problem solving cannot be initiated unless information related to the selling environment is communicated to the appropriate person. Also, goal development and personal improvement cannot be implemented effectively unless the manager communicates decisions and information back to the sales representatives. In fact, many organizational conflicts and problems result from or are amplified by poor communication. Because of the apparent importance of information communication to the sales function, this chapter introduces the reader to the communication process and barriers which may restrict employee ability to obtain and relate information.

COMMUNICATION PROCESS

The most important attribute which distinguishes humans from other animals is the ability to develop new ideas, theories, concepts, and opinions, and pass this information to others. Similarly, organizations develop procedures and techniques for handling business problems which can be utilized by successors in order to avoid the inefficiencies of trial and error. Salespeople and sales managers, for example, can continuously monitor the attitudes and needs of various customer groups, then develop standard presentations, product designs, and call procedures which reflect the customers' unique desires.

The point is that transference of information and knowledge is made possible by the communication of language. According to S. I. Hayakawa, "language . . . is the indispensable mechanism of human life . . . of life such as our that is molded, guided, enriched, and made possible by the accumulation of past experience."[1] Although being one of the most pervasive and important of human activities, efficient written and oral communication of language is one of the most difficult and neglected. The purpose of this section is to review the elements of the communication process which will serve as a reminder of how difficult it is to ensure the meeting of our responsibilities as both senders and receivers.

As shown in Figure 11-1, the communication process begins with an idea or a concept that the sender wishes to transmit to a receiver.[2] The concept can be a suggestion, warning, directive, observation, or any-

---

[1] S. I. Hayakawa, *Language in Thought and Action* (4th ed.; New York: Harcourt, Brace, and World, Inc., 1978), p. 13.

[2] C. Shannon and W. Weaver, *The Mathematical Theory of Communication* (Urbana, Ill.: University of Illinois Press, 1949); William F. Glueck, *Foundation of Personnel* (Dallas, Texas: Business Publications, Inc., 1979), p. 65; Robert L. Mathis and John H. Jackson, *Personnel* (2d ed.; St. Paul, Minn.: West Publishing Company, 1978), p. 69.

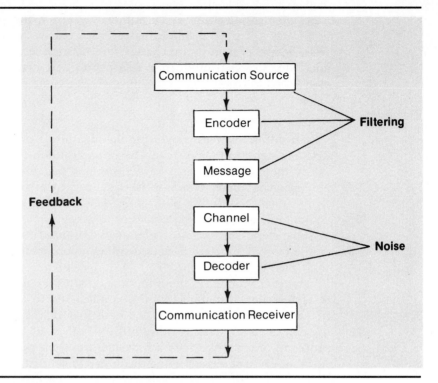

Figure 11–1
Communication
Process

thing else the sender needs to communicate. The idea is developed into a symbolic representation, transmitted through an appropriate channel, and interpreted by the receiver. Finally, the receiver responds to the translated message which may stimulate subsequent communication from the original sender. Although the model may seem simple, there are numerous problems and considerations at each phase of the model.

Source

The **communication source** is an individual with a reason for communicating. The individual could be a sales representative with an idea for a prospective buyer or the sales manager. It could be an executive who could improve sales efficiency with a changed sales strategy or technique to be used by salespeople in their presentations.

In order to effectively communicate, the communicator must *empathize*. In other words, before the message can be formulated, the source must consider the receiver's position and look at the situation from the receiver's perspective. For example, the executive must understand the effect of a new policy or an organizational change on cooperating salespeople and their support team. Although top management may view an organizational change as an improvement in efficiency, sales management and/or the salespeople may see it as a threat to their earnings, jobs, responsibilities, or authority. Thus, when an executive communicates a change to subordinates, the executive must carefully explain why, when, and how the change will take place. In fact, it may be a good idea to solicit input from salespeople and customers before a decision is made in order to identify their reactions and feelings.

Encoding

Encoding involves converting the idea into a symbolic form that will be meaningful to the receiver. The important point concerning encoding is that the translation must have a common meaning for both the sender and receiver. Since everyone is socialized in a different environment, many ideas, words, or phrases have various meanings. For example, computerization suggests efficiency to many top managers and a threat to some clerical workers. In fact, everyone in a firm has a different conception of computerization depending upon their position as well as their past experience.

Another problem is the intentional distortion of information referred to as **filtering**. Although filtering is discussed in a later section of this chapter, it must be pointed out here that deliberate manipulation of information is frequently practiced by both sales executives and salespeople in order to facilitate achievement of their personal goals. If management gives salespeople the flexibility to set price, they may envision it as a chance to increase sales volume at the expense of profit rather than expanded decision-making authority as may have been intended by management. If the salespeople are given pricing flexibility and are evaluated based upon gross sales volume, then excessive discounts may be given to achieve higher sales and, therefore, higher commissions. The result to the organization will probably be lower profit and, in many cases, lower sales volume.[3] The point is that management communicated their intentions to the sales force without proper consideration of how the salespeople would interpret and react to the directive. The result was intentional manipulation of the directive to satisfy their own objectives.

Message

The **message** is a systematic set of symbols. It is a symbolic model designed to transfer meaning from the sender to the receiver. The effectiveness of communication is contingent upon the sender's ability to build a verbal or nonverbal model of the intended message. It may be in the form of a written word, a spoken idea, a sensuous look, a laugh, a mode of dress, or any number of additional suggestions.

It is important that salespeople and sales managers remember that a single message may be interpreted as several messages by the receiver.

---

[3] P. Ronald Stephenson, William L. Cron, and Gary L. Frazier, "Delegating Pricing Authority to the Sales Force: The Effects on Sales and Profit Performance," *Journal of Marketing*, Vol. 43 (Spring, 1979), p. 27.

A manager may be training the sales force on telephone prospecting. Although the manager emphasizes the importance of telephone prospecting, his or her lack of enthusiasm or unwillingness to actually demonstrate its use may suggest to the trainees that the manager does not effectively practice the techniques. The salespeople may, therefore, also be uncertain about the telephone as a prospecting tool and resist its use. Sales managers should, therefore, be fully aware of implications associated with verbalized communications, as their attitude will be revealed by their expression, tone, and behavior.

Channel

Channel refers to the medium through which the message travels. It may be a sound wave, a touch, or a written note. Some writers have suggested that the channel is so important that it is the influential agent in determining how a person perceives the communication. If its importance is in fact justified, it is critical that marketing people select the appropriate medium to accomplish a particular communication.

For purposes of managing the sales force, *personal* communication between salespeople and sales managers seems to be most effective. Although written messages are effective for informing salespeople of new developments, studies have indicated that eyeball-to-eyeball contact is the most effective.[4] Interpersonal communication is also considered to be most effective in communications between the salesperson and the buyer. Cassettes, telephone calls, letters, and audio-visual equipment are felt to be significant but inferior to personal contact.

In addition to problems created by the intrinsic nature of the channel, miscommunications also result from noise. **Noise** refers to any unplanned interruption of the communication process. It can be an external distraction such as an extraneous sound or an internal diversion such as anxiety or stress. Since the sender can only be responsible for selecting the channel that minimizes the chance of noise, success or failure of the communication may largely rest at this step on random occurrences of noise. The presence of noise, however, may suggest to a salesperson the utilization of techniques designed to gain a buyer's attention (i.e., unusual phrases, unique presentation materials and short concise messages). In other words, use noise producing phenomena to divert attention.

Receiving

One of the most difficult and neglected aspects of communication is receiving. The receiver must accumulate information either by listening, watching, feeling, or reading. In many respects, the process is analogous

---

[4] "Sales Communications, Inside and Out," *Sales Management*, Vol. III (November 26, 1973), p. 7.

to data processing utilizing a computer. When information is received, it is filed in short-term memory similar to the core memory of a computer. Information that is analyzed and considered important may be moved from short-term storage and filed in long-term memory. This is similar to the computer process of moving data from core to a tape for storage. After information is filed in an appropriate storage location, short-term memory is ready to receive new information. Since the process can occur in an extremely short time period, analyzing and storing information for processing can be greatly impeded if the receiver is not paying attention.

Decoding

Once the message is received, it is ready for decoding. **Decoding** refers to the conversion of the message into a meaningful form. The effectiveness with which decoding is accomplished depends upon (1) the number and nature of distractions, (2) the receiver's needs at the time of the message, (3) the accuracy and fidelity of the message, (4) the experiences, attitudes, and values of the receiver and sender, (5) the receiver's desire to perceive, and (6) the effectiveness of encoding.

An example of communication inefficiency caused by several of the problems involves an international promotional strategy implemented by Exxon Oil Company. They utilized the well-known phrase "Put a tiger in your tank" in a small country that did not consider lions and tigers as superior beasts. As a result, the people could not interpret the meaning favorably since their frame of reference was not consistent with that of Exxon management.

Action/Feedback

The last step in the communication process is really the first step in a new communication process: physical or verbal reaction to a message. Action/Feedback may be in the form of a raised brow, a smile, a positive or negative reply, or some other reaction. It indicates to the source whether the meaning of the message is understood, as well as the receiver's general reaction. If the message is not understood, it can be changed to facilitate effective communication. If the message generates a physical response not consistent with the verbal reaction, the sender can get better insight into the receiver's true feelings.

An important but often overlooked point about action/feedback is that the receiver becomes the sender, and the originator of the message assumes the receiver's role. The receiver, therefore, must confirm that the idea or concept was received and understood and the original sender must receive the feedback, interpret it correctly, and act accordingly. One of the most frustrating experiences for salespeople seems to be a sales manager putting on a sales meeting who talks to a chalkboard or flip chart. A message is being sent by the presenter, but reception is never confirmed. The communications cycle is incomplete as the sender has not fulfilled the second part of his or her responsibility in observing feedback from the participants.

BARRIERS TO EFFECTIVE COMMUNICATION

The identification of problems is facilitated by effective, free flowing communication. When communication is open, sales managers are more aware of the needs and problems of customers as well as their sales-people. When the efficient functioning of a communication system is restricted, management awareness of problems and opportunities decreases, thus restricting effective decision-making. There are numerous explanations for the restriction of effective communication. Since specific barriers to communication are too numerous to discuss in this section, the general categories of physical, personal, and semantic barriers have been developed to facilitate examination.

Physical Barriers

Physical barriers (noise) refer to external distractions or limitations which suppress fidelity of messages. Examples of these noise producing phenomenon include a change in temperature, the presence of an attractive person of the opposite sex, a disturbing sound, competing messages, or the simple fact that salespeople seldom work in the presence of their managers. Most physical barriers are so obvious that most people have learned ways to overcome or avoid them. In fact, when the noise level surpasses a specific level, people use gestures, signals, or other body language devices to communicate. Also, sales managers may use the telephone, memos, or videocassettes to bridge the physical, geographical gap between them and their salespeople.

Personal Barriers

Most of the psychological barriers to communication can be categorized under the general term of personal filters. People are literally deluged with available information or data which supress fidelity of messages. They hear numerous sounds, see a wide area of space, feel and touch many objects, and smell countless odors. If there were no systematic way to screen out or filter this infinite amount of information, the processing of information would be impossible. In management, as in personal experience, people develop ways of categorizing data and learn how to focus upon the important information while ignoring the unimportant (i.e., selective attention or exposure). The definition of important information is determined for each individual by being told what to look for or observe by parents, peers, or other members of our culture. Individuals learn by trial and error to select certain pieces of information and to ignore others. The important point is that such screens or filters are learned behavior based on experience and teaching, and are very useful in preventing people from being overwhelmed by information.

In the communication process, the same filters that facilitate decision-making may prevent effective communication with others. For example, meaning attributed to a particular idea is based on one's preconceived attitudes and values, as well as on the nature of the language. Attitudes of individuals on one level or in one department of an organization are often in conflict with those of people in other areas. The sales manager, for example, sees problems from a sales or marketing perspective (e.g., reduction in inventory levels and eventual stockouts reduce sales, revenue, and customer satisfaction). The production manager, on the other hand, envisions a reduction in inventory as a threat to continuous, smooth production. Finally the finance manager sees inventory as an opportunity to maximize profit by balancing carrying and ordering costs. If a synergistic effect is to be gained, all people involved must have the same viewpoint and work willingly and effectively together to accomplish common objectives—which is really the essence of the marketing management concept.

The result of the incongruence of meaning is distortion and misunderstanding—the individuals change the meaning to fit their own ideologies, attitudes, values, concepts, and beliefs. Referring to the above example, when top management sends a memorandum indicating an inventory problem, marketing thinks the plant is not producing enough, production believes marketing is not selling, and finance thinks the plant is overproducing and marketing is underselling. These opinions are internalized by individuals in each department and no amount of evidence or rational persuasion will change their minds. They may implement corrective measures via top management order, but they will never admit failure or responsibility. This phenomena is referred to as **selective distortion.**

A related barrier is **intentional distortion** or **filtering** of information. The objective of intentional distortion, or falsification of information, is to facilitate attainment of the sender's objectives. Salespeople will manipulate information given to their managers. Sales managers often filter information received from their superiors. The result is distortion of information by the sender and, if frequently practiced, skepticism on the part of the receiver concerning accuracy of the information. The obvious implication is that accurate data is viewed with a grain of salt and the information system becomes inefficient.

Another personal barrier relates to the evaluation of statements, data, or situations based upon personal objectives and habits without application of logic or objectivity. The primary reason for nonobjective evaluation is prolonged application of a given method or idea that yields positive reinforcement. In other words, a company is run a certain way, a sale is made in a particular manner, or a buyer buys from a certain supplier. If the experiences are positive in terms of profit or satisfaction, the same procedures will be applied repeatedly. The person (or people) develops a case of tunnel vision, and cannot understand or does not *want* to understand different perspectives.

An additional personal barrier is a hierarchial or social status barrier. For example, the vice president of marketing of a large corporation who goes to an annual sales meeting to rap with the people on the line will likely be no more successful in establishing effective communication than the army general who decides to inspect the privates. There is, unfortunately, a problem with understanding communications between various levels. For example, an operations research team develops and proposes an idea designed to improve sales strategy. Although management tells the team that it is not acceptable because of initial costs, it may really be rejected because it was presented on a level not understandable to the decision-making executive.

A final personal barrier is attitude toward the sender or receiver. Oftentimes antagonism between two individuals causes miscommunication. For example, a major retail chain in the Southwest had a divisional merchandise manager that had a personal conflict with one of the buyers. This conflict resulted in instances where they would not communicate at all and in other situations where they would intentionally distort messages. The merchandise manager was uncooperative in supplying the buyer with information concerning fashion, suppliers, and potential availability, and the buyer would not consult the manager on merchandising decisions. The result of the conflict was decreased productivity, demotion of one individual, and termination of the other.

Personal communication barriers have no quick and easy solution. By definition they are both personal in nature and subject to the many aspects of interpersonal relationships. The most important point to be gained is to realize their existence and understand how they can occur. To overcome these barriers, the most important thing a sender of communication can do is to carefully observe the receiver's feedback and respond accordingly. It is the sender's responsibility to ensure that the message is received. Only by watching and listening for feedback can the sender ensure the fulfillment of that responsibility.

Semantic Barriers

Although language facilitates learning and communication, it must be remembered that it is simply a representation of reality and is not reality itself. Because people tend to interact with people like themselves, the phrases, mannerisms, and terms common to them become their representation or image of reality. Outside their grouping, however, these common interpretations lose precision in meaning and cause communication problems. A classic illustration of this is the data processing manager who tries to explain the computer system to a field sales manager. The terminology (or jargon) of data processing is both complex and elaborate, and all too often has no meaning to people outside the area of computer systems. When phrases such as consistency paradigm, contingency tables, histograms, perceptual mapping, and stochastic models are used, salespeople and sales managers are typically unable to comprehend concepts that are really rather simplistic in nature.

This semantic barrier is made clear by Korzybski in his widely accepted approach to perceiving reality known as general semantics. According to Korzybski, language is like a map while reality (actual events, objects, or things) can be compared to a territory. Maps are not territories, but are simply abstractions or symbolic representations of the actual event. In essence, what the general semantic approach does is reject many Aristotelian ideologies in favor of a more scientific approach to the study of the empirical world. Specifically, the Aristotelian perspective argues that one can perfectly identify the empirical world through language. General semantics or the non-Aristotelian perspective, on the other hand, recognizes the limitations of language and the impossibility of understanding and representing reality in its entirety. The best that can be done is to develop languages that are similarly structured to the real world.[5]

The map-territory dichotomy envisioned by Korzybski and the problems associated with identifying reality become evident when one attempts to describe a human being. In actuality, a human consists of many characteristics and materials unique only to one person. It is impossible for a word or group of words to perfectly represent the reality of the person or differentiate between several people unless, of course, the word is the person.

One of the most significant semantic barriers to effective communication is ambiguity created because the sender assumes the receiver understands. It may be in the form of an incomplete memorandum, an ambiguous questionnaire, an unempathetic salesperson, or a technical report. The fallacious preconception can be particularly devastating in a one-way communication such as a mail survey or advertisement. The receiver, of course, does not respond and the miscommunication continues until the message is changed because of negative results. In interpersonal communication, the receiver can ask for additional information or communicate ignorance by a raised brow or blank stare. This can subsequently be detected by the sender and stimulate explanatory statements.

Summary of Communication Barriers

As indicated in the preceding discussion, physical, personal, and semantic barriers to communication can create problems for sales executives in decision-making. Decision activity does not even begin unless the decision maker is aware that a problem exists. Problem awareness is directly dependent upon the identification of accurate data or informa-

---

[5] Alfred Korzybski, *Science and Sanity* (4th ed.; Lakeville, Connecticut: The International Non-Aristotelian Library Publishing Company, 1958).

tion coming from the environment and signaling the need for problem solving. If the communication process that alerts the decision-maker is faulty or incomplete, timely identification of problems will be practically impossible. In a similar sense, search for alternatives, evaluation of alternatives, and implementation of an optimum solution will be diminished in efficiency and effectiveness.

Most sales managers are fully aware of problems associated with communications and can cite numerous examples of misinformation causing delays, errors, and other organizational problems. While most of our discussion is focused on interpersonal oral communications, the same type of problems can occur with any medium. In fact, the potential for communication barriers increases when the interpersonal process is replaced by some other communication medium. One of the primary reasons for communication problems in written and mass media is the problem of recognizing action needed based on feedback. For instance, a memo directed at field salespeople may be understood by the sales manager but may be ambiguous to a particular salesperson. Since there is often a time lag between sending the written message and receiving a response, the sales manager can easily forget to check for feedback. Although organizations spend considerable amounts of money on programs to train their managers in writing skills, communication problems still remain as the prime concerns.

TWO-WAY COMMUNICATION — A NECESSITY

In many organizations, sales managers dictate policy to salespeople, provide salespeople with product and sales information, present ideas at sales meetings, and, in general, make numerous decisions that have significant impact on the salesperson's job. Many of these same managers, however, are reluctant to allow input from salespeople on matters that the salespeople may be more qualified to assess. These sales managers are more interested in both preserving their own philosophies on managing and protecting their power position within the organization than in considering the actual needs and desires of their salespeople.

When a sales manager communicates without consideration of feedback from field representatives, not only can morale be damaged, but much vital market data can be lost. Effective decision-making is largely dependent upon the collection and evaluation of timely data about such variables as markets, competition, and technological developments. No individual in an organization is in a better position to inform management of these developments than salespeople. When sales managers constantly ignore salesperson input on these matters, however, continued upward communication of information related to markets and competitors may be lost. In fact, in one study it was found that the two most significant reasons why salespeople do not communicate information to management are that (1) management does not use the information, and

A Company Profile

Exxon Corporation was formed on August 5, 1882, and has developed into one of the largest, most efficiently managed corporations in the world. Exxon has an interest in 54 oil refineries, 65,000 service stations, 25,000 miles of pipeline, 24 million tons of tankers, and operates in approximately 100 countries. Although its primary business is oil and gas, Exxon Corporation is heavily involved in coal, synthetic fuel made from oil shales and coal, solar energy, electrical equipment, minerals, chemicals, and office equipment. These activities translate into a total revenue of approximately $103 billion and profits of approximately $5.6 billion.

Although there are numerous reasons for Exxon's success, there are several facts about Exxon that will help ensure its continued growth and prosperity in the future. First, Exxon effectively anticipates the future needs of society and directs its resources toward the satisfaction of those needs. This orientation to the future is reflected in its $2 billion budget for research and development, its investment in the energy forms of the future, and its diversification into other contemporary business products such as electronic mail. Second, Exxon Corporation has an uncompromising commitment to the selection and development of its employees. Approximately two-thirds of Exxon's employees hired in recent years have university degrees. Also, all new recruits go through a comprehensive, competitive training and development program that touches most areas of the organization.

Exxon's sensitivity to its employees and other publics is reflected in its long-established commitment to effective intracompany and intercompany communications.

Similar to other large, multinational corporations, effective communications at Exxon are complex and difficult. While small companies can communicate directly to their employees, markets, and other publics, large companies must employ sophisticated mass media channels to accomplish the same objectives. Exxon Corporation, therefore, utilizes a large number of approaches to simply help people maintain an awareness of its many programs, products, activities, and people. The approaches include print media, broadcast media, video cassette programs, and face-to-face communication. Exxon Company U.S.A., Exxon Corporation's principal domestic operating division, for example, produces and distributes a video tape, This Week in Exxon, that reaches 70 locations on a weekly basis. It reports on activities in various areas of Exxon's operations and highlights new developments and innovations.

Exxon's approach to the development of communication vehicles is similar to the development of new products: develop products that satisfy the needs of specifically defined market segments. Exxon's publications and programs for maintaining effective communications are developed for clearly defined segments of the population. Also, their content is consistent with the recognized needs of each group.

Some of Exxon's target audiences include (1) current and retired employees of Exxon, (2) the consuming public, (3) Exxon distributors, (4) Exxon dealers, (5) higher education personnel, and (6) stockholders. Exxon employees, for example, are informed of human interest activities and achievement milestones through Profile, a monthly, in-house publication. The consuming public is informed of the numerous activities and businesses of Exxon in Exxon U.S.A., a quarterly publication, as well as through its television and newspaper advertisements. Distributors receive Energy which focuses on human interest and case studies. Also, dealers, higher education personnel, and stockholders are informed of activities through Exxon Extra, Dimensions, and Lamp, respectively.

In addition to mass media communication with its publics, Exxon also has a formal program for facilitating face-to-face communications. One such program is a quarterly meeting to bring all dealers together to talk about new programs, equipment changes, inventory verification, and so on. Exxon utilizes slides, films, and other audio/video equipment to communicate its message. Then the dealers provide feedback to management on each issue.

To further facilitate communications with customers, Exxon employs advisory councils at the dealer and distributor levels. Exxon Company, U.S.A. has four regions, and each region is divided into districts, zones, and territories. Advisory councils are organized at the district levels. In addition, dealers and distributors in each district separately elect representatives to regional advi-

sory councils, and each regional council elects members to national advisory councils, one for dealers and one for distributors. The agenda for meetings is prepared by the council which discusses a wide variety of problems and opportunities. The result of these advisory councils at each level of the organization is direct, undistorted communication from the lowest levels in the distribution channel to the top management of Exxon Corporation.

Communication between dealers and management is also facilitated by a formal grievance procedure. If a dealer or distributor is not satisfied with a district level action, the middlemen can appeal the action to dealer/distributor relations committees at the regional level and headquarters level.

Exxon apparently understands and responds to the importance of effective communication. It has shortened the distance between top and bottom management, reduced the probability of unresolved grievances, and ensured that its customers and publics are involved in the communication cycle on a regular basis. Finally, Exxon makes certain that orientation toward communication excellence is preserved through special management seminars and programs on effective communication.

(2) salespeople are too busy with other activities.[6] In other words, some sales managers believe that salespeople should just sell and not be involved in decision-making activities.

In summary, more emphasis should be placed on the upward transmission of ideas, feelings, and attitudes in an organization. Downward communication is necessary, but without proper consideration of feedback its value is significantly limited. As was pointed out by Roethlisberger years ago:

> One simple, genuine move on the part of management to understand employees from their point of view is worth ten moves on the part of management to get the employees to understand the

---

[6] Dan H. Robertson, "Sales Force Feedback on Competitors' Activities," *Journal of Marketing*, Vol. 38 (April 1974), p. 71.

problems of management. One move to find out why people at work behave and feel the way they do is worth ten moves in the direction of telling people how they ought to feel and behave.[7]

GUIDELINES FOR EFFECTIVE COMMUNICATIONS

Most problems in an organization result from or are exaggerated by poor employee communications. As indicated earlier, the communication process is complex and the barriers to effective communication are numerous. However, since communication is the coordinating phase of management, it is vital that a program for the perpetuation of employee communication be implemented at all organizational levels. The purpose of this section is to translate communication theory into specific guidelines which should be considered by management when developing such a program. Such guidelines include the following:

- Solicit ideas from salespeople and other employees before making policy and strategy decisions. Also, in order to perpetuate two-way communication, let them know that these ideas are important decision variables.

- Evaluate communication from the perspective of the sender and carefully examine how receivers of your communications perceive your messages. In fact, try to anticipate how they will react.

- Express ideas in terms which can be easily understood by the receiver.

- Observe body language, gestures, and expressions to determine genuine attitudes toward a communication.

- Continuously improve communication skills by evaluating the success of each communication to determine why it is successful or unsuccessful.

- Frequently use personal, face-to-face communication with subordinates. Make these encounters seem important to the subordinate by minimizing interruptions.

- Restrict unimportant communication and demands on subordinates.

- Identify personal antagonism which may stifle effective interaction.

---

[7] "A 'new look' for Management," *Worker Morale and Productivity*, General Management Series No. 141 (New York: American Management Association, 1948), p. 20.

COMMUNICATION AIDS

Previous sections of this chapter outline the communication process, identify barriers to effective communication, and recommend ways to improve communication skills. This section identifies various tools which may facilitate communication among salespeople, sales managers, customers, and suppliers. These sales aids include sales bulletins, advertising, trade shows, and audio-visual equipment. Other communication devices such as sales reports are discussed in Chapter 10.

Sales Bulletins (Newsletters)

Sales bulletins are one way of communicating new product information, economic data, company policy changes, sales techniques, and company performance data to salespeople. They are also an excellent vehicle for soliciting input from salespeople concerning these organizational activities. Bulletins are generally developed by the sales manager or assistant and are usually presented in a one page leaflet format or a more expensive magazine format. Regardless of the format selected, they should be concise, interesting, and utilize numerous illustrations and subheadings.

Ideas for bulletins come from the sales manager, company executives, salespeople, customers, and suppliers. Not only should bulletins reflect corporate ideas and communications, but they should also provide salespeople with a forum for presenting their ideas and interests. For example, a regular column in which a salesperson can discuss how a particular type of account was sold can be useful to other salespeople that are confronted with similar problems. Another idea which utilizes upward communication is a question-answer section. Salespeople should be given the opportunity to direct questions to various executives and then these managers can develop an answer which will appear in a subsequent issue. Figure 11-2 lists additional information salespeople would like to have appear in bulletins.

- How to meet buyer objections.

- News of competitors.

- New selling strategies.

- New product applications.

- Reasons for price changes.

- Current summary of market conditions.

- Sales promotion ideas.

- Product sales volume and techniques in other territories.

- Features by well-known sales authorities.

Figure 11-2
Bulletin Topics

Not only do sales bulletins keep salespeople informed of industry, company, and economic events, they also minimize the need for expensive, time-consuming sales meetings. Employees can benefit from a sense of interaction through bulletins and can feel more a part of the team without frequent personal contact. Also, information in bulletins can help sales representatives become better salespeople and more effectively meet and satisfy the needs of customers.

Audio-Visual Communication

Another powerful communication tool is audio-visual equipment which sales managers can utilize to present sales approaches, product demonstrations, and company information to field sales representatives. With costs of travel increasing substantially, investments in this type of equipment can be less expensive than frequent sales meetings and conferences in the long run. Doubleday and Shell Oil Company, for example, use audio-visual programs to train salespeople.[8] Montgomery Ward has gone even further by utilizing live, telecommunications devices to introduce new products and advertisements to sales managers at remote locations.[9] This equipment also facilitates instantaneous feedback from sales managers by way of question and answer sessions.

To spread costs of such audio-visual equipment, it can also be used by salespeople to present ideas to buyers. Pacific Telephone & Telegraph Company's salespeople for example, are all supported by professionally developed slide tape programs. Success from the program has motivated management to extend the program to the point that over 250 programs have been developed, some of which are customized for the governor and cabinet of California and the presidents of more than a dozen major corporations.[10]

Advertising

Advertising has traditionally been considered an effective communication tool for obtaining leads for salespeople and for paving the way for sales calls. Many managers believe that company advertising impacts on the credibility of the advertiser. Because the company does advertise, customers will envision it as a more credible, viable organization and be more receptive to messages presented by company representatives. This makes it easier for salespeople to not only get an audience with prospective buyers, but also to stimulate them into accepting sales ideas. In fact, in one study Morrill indicates that not only does advertising pave the

---

[8] "Suddenly the Aid is a Full Partner," *Sales and Marketing Management* (December 12, 1977), p. 41.

[9] "On-Camera vs. Face to Face," *Sales and Marketing Management* (April 3, 1978), p. 12.

[10] "Plugged-in Selling at Pacific Telephone," *Sales and Marketing Management* (December 12, 1977), pp. 42–43.

way for salespeople, but it also reduces costs associated with selling the prospect by as much as 28 percent.[11]

Trade Shows and Exhibits

Trade shows and exhibits can serve as effective media for communicating ideas to potential customers. National trade shows give companies exposure to potential customers from all areas of the country. Also, regional meetings can be used to get additional exposure in those areas where market penetration has been weak. In addition to being a common ground for meeting customers at a reduced cost, trade shows may also be used to test new ideas or products. Valuable input from prospective buyers can be obtained before the company invests significant sums of money in the idea.

Trade shows and exhibitions should be taken seriously and the firm should formulate objectives to be accomplished at the show. A firm's rationale for attending a show should not simply be that it (the firm) has always attended or that competitors will be there. If the firm cannot state some specific objectives it hopes to attain by attending a trade show, it probably should not attend.

Assuming, however, that management has decided to participate in a show, how can it be sure of maximizing its benefits from this promotional investment?

1. *Plan development of the exhibit far in advance of the show.* Display firms need a minimum of 60 to 90 days to construct an exhibit. If sufficient time is not allowed, then resultant increased costs of overtime can significantly reduce the amount of budget available for additional expenses.

2. *Carefully evaluate and select display firms.* A full-service display firm is equipped to design, build, ship, and dismantle exhibits. Evaluation of alternative designs and proposed bids, however, should begin several months prior to commencement of construction. This decision is extremely important to success of the trade show and should be considered as important as the selection of an advertising agency.

3. *Be open-minded to the display firm's ideas.* Do not predetermine the type and design of exhibits. The display firm is familiar with convention facilities, electrical and fire codes, union contracts for building and dismantling, installation of lights, and facility rules for displays. They have also observed the effectiveness of various types of exhibits and can provide valuable input on design effectiveness.

4. *Anticipate problems during the preliminary design stage.* Although design and building of exhibits may seem simple, it is difficult to build a display which maximizes effectiveness and is within budget

---

[11] John E. Morrill, "Industrial Advertising Pays Off," *Harvard Business Review*, Vol. 48 (March-April, 1970), p. 12.

constraints. When evaluating preliminary sketches, ask the following questions: Are the designs practical from the standpoint of traffic flow? Will they gain attention among the numerous other displays? Is there adequate company identification? Is there sufficient lighting? Is there enough graphic or pictorial content?

Although design and development of appropriate exhibits is important to the success of trade show promotion, the exhibit is primarily designed to initially gain attention and interest. It is also vital that the appropriate mix of employees be present to offer ideas and answer questions. Do not have only salespeople or only engineers working the display at one time. Since salespeople are often not technically competent to answer all questions and engineers are not always good salespeople, communication of ideas can be facilitated with a mix of employees.

As with most sales and sales management activities, it is also appropriate to evaluate effectiveness of the trade show exhibit. It is appropriate to audit the number of visitors attracted to the exhibit and maintain a file of prospects. As these prospects become customers, these records can be added to audit information to determine long run contribution of the show. Figures from various shows can be maintained to compare relative effectiveness and subsequently establish a benchmark for effectiveness.

SUMMARY

Interpersonal communication is mandatory for effective selling and sales force management. Since both activities are problem solving disciplines, it is critical that data be collected and disseminated in such a way that problems can be identified, understood, and handled.

The communication process begins with an idea or concept that the sender wishes to transmit to a receiver. The concept is developed into a symbolic representation, transmitted through an appropriate channel, and interpreted by the receiver. The receiver responds to the translated message which may stimulate subsequent communication from the original sender.

Although effective communication can help sales managers identify and solve problems, ineffective communication can create an entirely new set of problems. Some of the major problems that can distort the communication process are physical barriers (i.e., external distractions which suppress fidelity of messages), personal barriers (i.e., information overload and personal distortion of messages), and semantic barriers (i.e., inconsistent meaning of words, phrases, and other symbols of reality).

QUESTIONS

1. List and define three barriers to effective communication.

2. What are the components of the communication process? Why is it important for salespeople to understand this process?

3. Discuss decoding and the factors that are associated with effective decoding.

4. The author discussed two-way communication. Why is feedback from field representatives so important to sales managers?

5. What are the advantages of sales bulletins?

6. Explain the differences between selective and intentional distortion.

7. What can be done to overcome personal communication barriers?

8. How could management improve two-way communication?

9. Does company advertising aid salespeople? Support your answer.

10. What can be done to improve the effectiveness of exhibiting at trade shows?

Chapter 12 _____

Motivating
Salespeople

After completing this chapter, you will be able to:

- Identify the meaning and importance of motivation.
- Discuss theories of motivation and the impact of theory on sales management.
- Identify and explain techniques for motivating salespeople.

Since motivation results from an individual's drive to satisfy needs, it is imperative that sales managers understand the needs and, therefore, the motivations of salespeople. For example, a particular salesperson's productivity may decline for two or three periods. Although the primary cause of reduction in productivity may relate to family problems, the sales manager may interpret it as laziness or ineffectiveness in some aspect of the selling process. The salesperson's behavior is directed toward a goal of satisfying a personal problem or, in other words, the salesperson is motivated to alleviate an imbalance in his or her personal life. A manager who is not sensitive to the salesperson's immediate needs and motivations may possibly work on the salesperson's presentation or product knowledge, evaluate the salesperson's call performance, or even criticize and intimidate the salesperson in front of peers. Until the person's motivating needs are satisfied, there is a good chance that the sales manager's activities will cause either no change in productivity or, in the latter case, demotivation in behavior.

The point is that motivation is complex, personal, and constantly changing. Each person is motivated by different stimuli depending on which needs are aroused at a particular time. Simple group methods that are designed by managers to improve morale and motivate salespeople to higher levels of productivity may be effective for some salespeople (i.e., those whose needs are consistent with the need-satisfaction technique) but have no effect on other members of the sales force (i.e., those whose needs are inconsistent with needs which are being appealed to by the technique). Also, as a need is satisfied it may cease to be important and a sales manager's efforts to improve morale of a salesperson by appealing to the need may be futile. Therefore, what worked to improve morale during one week may be completely ineffective the next week.

THEORIES OF MOTIVATION

As was indicated previously, motivation is goal-directed behavior intended to satisfy some aroused need(s). The sales manager's role in motivating salespeople is to help salespeople satisfy their needs, or at least to help them strive toward need satisfaction. To effectively accomplish this goal, the sales manager must either analyze and individually deal with each salesperson's needs and goals, or make certain assumptions about need structure and the impact of certain needs on behavior. If those theories of need structure can reasonably be applied to a majority of the population, then general programs of motivation (i.e., theories of motivation) can be implemented for an entire sales force. Remember, however, that even when applying general theories of motivation some salespeople will have needs that are not met by the program.

Hierarchy of Needs

A.H. Maslow theorizes that there is a hierarchy of needs which can be helpful in explaining motivation. Figure 12-1 shows Maslow's hierarchy of needs.

According to Maslow's theory, the five categories of needs are arrayed in a hierarchical arrangement from the most basic, low order needs (i.e., physiological) to the most complex, high order needs (i.e., self-actualization). People are initially motivated to satisfy physiological needs. Until these lower order needs are partially satisfied, other need categories are not important motivators of behavior. Once physiological needs are satisfied, individuals are motivated by the next group of needs in the hierarchy. For example, if a person is hungry (a physiological need), all energy and motivation will be directed toward satisfaction of that need. Once hunger is satisfied, the person's attention is turned to the need for security, protection of one's property and family, and development of order in one's life (i.e., safety needs). After the person is secure and safe, the need for social acceptance and approval becomes the primary motivator of behavior. When social needs are satisfied, the person looks for status and recognition within the group (self-esteem needs), and finally attempts to achieve his or her full potential (self actualization).

Although Maslow provides a general hierarchical need structure, utilization of the theory to sales management problems is somewhat difficult. When one progresses beyond safety needs, ways in which higher order needs may be satisfied are numerous and unique to each individual. For example, one salesperson may find association with the sales group to be rewarding and may not need any additional social acceptance. This person may also seek recognition and esteem from work activities. In order to motivate this person, the sales manager should provide opportunities for advancement, contests, and other challenges. Another salesperson may not realize any satisfaction from associating

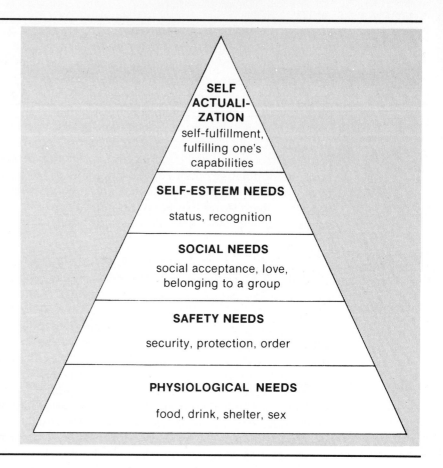

Figure 12–1
Maslow's Hierarchy
of Needs

with the sales group. Satisfaction of the need for social acceptance may come from association with a charity, a religious group, or a sports group. Opportunities for advancement and challenges may have little impact on such a person's motivation to perform.

Since salespeople are gratified by different types of group interaction and recognition, it is imperative that sales managers identify the methods of need satisfaction desired by each person. Salesperson A, for example, may believe that an office window reflects a certain amount of status. In order to have and maintain an office with a window, salesperson A may increase performance. Salesperson B may equate status with a particular model of car. For this person, if a particular sales level is accomplished and maintained, he or she may be given that particular model as a company car. If the sales manager understands each salesperson and is sensitive to each one's unique needs, then the manager can develop motivational programs which help each one progress toward satisfaction of those needs and, therefore, motivate them to higher performance.

Job Satisfiers and Dissatisfiers

From a study of accountants and engineers, Herzberg, Mauser, and Snyderman identified two groups of factors which impact on job satisfaction (i.e., two-factor theory).[1] One category of factors, known as **hygiene factors**, are associated with conditions surrounding actual performance of a job and are listed in Figure 12-2.

Figure 12–2
The Hygiene
Factors

- Supervision-technical

- Interpersonal relations

- Physical working conditions

- Salary

- Company policies and administrative practices

- Benefits

- Job Security

These hygiene factors are a source of dissatisfaction if they are not present, but their presence does not improve job satisfaction. For example, if salary is at an acceptable level, employee attitude will be at a level of indifference, but if salary is below this level of acceptability employees will be dissatisfied. Also, if salary is above an acceptable level, improved satisfaction will not occur. In other words, manipulation of hygiene factors will not motivate a person to perform at higher levels but can keep a person from being dissatisfied, changing jobs, or performing poorly.

The other group of factors, referred to as **motivators**, relate to the job itself and are shown in Figure 12-3. While absence of these motivators will not cause dissatisfaction, their presence can motivate employees to higher levels of satisfaction and performance. Recognition of salespeople for their ideas, therefore, may positively influence performance. If they are not recognized, however, they will not necessarily be dissatisfied.

Although some research partially confirms Herzberg's findings on motivation, most research suggests that employee motivation is not as cut and dried as Herzberg implies. From a study by Edwin Locke, for example, it was concluded that the presence of Herzberg's motivators may cause satisfaction among some employees and dissatisfaction in

---

[1] Frederick Herzberg, Bernard Mauser, and Barbara Block Snyderman, *The Motivation to Work* (2d ed.; New York: John Wiley and Sons, Inc., 1959).

Figure 12–3
The Motivators

- Achievement
- Recognition
- Work itself
- Responsibility
- Advancement
- Growth potential

others.[2] To be specific, Herzberg suggests that satisfaction is related to the work itself. According to Locke, however, satisfaction only occurs if the assigned work is both challenging and can be coped with successfully. If it is challenging but is beyond the person's capabilities, it will result in dissatisfaction. Locke's studies have provided the following conclusions about factors which employees want from a job:

- Challenging work he or she can cope with successfully.

- Just rewards for performance which are in line with his or her applications.

- An understanding of what is expected by others.

- Appreciation and acceptance by supervisor and co-workers.

- Working facilities and resources which facilitate task performance.[3]

Herzberg and Locke's ideas on motivation have significant implications for sales management. Many sales managers provide new salespeople little training or support. These salespeople are simply assigned an uncultivated market and told to sink or swim. There is a very good chance that they will confront numerous problems when initially attempting to develop the territory. If the salespeople are not experienced or adequately trained to overcome these problems, they may become discouraged and look for another challenge that can reasonably be met.

Other Theories of Motivation

In addition to Maslow and Herzberg, other researchers have provid-

---

[2] Edwin A. Locke, "Satisfiers and Dissatisfiers Among White-Collar and Blue-Collar Employees," *Journal of Applied Psychology*, Vol. 58, No. 1 (1973), p. 67.
[3] In: Henry L. Tosi and Stephen J. Carroll, *Management: Contingencies, Structure, and Process* (Chicago: St. Clair Press, 1976), pp. 126–127.

ed insight into factors which motivate individuals to perform. McGregor, for example, explained that managers should first attempt to understand general human nature and then develop organizational programs and policies which are consistent with that behavior.[4] To give management insight into the behavior of employees and provide a basis for program development, McGregor proposed two theories: Theory X and Theory Y. **Theory X** suggests that humans have an inherent dislike for work, avoid responsibility, and must be coerced, controlled, and threatened with punishment to get them to exert effort toward accomplishment of goals. On the other hand, **Theory Y** indicates that work is a natural phenomenon, individuals will exercise self-direction and self-control in accomplishing objectives, the capacity to exercise imagination is widely distributed in the population, and commitment to objectives is a function of the reward associated with their achievement.

McClelland's research indicates that motivation is strongly correlated to achievement.[5] In other words, people that are motivated to perform at relatively high levels have a strong need to achieve in terms of successfully solving problems and advancing professionally. While many of the other ideas on motivation focus on procedures which will motivate current employees, McClelland identifies a characteristic of prospective and current employees which can serve to predict whether they have the capacity to be motivated. By testing the strength of their achievement need, one can predict their response to various job responsibilities.

While subordinates should have a high need for achievement, McClelland has indicated that successful managers have a high need for power.[6] Studies of managers indicate that while the achievement motive may be high, the need to influence others should be higher. McClelland also points out, though, that this power motive should be controlled so that efforts are directed toward benefiting the organization and not the manager's personal well-being.

TECHNIQUES OF MOTIVATION

The theories of motivation discussed in the preceding section reflect results of research into employee performance and variables which impact on that performance. Although these theories cannot be universally applied to all employees on all organizational levels, they do provide insight into the complexity of the motivation problem and suggest procedures which should be followed by managers in order to stimulate employees to higher levels of performance. Sales managers should be

---

[4] Douglas McGregor, *The Human Side of Enterprise* (New York: McGraw-Hill Book Company, 1960).

[5] David C. McClelland, *The Achieving Society* (New York: Halsted Press, A Division of John Wiley & Sons, Inc., 1976).

[6] David C. McClelland and David H. Burnham, "Power is the Great Motivator," *Harvard Business Review* (March-April, 1976), pp. 100–110.

familiar with these ideas and give salespeople the opportunity to benefit from their application. Many sales managers have a tendency to use their own experiences and ignore the abundance of empirical data about human behavior and motivation. Although experience is important, it certainly should not replace concepts and procedures advanced by people who spend all their energies attempting to better understand human behavior.

Theories of behavioralists and the insight of sales managers are brought together in this section to identify and analyze the feasibility of alternative techniques of motivation. Since some of the techniques have much broader application than simply motivating, they will be discussed both in this section and in other sections of the book.

Sales Meetings

When the same salespeople are brought together for regularly scheduled meetings, such meetings tend to become uninteresting, a chore for the meeting leader, and a bore for the salespeople. Although managers often try to use these meetings to improve morale, educate salespeople on new product information, train salespeople on new sales techniques, or allow salespeople to share ideas, they are usually nothing more than an inconvenience and do not improve morale. In fact, they may have a negative impact on the organization by reducing the salesperson's time in the field.

Although there is no evidence to suggest that meetings have any impact on motivation, they can serve as a medium for praising the performance of certain salespeople. Consistent with the theories of Herzberg and Maslow, an awards meeting can be used to publicly recognize performance of outstanding salespeople. Since salespeople generally work alone and are not in constant contact with other employees of the firm, there is little chance to publicly recognize their performance. With an infrequent but important awards program, salespeople can have the opportunity to be recognized in the presence of peers and possibly receive recognition in local media, company bulletins, and association publications.

In addition to meetings which are designed to recognize performance, meetings may also be necessary to accomplish other objectives. In many cases, these are the meetings that negatively impact on productivity and morale. If such a meeting is necessary, however, it is important that sales managers follow some rules to realize maximum benefit from such activity and insure that the meeting does not demotivate the salespeople. (See Figure 12-4 for a summary.)

First, make certain that meeting objectives cannot be better accomplished by some other means such as field contact, office conferences, a letter, or a bulletin. In many cases, new product information and company performance can be related to salespeople with one of the alternative techniques.

- Identify alternative ways, other than a meeting, that objectives may be accomplished.

- Specifically define the meeting's purpose.

- Select a meeting leader who can most effectively accomplish its objectives.

- Minimize the length of the meeting.

- Emphasize meeting benefits to salespeople.

- Solicit questions from salespeople prior to final meeting preparation.

- Refer to a written checklist of details.

- Rehearse meeting content for timing purposes.

Figure 12–4
Rules for Sales
Meeting Planning
and Organization

- Evaluate its effectiveness.

- Use meetings to recognize outstanding accomplishments, but never criticize for inadequate performance.

Second, the purpose of the meeting should be clearly defined prior to its announcement. It is a good idea to attach a theme so that salespeople may be better able to remember the major thrust of the meeting.

Third, determine which persons can make the best contribution in attaining meeting objectives. The sales manager, management people other than the sales manager, management people from other companies, selected customers, selected representatives from suppliers, and professional trainers are all potential contributors.

Fourth, make the meeting as short as possible. If the manager adequately prepares meeting objectives and identifies how those objectives are to be accomplished, the meeting will generally be much shorter than one which lacks necessary preparation.

Fifth, specify time and place and emphasize benefits to salespeople when announcing a forthcoming meeting. Several years ago International Harvester used the curiosity approach to build interest in forthcoming dealer meetings. A man with HUET printed on him was sent to dealers to stimulate curiosity about the acronym's meaning. After weeks of guessing its meaning they were eventually informed that it meant "Harvester Used Equipment Training."

Sixth, solicit questions from salespeople that they would like answered prior to final preparation of the meeting agenda. These questions should be distributed to the appropriate executives and answers should be formulated and returned to the sales manager. Another important rule is to use a written checklist of meeting details. For exam-

A Company Profile

Moore Corporation was formed in 1882 by Samuel J. Moore to provide products and services which facilitate the recording, communication, retention, and retrieval of business information. The company's first product was the Paragon Counter Check Book, a duplicating salesbook operating on the principle, "Let one writing serve many purposes." This ingenious idea was initially responsible for Moore's early growth and gave it the impetus to develop into a multinational corporation with approximately $2 billion in sales, $115 million in profit, 27,000 employees, 131 plants, and 5,500 sales representatives.

During the late 1800's and early 1900's most of Moore's efforts focused on improving manufacturing efficiency by upgrading state-of-the-art printing technology, simplifying paper handling, achieving longer and faster press runs, and reducing overall costs. Moore's salespeople also evaluated customer requirements and problems to identify new products that could help customers cope with increasing demands and pressures. The counter check book, for example, provided retail merchants with a permanent record of transactions. It was invaluable to business people because it helped them check accuracy of bills, track credit, control inventory, and minimize the hazard of theft. In developing another product, the Speediset multipart form, Moore responded to the need of a single poultry raising business in California, and opened the door to hundreds of thousands of other opportunities.

Moore is the world's largest manufacturer of business forms, and in fact can be credited with initial development of the forms industry. Its forms division, which is responsible for 90 percent of Moore's revenue, provides business with a comprehensive array of products, from simple handwritten types to highly complex forms, and systems for advanced data reading and writing equipment. The company also supplies a complete line of computer supplies and related products, including continuous forms handling equipment.

Moore's other product offerings include business systems, response graphics, and computer graphics. Moore Business Systems offers small and medium sized businesses computer-based information systems tailored to the needs of their particular industry. The division offers its customers computer hardware, industry-related software, service, and supplies. Another division, Response Graphics, serves the direct mail and lottery industries with new and innovative systems applications which link patented ink jet printing processes with computer control and press speeds. Mailings are printed, personalized, and posted in a mass production operation to meet the needs of direct marketers. Finally, Moore's computer graphics division, International Graphics, serves those firms which demand access to large quantities of changeable printed reference materials on a regular or recurring basis. Data base information, computer typesetting, and high-speed printing are combined in one package to produce updated parts/price lists, directories, rosters, realty books, and tariff schedules.

Moore's salespeople have always been an important part of its success. They help customers reduce the costs of doing business by working with them on a total forms program. In the past when companies needed large quantities of forms they would invite several forms suppliers to bid on the order. Moore changed this approach by working with customers on a program of combining individual orders into large orders. Instead of printing 50,000 forms at a time for a customer, Moore may print 1 million forms, warehouse the products, then defer charges until the product is needed. Another part of this systems approach is the efficient construction of a format for each form. Forms may include such cost reduction features as size reduction and the elimination of multiple copies. Smaller customers are served with traditional programs or telemarketing.

Motivating salespeople is an important aspect of Moore's total management program. Although variable compensation (i.e., salary plus commission plus bonus) is an ingredient in its motivation mix, recognition, training, and performance review are the most significant elements of the company's program. Exceptional performance is recognized throughout a salesperson's career at Moore. One of its most successful programs is the Achievement Club. In order to become part of Moore's Achievement Club, salespeople must reach quota as well as sell more than 50 percent of the people in their peer group. The company has four peer groups consisting of salespeople with similar sales volumes. All salespeople qualifying for the Achievement Club attend a five-day business and awards meeting with their spouses.

Recognition is also accommodated in Moore's Summer Sellathon contest and career path program. During the Summer Sellathon, salespeople accumulate prize points that can be converted into merchandise or cash for exceeding sales quota. Moore's sales career path program involves four steps. In order to reach step one, salespeople must successfully complete phase I and phase II of the training program. The

company recognizes accomplishment of step one by granting the salesperson the title, "sales representative." Criteria for reaching step 2 are personal sales of at least $300,000, phase III training, and one Achievement Club membership. For accomplishing step 2, salespeople earn several prizes and the title, "account representative." Criteria for realizing step 3 are $750,000 in sales, phase IV training, and 3 Achievement Club memberships. Step 3 salespeople receive a publicity press release in local newspapers, a customer announcement, numerous personal awards and prizes, and the title "account executive." Criteria for reaching step 4 are personal sales volume of at least $1,200,000, phase V training, and 10 Achievement Club memberships. Step 4 salespeople are recognized with the title, "senior account executive," private office accommodations, customer announcements, paid advertisement in local newspapers, and numerous awards and prizes.

Moore's five phase training program is an important ingredient in its motivation program. Initial training involves a comprehensive self-study course on product knowledge, pricing techniques, and company policy. Phase I training is followed by a two week program on basic selling techniques, presentations, and systems selling at the Moore Education Center. Phase III training is a products and systems selling seminar which encompasses data processing fundamentals, complex forms construction, advanced systems applications, and marketing objectives. This is followed by an advanced seminar, which covers advanced product knowledge and forms management programs. Final training includes a senior representative's course for those involved in major account selling and servicing, and management seminars for supervisors and managers.

Motivation is also facilitated by per-

formance evaluation. Moore utilizes quantitative and qualitative indices to assess each salesperson's performance. Since some salespeople are motivated by advancement and new challenges, performance review includes a career plan section. If a person *wants to be a sales manager, this desire can be indicated on the review form. Management will then attempt to accommodate the desire of qualified salespeople for management responsibility.*

ple, find proper facilities, arrange meeting rooms to accomplish objectives, arrange for breaks, check ventilation, lighting, sound, and props, and start on time.

Seventh, if the meeting is going to be a large formal gathering, rehearse it from beginning to end in the room in which it is to be held. Time each segment. Start on time and quit at the stated time. Make certain breaks are no longer than scheduled.

Finally, appraise each meeting immediately after it is over as to its effectiveness. In addition to the sales manager's observations, a questionnaire can be used to solicit input from all participants. This data can then be used to insure that the next meeting is better planned, better prepared, better conducted, and better received.

Sales Contests

Another common technique for motivating salespeople is the sales contest. A contest is a competitive event in which salespeople are encouraged by the probability of winning a prize to achieve a stated sales objective. The time span of the event should be limited to several months or less, and the objective should not relate to daily sales objectives. The objective of the contest is to provide short run incentive to earn both additional financial reward and possible recognition. If contest rules and objectives do not vary significantly from the daily job function it will not be perceived as a unique chance for recognition. Also, if the contest lasts for more than a month or is frequently repeated, rewards will be perceived as part of normal compensation and cease their role as incentives.

Rules. In addition to varying salesperson objectives and limiting contest time frame, there are several other rules which sales managers should strictly follow in order to insure a successful incentive program. First, objectives should be specifically stated and realistically attainable. Some objectives that fulfill this requirement are as follows:

- Open new accounts (including new business, dead accounts, and competitors' accounts).

- Introduce a new product to various markets (i.e., penetration of channels during initial introduction).

- Sell distress merchandise.

- Penetrate a specifically defined market segment (i.e., a certain sized category of firms, a geographical area).

- Obtain dealer cooperation in a manufacturer-sponsored promotional campaign. Salespeople can be scored based upon the number of dealers participating and the extent of participation by each dealer.

Objectives such as increasing sales volume, profit margin, or market share are part of the salespeople's long range sales objective and cannot be effectively implemented in a short run contest. Also, since potential often varies between territories, it is difficult to structure equitable contest rules.

Another rule for contests is that each salesperson should have an equal chance of winning. This can be accomplished by using one of the practical objectives listed above, establishing quotas if increased sales volume is the contest objective, or by establishing group competition. Group competition is effective because teams can be balanced with salespeople of various experience levels and potentials. In addition to making competition more equitable, salespeople realize the benefits of teamwork and team building.

Third, many managers suggest that all salespeople should win. The salesperson that receives the highest contest score may possibly receive an around the world cruise while the person with the lowest score may receive a bicycle, but everyone should win something. Also, the prizes should be attractive and desirable so that salespeople are encouraged to expend extra effort to win.

Finally, the firm should maintain contact with salespeople during the contest period. As the contest continues, initial enthusiasm generated at its announcement may be lost. In order to insure that contest benefits continue past the first few weeks, memoranda, reminder letters, media announcements, and personal calls should be utilized. In many cases, communications may be consistent with the contest theme. For example, it may be a "South Sea Islands" contest. Every week of the contest, top management could send to each salesperson items from an island. They could also arrange for local travel agents to call the salespersons' spouses to make arrangements for the winning vacation.

Incentive Capacity of Contests. If contests are properly structured and objectives are beyond normal sales goals, certain advantages may be realized by the sponsoring firm. The firm may be able to open new markets, effectively introduce a new product, move distress merchandise, or stimulate reseller support. At the same time, sales staff morale may be boosted during a time when sales and motivation are low. Many salespeople work by themselves and only compete against themselves. The contest gives them a chance to work with other salespeople at an exciting, rewarding, and enjoyable project as well as engage in challenging competition. Although there is no empirical proof that contests have significant motivational characteristics, they are a good change of pace and, if properly handled, may produce stimulating and rewarding fun for the sales force and may even help profits for the firm.

Direct and Indirect Costs of Contests. In addition to costs of contest prizes and promotion, there are several indirect costs that management should evaluate before implementing such an incentive program. They include:

- Management time associated with developing, coordinating, and controlling contests.

- Impact of contest on low-level performers.

- Post-contest sales levels.

- Effect of contest on customer servicing.

Not only should direct contest costs be deducted from sales increase, but indirect costs should be evaluated and also subtracted from revenue. For example, management must spend a significant amount of time developing and administering the contest. Costs associated with these activities may involve telephone calls, travel, and contest materials. The most important point management should remember when utilizing a contest as an incentive is that it should be set up according to the rules detailed above and its *net effectiveness* should be objectively monitored.

In addition, if contest rules are not properly followed, the contest may have no impact or a negative impact on all salespeople except the top producers. Other salespeople simply accept the fact that one of the top producers will win and, therefore, do not actively participate.

Another variable that should be monitored by management is the sales level immediately after the contest ends. If it is lower than prior years' sales levels during the same period, the reduction in sales should be deducted from contest revenue. Although not all companies experience a letdown from salespeople after a sales contest, it can happen and should be considered.

Several final contest costs deal with salesperson interaction with buyers. First, if the contest objectives emphasize sales volume, some salespeople may ignore customer servicing—which is, of course, a significant aspect of selling. This may lead to customer dissatisfaction and possibly lost customers. Second, some salespeople will ask their well-established customers to buy additional units during the contest period. This overstocking strategy may distort actual results of the contest, reduce sales during the period immediately after the contest, or result in a high rate of merchandise return.

Sales Training

Although a separate chapter has been devoted to sales training procedures, the role of sales training in motivation of salespeople is briefly discussed in this section.

A review of motivation theory indicates that employees may be motivated to higher levels of productivity through recognition, growth potential, advancement, and the successful completion of challenging work. In other words, salespeople that accomplish stated objectives realize positive reinforcement from their success, develop an optimistic and confident attitude toward their position, and are motivated to successfully confront additional challenges. On the other hand, salespeople that receive negative reinforcement early in their sales career may internalize these negative experiences and become reluctant to seek higher, more challenging goals.

Since successful accomplishment of tasks is highly correlated to motivation, it is imperative that sales managers help facilitate success among their salespeople. The best way to ensure a winning attitude and success among salespeople is to teach them the newest, most effective selling techniques. Also, they should be trained to handle all customer problems, react to market changes, and motivate customers to buy. Because it directly helps salespeople accomplish both short and long-term objectives, training is one of the most essential ingredients in the motivation mix.

This training should be directed at both the new recruit and the seasoned sales veteran. The new recruit is in an extremely vulnerable position and future sales habits and performance will be influenced significantly by early experiences and learning. Also, young salespeople are more educated and will not only respond favorably to, but will demand, extensive training programs. Experienced salespeople must also be trained and retrained. Although they may be successful and motivated early in their careers, events may affect their success and attendant enthusiasm. These salespeople, therefore, should receive continuous product and sales training to ensure that new technologies do not render their talents obsolete and ineffective.

Financial Incentive

Although financial rewards have traditionally been utilized to stimulate salespeople to achieve higher levels of performance, most authorities on both motivation and compensation agree that financial incentives do not necessarily accomplish their stated purpose. Lack of adequate financial rewards may hurt morale and increase turnover, but the presence of adequate compensation will not necessarily motivate. As was indicated by Yankolovich, employees desire more leisure and external rewards, and demand money to compensate them for engaging in a relatively unappealing task—work.[7]

Other observers indicate that sales managers should create a total environment within which salespeople can motivate themselves. Although compensation may be one variable among the total mix of motivators, it is not a panacea. John Moynahan, for example, suggests that the following additional elements play a significant role in motivating salespeople.[8]

- Peer recognition and perception of career opportunities.

- Salesperson's respect for the company, its products, and its management.

- Adequacy of fringe benefits.

- Equitable distributions of territories.

- Customer perception of the company's image.

Other studies have helped confirm the fact that compensation level does not positively impact on motivation. Newton found in a study of over 1,000 sales organizations that low compensation will lead to higher turnover and, conversely, high pay will reduce turnover, but a high compensation level will not result in high performance. The type of compensation plan (i.e., mix of salary and commission), however, will impact on productivity.[9] In addition to the type of compensation plan, the openness of the compensation plan may also impact on productivity. A recent study found that secrecy in salesperson compensation will negatively affect motivation while an open pay plan where salespeople are free to identify the compensation level of peers has a "positive impact on salespeople's job performance and their satisfaction with pay, company promotional policies, and work."[10]

The implications of recent research for sales managers is that they should be more innovative in their utilization of pay as a motivator. Rather than simply adjusting pay levels or using a straight salary or commission plan, they should study the impact of commission and salary levels on productivity, develop equitable compensation plans which reward productivity, and allow salespeople to identify the compensation levels of peers. In addition, sales managers should remember that compensation is only one variable impacting on motivation, and, therefore, they should not overemphasize pay at the expense of other, more important motivational factors.

---

[7] "Motivating the 'New Breed' With New Incentives," *Management Review*, Vol. 67, No. 11 (November, 1978), p. 4.

[8] John K. Moynahan, "The Incentive Compensation Plan Won't Necessarily Turn your Sales Force On," *Sales and Marketing Management* (March, 1978), p. 106.

[9] Derek Newton, "Get the Most Out of Your Sales Force," *Harvard Business Review* (September-October, 1969), p. 132.

[10] Charles M. Futrell and Omer C. Jenkins, "Pay Secrecy Versus Pay Disclosure for Salesmen: A Longitudinal Study," *Journal of Marketing Research*, Vol. 15, No. 2 (May, 1978) p. 218.

Team Building _____

Motivation theory suggests that people are motivated by group interaction, recognition, and appreciation and acceptance by co-workers. Team building represents a powerful technique which incorporates existing theory into a motivation program. Specifically, team building consists of periodic meetings by a group of people whose jobs are inter-related to examine how effectively they function as a team, to identify barriers to their collaboration, and to mutually attempt to reduce or eliminate any existing barriers. Similar to sensitivity training, team building attempts to enable individuals to contribute more effectively to their team by making them more aware of how their behavior affects the performance of other members. The synergistic effect of bringing a group of salespeople together to share ideas and problems may result in a stronger feeling of togetherness and a commitment to succeed.

Elements in Team Building. So that the firm realizes maximum benefit from team building, the following rules should be incorporated into the program.

- The sales manager should gain the trust of subordinates. The manager should be open and honest with salespeople and, at the same time, assume a low profile and maintain control over the group.

- Prior to a team building meeting, salespeople should be informed of specific meeting objectives. Also, so that issues are more clearly defined and thoroughly dealt with, no more than two objectives should be stated.

- Although the manager should maintain control, he or she should become part of the team and not stifle the creative input of the individuals. All ideas of team members should be accepted and not criticized prematurely.

- Prior to a team building meeting, the sales manager should arrange a suitable place for the meeting outside of the work environment, notify participants, prepare all visual aids and equipment, and plan procedures to be followed during the meeting.

- Do not expect to uncover new ideas and identify behaviors and aspirations in one meeting. It is often necessary to conduct several meetings before the members become comfortable with each other and the team becomes effective.

- During a session, the group should prepare a list of "written action items" specifying the commitments that each member made with regard to facilitating each other's effectiveness. Subsequent sessions attempt to assess performance against these commitments as well as develop new objectives.

Weaknesses of Team Building.   Although new ideas and better interpersonal relations are facilitated through team building, there are some disadvantages which accompany such a program. First, team building can be time consuming. Although it may save time for the members in the long run, initial development of the program requires a substantial investment of time and effort. Second, new members that join an existing team often have difficulty in adapting. Third, dominant members of the team may overwhelm and control other members. The leader must identify these people early in the program and moderately restrain their activity. Finally, frankness of some team members may offend some of the more vulnerable members and cause resentments which interfere with effective working relationships. Although discussing some topics is often painful, experience has shown that candor and openness facilitate the solving of most problems more quickly and sensibly.

Salesperson Evaluation

A final technique for motivating salespeople is the evaluation or merit rating system. As was indicated previously, salespeople that successfully cope with assigned tasks and achieve objectives will be more highly motivated than those employees that consistently realize failure. Evaluation programs, like training programs, are consistent with this motivation theory in that they are (or at least should be) designed to help salespeople improve performance and achieve goals.

Although evaluation procedures will be extensively discussed in a separate chapter, several brief remarks are made here to point out how important such a program is to the performance and motivation of salespeople. Before a sales manager can help a salesperson satisfy his or her needs, it is mandatory that the sales manager understand those needs. Merit rating forces the sales manager to identify the needs of each salesperson; to uncover personal problems and habits which may constrain realization of one's potential; to evaluate the quality of the salesperson's presentation, customer relations, and other sales related activities; and to quantitatively evaluate all aspects of sales performance (i.e., from controlling costs to closing sales).

Salesperson evaluation programs, therefore, require that managers understand both personal strengths and problems, and business factors which impact on the salesperson's ability to perform. Such programs also require that the manager work with salespeople individually to help them capitalize on their strengths and overcome their weaknesses. By individually working with each person, unique programs for improvement can be implemented to fit each person's particular needs. This overcomes the problem of developing a general program which only impacts on a small percent of the sales force.

Motivation is an individual phenomenon and should be handled individually. Effective evaluation programs represent the only technique which employs an individual-oriented rather than group-oriented approach. It is also one of the few techniques that utilizes accepted motivation theory as the basis for its development. For these reasons it is possibly the most effective program for sales force motivation.

SUMMARY

Motivation is defined as goal-directed behavior to satisfy an aroused need. It is complex, personal, constantly changing, and is largely responsible for a salesperson's performance. Since motivation is complex and personal, the sales manager must develop individualized programs to stimulate salespeople rather than solely employing simplistic, group procedures such as contests.

Motivation theory has provided a significant amount of insight into the feasibility of various motivational programs. It suggests that people have a need for recognition, achievement, challenging work, just rewards, appreciation and acceptance by co-workers and supervisors, unambiguous role definition and working conditions which facilitate task performance.

Motivational techniques that are utilized by sales managers include sales meetings, sales contests, sales training, financial incentives, team building, and salesperson evaluation. Although sales meetings and sales contests are effective if precise objectives are identified, training, incentives, team building, and evaluation are normally the most productive procedures.

QUESTIONS

1. Define motivation and discuss Maslow's Hierarchy of Needs.

2. List the rules that must be followed when developing a sales meeting.

3. What are the two groups of factors which impact on job satisfaction? Explain.

4. Is a contest an effective motivational tool? What rules should be followed in order to maximize the benefits of contests?

5. Do you agree that sales training programs should be given only to the new recruit or young salespeople? Why or why not?

6. What elements in the business environment will encourage salespeople to perform at their best?

7. Is money an effective motivational tool? Why or why not?

8. Discuss the following veiwpoint: It is one thing to say morale is low, another to explain why, and still another to take proper action.

9. Is job enrichment always an effective solution for motivating salespeople to perform at a higher level of productivity?

10. Discuss the strengths and weaknesses of team building?

11. Should an individual's pay be open knowledge or be kept confidential? Support your opinion.

Compensation
of Salespeople

After completing this chapter, you will be able to:

- Identify the objectives and importance of a compensation plan for salespeople.

- Examine research studies which have explored the relative efficacy of alternative types of pay plans.

- Present a systematic procedure for establishing a compensation plan.

- Evaluate the feasibility, uses, and application of the types of compensation plans.

- Present the types of fringe benefits available to management.

Compensation refers to direct and indirect monetary payment for performance of work. By rewarding and recognizing salespeople for performance, a compensation plan should help a firm meet several objectives. First, it should help reduce turnover by satisfying salespeoples' need for monetary security. Second, as a tool for partially satisfying the need for recognition, it should help improve morale and performance. Third, the compensation plan should direct salespeople toward activities, territories, and customers which are important to the accomplishment of company goals.

The extent to which objectives of a compensation plan are accomplished depends on the procedure used to establish a payment plan, the dollar size of rewards, and the type of compensation plan employed. The purpose of this chapter is to examine aspects of sales force compensation which impact on accomplishment of stated objectives. Specifically, the chapter focuses on (1) the importance of sales force compensation, (2) current trends in compensation size and methods, (3) the procedure for establishing a pay plan, (4) types of available compensation plans, and (5) fringe benefits.

IMPORTANCE OF COMPENSATION

Although compensation is not the only factor influencing salesperson performance, it is one of the most important. For example, in a study of International Harvester salespeople, it was found that an increase in pay level positively motivated some salespeople to work harder.[1] In another study of approximately 1,000 sales executives, Derek Newton found that the method of compensating salespeople will impact on performance.[2] The common factor which emerges when one examines the importance of compensation is that some salespeople are positively motivated by pay while others are either not motivated or are *demotivated* by compensation plans. The International Harvester study, for example, also identified a group of salespeople who were negatively motivated by a new compensation plan which afforded the opportunity to earn more income.[3] The results of a study done by Morse and Weiss indicated that the sales performance of 90 percent of the salespeople they investigated would not be significantly motivated by satisfaction of the economic needs.[4] Another study suggests that personal characteristics of salespeople strongly influence the degree to which pay systems affect performance.[5]

The point is that management must evaluate the role and importance of compensation in light of the characteristics of people on the sales force. For some salespeople, pay may be an effective way to motivate and to increase satisfaction. For others, incentive compensation plans will not return to the firm the money which is invested in such plans. Although few studies have isolated the relationship between employee characteristics and the importance of compensation, some conclusions have been developed.

- Satisfaction with a reward system that is financially oriented increases with age. Also, older salespeople have a greater desire to obtain financial rewards associated with such a system than younger salespeople.

- People in higher level jobs value pay less than people in lower level jobs.

- Men are more significantly motivated by pay than women.

- Pay is valued most by people who have a high need for achievement.

- Pay is more highly valued by married salespeople with large

---

[1] René Y. Darmon, "Salesmen's Response to Financial Incentives: An Empirical Study," *Journal of Marketing Research*, (November, 1974), p. 422.
[2] Derek A. Newton, "Get the Most Out of Your Sales Force," *Harvard Business Review* (September-October, 1969), p. 132.
[3] Darmon, *op. cit.*
[4] Nancy C. Morse and Robert S. Weiss, "The Function and Meaning of Work in the Job," *American Sociological Review*, XX (April, 1955), p. 197.
[5] Gilbert A. Churchill, Jr., Neil M. Ford, Orville C. Walker, Jr., "Personal Characteristics of Salespeople and the Attractiveness of Alternative Rewards," *Journal of Business Research*, VII (1979), p. 48.

families than unmarried people.[6]

Sales executives, therefore, should not be too hasty in their attempt to solve all sales problems with changes in their compensation plan. Rather they should treat compensation as if it were just another tool which can be used to correct motivational problems. Its motivational characteristics should be compared to the motivational ability of programs designed to (1) improve salesperson recognition, (2) improve salesperson knowledge and skills, (3) allocate salespeople more equitably to territories, (4) improve working conditions, (5) improve interpersonal relationships between employees, (6) make salespeople feel more involved, and (7) improve company image, product quality, promotional support and pricing. Unless all of these programs work together to help improve company performance and accomplish salesperson objectives, no amount of money will increase motivation and improve performance.

PROCEDURE FOR ESTABLISHING A PAY PLAN

A number of years ago paying salespeople was a relatively simple matter. Outside salespeople usually received a straight commission and paid their own expenses. In some cases outside salespeople were given the opportunity to receive an advance to cover expenses which was deducted from future commissions. (This was known as a **draw**.) In contrast, retail clerks typically worked on a straight salary with no advances or commissions. Today, however, sales executives realize that simplification of compensation plans is often accomplished only by sacrificing overall company goals. Compensation programs oftentimes must be complex and unique to each salesperson or group of salespeople. For example, one textile firm with 33 salespeople has 33 individualized payment plans.

To effectively deal with the complex environment within which sales executives operate, it is necessary to develop and closely follow a precise procedure for establishing the pay plan. By doing so, the sales executive can be consistent in the establishment of each salesperson's compensation, consider all variables which impact on compensation, and uniformly consider the relative importance of those factors on compensation method and level. Also, if the sales executive changes positions or companies, information used to initially arrive at compensation levels of existing salespeople is maintained for use by the new sales executive. Without such a systematic procedure, compensation may result from whims of the executive, a recruit's bargaining ability, or other highly subjective factors.

To overcome potential problems and promote consistency in decision-making, therefore, the sales executive should employ the following

---

[6] *Ibid.*, p. 29 and p. 46.

procedure to arrive at an appropriate compensation plan:

1. Identify and recognize company objectives.
2. Identify the salesperson's role in accomplishing objectives.
3. Determine compensation level.
4. Determine compensation methods and mix of methods.
5. Evaluate payment method to insure that it includes essentials of a sound compensation plan.
6. Use historical sales and profit information to validate the payment plan.
7. Evaluate effectiveness of the plan.

Identify and Recognize Company Objectives

Similar to other sales management policies and strategies, the optimal compensation plan is contingent on company objectives. Does the firm need to reduce turnover? Are there specific product lines that need additional sales support? Does the firm need to attract better qualified salespeople? What growth is needed? Is the firm experiencing an excessive inventory buildup? What are the firm's profit and return on investment goals? Answers to these and other goal-related questions will serve as the basis for identifying which functions should be performed by company salespeople and, therefore, methods of compensating salespeople for performing the attendant functions.

Identify Salesperson's Role

After company goals are identified, it is then necessary to identify activities which must be performed to satisfy goals. Activities and factors which may influence both the level of compensation and type of compensation plan include the following: (1) the amount of servicing necessary to maintain existing customers; (2) the amount of cold calling in immature markets; (3) the extent to which salespeople must wait in offices, fill out reports, travel, and provide customer support; (4) the amount of advertising support provided by the company; (5) the intensity of competition in relevant territories; and (6) the extent to which salespeople contribute to revenue generation relative to other groups in the firm. A compensation plan can then be designed to satisfy the firm's unique objectives and sales activities. For example, if salespeople must provide a significant amount of support and servicing to customers, then the compensation plan should include a salary to cover the salesperson's time for performing service activities.

Determine Compensation Level

The compensation level of a salesperson should be based on (1) activities which are performed by the salesperson (listed above), (2) pay level of peers, subordinates, and superiors, (3) median industry compensation level, (4) the salesperson's experience and education, (5) market demand for the salesperson's talents, and (6) company objectives. Since these factors will vary for different companies and different people within the same company, sales executives should treat each compensation decision separately.

Although some people argue that salespeople should be allowed to earn an unlimited amount of money, most managers agree that some control over compensation levels should be maintained. The primary reason for maintaining control is that motivation of management may be reduced if salespeople earn more money than superiors. Also, it may be difficult to convince salespeople who could potentially be good managers to assume the additional responsibilities of a manager for less pay. In fact, in one study, it was found that performance is perpetuated if commissions and bonuses are limited to approximately 20 percent of one's total compensation.[7]

On the other hand, if salespeople are not allowed to earn an amount of income which is equivalent to the amount earned by salespeople in competing firms, turnover will be substantial. If turnover is allowed to exceed approximately 10 to 15 percent annually, it can result in a significant decline in growth and profits. These declines result because there are costs associated with selection and training of salespeople, a territory may remain uncovered while a new salesperson is being trained to assume responsibility for the area, or customers may begin to purchase from a competitor if the salesperson joins the competing firm.

Another compensation decision relates to the compensation of trainees. (Figure 13-1 shows level of pay for trainees and experienced salespeople.) The objective in paying trainees is to reduce turnover during training so that the training investment can eventually be returned to the firm. The best way to accomplish this is to pay a straight salary during training which is equivalent to the industry norm. Then after initial training the new salesperson should gradually be given incentive pay in proportion to the normal learning curve for the company.[8] For example, a person who is recruited from a competing firm will probably learn and become productive much faster than the new college recruit and, therefore, will receive maximum incentive pay at an accelerated pace.

Determine Compensation Methods

After a compensation level is identified, the firm must identify methods to accomplish that objective. Ingredients in the compensation mix can include salary, commission, bonus, fringe benefits, profit sharing, and special incentives (e.g., contests). Each method has certain advantages and disadvantages and should be applied to accomplish specific objectives. In a later section of the chapter, these methods are examined in depth.

---

[7] Newton, *op. cit.*, pp. 130–142.
[8] James F. Carey, "Paying the Sales Trainee," *Sales and Marketing Management*, Vol. 117 (August 23, 1976), p. 49.

Figure 13-1

How Salespeople's Total Compensation is Growing

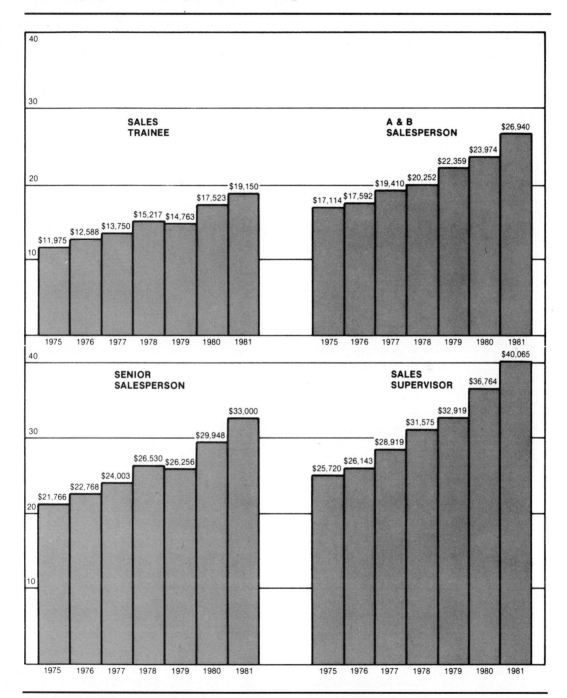

Evaluate Payment Method

During and immediately after development of a pay plan, the sales executive should evaluate the plan to insure that it meets all requirements of a good plan. The best way to accomplish this is to develop a checklist of considerations and compare elements of the plan to the checklist of factors. Such a list is presented in Figure 13-2. This procedure insures that all factors are considered and that the firm is consistent in the procedure employed to determine a compensation plan for each salesperson.

Figure 13–2
Preliminary
Evaluation of
Compensation Plan:
Checklist of
Considerations

1. Can salespeople measure their incentive pay at any point in time?

2. Does it expedite payment of rewards?

3. Is it large enough to attract and hold salespeople?

4. Are incentives built into the plan to encourage maximum sales effort and contribution to profit?

5. Is payment level too high or too low?

6. Is it operative during economic downturns or must compensation be adjusted downward?

7. Does the amount of incentive vary for different products and territories which have varying levels of profitability and market potential?

8. Is it adaptable to salespeople with varying levels of experience?

9. Are salespeople compensated for nonselling activity?

Validate the Compensation Plan

In order to determine whether the proposed compensation plan contains elements of a good plan, one must test its validity with historical information. The firm should use sales records for a period of time which include various economic and market changes. In some cases the firm may need to use ten or more years of historical data to effectively validate the plan. Next, salesperson compensation should be calculated for the prior years and compared against both actual compensation and industry norms. After historical compensation levels are calculated, they should be evaluated to insure that all elements of a sound plan are present (i.e., considerations in Figure 13-2). If the compensation plan is not adaptable to various economic conditions, market conditions, or territories, or applicable to salespeople with varying characteristics, the firm will be alerted of potential problem areas. It can then make necessary changes to alleviate the problems before the plan is implemented.

Evaluate Plan Effectiveness

Like other areas of sales and marketing, conditions surrounding development of a compensation plan change. The firm may develop new product lines which require additional sales effort. The firm may become more concerned with after-sale service and ask salespeople to devote more time to such activity. New distribution channels and, therefore, new customer categories may be opened. Management's perception of the importance of personal sales in the promotional mix may change.

Often changes take place without anyone considering the impact of change on the firm's operations. Compensation plans, therefore, become inappropriate, and decision-makers are unaware of their inadequacy. This may last for years until someone begins examining reasons for excessively high turnover, salesperson morale problems, or excessive sales expenses. By this time, however, damage to the firm has already taken place. To avoid such problems, the firm should periodically evaluate the adequacy of its compensation plan—not just when economic or market changes occur, but on a regular basis.

TYPES OF COMPENSATION PLANS

After company objectives are established and the salesperson's role is identified, the type of compensation plan which most effectively satisfies objectives must be established. It should be remembered that there is no perfect pay plan for a given situation. Each plan has advantages and disadvantages and these must be weighed to determine which is most appropriate.

Before deciding on the form a compensation plan should take, management must first make certain that it offers fertile ground in which the plan can take root. First a company's marketing plan must have strong, effective, and realistic policies related to its products, pricing, service, advertising, and so on. Management will soon be disappointed if it expects a compensation plan to overcome deficiencies in these areas. Second, the company needs well-qualified salespeople—thoroughly trained in the firm's background, policies, product lines, service, and strategies. In addition, the firm should have a sales control system of carefully plotted territories, reasonable quotas, and meaningful sales records and reports that management can use to develop a productive compensation plan.

Straight Salary

This method of monetary compensation is popular with well-entrenched companies selling a broad line of products and requiring salespeople to perform a large amount of servicing, prospecting, and promotional or engineering duties. It is also used when the salesperson

A Company Profile

S tandard Meat Company began operations as a local supplier of beef products to hotels, restaurants, and other institutions in the Dallas/Fort Worth area. In the mid 1960s, Standard's owner recognized the emergence of multiunit, nationally-oriented restaurant chains, and began to position the company so that it could effectively satisfy the needs of this attractive, new market segment. Standard established a distribution network that permitted it to deliver directly to individual units of the restaurant chains on a weekly basis, bypassing distributors and brokers. The company helped develop a packaging technology that gave chilled meat a two to three week shelf life. Standard also developed production and quality assurance programs that helped it maintain competitive prices and, at the same time, a product quality that was consistently within customers' specification requirements.

Standard Meat Company's growth in the 1960s and '70s gave it a dominant position in the market for U.S.D.A. choice, portion controlled steaks. By 1980, this privately held, Fort Worth meat company, supplied steaks to a majority of the national steak chains. It also developed a significant amount of expertise in processing and cooking the byproducts of the steak cutting operation into pizza topping, taco meat, chili, and a variety of other precooked meat products.

To maintain existing chain accounts and develop new business, Standard Meat Company employs national account managers. Each account manager coordinates all activities associated with the management of numerous chain accounts. If a new product is developed for an existing account, the salesperson (national account manager) will coordinate the development of samples, present samples to the customer, sell the customer on the idea of offering the product as a new menu item, help develop pricing strategy, insure that initial production is consistent with agreed upon specifications, alert quality control and distribution to the product line addition, and make sure that all other details are handled. Account managers also identify, qualify, and sell new accounts on the idea of buying one of Standard's existing or new products.

All national account managers are compensated on a salary plus commission basis. When the new compensation system was implemented in January, 1981, its objectives were to (1) maintain low salesperson turnover, (2) encourage salespeople to maintain existing customers, (3) motivate salespeople to develop new customers, (4) attract high quality sales trainees, and (5) encourage salespeople to maintain a reasonable gross margin.

Prior to development of the new compensation system, salespeople were paid a salary plus an end-of-the-year bonus that was subjectively determined. Although this helped provide financial security, it did not encourage salespeople to develop new business or develop new products for existing accounts. Compensation did not reflect productivity. Because the bonus was paid annually, it did not serve as a performance incentive.

The revised compensation system includes a base salary that is designed to reward salespeople for managing existing accounts and a monthly commission that serves as an incentive for developing new customers. Salaries are high enough to minimize turnover, and reflect a salesperson's *experience and qualifications. Since account managers have discretion to determine price, commissions are paid on gross profit margin. This insures that new business is sold at a profit. Also, since they are required to maintain existing business as well as develop new business, salespeople are paid a dual commission. One commission is calculated on the total gross profit contributed by a salesperson during each month (i.e., commission for account maintenance). The percentage used to calculate account maintenance commission varies from one-tenth of one percent to one percent, depending on the amount of business managed by a salesperson. If a salesperson manages a significant amount of business, that person does not have as much time to develop new business as a person that manages a smaller amount of business. The other commission is paid on increases in profit margin above the same month of the previous year. For example, if a salesperson's accounts contributed $100,000 in January, 1980, and $150,000 in January, 1982, then a commission was paid on $50,000. If gross margin declined from 1980 to 1981 then the negative balance was carried forward to the next month. Also, commission paid on increases in business (i.e., new business) is significantly higher than commission paid for account maintenance. If a salesperson loses an account or does not develop a new account, therefore, the accompanying reduction in commissions substantially affects total compensation.*

Introduction of the new compensation system accomplished anticipated objectives. Turnover of salespeople through dissatisfaction with income remained low. Salespeople increased efforts to sell new products to existing customers and substantially expanded their prospecting activity. In fact, during the first nine months of the system's implementation, the number of qualified prospects with which the same number of salespeople were working doubled. In addition, several high quality salespeople who were subsequently employed by Standard indicated that the compensation system was one of the primary reasons for their joining the company. Finally, efforts by the salespeople to promote higher profit product lines expanded significantly.

is not the person or entity that is primarily responsible for developing markets and making sales. Firms using straight salary claim to have:

- Better control over their salespeople, particularly for promotional and other activities that do not result in immediate sales.

- Less turnover, because their people, having a steady income and being well paid (the company assumes), are less inclined to leave.

- More freedom in changing customers and territories.

- Realization of greater profits when business is good.

- Better administrative control over compensation.

Companies paying straight salaries reason that once a salesperson and a market become established, increased sales are more often due to improvements in the business economy or factors which are controllable by the company than in the results of added sales effort. The thinking of such companies is that salespeople are paid well to do their job, so why should they receive an increase for something they did not create? Firms also argue that compensation is only one variable in the motivation mix. Individuals who are motivated to perform at a level of excellence will perform at that level regardless of the type of compensation plan. Conversely, if a salesperson is not motivated to perform, no incentive program will stimulate the salesperson to change this behavior.

On the other hand, it may be argued that a straight salary may breed complacency. Also, during economic downturns, the fixed cost aspect of salary can possibly create a burden for the firm. Third, the company assumes risks associated with development of new salespeople, since compensation is not a function of sales. A person may simply use the firm until he or she goes on a commission and then leave the firm for another company. Finally, salespeople on a straight salary may become order takers instead of aggressive developers of new markets.

Straight Commission

Straight commission simply means that the salesperson is paid an amount of money which is in direct proportion to productivity. Such a system of payment has the following advantages:

- It minimizes capital investment risks for the company.

- It relieves management of the responsibility of management. Frequently, top management is too busy to direct its salespeople; in other cases, the manager may not have the know-how.

- It encourages salespeople to act as if they were in business for themselves.

- It helps avoid losses when sales decline since selling expenses vary directly with sales.

- It attracts persons who have confidence in themselves.

- It encourages poor producers to weed themselves out voluntarily.

Generally, a straight commission plan is used by firms that are in a relatively weak financial position and cannot risk any arrangement other than one where selling costs can be related directly to sales. It is also used in industries where a commission plan is the norm (e.g., residential real estate), where it is not feasible to closely supervise salespeople, where salespeople are of such high caliber that close supervision is not necessary, or where salespeople are independent contractors.

From the standpoint of management, commission plans lead to highly independent salespeople and thus, a degree of control is sacrificed. Second, a danger in a multi-product firm is that if the commission rates are not coordinated and balanced against each other, salespeople will concentrate attention primarily on those products which are most important or profitable to them and not on products which are important or profitable to the firm. Third, there will be no consistency of income among salespeople. Fourth, service aspects of selling may be deemphasized or ignored. Fifth, changing territorial boundaries becomes difficult and a major source of demotivation. Sixth, pay level uncertainties lead to higher turnover. Finally, good salespeople normally will not consider promotions to management.

If a straight commission plan is adopted, commissions may be paid for profit contribution or contribution to sales volume. Although most companies utilize a volume-based commission plan, there are positive and negative aspects of each approach. A plan based on sales volume is easy to develop and administer. Also, growth in sales volume is the objective of salespeople; although it may not be the bottom line objective of management. Although a commission based on sales volume is easy to administer and is consistent with sales objectives, it does have some problems. First, some territories may have significantly lower potential thus making it more difficult for some salespeople to earn as much as others. Second, if salespeople have flexibility to set price, they may reduce price below cost to make a sale. The salesperson is rewarded, but the company loses money. Third, profit, not sales, is the objective of all companies.

A commission plan based on profit has several advantages. It is consistent with corporate objectives and reduces the probability of sales being made at a loss to the firm. Also, a profit-based commission directs salesperson attention toward higher profit items. In companies where the lower profit items are also the high volume items, salespeople may focus attention on selling the high volume products and deemphasize the sale of low volume/high profit products. A profit based system helps redirect salesperson effort.

There are also problems with a profit-based commission plan. First, although salespeople have control over sales volume, they do not have control over expenses such as maintenance, overhead, purchasing, and other corporate expenses. Their income, therefore, may be determined by corporate decisions over which they have no input. This can be a major source of frustration to salespeople. Second, some companies reward salespeople based on profit, but evaluate performance based on sales volume. This inconsistency between compensation and evaluation systems can be another potential inequity. Third, dissemination of cost information in order to effect such a system can lead to security breaches. Finally, newly developed products with a penetration price may not have a high profit. A profit-based system may direct attention away from these new products that require a significant amount of attention in order to survive.

Salary Plus Commission

A combination plan comprised of salary plus incentive (i.e., commission, bonus, etc.) is the most widely utilized compensation method. Under such a plan, salespeople are compensated for service and other specified activities with a salary, and are given an opportunity to earn additional income for accomplishments which exceed the expected.

The primary advantage of a combination plan is that it gives management effective control over sales expenses, but allows salespeople to earn an income which is proportional to their productivity. Also, the salary part of a combination plan helps reduce turnover by making salespeople feel as if they are part of the company instead of independent contractors.

The primary problem with a combination plan is in determining salary and commission levels. The most popular split between salary and commission is 80 percent salary and 20 percent commission.[9] According to one study an 80/20 split is optimal for missionary sales, technical sales, and new business sales, while a 60/40 split is optimal for consumer goods (trade) sales.[10]

Setting the Base.   The term **base** refers to the minimum sales or gross profit volume which must be achieved before any incentive pay can be realized. Determining an optimum base volume is the most difficult part of designing a combination salary and commission plan. If it is set too high, incentive aspects of the plan will be lost because salespeople will have too much difficulty in meeting the minimum volume or profit level. If the base is set too low, salespeople will earn more compensation than is reasonable and the firm will lose control over the plan. Another problem is that economic changes and territory changes may make the base too easy or too hard to meet.

Considering the problems associated with setting the base, there are several ways this task can be accomplished. First, the previous year's sales or profit level may be used as the base. As long as economic conditions do not change drastically, this method may be effective. If the industry faces an economic downturn, however, the base becomes too difficult to realize and, therefore, loses its effectiveness.

To overcome problems associated with unexpected economic changes, a three-year moving average may be used. The previous three years are averaged to establish the following year's base; then, for each subsequent year, the sales or gross profit figures for the first of the three years are dropped and the immediately previous year's sales are added. Also, a ceiling is established on potential earnings from commissions. This plan smooths out any wide year-to-year fluctuations but may still be ineffective if unusual economic conditions persist.

---

[9] John P. Steinbrink, "How to Pay Your Sales Force," *Harvard Business Review*, Vol. 56 (July-August, 1978), p. 112.

[10] Newton *op. cit.*, pp. 130–142.

Determining Incentive Pay.   Determining the level of incentive pay in a combination plan depends on company objectives and the nature of the sales task. A guide to establishing the size of incentive pay is presented in Figure 13-3.

Incentive pay is relatively high when the following conditions exist:

1. Salesperson's skill is the most important factor in making sales.

2. The firm is relatively unknown.

3. The firm uses a relatively small amount of advertising and sales promotion.

4. Product price and quality is undifferentiated among competitors.

5. The salesperson's primary function is developing new accounts and stimulating sales volume.

Incentive pay is relatively low when the following conditions exist:

1. The salesperson is primarily an order taker.

2. The firm is better known than most competitors.

3. The firm advertises extensively.

4. The firm has a significant competitive advantage with respect to product quality or price.

5. A primary function of the salesperson is providing customer service or technical assistance.

6. Factors such as economic trends which are beyond the control of the salesperson are significant determinants of demand.

Figure 13–3
Rules for
Establishing
Incentive Pay

Source: Richard C. Smythe, "Financial Incentives for Salesmen," *Harvard Business Review* (January-February, 1968), pp. 114–115.

In addition to establishing a precise commission or bonus for sales which exceed the base, some firms also build a competitive feature into the compensation plan. One such method, peer rating, rewards salespeople for their actual performance as well as their relative performance (i.e., relative to performance of other salespeople). Peer rating involves three steps.[11] First, the firm establishes marketing objectives and the

---

[11] "Peer Rating Compensation: A Peerless Plan for Salesmen," *Research Institute Marketing for Sales Executives* (September, 1972).

relative importance of the objectives to the firm. Second, once objectives are identified, an individualized quota which reflects each salesperson's sales history, stage of development, and territorial potential is established. Third, a salesperson is paid a commission which is based on (1) the extent to which his or her sales volume exceeds quota, and (2) the salesperson's competitive position among his or her peers. For example, the top 20 percent of the sales force might receive a 10 percent commission, the next 20 percent an 8 percent commission, then 4 percent, 2 percent, and 1 percent.[12]

Trends

The Dartnell survey of salespeople indicated that utilization of a straight salary to reward sales effort is becoming more widespread (see Figure 13-4). The primary reason for the increase in salary plans and the decline in commission plans is that economic conditions are becoming more uncertain and firms cannot, therefore, effectively control compensation levels. Also, the increase in costs associated with hiring and training new salespeople has forced firms to reduce turnover. Finally, with increases in the cost of living and economic uncertainties, employees are demanding a more secure form of income (i.e., salary).

FRINGE BENEFITS

In addition to paying a direct salary and/or commission, most firms reward salespeople with indirect benefits. Although fringe benefits do not necessarily motivate salespeople to be more productive, they do aid the firm in attracting qualified prospects and in retaining existing personnel. Also, profit sharing plans and stock options may cause salespeople to be profit-oriented. Table 13-1 on page 318 lists the primary fringe benefits which are offered by firms.

SUMMARY

Compensation refers to direct and indirect payment for performance of work. Although compensation plans are designed to reward performance, reduce turnover, and direct salesperson activity, various types of people are influenced differently by compensation systems.

The sales executive must, therefore, study the unique characteristics and motivations of each sales group and design a plan that is consistent with specific needs and desires. Management should (1) establish company objectives; (2) identify the salesperson's role in accomplishing

---

[12] "A Compensation Formula That Produces Results," *Research Institute Marketing for Sales Executives* (April 13, 1978).

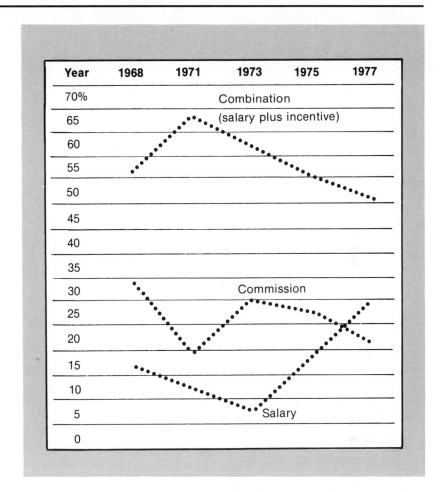

Year	1968	1971	1973	1975	1977

Figure 13–4
Companies Using
Various
Compensation
Plans

Source: *Harvard Business Review*, Vol. 56 (July-August, 1978), p. 27.

objectives; (3) determine compensation level; (4) determine compensation methods and mix of methods; (5) evaluate payment method to insure that it includes the essentials of a sound compensation plan; (6) use historical sales and profit information to validate the payment plan; (7) evaluate effectiveness of the plan.

The alternative types of compensation plans that may be employed include straight salary, straight commission, salary plus com-mission, or other incentives. Straight salary is utilized for well-entrenched companies, selling a broad line of products, and requiring sales-people to perform a wide range of other ser-vices. Straight commissions are utilized by firms that are in relatively weak financial shape or in industries that are traditionally character-ized by straight commission. Salary-plus com-mission is the most widely utilized approach and is, in most cases, the most effective.

Type of Benefit	Approx. percent of Firms Paying All or Part (1977)
Hospital Insurance	98%
Accident Insurance	85
Life Insurance	94
Dental Insurance	35
Educational Assistance	65
Profit Sharing	38
Pension Plan	57
Stock Purchase	21
Personal Use of Company Car	57
Club or Association Membership	48
Salary Continuation	73
Moving Expense Reimbursement	63

Table 13–1
Fringe Benefits

Source: John P. Steinbrink, "How to Pay Your Salesforce," *Harvard Business Review*, Vol. 56 (July-August, 1978), p. 112.

QUESTIONS

1. What are some major factors for assessing a salesperson's value to a company?

2. What are the general criteria for a good compensation plan?

3. A simple compensation plan makes it possible for the salesperson to calculate his or her earnings and expedites the payment of rewards. Why are these characteristics of a payment plan important?

4. How should the following salespeople be paid?
   (a) Airline ticket salesperson.
   (b) House-to-house vacuum cleaner salesperson.
   (c) Technical salesperson—making appointments for land development company.

5. What are some advantages of having a flexible plan vs. an inflexible plan?

6. Should a salesperson be paid a bonus for exceeding forecasted sales volume?

7. Should salespeople be given the opportunity to make more money than their manager?

8. Are turnover and productivity of salespeople influenced by their compensation level? Explain.

9. What programs other than pay systems could be used to motivate salespeople?

10. How could the sales manager determine the validity of a proposed compensation plan?

Case 11–1

Phil Crane*

Phil Crane, forty-two years old, joined the field staff of Glover Drug Company as a Professional Sales Representative in 1979. Prior to his employment, he had served as a captain in the clinical laboratory section of the U.S. Army Medical Service Corps. His duties were chiefly concerned with laboratory diagnostic procedures and blood chemistry studies.

Mr. Crane was first interviewed by Mr. Edward Black, Manager of one of Glover's sales divisions. Crane impressed Black with his knowledge of medicine and his many years of experience working with physicians and other members of the medical profession. Although Crane had no previous sales experience, Black felt that he had the personality, knowledge, and poise necessary for success as a professional sales representative. In addition, Crane professed an interest and enthusiasm for "detailing",[1] a major part of the Sales Representative's work.

Satisfied with his initial interviews with Crane, Mr. Black instituted a credit check on Crane through the Personal Credit Investing Company. These reports were favorable. Personal references also spoke highly of Crane's personal qualifications. Following receipt of these reports, Black employed Crane who was then relocated to the headquarters city of his territory assignment.

Black assigned Mr. Will Jackson, District Supervisor, to train Crane for one week according to the field training program then in effect. Jackson reported favorable progress to Black, and Crane commenced territorial coverage on his own.

Crane attended a Glover Sales Conference in 1979, and in early 1980 was assigned to the regular three-week Home Office Training Class. Although he appeared to be a diligent student, his performance was not outstanding. While at class it was observed on occasion that Crane drank, but he was always sober in the presence of his colleagues. His attendance was perfect, except for the last day when he failed to report to class. Upon checking his room, Mort Sayles, Assistant Professional Service Manager, found Crane ill in bed. He called a physician who diagnosed the illness as pneumonia. However, Crane did not agree with the diagnosis and refused to enter a hospital because he claimed it was only a recurrence of malaria. Sayles stayed with him the balance of the day and left only when Crane insisted he leave. The next morning, apparently feeling well again, Crane went home.

When these incidents were reported to Mr. Black, he rejected any suggestion of dismissing Crane. He firmly believed that Crane was under a strain at class and would straighten out when he returned to territory.

Back on territory, Crane's work appeared satisfactory. There was every indication that he was doing a good job, all of which supported Black's opinion. His oper-

---

* Adapted from PROBLEMS AND POLICIES IN PERSONNEL MANAGEMENT, Joseph W. Towle, Sterling H. Schoen, Raymond L. Hilgert; 1965 by Houghton Mifflin Company. Used by permission of the publishers.

[1] Professional Sales Representatives were assigned territories where they were responsible for calling upon drug wholesalers, distributors, retail pharmacies, hospitals, and other similar organizations. They were to encourage the Glover Drug products, check stocks, take orders, and many miscellaneous duties related to promotion of Glover Drug items. In addition, the Sales Representative was to call regularly upon physicians, dentists, hospital personnel, and people in related fields to discuss the chemistry, pharmacology, clinical use, and dosages of Glover products, and to provide them with samples and product literature. This latter function was commonly described as "detailing".

ation—on paper at least—was above average and his sales showed progress.

In mid-1980, Jackson was relieved of his duties as District Supervisor and was replaced by Ms. Janie Lewis. On her first trip with Crane, Lewis observed that his overall sales operation was good, although she noted that Crane was weak in detailing techniques. Crane spent several hours during the visit criticizing Jackson as being an inadequate supervisor. Crane was especially critical that his initial training with Jackson had been limited.

Sometime later, Crane made a long distance call to Mr. Fred Borden, Glover's Assistant Marketing Manager. Crane was almost unintelligible and gave the impression that he was intoxicated. Ms. Lewis had a similar experience. Also at about the same time, a physician from a city in Crane's territory called Joe Pfinster (Professional Sales Manager) to inform him that the Glover representative was acting "very strangely" on territory. This last incident was referred to Black who instructed Lewis to make an immediate investigation. Lewis flew to this city and contacted the local wholesaler and several retailers in an effort to get their reaction to Crane's behavior. They all endorsed Crane favorably.

Lewis immediately visited Crane "to lay the cards on the table" in an effort to get at the truth. Crane emphatically denied that he was under the influence of alcohol at any time on territory. He claimed his difficulty was a recent flare-up of malaria which he had contracted in the service, and undoubtedly this, plus the medication he was taking, accounted for his speech difficulties, as well as the report received from the physician. This information was forwarded to Black. It was at this time that Crane made arrangements to be hospitalized for a general check-up. Upon his release he wrote the following memo to Mort Sayles:

> This is to thank you for your recent memo regarding my hospitalization. They really gave me a real going over. I saw about nine different doctors during my relatively short stay there, had multiple laboratory examinations, and quite a number of x-ray examinations. However, they have not had a chance to completely evaluate all of their findings as yet and I am to go back there sometime in the near future (when they send me notice to report) and hope that they will have something definite to tell me. I returned to the territorial operation Wednesday at noon and made quite a number of calls that afternoon and will work this Saturday[2] so as to make the most of the time "off territory". Thanks again for your memo.
>
> Sincerely,
> Phil Crane

For the remainder of 1980, Crane's operation continued satisfactorily. Lewis was unable to contact Crane personally until early 1981, due to an expansion of territories. Following this visit she reported to Black that Crane's operation had deteriorated and that his detailing was far from effective. In addition, Crane's sales had begun to slip in late 1980 and continued to fall in the first half of 1981. On paper, however, Crane still presented a good call average. Lewis reported that Crane accepted supervisory advice and appeared willing to improve. Since there were several sales vacancies in the District, Lewis and Black were hopeful that Crane could be "salvaged" so as to prevent another vacancy in the sales organization.

In July of 1981, Lewis recommended a $50 salary increase for Crane which

---

[2] From the time he was employed, Crane customarily worked on Saturdays and reported his calls accordingly on a separate Daily Activities Report.

she hoped would serve as additional incentive for more rapid improvement. On a supervisory visit with Crane immediately after this, Lewis reported that she could see little if any improvement and counseled Crane accordingly.

In the last quarter of 1981 Crane's sales attainment had improved. During a supervisory visit, Crane declared he was working hard and promised that 1982 would be a much better year. He also stated that his health had improved and he thought his malaria had been arrested. On January 1, Lewis became manager of the division which included Crane's territory. Immediately following her promotion Lewis visited Crane and noted a somewhat improved performance. Crane was still weak in detailing techniques, but otherwise seemed to be making progress. He was strong in the retail trade and appeared to have the support of his wholesalers. Crane complained that his salary was inadequate and was disturbed that he did not get an increase in January. Lewis reviewed his operation in 1981 and told him in view of his record for that year, another increase in January was not justified. Crane vowed to work hard in the first half of 1982 so as to be eligible for a review in July.

In April of 1982 Lewis arranged to meet Crane in Pompano City, a town in Crane's territory. Upon her arrival, Lewis found Crane in his hotel room in such condition that he was unable to speak for fully twenty-four hours. The following day Crane explained that his illness was due to malaria, plus the medication he was taking which included "a small amount of whiskey".

1. Evaluate the supervisory style of Glover Drug Company.

2. What could have been done to prevent the final confrontation between Crane and Lewis?

Case 11–2

Robert E. Day Corporation

The Robert E. Day Corporation is a multiproduct manufacturer employing over 40,000 people and has manufacturing facilities in over 25 countries. Through growth and acquisitions, the company today produces a wide diversity of products which includes: food and agricultural equipment, industrial packaging equipment, material handling equipment, auto service and outdoor power equipment, chemicals, pumps, construction equipment, and power transmission equipment. Last year's sales exceeded three billion dollars.

The PTG Company, a subsidiary of the Robert E. Day Corporation, consists of four divisions. Division A manufactures industrial brakes, with manufacturing facilities in Los Angeles, California. Division B manufactures precision bearings, with plants in Dallas, Texas and Springfield, Missouri. Division C manufactures chain products, with plants in Dallas, Texas and Jacksonville, Florida. Division D manufactures gear reducer products with plants in New York City and Chicago, Illinois. The PTG headquarters facilities are in Dallas. The previous year's sales of the PTG Company were $100 million.

The Robert E. Day Corporation acquired the PTG Company in 1978. Prior to the acquisition of the PTG Company, the sales organization was structured by district offices. The structure consisted of seven regional warehouse/service centers located throughout the United States. Each service center was organized with regional sales and operations managers. Salespeople were geographically located within a region and reported to the regional sales managers. Salespeople were responsible for selling all the products of PTG Company to original equipment manufacturers (OEMs) and industrial distributors within their assigned territories.

In an attempt to gain market share, the Day Corporation decided to reorganize the sales staff into division and customer class specialists. The reorganization involved the hiring of additional division sales personnel including sales managers for each division. In effect each division would operate as a separate entity.

After a period of five years, Robert E. Day Corporation evaluated the reorganization. Some of the major conclusions are as follows:

1. Major accounts buying multidivisional products do not like dealing with more than one salesperson.
2. Increased sales expenses are due to the overlapping of sales efforts.
3. Regional managers tend to get more involved with administrative details than sales efforts.
4. Communications break down in the sales group.
5. Conflicts exist in selling efforts.
6. Morale is poor.
7. There is an increase in turnover of sales personnel.
8. The increase in sales is marginal.

Upon evaluating the major conclusions and findings, it was further concluded that service rather than quality of products and price was a determining factor for a need to create changes. The new reorganization is presented in Figure 1.

The structure in Figure 1 represents a continuation of diversification by division. The decision to continue this diversification was based on the need to control the manufacturing aspects of the business in order to better evaluate profit and loss statistics, market share data, new product development, and improved production techniques.

However, the overall sales structure of the PTG Company changed from division sales specialists to a "pooled" sales force. In addition, it was decided to diversify the sales force into two major groups: OEM Sales Group and Distributor Sales Group. These two groups would sell all products to the two major classes of customers respectively. The regional manager would now have direct control over the regional distributor sales people. The OEM sales people would report to the OEM regional managers located in Dallas. The divisional sales managers would offer staff support to the sales force.

The new structure has been operational for three years. The Robert E. Day Corporation has asked the PTG Company to prepare a five year long-range plan. The current sales structure will represent a prime concern.

The management of PTG Company interviewed various sales personnel and conducted attitude surveys to obtain current information. The following represents information from the studies that will be useful in analyzing the new structure and will aid in the preparation of the long-range plan:

1. There has been a moderate increase in market share.
2. There has been a moderate decrease in sales expenses.
3. The general attitude of the sales personnel has improved although there still exists an overlap of sales in certain areas where distributors sell to OEM accounts.
4. Sales personnel do not agree with quota selection.
5. Sales feels communications with the factories are a definite problem.
6. The past division specialists do not feel comfortable with new division products. Each division acts independently to include different terms

Figure 1
Current Reorganization

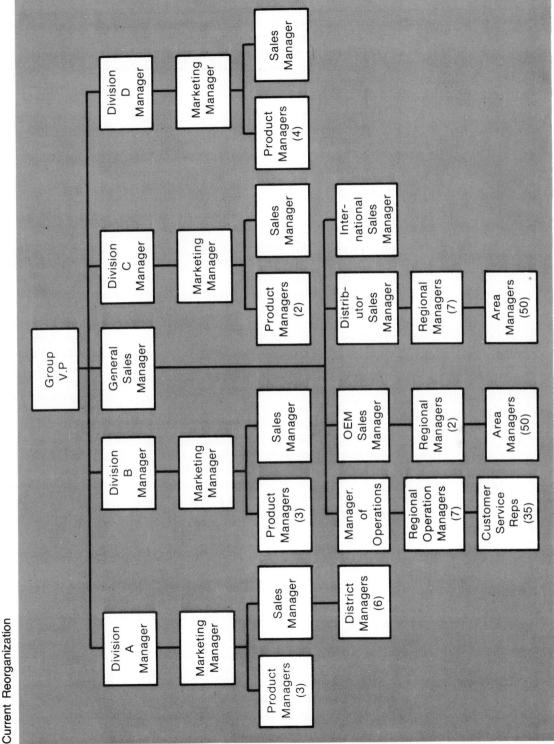

and conditions, marketing philosophies, and apparent indifference to salespeople.

7. There is dissatisfaction with commission structure.
8. A lack of consistency by the divisions exists.
9. There are conflicting viewpoints on sales efforts between the OEM and distributor sales groups.

1. Given the information in this case, what suggestions and/or plans must be incorporated in the long-range plan for the Robert E. Day Corporation?

2. Evaluate the impact of company policies and programs on communications.

Case 12–1

Lawrence Scott

Lawrence Scott joined the field staff of Stuyvesant Drug Products Company as a detail person early in 1980. He was a college graduate, having majored in physical education, and although extremely interested in sports and athletics, did not pursue a teaching career as originally planned.

Mr. Scott was first interviewed by Mr. Edward Graham, Midwest Division Manager. Scott impressed Graham as an aggressive, hard-working book sales representative who appeared eager to gain prestige and higher earnings by entering the pharmaceutical industry. Graham decided to consider Scott for the Louisville territory, and immediately instituted a personnel check through the Personal Credit Investigating Company. Character references and former employers spoke well of Scott and reported nothing unfavorable. However, Personal Credit reported that Scott was employed by the Post Office in his home town, Freeport, following his graduation from high school in 1970. (His application for employment stated that he graduated from high school in 1971 and made no mention of his employment by the Freeport Post Office.) The report stated that during February, 1971, a quantity of mail was found on a creek bank near Freeport that had never been delivered although it had passed through the Freeport Post Office. Upon investigation, a postal inspector discovered that Scott had disposed of two bags of mail by throwing them into the creek. Scott claimed that he had a date that night and had thrown the mail away to avoid being late. Scott was discharged by the Post Office for this offense, but no charges were pressed by the authorities.

Graham decided to employ Scott and arranged to train him in the technical aspects of the job and familiarize him with reporting systems and other paper work necessary to carry out his functions as a medical service representative.

Scott's territorial performance apparently pleased Graham. About a year after joining the company, Graham wrote Scott:

March 21, 1981

I should like to commend you on your splendid performance during the last half of 1980. You finished this half with 104.7 percent attainment of quota. What is even more impressive, Larry, you attained 106.8 percent of your quota in old products. Very nice work. I know you will do everything possible to retain or better this position next year. Best of luck to you.

Edward Graham

During the ensuing months, Graham was quoted by other representatives to remark about Scott's oustanding performance. Scott received salary increases in July of 1980, January of 1981, and again in July of 1981. Although this was considered unusual and was not in accordance with company policy, Graham insisted, and the exceptions to policy were made.

Scott seldom corresponded with the home office except for routine matters. The only knowledge the home office had of his performance was obtained through copies of memoranda from Graham to Scott.

By the end of 1981, Stuyvesant Drug Company had grown rapidly, and had expanded its field staff considerably since the early part of the year. As a result, several new sales divisions were to be created. Scott received word from the home office in December that effective January 1, 1982 he would be responsible to Mr. Douglas Rathbone, the newly appointed Cincinnati Division Manager. Rathbone was highly regarded by the home office and was considered to be very capable by Harry Lane, his regional sales manager.

Soon after his appointment to division manager, Rathbone went to Louisville to work with Scott and to get acquainted with him. As he was eager to get acquainted with all the representatives in his division as soon as possible, Rathbone spent only two days during this field visit with Scott. Following this trip, Rathbone reported to Lane:

TO: Mr. Harry Lane   February 17, 1982

FROM: Douglas Rathbone

SUBJECT: Field Visit with Lawrence Scott

Detailing—Not too strong here. Tries to cover too much in the allotted time. Didn't have calling cards with him.

Accounts—Very good support and cooperation with direct retailers and wholesalers. They all like him. He should know the names of more of the personnel in the stores.

Comments—Makes an excellent appearance—neat. Well groomed. Has a good general knowledge of his territory. He appears conscientious and a willing worker. Ambitious.

Doug Rathbone

About two months later, Rathbone again worked with Scott and reported:

TO: Mr. Harry Lane   April 23, 1982

FROM: Douglas Rathbone

SUBJECT: Field Visit with Lawrence Scott

Detailing—Weak. His detailing lacks enthusiasm and his delivery needs more modulation and variety. A dull and uninspiring detail.

Accounts—Has good wholesaler support. Could stand improvement with some of the retailers.

Comments—On the favorable side, the man has a nice appearance and is well groomed. He is also sales-minded.

On the negative side is his manner of expressing himself in the physician's office. Definitely a candidate for a Dale Carnegie course or Toastmasters. He was so advised.

His organization is just fair. His car and detail bag were poorly organized. We repacked his detail bag and I advised him to organize his car better. The man has the basic qualifications but needs development to become a first-rate detail person.

Doug Rathbone

During a telephone conversation a week or two later, Rathbone expressed to Lane his disappointment in Scott's performance. At that time, Rathbone was busy training the division in sales. However, he intended to devote extra time in Louisville just as soon as he completed training new men and a group of medical students he had employed for the summer.

On June 4, Lane received an announcement from Scott that his wife had delivered a baby girl, Louise, on May 29.

Rathbone had been traveling extensively during the month of May and by early June was in the midst of training summer students. On Wednesday, June 6, he was in Centerville, a town located on Swan River, about 300 miles from Louisville. Centerville was known to be a resort town offering various types of amusements and sporting facilities. Although he was training two students, Rathbone called Paula Norris, the local representative to accompany him on an afternoon appointment he had with the manager of the local wholesale druggist. As Rathbone and Norris were driving toward the outskirts of town at about 4:00 P.M., Rathbone thought he saw Scott on a miniature golf course with an unidentified young woman. Scott appeared to be attired in bathing trunks and an open shirt. As the two passed the golf course, Rathbone asked Norris to drive around the block. Upon returning to the scene, both Norris and Rathbone were certain that it was Scott who was playing golf. They did not stop, but continued on their way to the wholesaler.

As Rathbone drove home to Cincinnati that evening, his thoughts concentrated on the Lawrence Scott situation.

1. What action, if any, would you take with Scott?

2. Evaluate the impact of the company's management style on employee motivation.

Case 12–2

Better Machines, Inc.*

Better Machines, Inc., founded in 1904, was an industrial distributor selling a broad line. It was organized into three divisions: (1) the Machine Tool Division, which sold metalworking equipment, (2) the Materials Handling Equipment Division, which distributed specialized handling equipment, and (3) the Construction Service Division (CSD), which sold and serviced construction equipment. Early in 1968 Ted Logan, CSD marketing manager, identified his division's most important problem as that of motivating salespeople to perform effectively. He remarked, "Sales executives can give employees incentives, but motivation must come from within the indi-

* Richard R. Still, Clyde E. Harris, Jr., CASES IN MARKETING: Decisions, Policies, and Strategies, © 1977, pp. 147–151. Reprinted by permission of Prentice-Hall, Inc.

vidual." The division's representatives received considerably higher compensation than the average in the industry, but motivational problems persisted.

In 1982 CSD sold $23 million worth of equipment. It competed against thirty distributors serving the Indiana and southern Illinois market and attained a penetration ratio of 50 percent.[1] CSD's sales income came from equipment ($15 million), parts ($5.7 million), and service ($2.3 million). Sales of Goliath equipment, the leading line, amounted to $11 million in 1982.

CSD represented four manufacturers of such equipment as graders, loaders, stone crushers, earthmovers, rollers, bulldozers, cranes, power shovels, and asphalt pavers. Prices of different pieces of equipment ranged from ten thousand dollars for small loaders to three hundred thousand dollars for larger, heavier products. Management made gradual changes in the items handled, discontinuing some pieces of equipment from time to time, but had dropped none since 1978. The high quality of the equipment it distributed was a source of pride throughout the division.

Central headquarters were at Terre Haute, Indiana, and the CSD's sales area extended over Indiana and southern Illinois. Branch offices, with parts and service facilities, were at Decatur and Mt. Vernon in Illinois, and at Indianapolis, Fort Wayne, and Terre Haute in Indiana. Branches, each with a full-time manager, operated autonomously as profit centers.

Of the nineteen CSD field sales representatives, five worked out of Terre Haute, five out of Indianapolis, four out of Fort Wayne, three out of Mt. Vernon, and two out of Decatur. Each managed an assigned territory, made scheduled calls, prospected for new customers, developed mailing lists, and submitted weekly activity reports to the branch manager. Five specialty representatives, with engineering and application knowledge of certain equipment lines, covered the entire market area, assisting regular territorial salespeople. While on field assignments, specialty representatives were supervised by branch managers (see Figure 1).

Sales in different sales territories ranged from three hundred thousand dollars to $3 million annually. Territorial boundaries were drawn mainly on the basis of analyses of company and industry sales records indicating performances of both CSD and its thirty competitors. Further analysis of territorial sizes and potentials took into account the number of pieces of equipment already in each sales territory, their ages, and their models. After appraisal of these and other data, branch managers and the general manager determined market and sales potentials, made sales forecasts, and set the division's sales quotas. Experienced salespeople worked the larger-volume territories, newer reps the rest.

Management utilized a prospect classification system aimed toward improving control over field sales operations. All prospects for construction equipment were put into one of four categories:

1. Those who were *going to buy.*
2. Those who were *probably going to buy.*
3. Those *interested in buying.*
4. Those with almost *no interest in buying.*

Prospects in category 1 received the highest contact priority. Prospects remained in category 2 for two weeks and in category 3 for three weeks; during these periods, contacts by salespeople were used to qualify these prospects for other classifications. This system forced sales reps to gauge the degree of buying intent in customers' minds. After a prospect bought equipment and became a cus-

---

[1] A penetration ratio indicates the relationship between actual sales and market potential.

Figure 1
Organizational Structure

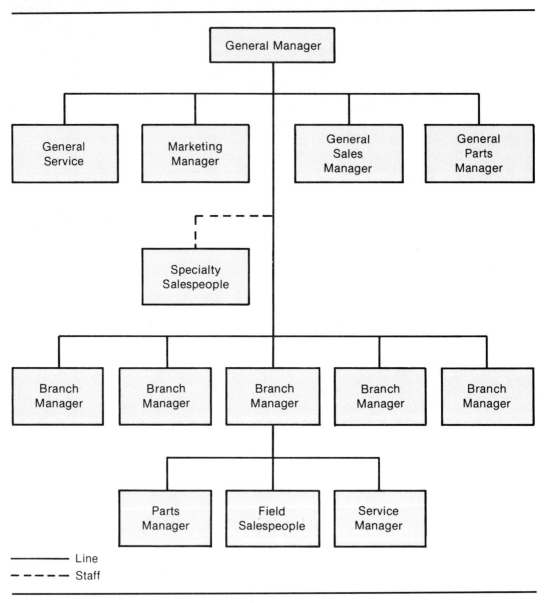

tomer, the division recorded the equipment's type, the date of sale, and the amount of sale. The company had recently computerized its prospect and customer classification system, utilizing the information to determine weekly routing schedules for the field salespeople.

Management assigned quotas to all field salespeople. Those failing to reach their quotas were required to submit written reports explaining the reasons for unsatisfactory performance. Branch managers reviewed these reports when considering sales rep's contract renewals.

Compensation of salespeople included a salary, averaging about 65 percent of the total income, and commissions on sales. Factors such as relative seniority, nature of territorial assignment, and recent performance compared with quota were used in determining base salaries. Commission rates varied according to the level of sales, and both rates and rate-break points differed among individual contracts. In addition, certain product lines carried varying commission rates; for example, the contract of one salesperson provided that on sales of Goliath equipment she be paid 1 percent up to $150,000, 1.25 percent from $150,000 to $225,000, and 1.5 percent above $225,000. Specialty salespeople also worked on a salary plus-commission basis, sharing commissions on joint sales made with field salespeople. Shared amounts varied with the type of equipment, the selling effort exerted by each person, and the provisions of individual employment contracts.

CSD paid each sales rep's travel and entertainment expenses in their entirety. In addition, all salespeople participated in a profit-sharing plan which paid up to 17 percent of base salary, depending upon company profits. Salespeople averaged between $22,000 and $31,000 in total compensation for 1982, compared with an average of from $18,000 to $24,000 for competitors's salespeople. Sales executives received base salaries plus profit-sharing bonuses. Top management reviewed all compensation plans annually; however, only minor changes had been made in recent years.

Salespeople reported to branch managers on their work plans, expense items, complaints and adjustments, and lost sales. They also submitted daily call reports. Copies of all these reports were sent to the central sales control unit, tabulated, and then forwarded to sales and marketing managers. Expense reimbursements occurred only after receipt of detailed expense reports. Selling expenses expanded rapidly in 1981 and 1982, though executives had been unable to determine the reasons.

When sales reps lost two or more consecutive sales to the same account, branch managers immediately tried to determine if the reason was salesperson-customer incompatibility. On occasion, management reassigned certain customers to different salespeople. Branch managers, the sales manager, and the marketing manager all spent considerable time traveling with the sales force.

CSD did not use sales contests or other devices involving special recognition for improved or outstanding sales performance. The management regarded such frills unnecessary in view of the high level of monetary compensation. CSD held seven formal sales meetings during 1982. Participants discussed such topics as new products, updating of sales techniques, and changes in company policy. "Improving morale" was a recurring and stated goal of such meetings.

CSD's annual sales representative turnover rate was 12 percent; this compared with the industry's rate of 9 percent. The company did not conduct exit interviews, but management was of the opinion that most salespeople leaving did so because of greater monetary opportunities elsewhere. Three of the last five representatives leaving the company, however, had gone to work for competitors.

1. What, if anything, should have been done to motivate CSD's salespeople to perform more effectively?

2. Had you been called in as a management consultant to CSD, what would have been your recommendations?

Case 13 – 1

Potter Office
Supply
Company

Potter Office Supply Company is a manufacturer of office supplies and office furniture. It has manufactured and sold its products in the northeastern United States for over 25 years.

Due to the success of the company, Potter has decided to create a new sales district in the southeastern United States. It has been the company's policy to give as much leeway as possible to district sales managers in designing compensation plans for their salespeople. Keeping with this policy, Ms. Donna Brown, the district sales manager of the newly created district, has been asked to suggest a basic compensation plan and justify it.

The objectives Brown hoped to achieve through implementation of a compensation plan were as follows:

1. Encourage salespeople to penetrate the new market to the fullest extent by encouraging missionary sales work. This is especially true for the first year.
2. Create a sales plan which is satisfying to the salespeople.
3. Encourage the sale of profitable products.
4. Encourage salespeople to meet sales quotas.
5. Minimize selling expenses.
6. Attract and keep competent salespeople.
7. Motivate salespeople to do a complete selling job.

In order to attract and keep competent salespeople, Ms. Brown felt she must try to establish a salary level which was competitive with the sales salaries of competitors. Surveys indicated that the median salary for salespeople in the industry was approximately $20,000 per year. This was approximately $2,000 more than the median salaries of salespeople within the Potter organization. In order to attract and keep qualified salespeople, Brown felt it necessary that a competitive salary goal be met within three years, while keeping the projected sales force cost within 20 percent of total sales.

According to the present marketing plan, the first year in the new district was not expected to return a profit for the company. The salespeople were to concentrate on penetrating the market and establishing the company's reputation in both the retail and the wholesale market.

During the first year, Brown suggested that a straight salary compensation plan be used. This would provide the salespeople with stable earnings during the period of time when a great deal of their effort would be spent on missionary work. By using this straight salary compensation method, Brown felt she would be able to more closely direct the activities of the sales force during the initial market penetration stage of the marketing plan, without running into conflicts which a commission or bonus plan might bring about. The salary suggested for the first year was $15,000 plus expenses. This plan would be used for the first year only, after which a combination salary, commission, and expense account plan would be used. The benefit claimed for paying a straight salary was that it would give a stable income to the salespeople, and they would be motivated to develop the market in their territory to the fullest extent in anticipation of sales commissions to be paid the following year.

The following sales projections per salesperson were made for the second and third year of Potter's marketing plan: Year 2—$80,000, and Year 3—$130,000.

The sales territories in the new district were designed so that each salesperson would have the same sales potential, and no overnight travel would be required. Potential customers were clustered in major urban areas so each salesperson would be required to call on approximately the same number of customers and cover approximately the same distance in order to service customers. After the first year, each salesperson would be allotted an expense account up to a maximum of $430 per month.

According to the present marketing plan, by the third year each salesperson's expenses, which include car expenses and entertainment, should account for no more than 4 percent of total sales. At the rate of $430 per month, over 12 months, this results in an annual expense account cost per salesperson of $5,160, less than the projected 4 percent of total sales.

Based upon the projected sales, a sales force compensation plan consisting of a maximum expense account allowance of $5,160 per year, a commission of 3 percent on gross sales for the first $40,000, 5 percent on $40,000–$100,000 and 6 percent on gross sales over $100,000 was proposed.

This plan would give adequate incentive to increase sales, while not wasting the company's money by over-compensating the sales force. The increased commissions resulting from over $100,000 in sales would provide an incentive to achieve high goals while not over-burdening the company with high commissions. Instead, the increased commissions would be conpensated for by not having more salespeople in the field, thereby minimizing expense account costs and supervisory costs which would be needed to properly supervise a larger sales force.

	1st year	2nd year	3rd year
Projected total sales per salesperson		$80,000	$130,000
3% of first $40,000	straight sal.	$ 1,200	$ 1,200
5% of $40,000-$100,000	straight sal.	$ 2,000	$ 3,000
6% over $100,000	straight sal.		$ 1,800
Commission	straight sal.	$ 3,200	$ 6,000
Salary	$15,000	$14,000	$ 14,000
Total Pay	$15,000	$17,200	$ 20,000

Third Year Total: $20,000   salesperson's pay
                   + 5,160   expense account allotment
                    $25,160   projected cost/salesperson

$$\frac{\$25,160 \text{ cost/salesperson}}{\$130,000 \text{ total sales}} = 19.4\% \text{ of total sales by the 3rd year}$$

1. Were Brown's goals realistic?

2. Evaluate Brown's procedure for developing a compensation plan.

3. Overall, how effectively will the plan accomplish the company's objectives?

Case 13 – 2

Avery Drug Company

On July 1, 1981, Avery Drug Company, a medium-sized pharmaceutical manufacturing firm, announced a major change in compensation policy to its sales staff of 14 salespeople. The Avery salespeople, officially known as "medical sales representatives," called mainly on physicians. Their selling efforts consisted primarily of what has been referred to as "detailing"—i.e., making physicians aware of what Avery Drug Company had to offer that physicians might prescribe to patients when appropriate.

Prior to July 1, all Avery salespeople had received a salary plus a semiannual bonus. The bonus was determined solely by management, primarily on the basis of the company's economic situation as shown on the semi-annual financial reports.

Although sales management realized that certain problems would arise as a result of this change, each salesperson was to receive an adjustment in base salary to compensate for the loss of the bonus. Adjustments varied in amounts. In some instances they were less, in others more, than the amounts that salespeople had been averaging.

Don Moran, a salesman with the firm for nearly six years, was earning a base salary of $25,200 per annum at the time the policy change was announced. His bonuses during the previous two years were in the following amounts:

1979, second six months: $3,250.00
1980, first six months: $2,825.00
1980, second six months: $3,100.00
1981, first six months: $2,400.00

In addition to salary and incentive bonuses, salespeople also participated in a year-end profit-sharing plan, which for the last three years had amounted to 15 percent of base salary. The policy change did not alter their participation in this plan in any way, other than to increase their future payments due to the increase in base salary resulting from the adjustment.

On July 23 Hank Logan, Division Manager, sent the following letter to Don Moran. Other salespeople received similar letters, except that the salaries varied according to the individual.

Dear Don:

It has always been one of your company's objectives to provide you with one of the best—if not the best—compensation plans in the pharmaceutical industry. To continually meet this objective, we have, over the years, made changes and adjustments in our medical sales representatives' compensation policy.

After months of careful study, I am happy to announce that we have been successful in instituting a new compensation plan for our field staff. This straight-salary plan has been made effective July 1, 1981. Many of its features are derived from those previously suggested by members of our field staff.

All adjustments are retroactive and will appear in August salary checks. Your salary has been adjusted to $28,200 per annum. Let me assure you that the opportunity to further increase your total compensation has never been greater. However, sales performance will be more critically evaluated in the future to determine equitable and deserving salary increases.

We are confident that our new compensation plan will effectively motivate our field staff to accomplish future objectives.

Kind regards,
Hank Logan

Adapted from CASES AND POLICIES IN HUMAN RESOURCES MANAGEMENT, 3rd ed. by Raymond L. Hilgert, Sterling H. Schoen, and Joseph W. Towle; 1978 by Houghton Mifflin Company. Used by permission of the publisher.

When Hank Logan entered his office on the morning of July 27, his secretary handed him a telegram which read:

HANK LOGAN,
AVERY DRUG COMPANY, NEW YORK, NY

THANK YOU FOR THE CONFIDENCE YOU HAVE EXPRESSED IN ME THROUGH THE RECENT SORRY ADJUSTMENT. YOUR SUPPORT WILL CONTINUE TO BE JUSTIFIED.

DON MORAN

Dismayed, Hank Logan dropped the telegram on his desk and pondered what, if anything, he should do to respond to the telegram.

1. Evaluate Avery's compensation program.

2. What procedure should have been employed in announcing the change?

Part 6

Future-Oriented Considerations

14. INFORMATION SYSTEMS FOR SALES MANAGERS

15. DEVELOPMENTS IN SALES FORCE MANAGEMENT

CASES

Chapter 14 _____

Information Systems for Sales Managers

After completing this chapter, you will be able to:

- Define and emphasize the importance of marketing information systems.

- Discuss the procedure for developing marketing information systems.

- Identify problems associated with the development and implementation of information systems.

A **marketing information system (MIS)** is a systematic procedure for providing timely, relevant, and understandable information to a marketing decision-maker. The system can be as simple as a memorandum that identifies the number of product displays a particular salesperson established during a particular period, or as sophisticated as a computer based information system that provides the sales manager with daily information on each salesperson's performance.

Regardless of the complexity of a specific system, the objective of an MIS is to reduce uncertainty surrounding marketing problems so that more effective decisions can be made. Many marketing decisions are surrounded by a complex set of variables that may bear significantly on the efficacy of a decision. If these variables are not identified, examined, and integrated into the decision process, the decision may be nothing more than a hunch or guess. When extraneous variables are systematically examined and their influence is measured, there is a higher probability that the decision will reflect reality and provide an accurate answer to complex marketing questions.

PROCEDURE FOR DEVELOPING A SALES INFORMATION SYSTEM

In order to minimize problems and realize the inherent advantages of an information system it is critical that development of a system proceed in orderly fashion. Steps involved in development of a sales information system include the following:

1. Educate potential users of the system on the characteristics, uses, and value of an information system.

337

2. Examine the existing information system to identify its strengths and weaknesses.
3. Identify all decisions made by sales executives and supervisors.
4. Determine what information is necessary for effective decision-making.
5. Identify methods of collecting data.
6. Design the system and develop necessary support programs such as computer software.
7. Implement the information system.
8. Evaluate the system to insure its validity.

Educate Users

Ignorance of the potential uses and advantages of an information system is one of the primary reasons for the inability of a system to realize its potential. Many sales executives and salespeople simply do not understand the specialized language of systems people and are wary of the computer and its functions. If the intended users of the system are not educated and intensively trained regarding its uses and benefits, the system may be doomed before it is even developed. In fact, several empirical studies have focused on this problem and conclusively found that information systems are more likely to fail when user reactions are not dealt with prior to implementation.[1] It is important, therefore, that systems designers not only educate sales personnel but also involve salespeople and managers in the actual development of a system.

Examine Existing Systems

The systems designer should study present decision-making procedures and identify current information flow. The designer may find that some decisions are supported with an adequate amount and quality of information while other decisions are made in an environment of complete uncertainty. Such analysis might indicate information priorities and aid the designer in pin-pointing specific areas on which to focus.

Identify Decision Areas

Actual development of any information system must begin with an identification of the types of decisions made by sales executives and supervisors. Since the objective of a sales information system is to help managers make better decisions, it is logical to base the information model on the characteristics of the decision-making environment. In sales management there are three general types of decisions: strategic decisions, coordinative decisions, and operational decisions.

Strategic decisions are future oriented and deal with the organiza-

---

[1] See Daniel Robey, "User Attitudes and Management Information System Use," *Academy of Management Journal*, Vol. 22 (September, 1977), pp. 527–538.

tion's relationship with its environment. Decisions to change a policy, product, or price in order to adapt to forecasted changes in the work force, the marketplace, a governmental regulation, or an innovation are all strategic decisions.

Coordinative decisions relate future direction with present conditions. Business firms have personnel, financial, and physical resources that are utilized to satisfy present objectives. When a decision is made to change the future direction of a firm, resources must be reallocated in order to accommodate those strategic decisions. Coordinative decisions, therefore, relate to the implementation stage of strategic decision-making. For example, if a firm decides to penetrate a new geographical territory with existing products, it must investigate personnel availability, capital availability, marketing expertise, and adequacy of production facilities to handle an increase in demand.

Operational decisions are day-to-day decisions designed to control sales force activity. When a firm develops a sales information system it will initially focus on operational decisions. The sales manager is provided daily status reports on each salesperson's performance by product, customer, and territory. They may also receive information on inventory levels, stockouts, and production levels to help salespeople identify potential delivery dates.

Determine Information Requirements

After the sales manager determines what long and short run decisions are to be made, information requirements for each decision area must be identified. For some decisions the sales manager must collect **primary information**—i.e., information which is collected by a researcher in order to solve a specific problem. In other instances the sales manager can rely on **secondary information**—i.e., information collected by someone other than the person or firm that uses the information.

For making strategic decisions the sales manager must rely on both primary and secondary information. One of the most important strategic decisions is sales forecasting. In order to accurately forecast sales, the firm must examine (1) information on anticipated marketing programs and the impact of such programs on sales, (2) competitive programs, (3) economic conditions, (4) changes in public policy, (5) shifts in consumer behavioral patterns, and (6) technological changes. For each information need the systems designer must develop a system for collecting the relevant information and disseminating it to the appropriate decision-makers.

Coordinative decisions are generally made with external secondary information and company records. Coordinative decisions may require information concerning capital and labor availability, demographic trends, market potential, and managerial expertise.

Operational decisions require the development and utilization of company reports. Goals are established for day-to-day activities and performance data are measured to monitor achievement of those norms. Reports utilized to collect relevant information include sales reports, call reports, and new business reports (see Chapter 10). Some systems may go beyond simple reporting systems by programming the computer to actually make decisions. For example, a computerized inventory control system can be instructed to check inventory levels after each transaction to determine if reordering is necessary. If the reorder point is reached, the computer may either instruct purchasing to place an order or automatically place an order with the supplier's computer. See Figure 14-1 for a list of information needs.

Information for Strategic Decisions	Information for Co-ordinative Decision	Information for Operating Decisions
Customer Characteristics	Capital Availability	Market Share
Customer Segments	Production Capacity	Competitive Price Changes
Purchase Behavior	Labor Supply	Brand Switching of Customers
Market Potential	Management Expertise	Sales Performance by Product
Price Sensitivity of Customers	Knowledge of Channels	Sales Performance by Customer
Social Change	Middleman Availability	Sales Performance by Territory
Where Customers Buy	Availability of Materials	Lost Sales
Usage Rate of Customer Groups	Existing Marketing Laws	New Customers
Benefits Derived from Product Use	Media Availability	Sales Expenses
Market Changes	Tax Structure of New Locations	Advertising Effectiveness
Seasonal Fluctuations		Sales Performance by Channel
Competitive Programs and Products		Gross Margin
Technological Change		Total Sales Volume by Salesperson
Legal Change		

Figure 14-1
Information Needs for Sales Managers: By Decision Area

Identify Data Collection Methods

Once the firm has developed a comprehensive list of information needed, it must decide how the information will be collected. Alternative methods for collecting marketing data include surveys, observation, experimentation, internal reporting, external secondary information, and qualitative research.

Survey.   Surveys are utilized to collect factual information about customer characteristics, attitudes, opinions, and behaviors. For example, National Bank of Commerce may want to identify the characteristics of its commercial customers in terms of size and Standard Industrial Classification. One way to collect such information is to survey a random sample of commercial customers and ask for such information. The survey might also ask for their attitudes toward the bank and services they desire.

Surveys always involve the administration of a questionnaire to a sample or census of target respondents. Surveys are the most widely utilized data collection procedure because they are relatively fast and inexpensive, and can be utilized to reduce uncertainty surrounding almost any problem. Implementation of surveys is accomplished by mail, telephone, or personal interview. Although personal interviews are used to collect large amounts of information, they are slow, expensive, and require extensive training and administration of interviewers. Telephone is the most popular medium for collecting data because it is fast, relatively inexpensive, and flexible enough to be utilized for collecting all types of information. The primary problem with the telephone survey is that large amounts of information cannot be effectively collected.

Mail is used for collecting a large amount of information and is relatively inexpensive. The primary problem with mail is that response rates are often low and, therefore, nonresponse error is high. Also, when response is low the researcher must mail additional survey forms which drives up costs and delays collection of relevant data. In addition, mail is inflexible in that probing for answers is not possible. Also, mail gives the respondent an opportunity to read the form and determine what the researcher is asking before answering the questions.

Observation.   Observation is used to study actual behavior. Sales managers use observation to collect qualitative information on salesperson performance. They accompany salespeople on calls, assess their performance, and make suggestions for improvement. They also utilize such input in yearly performance appraisal interviews. The same procedure may also be used to assess the effectiveness of training programs. Figure 14-2 suggests ways in which observation may be used in solving marketing problems. The primary advantage of observation is that actual behavior can be precisely identified and measured. The primary disadvantage is that the researcher cannot precisely determine reasons for behavior.

Experimentation.   Experimentation is used to determine the effectiveness of marketing programs. A sales manager may want to determine the effectiveness of a new point of sales device for a firm's paint brushes. In order to accomplish this objective, the firm might divide a randomly selected group of distributors into two groups, an experimental

Figure 14–2
The Use Of
Observation In
Solving Marketing
Problems

- Use an audiometer to measure television viewing habits.

- Use a psychogalvanometer to measure response to proposed advertisements or musical recordings.

- Use eye cameras to study eye movement when reading magazines or evaluating products at retail.

- Use cameras to study movement of people in stores.

- Count the number of automobiles that pass a particular intersection.

- Observe decision behavior at the point of purchase.

group and a control group. For a period of time prior to introduction of the display, sales of the paint brushes are measured in each store (see Table 14-1). Then a paint brush display is placed in the experimental stores while the traditional display procedure is maintained in control stores. For the same period of time after introduction of the display, sales of all stores are measured. The change in paint brush sales in experimental stores is compared to the change in control store sales. The difference between experimental and control stores represents the effectiveness of the point of purchase display.

Experimentation is the only procedure that can be employed to precisely measure the effectiveness of a marketing program. It is, therefore, utilized to measure the feasibility of new products, the effectiveness of package design changes, the effectiveness of an advertising program, the effectiveness of a training program, and the impact of a price change on sales. As indicated by the types of information obtained through experimentation, it is extremely valuable to the efficient functioning of an information system.

Table 14–1
Experimental Data
for Paint Brush
Display

Before Measure of Sales	150 units	169 units
Experimental Variable	Display introduced	No Display
After Measure of Sales	267 units	172 units

Effect of Display = (267 units − 150 units) =   117 units
                    (172 units − 169 units) = − 3 units
                                                114 units

The primary problem with experimentation is the cost and time associated with development and implementation of an experiment. There are also numerous design problems that can impede validity and reliability of experiments. For example, a firm may want to measure the impact of an advertising program on consumer attitudes. In such a study the premeasure of attitudes may make the respondents more sensitive to the introduction of the advertisement and, therefore, bias the after measure of attitude.

Internal Reporting.   Most firms maintain a data base of cost and sales information that can be utilized to identify marketing opportunities and weaknesses. Sales reports can be analyzed to determine salesperson efficiency in terms of sales volume, profit contribution, development of new business, ability to close sales, expense control, and time management. Also, accounting data can give the sales manager insight into the profit contribution of various products, customer groups, and territories.

External Secondary Information.   External secondary information is primarily utilized to support strategic decision-making. When forecasting sales, for example, the sales manager needs information on economic conditions, market conditions, growth of various market segments, technological developments, and social change. Such information can be found in government reports, technical journals, trade magazines, and private reports.

Another important strategic decision that requires input from secondary sources is the allocation of salespeople to territories. As was indicated in Chapter 5, the allocation decision is normally based on an estimate of market potential. For consumer or industrial products, market potential can be derived from *Survey of Buying Power* and *Survey of Industrial Purchasing Power* found in *Sales and Marketing Management* magazine. Industrial firms may also use the Standard Industrial Classification method which requires utilization of *Census of Business* information on the number of firms in various territories.

Once a problem has been identified, it is critical that the researcher identify all possible sources of information to help gain insight into conditions surrounding the problem. In order to insure completeness, the following systematic procedure should be employed:

1. Examine all information available in libraries. Search the *Business Periodicals Index*, the card catalog, and the *Dissertation Abstracts* for technical papers and general interest information on the subject.
2. Examine government agency information sources. The Department of Commerce, for example, has a users library that can provide valuable information on industry conditions and market trends. The user should begin a search of government data by examining *The Statistical Abstract of the United States* and the *Industrial Outlook*. These publications summarize data collected from numerous government sources. For each subject area, extensive footnoting is provided in

A Company Profile

Established in Dallas, Texas, in 1916, Mercantile Bank has grown into one of the nation's fifty largest banks with assets of almost $4 billion. Mercantile dominated the financial market in Dallas until the 1960s, when other banking institutions began to expand, build larger and more impressive buildings, and form holding companies that involved the pooling of assets of dozens of Texas banks. Instead of responding to these challenges, Mercantile continued to focus its attention on the past. The Bank's inactivity and conservative posture not only cost it a dominant market position but also impacted negatively on its identity. Mercantile emerged in the 1970s in a subordinate position with no identity and no growth.

In 1975, with the appointment of Gene Bishop as President, the direction and corporate philosophy of Mercantile changed. The Bank developed a holding company that has grown into a national financial leader with $6 billion in assets. It hired innovative and aggressive executives to help identify and manage new growth opportunities. Merchantile also recognized the importance of marketing, and developed one of the most outstanding marketing support groups in the Southwest.

Prior to 1976, the marketing department was comprised of a public relations/advertising person that interfaced with an advertising agency on the implementation of promotional strategy. There was no commitment to the development of a comprehensive marketing strategy or information system. The concept of marketing was reflected in the role of the bank's lending officers: they would generally sit at their desks and wait for new customers to approach the bank.

Mercantile's marketing support group now consists of at least 35 full time employees that work in 5 departments, all of which report to a senior vice president of marketing. The personal banking department focuses on the implementation of programs that are designed to satisfy the needs of individual customers. The marketing planning group isolates products and manages the life cycle of those new products. For example, this group assisted the development of MPACT, a network of automatic teller machines strategically located in Mercantile's market area. The communications department develops and implements external as well as internal advertising and public relations strategies. The bank card department processes transactions for merchants. Finally, the product development division develops and assesses the feasibility of new ideas. It is also responsible for collecting and analyzing marketing information that is utilized by all departments in decision making.

Concurrent with establishment of a comprehensive marketing department has been the development of a sophisticated marketing information system. In general, the marketing information system consists of knowing who Mercantile's customers are, and identifying what they want, how to translate the customer's needs into new products, and how to introduce the resultant product into the marketplace. For example, prior to fully introducing the MPACT automatic teller system into the marketplace, Mercantile's new product development group utilized research to identify potential target customers, their attitudes toward the concept, and the price they would be willing to pay.

The information system at Mercantile is

represented by the following activities:

- *On-going secondary research studies to monitor environmental developments that impact on the financial industry.*
- *Qualitative focus groups to identify new products as well as to measure advertising effectiveness.*
- *Identification of market segments such as the affluent and low income segments—What are their banking habits? Where do they go to obtain advice? What are their buying intentions?*
- *Monitoring of changes in the size and characteristics of target markets— i.e., number of new doctors, lawyers, petroleum companies, CPAs, etc.*
- *Conducting pricing research for all new products.*

- *Analysis of alternative site locations.*
- *Study of demographic characteristics of each census tract.*
- *Analysis of competition.*
- *Monitoring effectivness of new products.*
- *Organizing and disseminating data to each area of the corporation.*

In five years, Mercantile has progressed from a company that was losing market share to one of the fastest growing banks in Texas. The quality and sophistication of the marketing information system has contributed to this planned, manageable growth. The Bank now operates in an environment of certainty, and all departments understand that the identification and satisfaction of customer needs is the reason for their existence. The lending officers no longer wait for customers. They leave the bank to seek out customers.

the event that the researcher wants to examine more detailed information about the subject. Researchers going directly to the original sources will find an overwhelming amount of data, most of which will probably be useless. Other excellent sources of marketing information in the Department of Commerce include special industry reports and government representatives. The Department of Commerce employs representatives for each major industry group. These people are responsible for collecting and maintaining information on their respective industries and, therefore, can be a valuable source of current data.

3. Contact trade associations for information that is not available in libraries or from the Department of Commerce.
4. Contact professional research firms for private research on the subject area. An excellent index that lists all private studies conducted on every imaginable subject is the *Findex*.
5. Contact large businesses in the relevant industry. Many large business firms maintain comprehensive technical libraries for use by their employees and, in some cases, customers and suppliers.

In addition to insuring completeness, the research must insure accuracy of the secondary information. Methodologies should be examined to insure that the information is reliable, valid, and not biased by subjective interpretation or self-interest.

Qualitative Research. When appropriate information cannot be obtained by quantitative or secondary research, one might employ depth interviewing, focus group interviewing, or projective techniques. These techniques are primarily used to develop a general understanding of a phenomenon rather than to conclusively prove a hypothesis. The sales manager may want to develop a better understanding of the behavioral characteristics of successful salespeople or the attitudes of customers toward a new product idea. If a lot is already known about respondent attitudes and behaviors the researcher will probably utilize depth interviewing or focus group interviewing (i.e., a free flowing interview session, directed by a moderator and involving 10 to 15 respondents). If, on the other hand, little is known about the phenomenon a nondirected projective technique is most appropriate (i.e., ink blot test, word association test).

Design the System

Once information needs and data collection methods have been identified the firm must design the system for collecting and disseminating the appropriate information. Specifically, the system designer must (1) identify who is responsible for collecting the data, (2) determine who is responsible for disseminating data, (3) determine how and where data will be distributed, and (4) calculate the costs of developing alternative systems.

A good initial step is to flow chart decisions and the movement of data to various decision points (see Figure 14-3). By doing this, each person will know where to find needed information and what they should do with available information. The systems designer is then in a position to get feedback from sales management on the ability of the system to fulfill needs. Alternative system designs can then be developed, and a cost/benefit analysis can be performed for each alternative. Such analysis will indicate to management which system alternative is most appropriate for the firm.

Implement the System

Implementation of the sales information system involves the integration of the sales system with the corporate information system. Although the needs of each functional area should be examined and separate systems should be analyzed, all systems must be integrated into a company-wide information system. If a firm has a separate system for each area it may experience duplication of costs. For example, marketers may need financial data in order to monitor gross margin contribution of salespeople or to develop prices for potential customers. Instead of having two departments collecting and analyzing the same data, it is more efficient to have one department collect the data, then disseminate it to appropriate decision points.

Implementation also involves installation of systems and employee

Figure 14–3 A Sales Manager's Management Information System

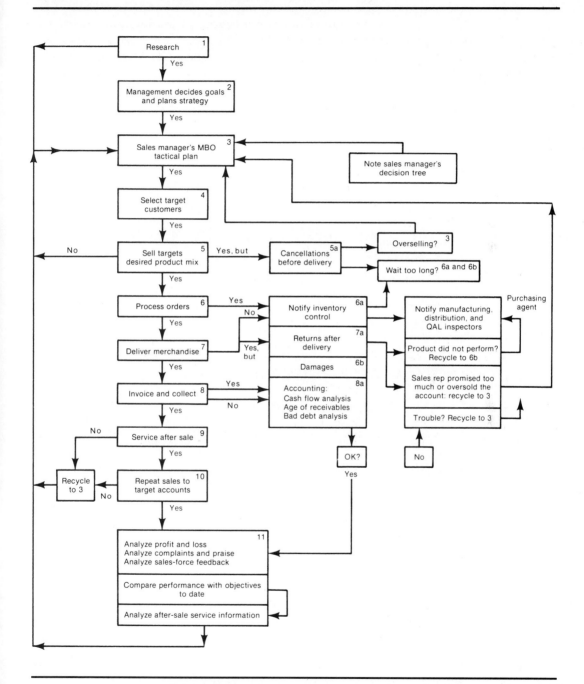

Source: Thomas F. Stroh, *Managing the Sales Function* (New York: McGraw-Hill, Inc., 1976), p. 101.

training. Hardware must be installed, data files must be introduced to the system, an instruction manual must be written for each user, every employee must be trained to insure proper utilization, and the system must be tested for accuracy.[2]

Evaluate the System

When a system has been in operation several months it must be evaluated to determine actual return on invested capital. Although it is difficult to precisely quantify return on investment, a subjective analysis can be performed to determine if the system is meeting expectations. Specific activities associated with implementation include the following:

- Insure that documentation is complete and accurate.
- Compare anticipated costs to actual costs.
- Compare anticipated benefits to actual benefits.
- Survey the attitude of users toward the system.
- Determine if internal controls are adequate.
- Identify weaknesses of the system.
- Make recommended changes.[3]

PROBLEMS WITH MARKETING INFORMATION SYSTEMS

When properly developed and implemented, an MIS provides timely and relevant information to decision-makers. Because of problems which are inherent in the decision-making and communication processes, however, efficient development of an MIS is not always possible. Although these problems cannot always be eliminated, they should be understood and accounted for. Common problems include information overload, inaccurate input data, language barrier, changing management requirements, failure to sell employees on the system, and assessment of costs and benefits.

Information Overload

An efficiently designed information system should focus on the collection of information that facilitates decision-making. Information that just satisfies a curiosity, is used to simply confirm one's suspicions, or is not utilized, should not be included in the system.

The problem, however, is that many sales managers do not know

---

[2] John R. Page and H. Paul Hooper, "Basics of Information Systems Development," *Journal of Systems Management* (August, 1979), p. 15.
[3] Page and Hooper, *Ibid.*, pp. 15–16.

what information is needed to make decisions. They simply ask for all available information and, therefore, waste the time of salespeople and researchers who have to collect the information and computer people who are required to process the information. For example, sales managers may require extensive monthly precall plans from salespeople. Then they simply file the plan instead of evaluating each one against actual performance in order to determine effectiveness. Although call plans can be helpful in measuring and improving performance, they can represent an information overload if they are not utilized.

In order to minimize the information overload problem, it is necessary to precisely define decisions to be made and identify information that is necessary to facilitate decision-making. Managers should also develop trial tables of information and simulate decision-making to determine if all data is relevant and necesssary, and that all required information is provided. Also, the firm can charge each operating manager for the information that they utilize.

Inaccurate Input Data

Inaccurate input data not only impedes decision-making but can destroy employee confidence in the information system. A manufacturer in the Southwest, for example, uses profit contribution as the basis for commission payments. Since the margin calculation is inaccurate, salespeople have little confidence in the firm's compensation plan and, in fact, are generally dissatisfied with management.

Language Barrier

People who develop MISs are often technical people who have little knowledge of the sales manager's requirements. Similarly, the sales manager is unaware of what can be provided by an effective computer based information system. The result is inadequate communication between the designer and the user.

The sales manager tells the systems designer what is needed and the designer then converts that request into a useable format. Often the request is either not interpreted correctly or the designer develops a format that will fit into the system rather than developing a system that will accommodate the request.

Changing Management Requirements

As firms grow and mature the amount and type of information needed to effectively manage the sales function changes. Sales managers need more information on territory potentials, customer characteristics, sales force productivity, competitive activities, and so on. They may also add new products, open new markets, such as international markets, and change compensation plans. These changes in information requirements lead to changes in data files and programs. Unless the system is flexible enough to accommodate these changes, extensive and expensive system modification may be necessary.

Selling the System

As was indicated earlier, research has found that MISs frequently fail when psychological reactions and organizational factors are not considered during system development.[4] Firms that do not train, educate, and involve employees in the development, uses, and strengths of an MIS may find that it is unacceptable to employees and does not function as planned. In order to avoid such problems firms should market the system to employees just like they would market a product to consumers. Specifically, they need to: (1) identify employee needs, (2) develop a system concept, (3) test acceptance of the concept among employees, (4) modify the concept to accommodate employee requests, (5) develop the system, (6) educate employees on the uses of the system, (7) promote the system to users, and (8) redesign the system when needs change.

Assessing Costs and Benefits

Although costs of developing a system can be calcuated and distributed to various operating divisions, benefits are not as easily identified and measured. Each operating manager must subjectively assess the impact of the system on the quality of decision-making. Are decisions made faster and more accurately? Are sales territories more productive? What effect has the system had on selling costs and gross margin? Has turnover been reduced? Has the system improved employee morale? What effect has the system had on the compatibility of various operating divisions?

SUMMARY

An MIS is a systematic procedure for providing timely, relevant, and understandable information to a marketing decision-maker. Its primary purpose is to reduce uncertainty surrounding marketing problems so that more effective decisions can be made.

In order to develop an effective information system, the designer must identify employee needs and educate potential users on the characteristics, uses, and value of an information system. Second, the designer must examine the existing system and identify its strengths and weaknesses. Third, the firm must identify all decisions that are made by sales executives and supervisors. Fourth, the firm should determine what information is necessary for effective decision-making. Fifth, the system designer should identify methods for collecting data. Sixth, the system is designed. Finally, the system is implemented and evaluated to insure validity.

Although information systems are designed

---

[4] Robey, *op. cit.*

to facilitate making decisions, they can be accompanied by certain problems. Too much useless information may be generated. Output data can be misleading because of inaccurate input data. Communications problems between the systems designer and user can cause the firm to collect too much or not enough information. Management requirements can change, thus invalidating the system. Employees may resist utilization of the system. Also, benefits derived from using the system are difficult to assess.

QUESTIONS

1. What could result from the lack of a marketing information system?

2. Why would management educate potential users of a marketing information system before examining the present system?

3. In development of a marketing information system, how does one determine which information is needed?

4. How are the best methods of collecting data determined?

5. How is the system evaluated after implementation?

6. Discuss the types of decisions made in sales management; give examples of each.

7. What must be examined in order to more accurately forecast sales?

8. Why are surveys the most widely used data collection procedure?

9. When would qualitative research be necessary?

10. What data collection procedure is most appropriate in measuring the effectiveness of a marketing program?

Chapter 15

Developments in Sales Force Management

After completing this chapter, you will be able to:

- Identify environmental changes that affect sales management programs.

- Assess the implications of environmental factors on sales managers.

- Identify and discuss the relationship between environmental analysis and sales planning.

Although procedures associated with managing sales forces are rather static, the environment in which those procedures are implemented is dynamic and constantly changing. The demographic, geographic, and psychographic characteristics of markets change. Economic conditions fluctuate randomly and frequently. The philosophical orientation of managers evolves to more effectively meet the challenges of business. Also, legal systems are altered when they inadequately reflect the needs of society.

Specific changes that characterize the selling environment include the following:

- The movement of females into sales and sales management careers.

- An expanding legal framework.

- Increasing costs of hiring, training, and maintaining salespeople.

- The changing character of the population and markets.

Although business firms are also influenced by other changes, these particular factors are having the most profound impact on sales management. A short sighted, status quo orientation that is insensitive to these changes can result in development of strategies that do not adequately take advantage of growth opportunities. The purpose of this chapter is to introduce existing and future sales managers to these environmental changes and discuss the impact of such change on managerial philosophy and practice.

WOMEN IN SALES

Inflationary pressures, increases in education levels, rising divorce rates, and changes in traditional role structures toward work and marriage have all affected the occupational behavior and aspirations of women. Specifically, the number of divorces have more than doubled between 1965 and 1979.[1] Although marriage is still popular among young people, it is being postponed until later in life. Also, of all bachelor's degrees earned in the United States, 25 percent were earned by women in 1950 as compared to 48 percent in 1980.[2] Furthermore, enrollment statistics in 1980 indicated that over 50 percent of all college students were female.

The result of these sociological developments is obvious. As shown in Table 15–1, the number of working women increased by approximately 71 percent between 1960 and 1981. Also, there are 73 women for every 100 men in the labor force. In addition, Table 15–1 shows that the increase in number of working women has been significant for all age groups except older groups.

Occupational and Income Inequities

Although the ratio of men to women in the total work force has narrowed during the past 30 years, the income levels and occupational positions of the two sexes are still distantly separated. Relative to income,

Table 15–1

Size of the Female Labor Force by Age (in 1,000s)

Age	1960	1970	1980	1981	Change 1960 to 1981 Number	Percent
16–19	2,062	3,250	3,471	3,303	1,241	60.2%
20–24	2,590	4,893	6,175	6,412	3,822	147.6%
25–34	4,140	5,704	10,311	11,144	7,004	169.2%
35–44	5,308	5,971	7,369	7,756	2,448	46.1%
45–54	5,280	6,523	6,015	6,130	850	16.1%
55–64	2,986	4,153	3,991	4,144	1,158	38.8%
65 & over	907	1,056	906	908	1	0.1%
Total	23,272	31,560	38,328	39,797	16,525	71.0%

Source: U.S. Department of Labor, *Employment and Earnings* (Washington: Goverment Printing Office, January, 1982), p. 178.

---

[1] U.S. Department of Commerce, Bureau of the Census, *Statistical Abstract of the United States, 1981.* (Washington: Government Printing Office, p. 80).

[2] *Ibid.*, p. 165.

women still earn less within particular occupational categories than men. Among wholesale sales representatives, for example, women earned 70.6 percent of what men earned in 1980.[3] Also, among manufacturers' sales representatives, women earned 68.3 percent of mens' earnings. Female retail clerks earned 65 percent of males.[4] Out of 67 major countries, the United States ranks 47th in economic divergence and 24th in occupational divergence (i.e., 23 other countries have less difference in occupational patterns than the United States).[5]

As indicated in Table 15–2, occupations representing the highest percentages of women include secretaries, registered nurses, and typists. Of the females employed in sales most are retail sales clerks. Table 15–3 on page 356 shows that industrial sales and management are still heavily dominated by men. In fact, 90 percent of wholesale salespeople and 85 percent of manufacturers' salespeople are men. A study conducted by the Research Institute of America indicated that 81 percent of all firms surveyed have not hired any women for sales positions.[6]

Sexual Stereotyping

One of the major reasons that women have had difficulty entering industrial sales is the stereotypes that have been attached to female salespeople. One study of 249 sales managers, 125 salesmen, and 125 saleswomen effectively illustrated this point.[7] The study was designed to determine (1) how sales managers perceive saleswomen, (2) how salesmen perceive saleswomen, and (3) how saleswomen view themselves. Variables tested in the study included aggressiveness, extrovert nature, trust, imagination, emotionality, open-mindedness, competency, career orientation, sales technique, intelligence, and self confidence.

Study findings indicated that salesmen and saleswomen perceive male salespeople to be at least somewhat strong on all factors except trustfulness, emotionality, open-mindedness, and imagination. They were neutral on the first three factors and somewhat negative about a salesman's imagination.

While males and females agreed on the strengths and weaknesses of salesmen, they did not agree on the strengths and weaknesses of saleswomen. Specifically, salesmen perceived saleswomen as (1) possessing poorer sales techniques, (2) having less career orientation, (3) being less open-minded, (4) more emotional, and (5) less self-confident than salesmen. Also, sales managers that had supervised both females and males envisioned males as being more assertive, more imaginative, more likely

---

[3] League of Women Voters, *Community Guide*, "Women and Vocational Training: A Step Up or Down?" (March, 1982), p. 1

[4] U.S. Department of Labor, Bureau of Labor Statistics.

[5] *Ibid.*, p. 30.

[6] Dan H. Robertson and Donald W. Hackett, "Saleswomen: Perceptions, Problems, and Prospects," *Journal of Marketing*, Vol. 41 (July, 1977), p. 67.

[7] This section is based on a study conducted by Robertson and Hackett, *Ibid*, pp. 66–71.

Occupation	% of women in occupation	% of all working women	median weekly earnings women	men
WHITE COLLAR				
Secretaries	99.2	11.5	209.16	268.54
Bookkeepers	89.4	4.1	202.95	306.08
Elementary teachers	81.9	3.6	289.38	338.67
Registered nurses	96.0	3.1	296.98	311.32
Managers administrators (except farm)	17.9	2.3	254.80	442.26
Sales clerks, retail	60.4	2.2	140.48	216.13
Office machine operators	72.4	2.1	200.89	295.77
Misc. clerical	81.6	2.7	202.01	292.58
Typists	96.5	2.7	189.06	231.19
Cashiers	86.9	2.0	149.27	216.47
BLUE COLLAR				
Nursing aides	84.5	2.5	154.86	191.52
Sewers/stitchers	87.9	2.5	143.42	185.78
Assemblers	53.7	2.1	186.46	272.33
Waitresses	83.1	1.6	133.51	204.92
Cooks (except private households)	52.6	1.4	139.04	188.26
Checkers examiners, inspectors manufacturing	52.0	1.4	203.68	314.06
Machine operators, misc.	29.2	1.3	179.87	283.52
Packers & wrappers, except meat & produce	64.7	1.2	176.21	216.40
Building interior cleaners	51.2	1.1	153.66	194.44
Practical nurses	96.5	.9	207.59	251.41

Table 15-2
Occupations Representing the Highest Percentages of Women, 1980

Source: Figures from the Department of Labor.

to utilize good sales technique, less emotional, not as open-minded, and less intelligent than females. Also, relative to the perception of men and women, sales managers rated saleswomen somewhat less competent than salesmen.

Not only is stereotyping indicated in research but it is also indicated in comments made by people in industry. For example, one person suggests that an average woman will fail faster than the average man.[8] Other

---

[8] Robin Brumett, "How to Pick an Ace Saleswoman," *Marketing Times* (May-June, 1976), p. 7.

Occupation	% of men in occupation	% of all working men	median weekly earnings	
			men	women
WHITE COLLAR				
Managers, administrators (except farm)	82.1	6.8	442.26	254.80
Secondary school teachers	50.8	1.3	346.50	289.97
Sales representatives, wholesale	90.4	1.5	368.01	259.91
Accountants	62.0	1.3	399.75	276.85
Bank officers, financial managers	65.9	1.0	472.01	270.20
Computer specialists	74.8	1.0	439.47	335.19
Shipping & receiving clerks	80.3	.9	250.20	191.19
Sales representatives, manufacturing	84.8	.7	408.33	278.88
Electrical engineers	96.0	.8	505.12	344.21
BLUE COLLAR				
Truck drivers	98.3	3.6	298.16	285.85
Blue collar supervisors	89.4	3.5	375.40	222.90
Heavy equipment mechanics	98.4	2.1	325.17	255.95
Janitors/sextons	86.9	2.0	211.09	175.61
Machine operators, misc.	70.8	2.1	283.52	179.87
Carpenters	99.2	1.8	304.03	196.40
Auto mechanics	99.5	1.8	282.11	265.10
Construction laborers	97.0	1.5	237.99	228.62
Welders/flame cutters	94.3	1.4	310.68	214.35
Electricians	98.9	1.3	398.21	273.02

Table 15-3
Occupations
Representing the
Highest
Percentages of
Men, 1980

Source: Figures from the Department of Labor.

people are more positive about the potential of females in sales. One survey, for example, indicates that female sales applicants are superior to male applicants for the following reasons:

- Because of the exclusion of women from high salaried, male-dominated positions, a large number of intelligent women are available for sales jobs.

- The socialization process has provided females with superior interpersonal skills.

- Women that apply for sales jobs seem to be more honest and ethical than their male counterparts.

- Because of the numerous financial and occupational opportunities associated with sales, women tend to work harder than men.

- Male prospects seem to respond more positively to saleswomen than salesmen.[9]

Attitudes of Women

Despite occupational and economic inequities as well as sexual stereotyping, the number of women in sales continues to climb. In a study of the paper and chemical industries it was found that the average firm employed 2.6 saleswomen in 1972. In 1977 the same firms employed 9.3 saleswomen.[10] As the trend continues, it will become increasingly important for sales managers to develop an understanding of females' attitudes toward job characteristics and rewards.

The findings of most studies comparing the attitudes of females toward job characteristics and rewards have been contradictory and inconclusive. Some studies have found that males are more interested in advancement/responsibility factors while females are more interested in work environment factors.[11] Other studies, however, indicate that such differences occur only when occupational and organizational level are not held constant. When the attitudes of males and females that are on the same organizational level are examined, no significant difference in work attitudes are revealed.[12]

One of the problems with studies of job attitudes is that they involve extremely small sample sizes and narrow populations. Also, since most of the studies do not examine salespeople, projecting the

---

[9] "When Hiring Women for Sales, You Get to Choose From the Cream of the Crop," *Research Institute Marketing for Sales Executives* (March 2, 1978), p. 4.

[10] Leslie Kanuk, "Women in Industrial Selling," *Journal of Marketing*, Vol. 42 (January, 1978), p. 88.

[11] Philip J. Manhardt, "Job Orientation of Male and Female College Graduates in Business," *Personnel Psychology*, Vol. 25 (1972), pp. 361–368.

[12] Arthur P. Brief and Richard L. Oliver, "Male-Female Differences in Work Attitudes Among Retail Sales Managers," *Journal of Applied Psychology*, Vol. 61, No. 4 (1976), p. 528.

A Company Profile

The Northwestern Mutual Life Insurance Company was founded in 1857, making it the eighteenth oldest life insurance company in the United States. Specializing in the sale of life insurance and disability insurance, the Northwestern has assets of over $11 billion and over $60 billion of insurance in force. It is a mutual company which means that the policyholders vote on proposed company activities, and, therefore, are the owners/stockholders. In a mutual company, dividends are paid to policyholders while in a stock insurance company dividends may be paid to both stockholders and policyholders. In 1981, approximately $545 million was allocated to Northwestern policyholders, an amount exceeding the annual premium of 550,000 policies or over 22 percent of premium-paying policies.

The Northwestern Mutual is a unique company that has identified a mission and business philosophy, and has steadfastly maintained that philosophy. Specifically, in 1889, the following company purpose was written:

> "The ambition of the Northwestern has been less to be large than to be safe; its aim is to rank first in benefits to policyholders rather than first in size. Valuing quality above quantity, it has preferred to secure its business under certain salutary restrictions and limitations rather than to write a much larger business at the possible sacrifice of these valuable points which have made the Northwestern preeminently the policyholders' company."

The Northwestern does lead the industry in benefits. A policyholder will earn more cash value on a policy than with any other mutual company, and will earn substantially more than with any stock company. The average size of new policies sold in 1980 was $47,000, substantially higher than for any other life insurance company. Policyholder satisfaction and company performance are also indicated by the fact that over one-half of its 1980 sales were to existing policyholders and it has the lowest lapse rate of life insurance companies.

Its dedication to policyholders is not only reflected in its dividend payments and overall performance, but also in its efficient management practices and controls. The Northwestern began utilizing electronic data processing in the mid-1950s—one of the first major companies to get involved in computer applications. It has made sound investments in oil leases in the Gulf, representing a significant departure from traditional mortgage loans and bonds that characterize the conservative investments of insurance companies. Northwestern needed to do this to keep the returns realized from an investment in life insurance competitive with other investments. It has effectively segmented its market to sell individualized life insurance rather than a variety of group plans, health, home, and auto insurance. Because the Northwestern primarily concentrates on one basic type of insurance, it has about one-fourth the number of home office employees as do most insurance companies, and has the lowest number of employees per $100 million of insurance in force.

Although the Northwestern has excelled in its overall management and performance, its primary competitive advantage is its sales force. It has over 4,000 full-time agents working out of 115 general agencies and over 300 district agencies. The top 25 agents for Northwestern earn an average of $315,414 per year, the top 100 agents earn $109,658, the top 500 agents earn $92,801 *per year, and the top 1500 agents earn over $50,000. The Northwestern has more members of the Million Dollar Round Table per agent than any other company. Approximately 62 percent of its agents have at least a college degree and another 28 percent have taken some college courses. Also, 29 percent of its agents were managers or professional people prior to joining.*

Finally, the Northwestern maintains a strong program to insure that it consistently

has a lower turnover than other insurance companies. In addition to carefully selecting only premium quality agents, it gives agents an enhanced commission for the first three years (i.e., 75 percent of premium instead of 50 percent). It also has a training program which includes field coaching, home office schools, field seminars, correspondence courses, clinics, study groups, and peer group meetings.

findings to this group can be dangerous. Recently, however, a study was conducted of 431 salespeople of two national pharmaceutical companies and one national hospital supply company. An analysis of the findings of this study revealed the following about the divergent attitudes of males and females toward their job:[13]

- Working in a male dominated industry is a source of dissatisfaction for female salespeople.

- Women are less confident in their selling skills and job security than males.

- Women show less interest in pay, promotion, and security and more interest in the "opportunity to meet different people" and "the opportunity for independent thought and action".

- Although men expressed more interest in pay and promotion than females, saleswomen are still significantly interested in these job related factors.

- Fewer women than men believe that the promotion system helps the best persons rise to the top.

While the findings of such studies are inconclusive, they should alert sales managers to the needs and problems of women pursuing careers in sales.

EXPANDING LEGAL FRAMEWORK

The legal environment in which salespeople operate continuously evolves and changes in order to accommodate changes in social norms

---

[13] John E. Swan, Charles M. Futrell, and John T. Todd, "Same Job-Different Views: Women and Men in Industrial Sales," *Journal of Marketing*, Vol. 42 (January, 1978), pp. 95–96.

and ideologies. Since the law is, in most cases, a reflection of society's attitudes, the law must change as behaviors, life styles, attitudes, and population characteristics change. Although changes in the law periodically reduce restrictions and vulnerabilities, they normally impose additional constraints on business activity. This being the case, managers and salespeople should be particularly sensitive to changes in the law and must develop timely and responsive contingency plans for reducing potential liabilities.

As was indicated in Chapter 2, the focus of legislation and court decisions has been on protecting product users and helping them make better-informed decisions. The credit laws, for example, were designed in part to make credit information more understandable. The Magnuson-Moss Warranty Act requires that businesses rewrite warranties in easily understood terms. The Fair Packaging and Labeling Act requires disclosure of extensive information on product labels. In addition, the government has made it easier for consumers to bring action against business firms that violate an antitrust or consumer law. Legislation has also given the Federal Trade Commission more power to establish rules and respond to improprieties.

The key rule for responding to changes in the legal framework is "awareness and education." Sales managers must maintain an awareness of legal developments, assess the impact of developments on the sales force, and then educate the salespeople on how they should respond to the developments.

One example of a recent legal development that has significantly affected sales and marketing activity is strict liability. This law is briefly examined in this section to indicate how sales managers should respond to such a development.

Strict liability means that a manufacturer is liable for any product defect that results in injury to a user of the defective product. There are three defects that may exist in a product. First, a design defect exists if injury results from a faulty design, and the risk of danger inherent in the design outweighs the design's benefits. Second, manufacturing defects arise when a malfunction in the manufacturing process produces substandard items. Third, a defect exists when the manufacturer fails to warn the user of risks associated with using or misusing the product.

Although there are many ways in which a firm should respond to strict liability law, a few of those potential reactions directly involve the sales department. For example, the sales department should be involved in the design safety review process from the time the product idea is conceived. At the concept stage of product development, the firm must evaluate alternative designs and identify the design that both minimizes liability and maximizes sales appeal. Since sales managers are more familiar with customer needs than are the technical people, it is critical that they give input at the initial stage of development. The sales department should answer such questions as: Which design will be most attractive to customers? What problems will the sales department experience with each design? What warning statements should be placed on the product? What effect will warning statements have on the product's saleability?

The sales force should also be utilized to educate customers on the appropriate uses of the product. Salespeople should be trained to help customers identify potential misuses and hazards associated with misuse. In order to accomplish this, salespeople should probe for every possible product application, examine actual utilization of the product in the manufacturing facility, avoid exaggerations about the efficacy of the product, contact a technical representative when in doubt about a potential use of a product, and correct any technical errors with the customers.[14]

INCREASING COSTS

Costs of finding, selecting, training and maintaining salespeople are increasing for all business organizations. With double digit inflation in the 1970's and early 1980's, the trend is almost certain to continue. Not only will it specifically affect selling costs, but it will also affect the cost of materials, production, labor, and distribution. Since costs cannot always be covered by higher prices, added pressure is placed on the sales department to insure that demand be maintained and costs be reduced.

One response to cost increases is to compensate salespeople for their contribution to profit rather than to sales volume. If salespeople have flexibility to negotiate price, such a compensation plan discourages them from using price as a primary vehicle for generating sales to the detriment of profitability.

Second, sales managers should become more concerned with efficiency. They should rigorously review salesperson performance with quantitative and qualitative criteria. They should also continuously monitor the profitability of product lines, customer groups, and territories.

Third, sales managers should do a better job of selecting and maintaining salespeople. More intensive interviewing and testing should be utilized so that the appropriate people can be identified for sales positions. Once recruits are hired they should receive extensive training and support in order to insure a higher level of morale. Salary plus commission plans can also be utilized instead of straight commission in order to reduce turnover.

---

[14] "Teaching the Sales Force to Stay Out of Court," *Research Institute Marketing for Sales Executives*, Vol. 4 (March 16, 1978), pp. 1–3.

POPULATION AND MARKET CHANGES

Changing characteristics of the population must be identified, analyzed, and monitored to determine their impact on sales management. The following represents a list of some changes that will continue to affect sales managers in the future:

- There will be a significant increase in the over 65 age group. This means that demand for products directed at this group will increase. It also means that sales managers will have a potentially large group of peope from which they can select for sales positions. One company in the Southwest, for example, employs retired people to sell industrial products part-time. They are given a limited line of products, trained on their application, and given certain accounts to call on. They are then paid a straight commission for their efforts. Before the plan was implemented it was not profitable to use company representatives to call on these smaller accounts.

- There will be a stabilization and possible decline in some younger aged markets. This should affect new product development efforts and cause firms to reposition their products for broader markets. If the trend results in an overall decline in the population, it may impede recruitment efforts of sales managers. Companies will have to respond by making sales an attractive alternative to other professions—something that has not successfully been accomplished among younger groups.

- There will continue to be large increases in the world population. This will have a profound affect on the size of potential markets and the relative importance of markets. Sales managers must respond by appropriately allocating resources to these markets. Shifts in emphasis will also be accompanied with problems of managing and maintaining salespeople in foreign markets.

- Geographic movement of the U.S. population will have a profound affect on the location and significance of markets. Territory potentials will have to be closely monitored and territories will have to be changed to accommodate market shifts. Also, new distribution outlets will have to be identified and cultivated, especially in high growth suburban areas.

  Geographic movement also puts pressure on sales managers to maintain existing salespeople as well as find new salespeople for geographically unattractive markets. Compensation and motivation programs may have to assume a regional flavor to encourage salespeople to stay in these areas.

• Increases in education cause changes in the motivation and behavior of potential recruits. Higher educated people are not as easily motivated by financial incentives as lesser educated individuals. Sales managers will, therefore, be required to develop a thorough understanding of the attitudes and behaviors of college graduates, and utilize this knowledge in the development of motivational programs.

MANAGING IN AN ENVIRONMENT OF CHANGE

As indicated in previous sections of this chapter, environmental change oftentimes has significant implications for sales managers. It affects the future direction of sales programs, the types and quality of programs, and the style of management employed by managers. Analysis of environmental factors also represents the starting point for development of sales plans.

Utilizing information collection and analysis techniques discussed in the previous chapter, the sales manager must monitor political, social, economic, demographic, and technological change. An analysis of these factors as well as an examination of the firm's current market situation serve as the basis for the development of goals and objectives. The development of objectives is then followed by the identification of target markets, the assessment of the impact of strategies on sales, and, finally, the organization and allocation of salespeople to accomplish objectives.

The point is that the effectiveness with which a sales plan is developed is related to the effectiveness with which the current and future selling environment is assessed. Each step in the planning process is predicated on effective analysis of environmental factors. The need, therefore, for accurate analysis of these factors is critical. On-going and comprehensive systems for collecting and analyzing information must be established. The importance of environmental factors on future directions of the firm must be assessed. Also, a planning framework within which environmental factors are placed must be implemented.

By assessing the importance of technological, social, political, and economic changes and utilizing relevant information to chart the firm's future direction, the sales manager can undoubtedly do a more effective and efficient job of recruiting, selecting, training, directing, maintaining, and motivating salespeople.

SUMMARY

This chapter identifies changes in the selling environment and assesses the implications of changes on sales management. Primary environmental changes include (1) movement of women into sales, (2) expansion of the legal framework, (3) increasing costs of hiring, training, and maintaining salespeople, and (4) changes in the characteristics of target markets. Sales managers must modify their philosophies and programs to accommodate change. They must also attempt to predict change so that plans are responsive to the future needs of customers. Most importantly, they must systematically monitor and assess environmental changes and utilize this assessment in the establishment of company goals and market plans.

QUESTIONS

1. What specific changes have impacted recently on the selling environment?

2. Discuss the reasons why more women are moving into sales and sales management?

3. Why is the concept of strict liability of particular importance to sales managers?

4. What can salespeople do to minimize their company's liability?

5. Discuss the defects which fall under strict liability law.

6. To a sales manager, what does the following statement indicate? "There will be a stabilization and possible decline in some younger aged markets."

7. What effect have recent legal developments had on the vulnerability of business organizations? Explain.

8. Why should sales managers be aware of the divergent attitudes men and women have concerning their job?

9. What future demographic changes will impact sales management?

10. What effect would increased levels of education have on the buying public?

Case 14-1

Pentax
Corporation

Pentax manufactured and sold expensive, complex, and highly sophisticated computers and electronic data processing equipment. The least expensive item in the line sold for $17,800; a number of standard items in the line sold for $100,000, and some for as much as $300,000. It was Pentax's product policy to specialize in the "high side of the industry's product line", and to leave the "bread and butter" items to competitors. As a result, the sale, installation, and proper use of Pentax equipment was considerably more difficult and complex than for the industry as a whole. Pentax equipment was sold primarily to large banks and insurance companies, to federal government agencies, and to private and university research facilities. No effort was made to sell to retailers or medium and small business firms whose data processing problems and operations would not justify the complexity and expense of Pentax equipment. Pentax had no plans to develop electronic equipment for home use.

The Pentax sales force of 150 people was organized by geographical area, and reported through five Regional Sales Managers to the Sales Vice President in the home office. The salespeople were all college graduates and some held advanced degrees. Their background was technical in either mathematics, science, or engineering. Salespeople turnover was normal for the industry, about 10 percent a year. All sales management functions were decentralized to the Regional Managers with headquarters supposedly acting in a supervisory capacity.

Clara Snodgrass was recently promoted to New England Regional Sales Manager from her old post of Assistant Regional Sales Manager on the West Coast. In her new job, she was responsible for all Pentax business in the states of Maine, New Hampshire, Vermont, Rhode Island, Massachusetts, New York, and Connecticut. There were 31 salespeople in the region.

The company followed a policy of a high degree of autonomy for Regional Sales Managers. In general, they were expected to do their own planning and to take complete administrative responsibility for their regions so long as they showed a satisfactory rate of profit and growth.

Since she had always been involved in sales, Snodgrass was not comfortable with her new management position. However, she was extremely aggressive and wanted to maintain a position of responsibility with Pentax. She, therefore, began gathering information from salespeople on market potentials, new sales opportunities, and potential vulnerabilities. Snodgrass wanted to quickly understand the current condition of her territory and identify strategies to promote immediate growth.

She also set up a regular, monthly sales meeting during which opportunities and problems could be discussed with salespeople. Eager to confirm her impressions from discussions with salespeople, she also called several customers to find out more about their needs and the extent to which the company had satisfied those needs.

1. Is Clara Snodgrass on the right track in her new role? Explain.

2. Evaluate Pentax Corporation and its ability to develop an effective marketing information system.

3. What organizational alternatives would you recommend, and what effect would they have on Pentax's ability to grow?

Case 14–2

Mohawk
Construction
Company*

Peter Farr, the sales manager in the Pittsburgh, Pennsylvania office of Mohawk Construction Company, was worried because the turnover rate in his sales force had increased, and sales growth rate had declined. In addition to the fact that growth in 1982 was 80 percent lower than its annualized growth of 20 percent, some outside sales reps had left Mohawk to work for direct competitors or for other building products firms. In discussing this situation with Joel Christensen, the production manager in Mohawk's Pittsburgh plant, Mr. Farr learned two things. First, a similar situation was developing to varying degrees in some of the other Mohawk sales offices. Second, it was possible that the sales force compensation plan did not provide sufficient incentive or motivation for the sales reps. This was leading to higher turnover and, therefore, lower sales volume.

The Mohawk Construction Company was a large manufacturer of prestressed concrete products, with its corporate headquarters located in a large midwestern city. Sales and manufacturing facilities were located together in four cities in the east and midwest. In each of the four plants, the chief executive was the general manager, under whom were a sales manager, a production manager, a chief engineer, and a financial manager. Sales in the Pittsburgh office alone last year were about $30 million.

Mohawk manufactured a full range of prestressed and precast concrete products. These products included flat slabs, girders, beams, columns, stairs, and T-shaped supports for floors and flat roofs. The product line also included a wide variety of structural and architectural walls. Mohawk's products were designed for use in the construction of office buildings, apartments, motels, factories, warehouses, schools, multi-storied parking structures, and bridges.

According to Mr. Farr, the prestressing of concrete enabled concrete to behave as an elastic, resilient material. This extended significantly the uses of concrete in construction. Because ordinary concrete performs well in compression, the prestressing process was designed to precompress the concrete during controlled manufacturing in a plant. Prestressed products were carefully designed to assure that this manufactured precompression was not lost when in use under specified loads. In comparison with non-prestressed concrete products, the prestressed units could carry larger loads, or could do the same job with reduced concrete weight. In effect, the prestressed products provided equal performance at lower cost.

Mr. Farr felt there was a favorable primary demand trend for prestressed concrete construction products. In conversations with architects and engineers he got the impression that their awareness and usage were increasing. Along with the increased rate of usage, competition had also increased. In the Pittsburgh area alone, there were five direct competitors for Mohawk. The direct competition among these firms made it essential that the firms all employ top-notch knowledgeable sales representatives. With direct product competition, it had become increasingly important to add extra amounts of goodwill and missionary sales work to protect one's accounts.

Mohawk, of course, also faced competition from other building-products systems such as wood structures, masonry buildings, and metal building systems. Salespeople estimated that the prestressed concrete industry had about a 10 percent share of the total market. However, they believed that market share was as high as 30 percent in some segments.

---

* Contributed by William J. Stanton, Professor of Marketing, University of Colorado, Boulder.

The Pittsburgh sales force which Peter Farr managed was composed of three outside sales representatives (also called sales engineers) and six inside sales-cost estimators. The outside people were responsible for calling on architects, engineers, developers, and contractors to promote the use of prestressed/precast building components. The tasks of the sales reps required that they be well versed in all types of building systems. They also had to have a thorough understanding of general construction practices and terminology. Many of the outside sales representatives were professional engineers, which provided them with the technical knowledge needed to market the products.

A fairly typical task of an outside sales rep was to consult with an architect or engineer about a job that was proposed for construction. Step by step, the salesperson illustrated how prestressed products could be incorporated into the project and the advantages of such a system. A sales rep typically would do preliminary design work, layout work, and budget analysis for the client. It was not uncommon for the sales rep to make many calls on a client during this planning stage.

Once the job was sold, the salesperson then became involved in several phases of Mohawk's operations. For example, the rep was involved in contract negotiations and credit checks of the new client. Upon approval of a sale, the representative then worked with Mohawk's drafting and engineering department to get the job underway. The rep also worked with the production and scheduling people to make certain that the products were made to specifications and delivered on time. All in all, the demands on a sales rep's time could be pretty heavy when he or she had four or five jobs going at the same time.

The inside sales-cost estimators performed many of the same duties as did the outside salespeople. The estimators handled many of the walk-in customers, doing the same pre-sale work which an outside representative would do in a client's office. The inside estimators handled 90 percent of all incoming telephone calls related to product usage and technical aspects. In addition, these workers handled most of the formal bid work for projects. Often these bid projects were very detailed and technical. An estimator may work on one project for several weeks or months, gathering all the necessary data from architectural or structural drawings. The estimators then made a detailed price analysis of all the products on which the company would be bidding. Prior to estimating a final price on a project, the estimator usually consulted with production, scheduling, and engineering personnel.

The estimators also had the responsibility of assisting the sales reps in several phases of an outside project. For example, an outside salesperson would bring to an estimator some preliminary designs. The estimator then would do an in-depth price analysis, plus would prepare all the promotional drawings for the project.

Mohawk's management recognized the potential pitfalls in this process. An estimator was often more familiar with a project than was the sales rep. An outside rep could be embarrassed if he or she did not fully understand what an estimator had done. Also, morale problems could develop when an estimator did all the groundwork, but the sales rep received the credit for the sale.

Mr. Farr felt that Mohawk had a very good employee-management relationship, at least as compared with other companies that Farr knew about in the industry. Mohawk had a policy of promoting from within the company. A typical career path would start in the drafting and engineering department. After some years of training and experience, a person would then move into the position of an estimator. Successful estimators were offered jobs as outside sales reps — a position that was considered prestigious in the eyes of most Mohawk employees.

Since its beginning, the Mohawk company had always used a straight salary plan as the basic compensation method for its office, sales, and management personnel. Mr. Farr believed that Mohawk's sales salaries were quite good. For outside sales reps, salaries ranged from $22,000 to $38,000 per year, usually depending upon the length of time a rep had been in that job. The company also provided an unlimited expense account, medical-dental-eye care insurance, three weeks of paid vacation, and a reimbursement of 22¢ a mile for auto expenses. The sales reps used their own cars when on business.

Both Peter Farr and Joel Christensen were concerned that Mohawk had been experiencing a higher-than-usual turnover rate in its sales department. As a side effect of this situation, Mr. Farr also had sensed a significant decline in morale among the remaining reps and estimators. During his exit interviews, Mr. Farr tried to find out why the people were leaving the firm. He was getting answers such as "I just felt like I needed a change," or "My new job offers a new challenge." Farr knew that these people were not giving him their real reasons for leaving.

Joel Christensen was a friend of Burt Pollak, a former Mohawk sales representative, who had left the company about nine months ago to work for a metal-building contractor. Pollak had been with Mohawk for eight years and was one of the company's top sales representatives. After playing tennis one afternoon, Christensen and Pollak were discussing the company and some of the turnover problems the firm had been experiencing. Christensen asked Pollak what he thought the problem might be. Mr. Pollak said that the reason he became frustrated and left the firm was because there were no incentives. Mr. Pollak went on to say that the company he now worked for paid him a base salary, plus a progressive commission rate, and also provided him with a company car for business and personal use. Pollak said that financially he was only about 5 percent ahead of what he was making at Mohawk. "But," he added, "with a company car and commissions, I really feel good about the compensation package. It gives me some incentive, and I feel more motivated to perform."

Mr. Christensen told Mr. Farr of this conversation with Burt Pollak, and both men considered what Pollak had said. They wondered if perhaps the time had come that the Mohawk company should revise its compensation plan to provide more incentive and motivation to the outside sales reps. They agreed to study their options and present the results to Mr. Frank Gray, the executive vice president in charge of sales and marketing.

After several weeks, Mr. Christensen and Mr. Farr developed what they thought was a fair and competitive plan. The proposed plan consisted of three elements: (1) the outside sales reps would be furnished with a company car; (2) the reps would have an opportunity to earn a semi-annual bonus; (3) a rep's base salary would be reduced as a partial offset to the cost of the bonus. Also under the new plan, the company would retain the existing fringe-benefit package.

The idea of a company car was justified by the fact that the annual mileage per sales rep averaged around 15,000 miles. Based on this, they believed that the company would actually save money in comparison with the existing plan. In addition, the sales representatives were to have full use of the automobiles for personal use. The only stipulation placed on that usage was that reps should pay fuel expenses if they used the car for vacation.

In connection with the proposed bonus, Mr. Farr reviewed the method presently used to estimate the costs and margins on a typical job. The following three groups of costs were added together:

1. Material costs — these costs included all the direct materials that were used in precast and prestressed members, plus machine and equipment costs allocated to each cubic yard of concrete produced.

2. Direct labor and overhead costs — these expenses included wages and benefits paid all hourly employees, plus all plant overhead allocated to the given job.

3. Outside labor costs and all administrative personnel costs—this category included outside crew salaries and benefits, plus administrative salaries and expenses.

To arrive at the selling price on a job, the company added to the above expenses a mark-up to cover selling expenses and net profit. Selling expenses typically averaged about 10 percent of sales. Net profits before income taxes ranged from 10 to 25 percent of the selling price. The bonus proposed under the new pay plan would be one half of one percent of net profits before taxes.

As an example of the arithmetic under the new plan, a sales rep now making $32,000 a year would have the base salary reduced to $24,000. The bonus that he or she would earn under normal conditions would bring total pay to the $32,000 level or higher. As Mr. Farr explained it, in an "off" year the company would have the benefit of a lower fixed salary cost, yet a sales rep would still be assured of receiving a reasonably comfortable salary.

Farr and Christensen had considered various other commission plans, but felt they might be too expensive to administer. Also under a commission plan, they feared the company might lose some of the control it now has over the sales force.

Farr and Christensen met with Mr. Gray and Mr. Arnar, another executive from the headquarters office, to review the revised compensation plan. The top executives were receptive to this new idea, but believed there might be some serious problems. Mr. Gray noted that it was a very good plan, but he was concerned about what the proposed plan might do to estimators' morale. Mr. Arnar thought that the new plan might be difficult to administer. He noted that varying territory potentials meant that some reps would have better bonus opportunities than other reps. Both Arnar and Gray also pointed out that net profit margins (the basis of the new bonuses) often were cut when competition forced Mohawk to bid low on a project.

Mr. Christensen and Mr. Farr left the meeting rather disheartened. They knew what the other executives said made sense, but they also knew they had a morale and incentive problem waiting for them back at the office.

1. What compensation plan should the Mohawk Company use for its outside sales representatives? Will this alleviate its sales growth problems?

2. What other problems could be contributing to Mohawk's slow growth and high turnover?

3. How should management approach its problems? Develop a sequence of steps that should be employed to solve existing problems and identify others.

Case 15–1

Miss Poly
Corporation

Dick Putmann, sales manager of Miss Poly Corporation, was faced with a problem created for him by an aggressive, talented, young woman who had come directly to him for the job as a sales representative. Miss Poly, a large manufacturer of moderately priced fashion apparel for young women, had an annual sales of over $80 million.

Miss Poly sold its dresses directly to dress shops and department stores. The firm employed 65 salespeople, who received a commission of 4 percent. Expenses were not covered.

In the past, Miss Poly had hired only male sales representatives, even though dresses were sold to both male and female buyers. Mr. Putmann had never before considered hiring a woman. One of the representatives in Los Angeles had resigned and an immediate replacement was needed. Miss Poly never had a shortage of good, experienced salespeople who wanted to represent the firm. Miss Poly was a very popular, fast selling line of merchandise. Mr. Putmann received many applications from experienced women's-wear sales representatives.

Miss Sandra Maria Burnett heard of the job opening in Los Angeles. She flew to company headquarters at her own expense, had an interview with Mr. Putmann, and made her presentation. She was completely aware that if the company did hire her, Miss Poly Corporation would be setting a precedent, because, as far as she knew, no woman had ever held such a position. She was quite confident that she was able to perform a top level job in the company.

Her background and experience were excellent. She was intelligent, and she made a very favorable impression on Mr. Putmann. Her previous work experience included employment at Brochus Marcus, Zest Cosmetics, and Princess, a young women's clothing store.

Mr. Putmann could not find anything in her record or interview that would disqualify her for the position. She proved to him during the interview that she was knowledgeable in her field and had some good ideas on how a company could increase its sales.

Miss Burnett was 33 years old, and had never been married. She had held responsible positions since graduating from St. Mary's College, Indiana. She told Mr. Putmann that her career was more important to her than having a family. She also made it clear that she would continue to work for Miss Poly even if she decided to marry.

1. Should Mr. Putmann hire Miss Sandra Burnett as a sales representative?

Case 15–2

Exco
Chemical
Corporation

Exco Chemical Corporation, in New York, N.Y., manufactures a highly diversified line of sanitation products, including soaps and soap equipment; floor maintenance products, sealers, cleaners, and waxes; disinfectants; insecticides and insecticide equipment; germicides; and sanitizers for personal protection. An average volume of $20,000,000 worth of these products is sold direct by more than 200 salaried salespeople who are distributed equally among 30 branch offices throughout the United States and Canada.

Exco products are sold direct to schools, hospitals, factories, offices and office buildings, hotels, restaurants, stores, automobile show rooms and service stations, public buildings, rail, air, and bus terminals, military bases, and other public places, in addition to leading resellers of sanitary supply houses, wholesale hardware, and paper merchants.

The 30 branch managers report directly to the two regional sales managers. The branch managers have authority to select, train, supervise and control salespeople operating out of their respective branches. They are required to report weekly on their work to the general sales manager. The branch managers were formerly successful salespeople, and variable amounts of their time are taken up with supervision.

At the insistence of the home office each branch manager must maintain coverage of a sales territory and meet a reasonable sales quota. Joe Branch is the Sales Manager of the Cincinnati branch sales office. Historically, his branch's sales have always been in the top 5.

This year's sales figures are running very close to last year's figures, which was a very successful year. A recent large order from AAA Department Stores, coupled with the efforts of his best salespeople, and Joe Branch's own strong sales, account for the lion's share of the Cincinnati Office total sales.

The following situations have developed recently:

(A) The Cincinnati Exco Company branch office has been working on a volume buyer, St. Mary's, for a large order for some time. The salesperson, Jim Johnston, had been unable (after numerous attempts) to negotiate a deal and had given up. Veteran salesperson, Sam Hill, was assigned to the St. Mary's account. One week later, Sam closed the sale at St. Mary's.

(B) Three years ago, Bob Edwards took over a territory that Sam Hill had previously developed. Hill was allowed to keep the three best hospital accounts and the two major industrial accounts. Bob Edwards had only four times in the past three years been able to earn his draw of $1,200 a month. Bob owed the company from his draw about $10,000. Branch knew that there were still several volume accounts remaining in Edward's territory. He had made field calls with him and felt Edwards' problem was that he was a weak closer.

(C) Jean Jones had been asked, as had all of the 200 salespeople, to make a forecast for one year in advance by product line and by customer type. Jean did not turn in her forecast at the requested time. Joe Branch was surprised as Jones always turned in reports on time with all details asked for. When Joe Branch asked Jean why she had not turned in the requested forecast, Jean became insolent and said, "Why should I? No one ever looks at them. Forecasts do not make sales and you know it—it's calls that make sales."

Joe Branch was a bit bewildered as to what to do since Jane was having one of her best sales years. Also, Joe did not want Paula Lane, one of the two regional sales managers, to learn of this situation with Jones as Lane might interpret this as being a weakness on Branch's part in not making his reps comply with such a request from headquarters.

(D) Paula Lane decided to go out into the sales territories. The first day out she spotted one of the company's best representatives, Sam Hill, a hundred miles out of his territory with a branch office secretary. At 2:00 p.m., the two were leisurely playing miniature golf and drinking beer. Lane knew Hill's wife had just given birth to a baby the week before. Lane phoned the Cincinnati branch office and asked the operator for the secretary. She was informed the secretary she saw with Hill had called in sick the last two days. Furthermore, a large Cincinnati hospital buyer called Lane the month before and said he had not seen Exco representative, Bill Jones, for three months. Lane, in checking, found that Bill Jones had reported making weekly calls on this account.

When Joe Branch arrived at the office the following day, several events developed:

(1) Bob Edwards was waiting to see him. Edwards stated that he had the worst territory in the Cincinnati Branch and unless he was assigned Hill's five accounts, he would quit.

(2) A letter (see Figure 1) came from AAA department stores.

(3) The phone memo shown below was on his desk.

> Paula Lane phoned. She had seen Sam Hill and Branch's secretary 100 miles from his territory at 2:00 p.m. Lane was furious and demanded that Branch fire Hill and the secretary at once. Secondly, Lane stated that she had not received the sales forecasts for next year from the Cincinnati Branch. She wants them in the mail tomorrow.

(4) A letter from the home office dated the week before stated that the three products Hill had sold St. Mary's were discontinued. These orders would not be filled.

1. What problems seem to exist in Exco Chemical Company?

2. What steps should be taken to remedy the existing problems?

AAA DEPARTMENT STORES
101 Stores Nationwide
200 Lakeshore Drive
Chicago, IL 60620

July 24, 1978

Joe Branch
Exco Chemical Corporation
123 W. 1st Street
Cincinnati, Ohio

Dear Mr. Branch:

Recently we purchased 2000 Model Number 201 insecticide spraying units from your company. When purchasing these sprayers I noticed a strange vibration when I first turned one on. The vibration would stop in a few minutes. I questioned your sales rep, John West, about this and he informed me his sample was defective and assured me there was no vibration in the actual production models.

They were delivered last month. I received a complaint from our downtown Cincinnati store last week about the unit's strange vibration. I called John West and he met us at the store. The unit did indeed vibrate. West became very defensive and abrasive. He called us liars and said even if there was a vibration it wouldn't hurt anything.

I'm assuming that this action is representative of your company. We are cancelling our order. The units will be returned at once.

Sincerely,

Mary Johns
Purchasing Agent

Figure 1
Letter on Joe's
Desk

MJ:ed

Index